EVERY INVESTOR'S
GUIDE TO

HIGH-TECH

STOCKS AND
MUTUAL FUNDS,
3rd Edition

EVERY INVESTOR'S GUIDE TO

HIGH-TECH

STOCKS AND MUTUAL FUNDS, 3rd Edition

*PROVEN STRATEGIES FOR
PICKING HIGH-GROWTH WINNERS*

MICHAEL MURPHY

BROADWAY BOOKS   New York

BROADWAY

EVERY INVESTOR'S GUIDE TO HIGH-TECH STOCKS AND MUTUAL FUNDS, 3rd Edition. Copyright © 2000 by Michael Murphy. All rights reserved. Printed in the United States of America. No part of this book may be reproduced or transmitted in any form or by any means, electronic or mechanical, including photocopying, recording, or by any information storage and retrieval system, without written permission from the publisher. For information, address Broadway Books, a division of Random House, Inc., 1540 Broadway, New York, NY 10036.

Broadway Books titles may be purchased for business or promotional use or for special sales. For information, please write to: Special Markets Department, Random House, Inc., 1540 Broadway, New York, NY 10036.

BROADWAY BOOKS and its logo, a letter B bisected on the diagonal, are trademarks of Broadway Books, a division of Random House, Inc.

Library of Congress Cataloging-in-Publication Data

Murphy, Michael, 1941–
    Every investor's guide to high-tech stocks and mutual funds :
    proven strategies for picking high-growth winners / by Michael Murphy.
    —3rd ed.
        p.   cm.
    Includes bibliographical references and index.
    ISBN 0-7679-0456-7
    1. High technology industries—United States—Finance.   2. Stocks—
United States.   I. Title.   II. Title: High-tech stocks and mutual
funds.
HC79.H53M87   2000
333.63'22—dc21   98-42585
                                                             CIP

THIRD EDITION

Designed by Stanley S. Drate/Folio Graphics Co. Inc.

00   01   02   03   04   10   9   8   7   6   5   4   3   2   1

To my beloved Lissa
And two kids I'm proud of, Christopher and Virginia
And to David, wherever you are

"I'll tell you why we were put on this planet. We were put on this planet to outperform the market!"

CONTENTS

PART I

THE TECHNOLOGY OPPORTUNITY

1 Why Buy Technology?   7

2 What Is the Market Telling Us?   14

3 What Is Technology?   37

PART II

THE TECHNOLOGY INDUSTRIES

4 Semiconductor Equipment   49

5 How to Make a Semiconductor   56

6 Semiconductors   62

7 Large Computers   76

8 Personal Computers   84

9 Software   91

10 Communications   104

11 The Internet   115

12 Medical Technology   129

PART III

PICKING TECHNOLOGY STOCKS

13 How to Pick Winning Technology Stocks:
The Growth-Flow Model   149

14 How to Spot the Great Growth-Flow Companies   156

15 What About the Little Guys? Finding Opportunities in
Development-Stage Companies (and Avoiding
the Dogs)   163

16 Controlling the Risk in Technology Stocks   *171*

17 Managing Your Technology Portfolio   *189*

18 Blue Chips 2010   *196*

19 Technology Convertible Bonds and Stocks   *228*

■■■■■■■■■■■■■■■ PART IV

CHOOSING HIGH-TECH MUTUAL FUNDS

20 Technology Mutual Funds   *241*

21 Twenty Technology Mutual Funds   *247*

22 Seven Medical and Biotechnology Mutual Funds   *269*

ACKNOWLEDGMENTS   *277*

APPENDICES

Appendix A   A Focus List of Great Growth-Flow
             Companies   *281*

Appendix B   A Focus List of Biotechnology Companies   *285*

Appendix C   Selected Technology Convertible Bonds and
             Preferred Stocks Available to Individual
             Investors   *289*

Appendix D   Changing Accounting Rules to Promote R&D
             Investment   *293*

Appendix E   Contacts and Sources   *295*

INDEX   *301*

PART I

The Technology Opportunity

EVERY investor's guide to

high-tech stocks and mutual funds. That includes you. There are only two kinds of people: those who already own high-tech stocks and funds, and those who will shortly. We are in the midst of a once-in-a-century revolution in the very foundation of our economy, the types of high-paying jobs, the sources of wealth, and the opportunities for investors.

If you own mutual funds, either directly or through a 401K plan, or if you have a pension plan or are the beneficiary of a trust, you probably already own a few technology stocks. But most people—including investment professionals—are woefully underinvested in the greatest opportunity of our generation.

Despite the amount of coverage volatile technology stocks get on financial television shows, fewer than 10 percent of Wall Street analysts cover stocks in the new technology economy. Despite the headlines garnered from time to time by some major growth mutual funds that own technology stocks, fewer than 90 mutual funds—out of some 9,000 in all—specialize in technology. Dominant companies like Intel are valued no more highly than the broad market averages, even though they are growing three times as fast.

Fear and ignorance keep most people—even professionals—at bay, yet you don't have to be an engineer or research scientist to do well in technology stocks. The real basis of a technology company's success is Research & Development. It is R&D that creates new products. New products drive rapid sales growth, often by creating their own demand. In 1994, how many people had an unmet need to be on the World Wide Web? New products also tend to carry higher profit margins because there is less competition. High rates of sales growth and high profit margins are a prescription for success. We will show you exactly how to factor R&D into your investment decisions without knowing a bit from a byte.

It is not only easy to get started in high-tech investing, but now is also the ideal time to invest. The world is no more than halfway through a massive thirty- to forty-year growth cycle in electronics and computer technology, and we are just beginning an equally massive thirty- to forty-year cycle in medical and biotechnology.

Depending on your individual situation, there are many ways to invest. Whether you decide to create a portfolio of individual stocks or mutual funds or technology convertible bonds, the most important message you will take away from this book is not how technology companies work, how to buy and sell the stocks, how to pick a high-tech mutual fund, or how to manage a technology portfolio—although you will learn all of these. This is the crucial message: You must sharply increase the percentage of your assets invested in technology to benefit from changing technology.

This asset-allocation decision will dominate your rate of return for the next three decades. Simply speaking, the specific stocks and funds you pick now will just make the difference between getting rich and getting really rich.

Over a full market cycle, you should target returns of 20 percent to 25 percent compounded annually. That means that $1,000 invested when your child is three will be worth $28,000 when the college tuition bill comes due at age eighteen. Or $1,000 invested in your IRA at age forty-five will be worth $87,000 at age sixty-five, or $808,000 if you let it ride to age seventy-five. Talk about beating inflation!

Of course, technology stocks are volatile. Virtually every year, the highs on most tech stocks are double the lows. As you get closer to retirement, you have less time to recover from a serious bear market. It is prudent to reduce your exposure to all equities, including technology stocks.

But most people are far too conservative in their asset allocation. How much should you target for technology investing? The answer may shock you: 100 percent minus your age. If you are 35, 65 percent of your total assets *including real estate* should be in technology. At age 50, 50 percent. At 75, you *still* need 25 percent of your assets in technology, because thanks to biotechnology you're going to live a long time.

Need current income? Buy technology convertible bonds (see Chapter 19). Don't have enough time to look at individual stocks? Buy technology mutual funds (see Chapter 20). Interested only in medical and biotechnology? Great. See Chapters 12 and 15 and concentrate your investments there. (Not only do we advocate 100 percent minus your age for your total investment in technology, we believe half of that should be in biotechnology. You may get up off the floor now.)

If you have the time and interest, you can short-term trade or even day-trade technology stocks, using the techniques described in this book to keep yourself in line with the fundamentals of a company. For either traders or the typical individual investor with a few free hours a month and a long-term investment horizon, the investment climate has never been better. Companies will ply you with information in hopes that you'll buy their stock. Most of them have investor-relations specialists to answer your questions, provide corporate profiles and technology backgrounders ("white papers"), and direct you to other helpful sources. If you have an Internet connection, the resources of the World Wide Web—from SEC filings to company press releases, to industry and stock chat groups—are available to you.

The few brokerage firms that specialize in technology stocks do a good job, with thoughtful background research on technology sectors and players. (Don't take their "buy" and "buy more" advice, though; make up your own mind.) Even the popular press and major newspapers do a far better job reporting on technology than they did when we started the *California Technology Stock Letter* back in 1982.

By the time you finish this book you will know more about technology investing than 99.9 percent of the people in the market, and in knowledge there is power.

Enjoy!

## CHAPTER ONE

Why Buy Technology?

Economies usually evolve slowly, but from time to time they go through a rapid, wrenching change that creates massive, new opportunities at the same time that old structures are destroyed. Each of these revolutions is caused by the emergence of a new, underlying economic driver, and brings with it new infrastructures that change society. We are living through one of those major changes right now, and it is creating once-in-a-lifetime opportunities to build new wealth.

When you are living through it, it can be difficult to put it in perspective. But ten thousand years back, your great-great-great-great-granddaddy[-10] was a hunter-gatherer. The economic driver was meat protein. Always on the move, taking what food and shelter he found along the way, our distant ancestor rarely deferred current consumption to make investments that would pay off in the future.

Not that there were many investment choices. Great-granddaddy[-10] and his mate may have smoked or salted meat to save for the winter, but that was pretty much the limit of their ability to invest for the future. They didn't build wealth, and there wasn't much of an infrastructure— little beyond animal trails through the woods.

Then—paradigm shift!—life evolved to an agrarian society where your great-grandparents[-8] farmed the land, saved seeds for next year's crop, developed water systems, and built houses. Towns sprang up to market crops and provide a center to buy supplies. The agrarian society lasted for thousands of years—until three hundred years ago, give or take.

What drove wealth building in this new society was land and crops. If you owned land, you were wealthy. If not, not. The enabling technology was pretty much limited to hand tools and horses. The infrastructure constituted dirt roads and couriers on horseback.

The United States was discovered and settled toward the end of this period. Having a limitless supply of land, lots of water, and not many regulations, the pioneers built great wealth rapidly. (Hong Kong did the same thing over the last fifty years on only 400 square miles, so we know that land isn't the issue anymore.)

Then came the Industrial Revolution, driven by cheap steel and a flood of new inventions. Wealth grew in steel, industrial machinery, coal, and transportation. The infrastructure changed to railroads, shipping, and the telegraph. The important economic indicators shifted to coal, iron and steel production, patent applications, and railroad operating income.

Great family fortunes were built in these new areas—glittering names, still well known, such as Morgan, Bessemer, Vanderbilt, Astor. Although investors could still make money buying and selling in the agrarian economy, it was much easier to get the wind at their backs investing in the new areas, side by side with the entrepreneurs.

But they weren't dubbed "entrepreneurs" in those days. They were called "robber barons."

After World War I, the United States and most of the developed world shifted to mass-production and consumer-based economies, thanks, in some measure, to Henry Ford. The economic driver changed to cheap energy—especially oil. The middle class grew faster, with enough income and an enabling technology (the automobile) to move out of the noisy, polluted cities. People did not have to live within walking distance of the factory anymore.

At that point, the growth industries changed to autos, housing, and retailing. The infrastructure shifted to highways, airports, telephones, and broadcasting. The important economic indicators changed to retail sales, auto sales, housing starts, and capacity utilization.

Again great new family fortunes were built in these areas. Automobile families were the royalty of the Midwest; home building created many multimillionaires after World War II. The Walton (Wal-Mart) success story may be the last example of that era. Again, investors earned the highest returns by focusing on rapid growth areas in the new economy.

Then came the technology economy.

As with all generalizations, it's easy to argue about when the Digital Age began. Mainframe computers went commercial in the 1950s; Digital Equipment Corporation was founded in 1957. But it was the demands of the Department of Defense plus NASA that drove the process of miniaturization to the point where Fairchild and Texas Instruments invented semiconductors. And Intel, descendant of Fairchild, gave birth to the microprocessor in 1971.

Microprocessors powered the digital watches and hand-held calculators of the mid-1970s. By the late 1970s, personal computers were spreading by the tens of thousands. Apple computers could even be seen on the desks of non-wonks in ordinary companies.

But this was not yet the Age of Empowerment, when anyone could own a personal computer for less than $5,000 and make it do useful things. It took IBM to put the Good Housekeeping seal of approval on personal computers by coming out with its own in 1981, clearly marking the latest change in the economy.

Now there's no question: This is the technology economy, and the economic driver is ever-cheaper semiconductors. Underlying all the advances in computing and communications are unbelievable price drops in semiconductor chips. Gordon Moore, the founder of Intel, propounded Moore's Law twenty years ago:

> # The Cost of Making a Semiconductor Drops 50 Percent Every Eighteen Months

He's been right thus far, and we expect that his law will continue to hold true for the next ten years at least, at which time the physical limitations of silicon may force a rethinking of the whole technology. But you never know. Ten years ago, it was thought that microprocessors could never go faster than 100 megahertz. Now you can buy 600-megahertz Intel processors, and people are waiting impatiently for 1,000-megahertz models.

The growth industries in the new economy are computers, software, semiconductors, communications, the Internet, and medical technology, and the infrastructure is changing to satellites, fiber optics, networks, and wireless connectivity. Again, the great new family fortunes are being built in these areas—just ask Bill Gates, or Jim Clark of Netscape/Healthion.

So how do we measure this?

Of course, the relevant economic indicators have changed again. It's just that the government and the media haven't quite figured it out.

We used to get ten-day auto-sales figures; where are ten-day computer-sales figures?

Why don't we hear about the high-tech trade balance (which shows a multibillion-dollar surplus)?

How about knowledge-intensive employment, which grew rapidly through the last recession and continues to show little unemployment? Of the U.S. regions with the fastest job growth in the early 1990s, San Jose and San Francisco (at either end of Silicon Valley) were first and third.

How about the *de*flation in high-tech prices, which drop reliably every year? One hundred megabytes of hard-disk-drive storage cost $250 in 1988, $35 in 1994, and $2.50 in 2000.

Year after year, technology companies grow about 20 percent with no inflation, while the rest of the economy plods along at 2 percent to 3 percent real growth. Although technology started as a small, specialized segment of the economy in the 1970s, after several years of rapid relative growth, the new technology economy accounts for almost 20 percent of the total economy.

Well, 20 percent times 20 percent is 4 percent growth. That's real GDP growth of 4 percent per year from the technology sector alone, no matter what the Federal Reserve Board does.

Yet, for the last few years, the Fed, in its wisdom, would not allow the total economy to grow faster than 4 percent. That means the acceptable growth rate for the entire nontechnology economy is 0 percent. Worse, the mass-production and consumer economy is saddled with debt, running a huge trade deficit in oil and automobiles, and suffering low growth due to the demographics of aging baby boomers. No wonder people are feeling financially stressed!

In this foot-on-the-brake environment, investors should be bailing out of the old mass-production economy, not to mention the even older industrial economy. (The latter is extremely vulnerable to foreign competition from the newly industrializing countries.) There should be a rush to align investment capital with the new entrepreneurial areas—especially in the United States. Except for robotics, where Japan is first, the United States dominates the new technology economy. Seven of the top ten personal-computer manufacturers are U.S. companies, including all of the top four. Now that technology markets have expanded to include consumers as well as corporations, and the entire world—instead of just the United States, Europe, and Japan—U.S. dominance of most technology industries is likely to produce domestic wealth comparable to Britain's in the Industrial Revolution of the 1800s. Judging by the performance of technology stocks over the last several years, many investors already have begun switching their investments from the old economy to the new one.

Why, then, do more than 90 percent of Wall Street analysts follow the old-economy industries? Of nearly 9,000 mutual funds, why are only about 90 classified as science and technology? With the tremendous demand for data storage, why does Seagate Technology sell for less than half the average price/earnings multiple?

Several years from now, all this will be different. There will be hundreds of technology mutual funds, serviced by hundreds of Wall Street analysts retreaded from old-economy industries. Intel will be in the Dow Jones Industrial Average, as will Microsoft. Investors may even be focused on the real driver for long-term technology profits—the research-and-development programs that create future earnings.

Why is R&D such a powerful economic driver? Information and knowledge are the essence of any economy. In the agrarian economy, knowledge was passed along orally and recorded in a few books and journals. The industrial and mass-production economies added blueprints, magazines, newspapers, and inexpensive books. In a technology economy, information is also gathered in databases that reflect the experience and know-how of millions of people, networked to the data and to each other. The knowledge explosion is both the cause and the effect of technological progress.

Information gets into the economy primarily by lowering costs. Real costs always fall. That is, adjusted for inflation, the real cost of creating something is under constant competitive pressure. This is the definition of productivity, and the direct cause of an increasing standard of living.

"Learning-curve" economics is best illustrated by the semiconductor industry. Since 1970, the cost of manufacturing one bit of random access memory has fallen 28 percent per year. By increasing wafer sizes, shrinking transistor sizes, and improving production equipment continually, semiconductor companies make the same profit margin today as they did over twenty years ago—on much larger sales. Now the cost of memory is so low that demand has exploded and it is used to improve hundreds of low-priced ordinary consumer goods.

No companies are more leveraged to the knowledge explosion than technology companies, which use technical information to create information-processing products, then reinvest 5 percent to 25 percent of sales in R&D to create new information. This is the source of tech companies' dynamic growth, and it's this kind of growth that you should seek as a technology investor. These companies often have to educate their customers on how to use information in order to create a demand for technology products. They almost always have to demonstrate an attractive return on investment to get the customer to sign on the dotted line, so every time they can cut the price (reduce the investment) it becomes easier to sell the product to a larger potential audience.

The fastest-evolving, most prolific corner of capitalism is technology. The nontechnology U.S. economy has settled into a mediocre 2 percent to 3 percent growth rate. As the 78 million baby boomers age, they spend less on the major family-establishing expenses of their thirties: houses, cars, kids, educations. They save more and provide less push for growth. Consumers are still burdened with debt; commercial real estate prices remained subdued; for years the federal government seems politically unable to truly balance its budget. The old mass-production economy is in trouble.

In a relatively slow-growth U.S. economy, it will not take technology long to become the largest, most important sector. If the old economy grows 2 percent a year while the new economy continues to grow at 20 percent a year, within seven years the new economy will comprise over one-third of the total, and within eleven years over one-half.

SHIFTING SECTORS OF THE U.S. ECONOMY

Year	Technology	Nontechnology
1997	15.0%	85.0%
1998	17.2	82.8
1999	19.6	80.4
2000	22.3	77.7
2001	25.3	74.7
2002	28.5	71.5
2003	31.9	68.1
2004	35.5	64.5
2005	39.3	60.7
2006	43.2	56.8
2007	47.3	52.7
2008	51.3	48.7

That's why we always rejected Peter Lynch's dictum that you can't invest in things you don't easily understand; that's a bus ticket up a dead-end road. Virtually all the net growth in the economy will come from technology: electronics technology, entertainment technology, communications technology, technology exports, new medical technology, and biotechnology drugs. Investors in technology are buying into inevitably superior long-term performance. The table above shows why the opportunity needs to be seized now, while this huge transition is happening.

In addition to the steady trend to lower costs, there are long waves in economic history with rising rates of growth for roughly a quarter-century followed by falling rates of growth for roughly a quarter-century. The economy expanded rapidly from the early 1900s through 1929. It then contracted until the artificial stimulus of World War II cut short the down-cycle in 1942, even though the consumer economy remained depressed for another four years. The post–World War II expansion peaked in 1969, followed by twenty-two years of economic difficulties, including corporate restructurings in most old-economy industries and outright depressions in the energy business, commercial real estate, and the savings and loans. In the early 1990s, the U.S. economy began a rising phase that will prompt an economic boom for two or three decades.

At the same time, we are in the midst of one of the occasional periods of surging technological change. The economy is adapting to new technologies, new consumer demands, new cost structures, and new educational needs. Retraining workers is a political battle cry. The combination of a rising long wave of growth and a high rate of technological change will bring about a radical economic and social transformation, providing extraordinary investment opportunities.

The fall of communism added over two billion people to the world's labor and consumer force. The internationalization of the world economy will intensify competition, forcing all companies to use the latest technology. Thus, high rates of economic growth will have a worldwide impact.

Technology companies tend to sell worldwide, with 20 percent to 70 percent of sales overseas. No matter how fast the United States grows, we can be sure that Latin America and the industrializing Pacific Rim will grow faster. Europe may struggle with lower growth due to its high-cost, social-welfare economies, and Japan may be fighting a depression for many years. But most of the world is a wonderful market for U.S. exporters; first among them are the technology companies.

If you want the investment winds at your back, you must invest in technology. The old days of "growth" by raising prices are over. Technology companies cut prices every year; technology managements know how to manage for growth in a deflation—they've never known any other environment. These are the managers for the twenty-first century.

Investors who are clever at buying low and selling high can still make money investing in the old cyclical consumer economy, outguessing all the other analysts and portfolio managers looking at the same dumb lists of comfortably familiar names. With luck, they might achieve the 10 percent long-term average equity return, even if the broad market does somewhat worse than that for a while.

But we'll take companies growing 15 percent to 50 percent a year with no debt, shipping 20 percent to 70 percent of their products overseas, investing 7 percent to 20 percent of sales in R&D to invent new products that create sales growth and carry high profit margins to boot. We suspect that more and more investors will join us as massive amounts of money flow out of the mass-production economy, and the even older industrial economy, into the technology economy in search of higher growth and a better return on investment.

During the next six years, the cost of computing will fall by 90 percent. The personal-computer market will nearly triple. The communications business will increase by a factor of five. There will be at least 2,000 percent growth in Internet accounts. Almost 200 biotechnology drugs will be approved by the Food and Drug Administration, many to treat previously untreatable chronic diseases of aging that cost the health-care system billions of dollars every year. It is indeed the best of times to be a technology investor.

## CHAPTER TWO

What Is the Market Telling Us?

Even though most individuals and institutions are underinvested in technology, if we are right about the momentous changes in the world caused by accelerating electronics and biotechnology, these changes should show up in some economic indicators and in the stock market.

And they have.

The new leading indicators of the high-tech economy are computer production, chip production, the high-tech trade balance, medical building starts, and knowledge-intensive employment growth. But these numbers are still hard to get. For example, the *Business Week* Index tracks steel production, housing starts, auto production, railroad carloadings, and the like to determine how the economy is doing. Those were important in the old mass-production economy or the even older industrial economy, but they mean almost nothing in the new economy. Consider the following:

- The U.S. health and medical industry is already larger than oil refining, mining, and production of aircraft, autos, auto parts, textiles, and steel COMBINED.
- The aerospace industry employs more people than the auto and auto-parts industries combined, and has a huge positive trade balance, while the automobile industry has a huge negative trade balance, second only to oil—the economic driver of the old economy.

- More Americans make semiconductors than construction machinery; more people work in data processing than in oil refining; more people work in biotechnology than in the machine-tool industry.

Although the change to a technology economy is fifteen years under way, historical reliance on the economic indicators from the mass-production and commodity economies is fooling industry and government. At the end of 1996, Federal Reserve Chairman Alan Greenspan finally said:

> While there can be little doubt that major gains are being made in today's market in the quality, choice, and availability of goods and services for American consumers, it is also clear that we measure these trends rather poorly. First, there are questions about the quality of the data we employ to measure output in today's economy. Second, like the major technological advances of earlier periods, it will take time for our newest innovations to work their way into the nation's infrastructure in a productive manner.
>
> In the computer software industry, for example, what is its price per unit and how does that price move from one period to the next? Also, we know that we are expending an increasing proportion of our gross domestic product denominated in current dollars on medical services. But what is the physical equivalent unit of output of medical care? What is the true price trend for the removal of cataracts when the technology and the nature of the whole procedure is so dramatically different from what it was, say, forty or even twenty years ago?

Wall Street seems just as far behind and equally duped: Dozens of Wall Street analysts are assigned to analyze the airlines, but very few are looking at video-conferencing systems than can substitute for much air travel. Hundreds of people are trying to figure out whether Philip Morris, with revenues growing a measly 3 percent a year, has enough cash flow to buy out its shares at a profit as the company liquidates itself into oblivion. Almost none are looking at the recent crop of biotech initial public offerings, several of which have bulletproof patent positions on newly discovered lung-cancer drugs.

In fact, the ratio of brokerage-firm analysts who work in New York City to those who work in California must be 100 to 1, while the ratio of technology companies headquartered in California to those headquartered in New York City must be 100 to 1 the other way. If all those New York analysts are playing tennis and golf with bankers, consumer-products-company officers, retailers, and real estate mavens, is it any surprise they do not even notice that technology companies have taken over the world?

We are at an important inflection point in the investment history of technology. Chart 2.1 shows the growth in capital spending in a new

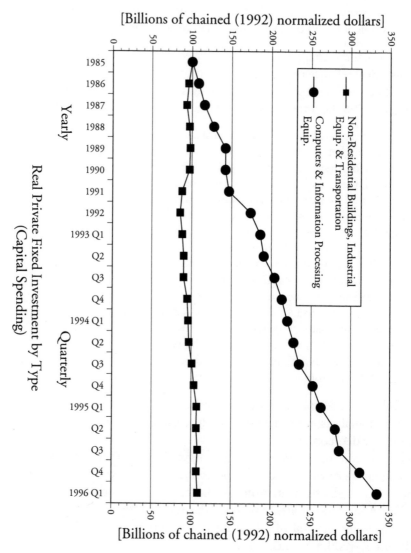

CHART 2.1

way—divided between traditional spending on bricks and mortar, industrial machinery and transportation equipment (squares), and computer and communications equipment (circles). Spending on low-tech equipment was flat for over ten years in real terms (adjusted for inflation). Computers and high-tech equipment outgrew low-tech spending in the late 1980s and then flattened during the 1990–1991 recession. Coming out of that recession, though, the growth rate of spending on computers accelerated. The share of Gross Domestic Product invested in capital spending increased from 6 percent to 9 percent, with virtually all the incremental spending going for high-tech gear. This is a direct reflection of MIT Media Lab Director Nicholas Negreponte's dictum that we are becoming a society that moves electronic bits around, rather than physical molecules. Information in the broadest sense replaces physical goods as the central product of a technology economy.

Chart 2.2 shows the U.S. population of primary childbearing age, 20 to 34 years old. Women have to average 2.1 children each just to replace their generation with a new one of equal size. The generation of the 1920s (Point A) increased its size 33 percent to the generation of the 1950s (Point B). The generation of the 1950s produced a whopping increase of 67 percent to the baby boomers (Point C). But the baby boomers will produce only a 1 percent gain, barely enough to reproduce themselves (Point D). Consequently, many of the mass-production industries are in trouble. Charts 2.3 through 2.7 show the relative-strength breakdowns (the performance of an industry stock index relative to the performance of the Standard & Poor's 500 Index) in the stocks of some U.S.–oriented industries: home building, household furnishings, textiles, building materials, and retailing.

In its usual mysterious way, the stock market seems to be stumbling toward the truth. Charts 2.8 through 2.13 show the difference between the stock prices of global consumer-branded companies (soft drinks, tobacco, household products) and global commodity-products companies (steel, aluminum, paper, and forest products). Paper and forest products approached a twenty-five-year, relative-strength low in 1996. Steel broke below a fifty-year, relative-strength low. The United States is no longer competitive in these products now that over one billion low-wage workers in Russia and China have joined the global labor force. Our comparative advantage lies in product development and marketing—even if the product is beer or shampoo, rather than microprocessors and operating systems.

If it is true that less stuff is being moved around, we would expect to see trouble in an industry like trucking. Chart 2.14 shows that we did—trucking stocks fell near a twenty-five-year relative low. And because it is much less expensive to move bits than to move molecules,

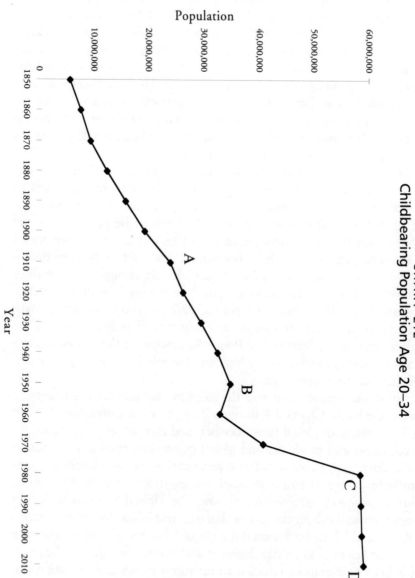

CHART 2.2
Childbearing Population Age 20–34

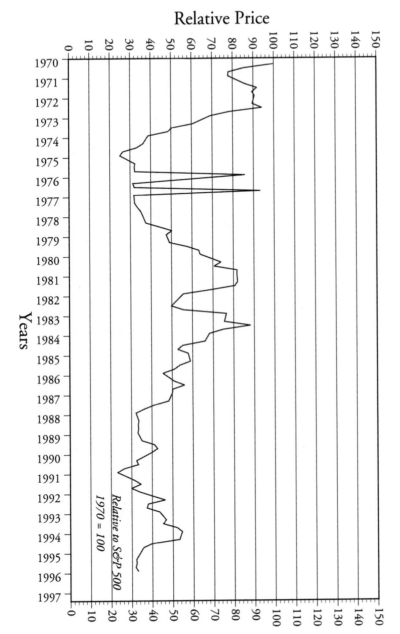

CHART 2.3
Home Building

Relative Price

Years

Relative to S&P 500
1970 = 100

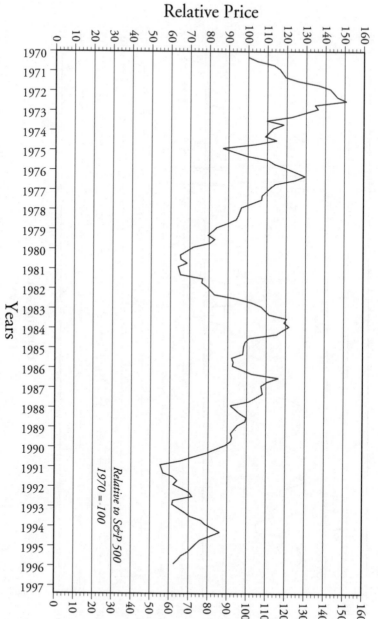

CHART 2.4
Household Furnishings & Appliances

Relative Price

Years

Relative to S&P 500
1970 = 100

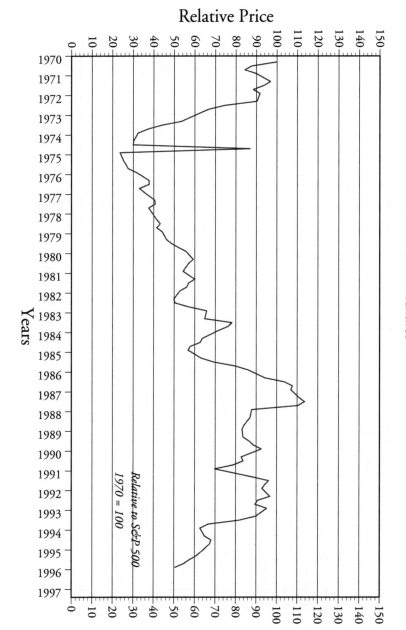

CHART 2.5
Textiles

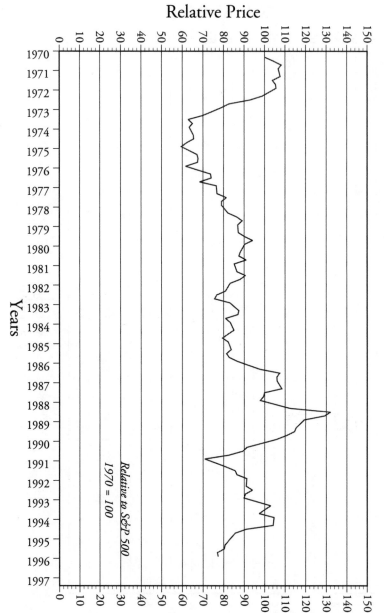

CHART 2.6
Building Materials

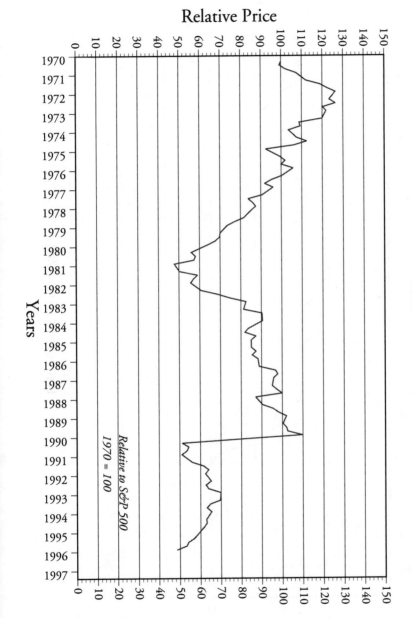

CHART 2.7
Retail

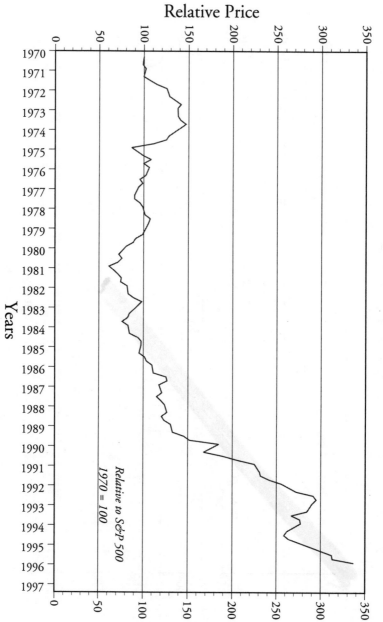

CHART 2.8
Beverages (Soft Drinks)

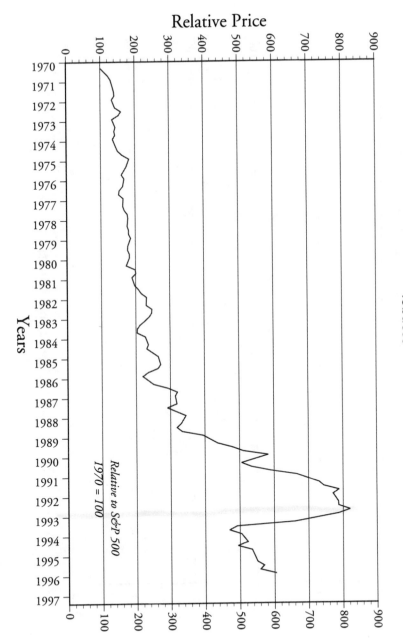

CHART 2.9
Tobacco

Relative Price

Years

Relative to S&P 500
1970 = 100

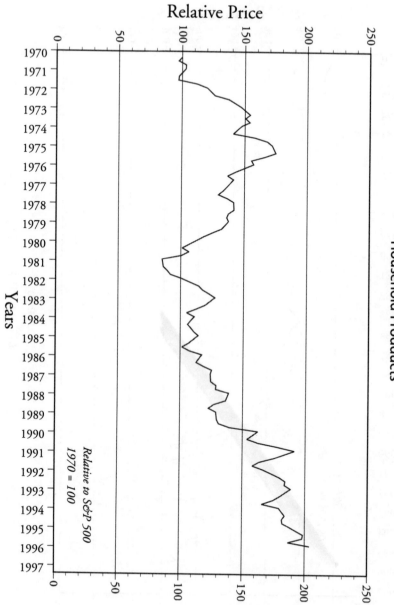

CHART 2.10
Household Prodducts

Relative Price

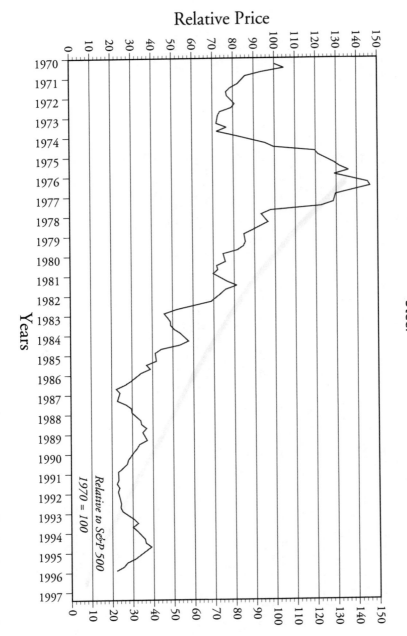

Years

CHART 2.11
Steel

Relative to S&P 500
1970 = 100

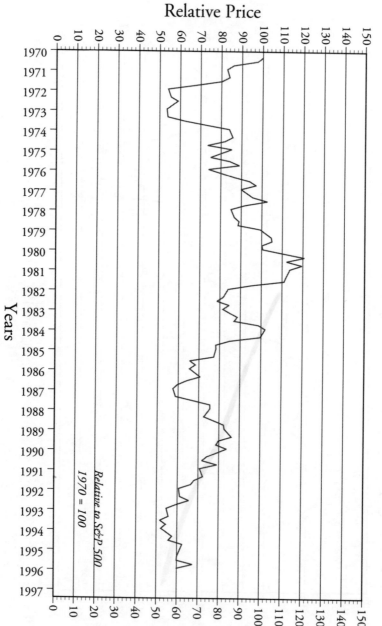

Relative Price

Years

Relative to S&P 500
1970 = 100

CHART 2.12
Aluminum

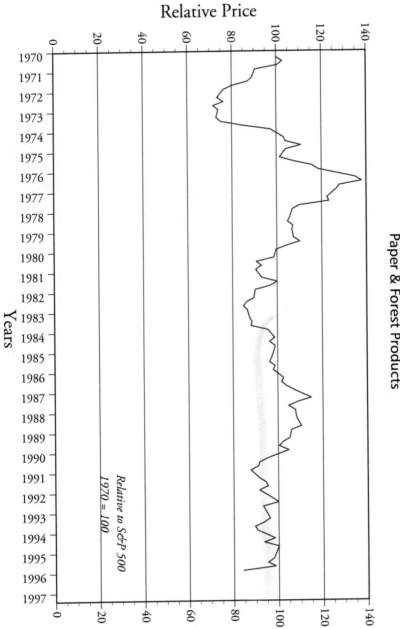

Relative Price

Years

CHART 2.13
Paper & Forest Products

Relative to S&P 500
1970 = 100

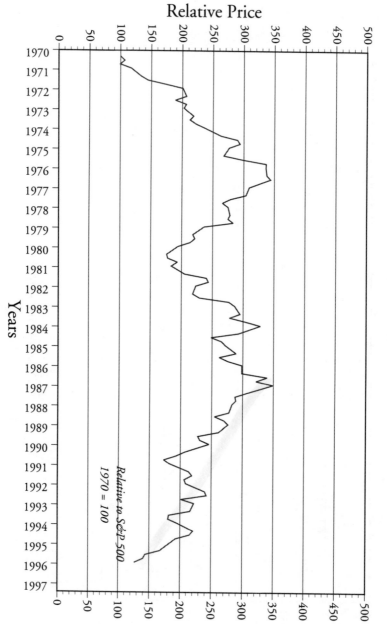

Relative Price

Years

CHART 2.14
Truckers

Relative to S&P 500
1970 = 100

energy also should be weak. Chart 2.15 depicts the domestic oil industry at the end of 1996—also near a twenty-five-year relative low.

While the paperless office is still a distant dream, e-mail and computer-to-computer faxing clearly reduce paper usage. Surprise, surprise, Chart 2.13 shows the paper industry stocks breaking down after 1994 as e-mail began to explode.

Who gains? With many underdeveloped countries using technology like computers, the Internet, and cellular phones to propel their citizens into the twenty-first century and sharply increase average incomes, one would expect to see the demand for food picking up. Chart 2.16 shows the price of wheat breaking a fifteen-year high in 1996, Chart 2.17 shows the price of corn breaking a twenty-two-year high in 1996, and Chart 2.18 shows soybeans breaking above a long trading range. U.S. farmland accounts for 26 percent of the world's productive land, and advances in biotechnology and sustainable farming are increasing food production.

Of course, the biggest beneficiaries are in technology. Chart 2.19 illustrates the performance of thirty technology leaders like Intel, Microsoft, and Cisco Systems. The stock market is confirming that the United States is changing into a technology economy. We are watching history being made.

Massive as they already have been, these changes are still in their infancy. About 90 percent of all the computing power that was ever built was generated in the last two years. There are about 430 million personal computers installed today; does anyone seriously think the computer revolution will stop before at least 2.4 *billion* PCs are in use? Less than a hundred biotech drugs have been approved in the last thirteen years. Only one-third of the people living today have ever made a telephone call. How big will those numbers be in five or ten years? What will the charts for semiconductors, personal computers, communications, and biotechnology stock indices look like then?

The stock market is a great reality test, and the reality of this economic transformation will be reflected in continued outperformance by the industries of the new economy.

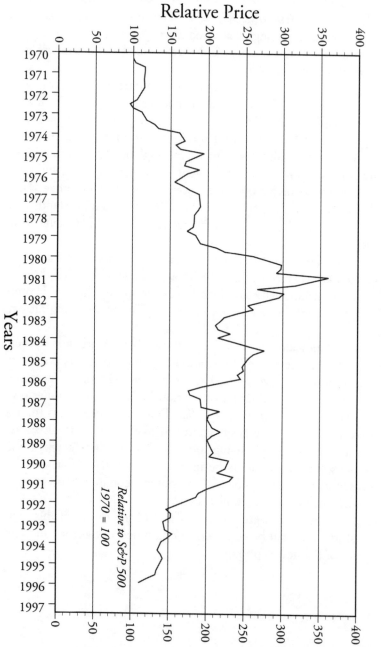

Relative Price

Years

CHART 2.15
Oil (Domestic)

Relative to S&P 500
1970 = 100

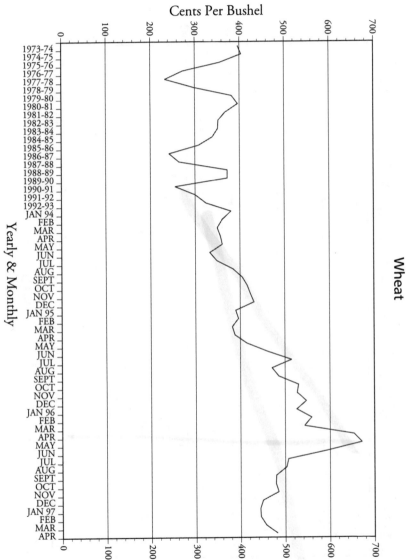

Cents Per Bushel

CHART 2.16
Wheat

Yearly & Monthly

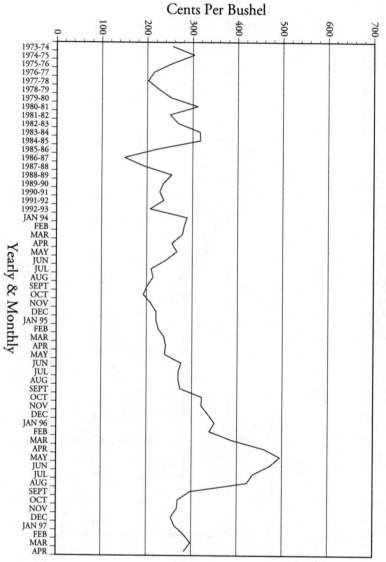

Cents Per Bushel

Yearly & Monthly

CHART 2.17

Corn

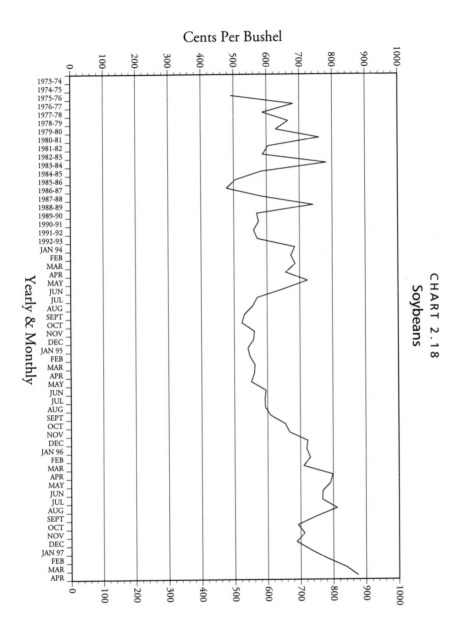

Cents Per Bushel

Yearly & Monthly

CHART 2.18
Soybeans

CHART 2.19
CTSL 30 Technologies

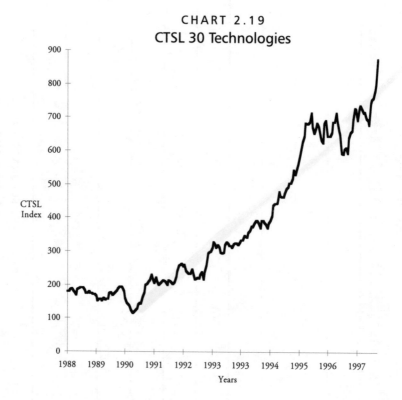

## CHAPTER THREE

What Is Technology?

When caveperson Oog made the first wheel, the rest of his or her society must have been dazzled by this stunning advance. It probably took Oog many weeks and several tries to get it right—square, triangle, or round? Thicker than it was high, or thinner? And what the heck would make it stay on the axle?

Oog was going through a process of research and development, investing human intelligence in a series of experiments and test projects to work out the final product. The wheel was a technological advance, and a series of improvements undoubtedly followed. Imagine the laughter that greeted the first proposal for spokes!

There wasn't a lot that could be done to improve the wheel, and it quickly became a stable, low-technology product. But not just because it was simple.

Consider the automobile. This incredibly complex product incorporates thousands of moving parts; interacting electrical, hydraulic, and chemical systems; and rugged mechanical demands, but it is not high technology. It *was* high-tech in 1920, but it is not today. Why?

The essence of high technology lies in rapid advances in product design because of heavy spending on R&D. R&D is the key to both identifying high-tech companies and identifying profitable investments.

R&D includes both "basic research" carried out in universities, think tanks, research centers like SRI (Stanford Research Institute), or under advanced military contracts, and "applied research" aimed at bringing to market a specific product featuring leading-edge advances.

As an example of the differences, look at thermogenic plants. The flowering voodoo lily is a spectacular, three-foot-tall version of the jack-in-the-pulpit. The central purple spike, drenched in hormones, emits waves of heat. Given an ambient temperature of 68° F, the voodoo lily can heat itself to 93° F. As a by-product, the lily produces salicylic acid—the active ingredient in aspirin.

There is considerable basic research going on around the world into why and how the lily generates so much heat. Plants usually compete for a limited amount of food, so for one to accelerate its metabolic rate and work like mad to spew "waste" heat into the atmosphere doesn't make obvious sense.

Botanists and biochemists are trying to figure out why these lilies heat up. Their current theory holds that the salicylic acid switches the entire metabolic path of the plant from energy storage to heat production just when it needs to be pollinated. The voodoo lily is best pollinated by carrion-loving insects, and the hot central spike emits an odor like that of rotting meat.

Ultimately, the voodoo lily will yield its secrets, papers will be written, prizes handed out, professors awarded tenure; attention will then shift to the next problem. Such is the nature of basic research.

By contrast, applied research on the voodoo lily is just getting under way. Du Pont, Inc., for one, is working with university scientists on possible practical applications for the voodoo lily's heat-generation mechanism. What sort of products could they be after? Let your imagination run free:

- a new herbicide that will interfere with a weed's metabolic path, causing it to self-destruct without drenching the soil with poisons?
- a genetically altered orange tree that would respond to cold snaps by releasing some stored energy as heat, maintaining itself above the freezing point?
- vegetables that could be kept in cold storage at an average temperature of 33° F, without fear that "cold spots" would cause freezer damage, because the vegetable would "turn on" enough heat to stay above 32° F?
- an energy-free way to heat a greenhouse? How about a *whole* house—piping the offensive smell away? Could enough heat be captured to make industrial steam?

Applied research is the art of the possible. Sometimes it's the just-barely possible, or the we-hope-the-other-guy's-chips-will-be-ready-when-we-are possible, in which case we call it "state of the art" or "leading edge" (wryly referred to in Silicon Valley as "bleeding edge"). It is the ability to realize the *product implications* of basic research that makes entrepreneurs and venture capitalists rich. A filmless camera, a Walkman, a massively parallel computer, a two-pound, full-feature portable computer—these are ideas that became possible through applied research because basic research had pushed some frontier back a little farther.

R&D spending creates new products and new variations of old products. Because these products are new, they can fetch premium prices and generate above-average profit margins. The first one or the first few companies to commercialize a new technology successfully reap the rewards of high profit margins and dominant market share.

If managers of a technology company understand their opportunity, they will reinvest a large portion of those above-average profits in further successful R&D. They will bring out a steady stream of new products and build a large, rapidly growing business. They will make their own products obsolete rather than letting some competitor do it for them. Before older companies know what's happened, the newcomer will take over a market or market niche, change the way an industry does business, accelerate the productivity and importance of a skill—you name it.

By sacrificing current earnings (in the face of Wall Street pressure to produce growing quarter-by-quarter results), they can get themselves on the Virtuous Circle, riding a cycle of high revenues—high profits—high R&D—high revenues up to a position as a large, dominant technology company. This is how an Intel, Microsoft, or Cisco Systems is built. Investors who buy into an innovative, R&D-intensive company at an attractive price will reap high profits over the long run.

How to Quantify R&D—The 7 Percent Solution

You know that the touchstone of a technology company is applied research and development. By quantifying their R&D efforts, you can make your first decisions on which high-tech stocks to buy.

If a company is spending a significant amount of money on R&D, it will list R&D as a separate line item on its income statement (certainly in annual reports, and usually in quarterly reports as well). If it claims to be a technology company but doesn't specify an R&D figure, look out.

We like to see companies spending at least 7 percent of revenues on R&D. To calculate this percentage, divide annual R&D by annual revenues for the last year or divide quarterly R&D by quarterly revenues. We arrived at the 7 percent hurdle rate by examining the income statements of hundreds of technology companies. There is a cluster of companies spending 20 percent or more of sales on R&D, another cluster in the 15-to-18 percent range, and another in the 10-to-12 percent area. These seem to be popular business models in several different industries. There is another cluster in the 7-to-10 percent range; below 7 percent, we found few companies that bothered to report R&D at all. Accountants do not require managements to break out R&D as a separate line item if it is not significant, and below 7 percent many companies seem to feel it is not significant. We agree!

There are a few legitimate exceptions. Some companies let their *suppliers* spend the money on R&D, yet still position themselves to benefit. For example, Seagate Technology is the leading disk-drive manufacturer, but this industry is characterized by brutal price competition that keeps gross profit margins at half the levels of many hardware companies. Seagate can afford to spend only about 5 percent of sales on R&D. However, Seagate's suppliers of recording heads and disk platters have higher profit margins than Seagate and spend 6 percent to 14 percent of revenues on R&D. Seagate works closely with them during the design phase of a new product and benefits from the suppliers' R&D spending.

Even starker examples are the computer retailers like CompUSA or Gateway 2000 that spend so little on R&D, they don't bother to list it as a separate item on their income statement. But clearly they benefit from everyone else's investments in R&D that keep pushing the performance of personal computers up and the prices down. We are willing to buy the computer retailers' stocks from time to time as legitimate investments in advancing technology, but we are always aware that these investments lack the proprietary edge R&D spending gives a company.

At the other extreme, technology defined by high R&D spending includes more than the usual electronics, computer, and medical industries. An example: Specialty-materials companies often qualify because they spend 10 percent to 20 percent of sales on R&D. Yet they are poorly followed by Wall Street and many are chronically underpriced.

That's not too surprising because Wall Street has been lazy in following technology. For many years, hiding behind the rubric "Don't buy what you don't understand," traders refused to buy computer or electronics stocks because they didn't know how to make a semiconductor, program a computer, or wire a local area network.

Instead they bought GM or Du Pont, Inc.—as if any of those traders could design an engine or even rebuild one themselves, much less manage a chemical reaction. Ludicrous, but it allowed lazy people to refuse to learn about new things and just keep investing in the old stuff.

Enter the personal computer: Everybody's got one. Most are networked or have a modem. Everyone understands the difference between software and hardware. To illustrate how far we have come, when we started the *California Technology Stock Letter,* we always said "random-access memory," not RAM; we never just said "byte," but always added in parentheses "a byte is one character made up of 8 bits, each bit is a 1 or 0." So the jargon of 1982 has become cocktail-party chatter in 2000.

Technology has been demystified. People not only lost their fear of the unknown when it comes to technology, they are actively embracing it. The hottest market in personal computing is the SOHO market: small office/home office. These are the PCs bought to run the home office or consulting job by day, and then educate and entertain the kids and family at night. The home PC used to be a low-power version about three years out of date. Today, many people have a more powerful PC at home than they have at work. The demand for technology will end when everyone in the world has a PC that can be asked in any language to provide any desired data or calculation, and it does so instantly. Anything less can be improved upon—and therefore will be.

What If They're Wasting the Money?

One question that always worries individual investors is "How can we tell whether R&D is being spent intelligently or being wasted?"

Fortunately, virtually all companies have more ideas than they have R&D money. Projects have to compete for funds internally, so a surprisingly small amount of money is spent in pursuit of totally off-the-wall ideas or, even worse, fraudulent research.

However, both happen. Sometimes companies overreach, too. Say a computer manufacturer is designing a machine that depends on a chip being developed simultaneously by another company. If the chip maker has a major problem or runs into a delay—they often do—the computer company may be out of luck.

Sometimes companies spend money on dumb things. Did you ever see Convergent Technologies' "WorkSlate," which came out in the mid-1980s? It was a little notebook computer, about the size of a Tandy 100, but it did only one thing: spreadsheets. With word processing the most popular application on personal computers by far, and with the then-rapidly-rising popularity of Lotus 1-2-3, the WorkSlate was doomed from the start. The round-rubber-button keyboard didn't help.

You don't have to be an engineer or understand exactly how a technology works to form an opinion about whether something makes sense. If it doesn't make sense to you, or someone cannot explain it clearly enough to let you form an opinion, don't invest. There's always another great stock with another great story just around the corner.

Sometimes companies falsely represent the validity of their R&D. According to *The Wall Street Journal,* ICN Pharmaceuticals was the subject of a four-year SEC investigation into alleged violations of antifraud and reporting provisions of the securities laws in connection with its application to the FDA for approval of a drug, ribavirin, which purportedly cured AIDS. At the time, ICN had low earnings and a high P/E multiple, but it looked pretty attractive based on its high spending on R&D. However, a little reading on ribavirin revealed that the company had previously touted it as a potential cure for several diseases, and it had never worked, except for one small indication in children. So we never bought the stock. We were in the audience when ICN management presented their data on how many AIDS patients died on ribavirin versus how many died on the placebo, and it was immediately obvious that the death rate on the placebo was four or five times higher than the normal AIDS death rate. They had stacked the deck by assigning the sickest patients to the placebo group and reserving the healthiest patients to test their drug—a gross violation of the requirement to divide patients randomly in double-blind studies. When a company has the kinds of problems with the SEC that ICN had, it makes it very difficult for us to trust management and buy the stock in the future—at any price or valuation.

There is an acid test for whether R&D is being wasted: Does the company turn out a steady stream of successful, new products? You can tell by reading successive annual reports if the research being undertaken one year becomes the product launch of the following year and the success story of the year after that. Or you can tell from the marketplace. Any computer retailer will tell you that Adobe Systems, for example, makes excellent software and introduces winning products and upgrades year after year.

If you want to be precise, phone the company and ask the investor-relations person this simple question: "What percentage of your revenues today come from products introduced in the last three years?"

The answer ought to be "over 50 percent," if the company's research is at all productive. In a fast-moving industry like disk drives, you'll find that 100 percent of the sales come from products introduced in the last twelve months! Now, *that's* productivity. If a company's been spending too much on R and not enough on D, you may get answers as low as 33 percent, 20 percent, or even 10 percent. If so, smile sweetly and tiptoe away. There are better places for your money.

However, if the company *does* meet the 50 percent test, ask the investor-relations person another, more open-ended question: "What are you spending your R&D money on?"

Of course, you won't hear about new projects in excruciating detail, but company representatives are surprisingly willing to talk about broad areas of effort. They may be furiously improving their current products, investing in a related product line, or even starting a new business venture. Sometimes, if you ask enough questions, the investor-relations person will pass you on to a scientist or strategic planner, who will be even more candid.

Incidentally, don't ever hesitate to pick up the phone and call investor relations, whether you own the stock or not. The phone number will be listed in the annual report, at the end of any press release, or on its Web site. Many companies have toll-free numbers for potential investors and shareholders, and several have fax-back systems to rush documents to your fax machine any time of the day or night. Technology companies know exactly how to get to institutional investors through their investment bankers, securities analysts, and brokerage-firm conferences. But high-tech companies, especially smaller ones, have a hard time reaching individuals. Many companies prefer individual shareholders; with a solid corps of individual backers, the entire company's stock valuation does not depend on one Wall Street analyst who might wake up in a bad mood someday. So they will welcome your call.

IBM's goal has been 50 percent institutional/50 percent individual shareholders for many years, and from 1993 to 1996 Intel deliberately boosted its constituency of individual holders from 30 percent to 50 percent. During that period, Intel stock increased 522 percent, so they have a lot of happy individual shareholders.

In fact, if you *don't* call, the investor-relations person might get fired for having nothing to do. You wouldn't want that to happen.

Keeping Up with Technology

Is it realistic for an individual to keep up with technology? The truth is that no one person can stay 100 percent on top of all the niches in technology today; there's too much going on. But it's easy to maintain a broad overview of the major trends and then focus on the few technologies and stocks that interest you.

For a broad background, read the Tuesday Science Times section and the Sunday Technology section in *The New York Times,* the science-and-technology section of *The Economist,* and a wonderful weekly digest, *Science News.* (All contact information is in Appendix E.) *Scientific American* is an old favorite that covers a wide range of technologies from biotech to space travel. Specific, thoughtful articles on electronics technology can also be found in *Wired, Upside, The Red Herring,* and *Forbes ASAP.* In biotechnology, *Bioventure View* is a monthly publication with a good mix of articles on people, companies, and technologies. To keep up with the science, we like *Nature Biotechnology.* For $105 you can join the American Academy for the Advancement of Science, impress your friends, and receive its superb weekly magazine *Science,* plus access to an equally superb Web site.

For roundtables with Wall Street analysts and interviews with chief executive officers, check out the weekly *Wall Street Transcript.* A subscription costs $1,890 a year, but it can be found in many libraries.

Brokerage firms specializing in technology turn out a lot of good research. Open an account and do some trading; you'll be surprised at what you get. Hambrecht & Quist; DB Alex. Brown; and Cowen & Co. all welcome individual investors. Those with bigger accounts could add Nationsbank Montgomery Securities; BancBoston Robertson, Stephens & Co.; and Goldman Sachs.

On many cable TV systems or with a satellite dish, you can pick up CNBC, C/Net, the Computer Television Network, "Science & Technology Week" on CNN, and ZDTV.

If you are on the Internet, try the free Yahoo stock forums (http://messages.yahoo.com/index.html), the subscription-based *Silicon Investor* (www.techstocks.com), our Web site (www.ctsl.com), the SEC filings in the Edgar system (www.sec.gov), and each individual company's Web site.

Companies are more and more inclined to publish management and industry presentations, research papers, and detailed company backgrounders both on their Web site and in an "investor's packet" they will be glad to mail to you. Many of these include reprints of brokerage-firm recommendations. Just ask that nice investor-relations person. Try to get a copy of any available prospectus, even if it's out of date—the "Business" section will almost always teach you something. Many companies broadcast their earnings conference calls on their Web site, as well as special analyst presentations.

Finally, there are many good technology newsletters that don't make stock recommendations, including Dick Shaffer's *Computer Letter,* Chris Shipley's *Demo Letter,* Jeffrey Tartar's *SoftLetter,* and Steve Szirom's *SIBS.*

For stock recommendations, our *California Technology Stock Letter* is the main newsletter for electronics, computer, and communications. We also cover biotechnology and medical devices, and there are several specialty newsletters for medical stocks, including Jim McCamant's *Medical Technology Stock Letter* and *AgBiotech Letter,* and Harry Tracy's *NeuroInvestment.*

PART II

The Technology Industries

IN April 1981, IBM introduced

its personal computer; two months later, I left Capital Research Company to start the *California Technology Stock Letter*. It was obvious that personal computing would change the world, sharply increasing the size and diversity of the markets for technology products. We started *CTSL* with fewer than fifty subscribers, but I hoped there might be a few hundred more individuals who would pay for institutional-quality research on these rapidly growing new companies.

During the previous eleven years, as I was following technology stocks, there were only two major customers for technology products: Fortune 500 companies and the Department of Defense. There were also only three major technology industries: large computers; suppliers of transistors, capacitors, and other components; and companies like Hewlett-Packard and Tektronix, making oscilloscopes and other specialty instruments. Even these three industries were closely intertwined. In an economic downturn, Fortune 500 companies would cut capital-spending budgets, and the mainframe and minicomputer industries would sneeze. All their suppliers—primarily the electronic-components companies—would then catch cold. Component companies, in turn, would cut back spending on instruments. Eventually, the recession would end, capital-spending budgets would grow, and technology stocks—moving as a group—would head back up.

Today, due in large part to that one significant product introduction by IBM in 1981, virtually every person, company, and government in the world is a customer for technology products. The technology industries now encompass not just large computers but personal computers, software, semiconductors, semiconductor equipment, communications (both telecommunications and data communications), the Internet, and medical technology (biotechnology and medical devices) as well.

Driven by a vast number of variables that include how we play, eat, talk, cure ourselves, and more, technology is no longer a mono-lith. The good news is that you now can build a nicely diversified portfolio while staying in the high-growth, broadly defined technology sector. The bad news is that you need to be familiar with the different business models and economic drivers of these eight very different industries if you want to understand your investments. Fortunately, you don't need an MBA or CPA to get enough background in these areas. For each industry, you just need to know the answers to seven questions:

1. How fast is this industry growing?
2. What drives the growth cycles?
3. How profitable is it?
4. Who are the customers?
5. Which competitive strategies win?
6. How will the Internet affect it?
7. What is the next big change?

The next several chapters answer these questions for the eight crucial technology industries. By the end of this part, you will have enough information to invest with confidence in any of these fast-growing areas. If one or two intrigue you more than the others, you will have a solid base of information on which to build a deeper understanding using the sources we will give you. There is nothing wrong with specializing and concentrating your investments in a single group like semiconductors or biotechnology, if you know what you are doing.

## CHAPTER FOUR

Semiconductor Equipment

The underlying reason that technology is taking over the world is that the cost of doing anything electronic—storing data, performing calculations—falls 50 percent every eighteen months. When costs are falling so rapidly, the power and productivity of a device at any given price point—say, $1,800 for a typical personal computer—rises 1,600 percent every six years. That means dramatic breakthroughs in the amount and kind of work you can do with your PC.

(You've probably heard the comparison that if the automobile industry had advanced at the same rate as the computer industry, your car would be a Rolls-Royce that goes 2,000 miles an hour on one cent of gas. To which the automobile manufacturers add: ". . . and crashes three times along the way.")

Many people think this terrific rate of advance is driven by the semiconductor industry. Not true. While that industry has the smarts to design great new chips, none of those designs would see the light of day without continuous advances in the semiconductor-equipment industry. If semiconductors are "the oil of electronics," then the equipment to make semiconductors is the drilling rig, tool bit, and pipeline.

The equipment manufacturers figure out how to make the electrical circuit lines on the chips thinner and thinner, and pack them closer and closer together, without having everything short out. Today they can put 550 circuit lines in the width of a human hair. In five years, 1000.

The equipment manufacturers also realized that the cost of processing a wafer full of chips was about the same, no matter how big the wafer was or what kind of chips were on it. Starting with 2-inch-diameter wafers, they have led the industry through several generations of equipment:

4-inch, 6-inch, 8-inch (now widely employed), and 12-inch (to be deployed beginning in the year 2001). A 6-inch-diameter wafer can hold about 225 typical chips. An 8-inch-diameter wafer holds 425 chips, and imagine a wafer of silicon a full foot in diameter stuffed with 975 chips. Obviously, if the cost of processing the wafer is about the same, the cost per chip is falling rapidly.

How Fast Is This Industry Growing?

The semiconductor-equipment industry grew 18 percent a year from 1987 through 1997. That included some slow years around the 1990–1991 recession and a boom year in 1995. Growth slowed in 1996 to about a 10 percent rate, and the industry topped out at about a $25 billion annual shipment rate. The second half of 1996 was weak, as was the first half of 1997, as semiconductor companies used up the excess capacity they had installed in 1994 and 1995. The Asian financial crisis caused further postponements of capital additions, even those needed to keep up with growth in the computer- and communications-equipment industries. While total 1998 sales were projected to fall below 1997 levels by about 15 percent, the equipment industry passed its trough at the end of 1998 and started a multiyear upturn.

Over 100 major semiconductor-fabrication factories are scheduled to be built in the next three years alone. Virtually every developing country's government wants to build a semiconductor fab, in the same way they used to want to build automobile factories. China alone may build as many as 300 fabs during the next ten years. As computers and communications spread around the world to newly affluent consumers everywhere, tremendous quantities of silicon will be sucked up. Those chips have to be built somewhere, so the equipment industry is likely to resume an 18 percent annual growth rate for the next seven to ten years.

What Drives the Growth Cycles?

Semiconductor equipment is a major capital investment, often involving millions of dollars for one machine and $1 to $2 billion for an entire fabrication facility. That means money is allocated by the chip-manufacturer customers through a careful capital-budgeting process, which takes some time. Consequently, *orders* for semiconductor equipment tend to *lag behind* conditions in the chip industry. Coming out of a slow period for chip sales, orders for new equipment will be low because chip makers have plenty of unused capacity from the prior cycle of factory building.

As chip sales pick up, spot shortages will develop and the prices of some chips will stop declining or even start to rise. Suddenly, the economics of making those chips justifies expanding production, and the chip makers will order more manufacturing lines for their current factories. This is when the semiconductor-equipment industry feels the first benefit of the upturn, as at the end of 1998, and its stocks start to outperform the market. Typically, chip makers just order more of what they already have—it is easier to get a new line into production if it is identical to others that already are producing chips.

In the next stage, their factories are nearing full capacity with no room for additional lines, so the manufacturers commit to new "greenfield" plants. These factory designs start with an empty plot of land—a green field—and take more than a year to build. During construction, the manufacturers will evaluate and test all the latest semiconductor equipment and issue purchase orders. At this point, new manufacturers have their best chance to get a foot in the door, because rather than just duplicate existing production lines, chip makers will be looking for newer equipment that can cut costs or produce higher manufacturing yields.

After the factory is built, it takes another six to nine months to bring in all the equipment and test the production process. This is the best of times for semiconductor-equipment stocks. They often surge on the announcement of orders won, and then move up again when the equipment is shipped and revenues are booked. This period can go on for quite a while, depending on what is happening to end-user demand for computer and communications products. Eventually, though, too much production capacity is built, chip prices fall, and the manufacturers back off from their expansion plans. They may even put projects on hold, pending the next up-cycle.

We used to say that the top of the market was always marked by Intel, which would decide to build a huge factory right at the peak of activity. By the time the structure was completed, the market would be headed down, and Intel executives would lock the doors before they equipped it. A year or so later, when Intel announced it was going ahead with the equipment orders, we knew that the bottom of the market was behind us. Early in 1997, Intel began placing massive orders for new equipment. Sure enough, we got a semiconductor upturn in 1999. You can track this cycle by getting the monthly press release on equipment orders and shipments from the Semiconductor Equipment & Materials Institute (see Appendix E for contact information).

When monthly orders exceed shipments, the ratio of orders to shipments is above 1-to-1. This ratio is called the book-to-bill ratio. Although the book-to-bill ratio for chips was more widely known until it was discontinued at the end of 1996, in many ways, the book-to-bill ratio for equipment is more useful. It is reported in SEMI's monthly press release; the data can be found on the Institute's Web site. The best time to buy a stock is when their book-to-bill ratio is below 1-to-1 but starting to rise, and the best time to sell is when the ratio is at a cyclical high but starting to decline.

If the supply/demand cycle for semiconductors was the only force driving the semiconductor-equipment cycle, it would not be a hard business to forecast. But there is another major force: the march of technology. The cost of making a semiconductor falls 50 percent every eighteen months *only* if the manufacturers have the latest equipment. Even in the middle of a downturn, manufacturing technology is advancing. Chip makers have to make constant trade-offs between adding to excess capacity today or being caught tomorrow with a high-cost process in an industry upturn. If a company decides to slide by without updating its technology, what will happen to it if a competitor *does* buy the new equipment?

Sometimes these issues assume national importance, as in the competition between the Japanese and the Koreans to build DRAMs—dynamic random-access-memory chips. In the 1996 personal-computer inventory correction, the price of DRAMs fell 80 percent. Japanese manufacturers were losing money, and the last thing they wanted to do was buy new equipment and increase capacity.

But the Korean manufacturers, who were also losing money, saw an opportunity to get a leg up on the Japanese by plunging ahead with new factories. On a strict return-on-investment analysis, it might not have made sense. But as a geopolitical decision, it was an investment worth making. After all, Korea needs to compete in something, and the country's other businesses—steel, shipbuilding, automobiles—are not especially easy to build up.

There is a possibly apocryphal story that after the founder and head of Hyundai retired in 1996, his son was promoted. The son had spent his entire business career in Hyundai's automobile business, and in order to understand the electronics side, he went on a tour of a Hyundai DRAM plant. At the end of the production line he held up an eight-inch wafer full of chips and said, "Let me get this straight. We sell this wafer for more than we sell a car?"

The plant manager said, "Yes."

"And we make more money on this wafer than we do on a car?"

"That's right."

The son made his first executive decision. "Build more semiconductor plants!"

Shortly after that, Hyundai announced new $1.5 billion projects in Scotland and Oregon, with a second follow-on project in Scotland in 2001. Korea's economic problems delayed those plants, but the transition from old-economy automobile manufacturing to new-economy semiconductor manufacturing is inevitable.

How Profitable Is It?

Very. Semiconductor equipment is a manufactured product sold to a small number of customers. The big three of the industry—Applied Materials, Lam Research, and Novellus Systems—average gross profits of 50 percent. Out of that they spend a lot on R&D, an average of 12 percent. They spend 18 percent on selling, general, and administrative expenses (SG&A), which is not bad, considering the long selling cycle and the extensive customer hand-holding required to get equipment installed and accepted in the customer's production process.

This leaves the three companies with average operating profits of 20 percent, superb by any standards. This financial model is typical for the industry, although smaller, newer companies may be using it as a target to reach.

What Competitive Strategies Win?

The most important strategy for these companies' success is to have the best price/performance equipment, which usually means the latest technology. Equipment that can build the most advanced, complex chips is worth a premium price, because that price is amortized over the number of bits or wafers it will process in a given period of time.

In an interesting corollary approach, some companies deliberately choose not to make the most advanced product, opting instead to drive the cost out of the previous generation of products and then sell the customer on a "mix-'n'-match" strategy: Use the old process wherever you can and the new, expensive process only where you have to. This method is practiced most successfully by Ultratech Stepper, which makes equipment to print the fine electronic circuit lines onto the silicon wafer.

The second most important strategy is to offer global service and support. Of course, this can be difficult and expensive for a small company that may have the latest and greatest gear, but does not have the size to support it worldwide. The usual solution is to sell and service direct in the United States and possibly in Korea, where there are only four major customers, and then use well-known equipment distributors to handle sales and support in Europe and Japan. The downside is that the distributor takes a hefty cut of the profits, which leaves less to reinvest in new R&D to stay ahead of the big boys. But if the equipment is good enough, it will generate lots of revenues and a big installed base, whereupon the manufacturer can eliminate the distributors and begin direct sales and support.

How Will the Internet Affect It?

The Internet will not have a major direct effect on semiconductor manufacturers because they deal directly with their customers or distributors. The face-to-face sales in this business takes a long time; the Internet is best at replacing long distribution chains with one-to-one customer contact.

Indirectly, though, the Internet is causing an explosion in data communications and the required computing power. Consumers in newly developing countries need a much cheaper device to get on the Internet than the traditional personal computer. This "Internet appliance" will cost less than $500—perhaps much less—and consist mainly of a keyboard and a few chips. The demand for silicon, both for the appliance and for the communications links to connect it to the Internet, will drive the semiconductor-equipment industry for years to come.

What Is the Next Big Change?

The next big change in the semiconductor-equipment industry is to move from today's 0.25-micron equipment to 0.18-micron equipment. This is the equivalent of going from 280 circuit lines in the width of a human hair to 400 lines.

Following a little behind, but essentially in parallel, is the move to twelve-inch-diameter silicon wafers, which should be well under way by the year 2001. These two changes will drive the next sharp drops in chip cost-per-bit, and essentially require that almost every semiconductor factory in the world be reequipped by 2005.

When you are looking at semiconductor-equipment companies, ask each how these two trends play into the company's business strategy. Call the investor-relations people at the company, or check the company Web site for a company backgrounder. For example, in order to make such fine lines, the current method of etching circuits—using high pressure, low-density reactive gas—has to change to low pressure, high-density reactive gas. Trikon Technologies licensed its technology in this area to

Applied Materials and Lam Research. The investor-relations contacts at other companies that make etching equipment will give you their perspective on this change in technology and tell you what they are doing to respond to it.

Today, most semiconductors are processed on single-wafer systems to maintain quality control. But processing wafers one at a time creates a real bottleneck. Mattson Technology has a robotics platform that handles four wafers at once, with no loss of quality. Innovations like this give new companies a chance to break into the big time as the chip makers upgrade their fabs for the twenty-first century.

## CHAPTER FIVE

How to Make a Semiconductor

You do not have to understand how semiconductors are made to be a successful technology investor—truth is, you can skip this chapter altogether. But this is the only technology we will explain in any depth because it is the basis for almost everything else that happens in the new economy. In the next five minutes, you will learn how to make a semiconductor—this technology stuff isn't so hard, is it? Diagram 5.1 shows how a semiconductor is made.

First, a single-crystal cylindrical ingot is pulled from a vat of pure, molten silicon (Figure 1). The ingot is polished and sliced into thin wafers with a diamond saw (Figure 2). These wafers are ground perfectly flat and polished to a mirror finish. This step is handled by some big specialty-chemical companies like Shinetsu and MEMC Electronic Materials.

Next, a very thin layer of pure single-crystal silicon is deposited on the surface of the wafer (Figure 3). This *epitaxial* layer is used to change the electrically conductive properties of the wafer, and is applied only once. Epitaxial reactors are an important submarket in the semiconductor equipment business. Competitors include Applied Materials, ASM International, and EMCORE.

The wafer then undergoes a series of processes that are repeated for each layer of the electronic circuit. In a *diffusion* furnace, dopants (impurities such as boron and arsenic) are diffused into the surface of the wafer to change its conductivity. This layer will be used to form base emitters, sources, and drains to move electricity around the chip (Figure

DIAGRAM 5.1

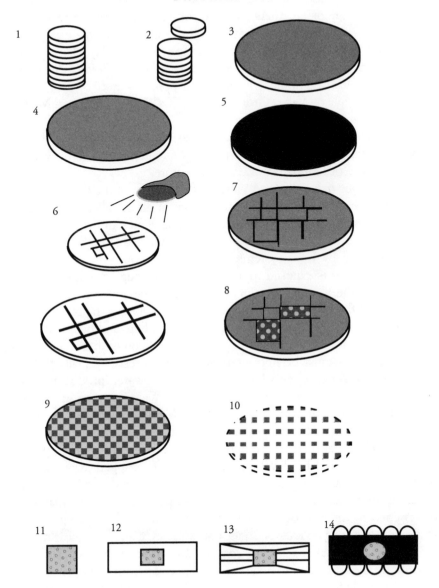

4). Diffusion furnaces are built by such companies as Tokyo Electron, Kokusai Electric, and Silicon Valley Group.

In the next phase, the wafer is placed in a cloud of vaporized film, which may be an oxide, metal, nitride, or other material. The cloud will deposit a very thin film of material on the wafer. This material may be destined to carry electricity within a layer, connect layers of other films, or to insulate one layer from another (Figure 5). *Chemical-vapor-deposition* (CVD) equipment is built by Applied Materials, Novellus, Lam Research, Silicon Valley Group, Genus, Watkins-Johnson, and Mattson Technology.

This layer is covered with a *photoresist layer,* which is a light-sensitive coating that can be used to print the circuit pattern on the wafer. It is like a piece of film before you snap a picture.

Next comes *lithography.* A picture of each layer of the desired electronic circuit has been transferred to a piece of glass, called a *mask* or *reticle.* Masks are made by companies like Photronics and Micro Mask, a division of Hoya Glass in Japan. The equipment used to make the mask is manufactured by Etec Systems. As Figure 6 shows, the photoresist layer on the wafer is exposed to a light shining through the appropriate mask. Where the light hits the photoresist, the material is hardened in the pattern of the mask. Hardening is done by developing the photoresist layer, just as a negative is developed from camera film, and baking it.

Because hundreds of identical chips are made on each wafer, many identical pictures must be imprinted on the photoresist. Usually this is done with a *wafer stepper,* which moves over the wafer, producing precisely aligned copies of the circuits on the mask. Wafer steppers are made by Nikon, Canon, Ultratech Stepper, and ASM Lithography.

After hardening, the wafer goes into *etch.* Using a reactive gas that acts like a chemical solvent, the deposited vaporized film from Figure 5 that is not protected by developed photoresist is stripped away. Selectively removing areas of deposited film leaves the circuit lines on the wafer, in the pattern determined by the mask pattern and in the material determined by the type of film deposited (Figure 7). The leading etcher manufacturers are Applied Materials, Lam Research, and Tokyo Electron.

The wafer then may go to *ion implantation.* More dopants are forced into the surface of the chip with an electron beam. These ions are placed precisely to control the electrical conductivity in a selected region (Figure 8). Varian Semiconductor Equipment and Eaton Corp. are major suppliers of medium-energy ion implanters; Genus dominated the high-energy market until the company sold its product line to Varian in 1998.

A *photoresist strip* machine then removes the developed photoresist; manufacturers include GaSonics International and Mattson Technology.

In an *oxide-deposit* step, a layer of silicon dioxide is placed on the chip via a gas discharge at relatively low temperature and pressure. This insulates circuit lines and prepares the chip for *metalization* (Figure 9). A thin layer of aluminum is sputtered by gas discharge onto the chip. The aluminum connects the circuit and interconnects various components of the chips. (In a recent technology advance, IBM began using copper to do the same thing.) For these steps, manufacturers usually employ chemical-vapor-deposition equipment, so the competitors are the same as for CVD: Applied Materials, Novellus, Lam Research, Silicon Valley Group, Watkins-Johnson, and Mattson Technology. Steps 5 through 9 may be repeated several times until the chips are complete.

The wafer is then *diced,* or cut into separate identical chips with a precision diamond saw (Figure 10), usually made by Kulicke & Soffa Industries or Disco. Each chip or die (Figure 11) is *bonded* to a package base, which contains the electronic leads that will connect the chip's electronic circuits to the outside world (Figure 12). *Wire bonding* connects the package leads to the chip leads (Figure 13); Kulicke & Soffa is the main supplier. Finally, *encapsulation* provides a top to the package, sealing the chip inside in a corrosion-free, protected environment (Figure 14).

Throughout this process, the wafers and die will be *inspected visually* by microscope for surface defects, often using equipment made by KLA Tencor or FEI Corp. (which bought Phillips ElectronOptics), and *probed electronically* for electrical faults using wafer probes made by Schlumberger or Advantest. Obviously, the earlier in the process a bad batch of chips can be caught, the fewer resources will be wasted on further processing.

After the chip is manufactured, it is examined by a *tester,* probably made by Credence Systems, Megatest, GenRad, LTX, or Teradyne. Depending on how the chip was designed, some problems can be corrected with lasers (Electro Scientific Industries) or by other means.

How to Make Money Making Semiconductors

Most of the over one hundred semiconductor fabrication facilities scheduled to be built in the next three years are designed to make chips with much finer 0.25-micron lines on much bigger 300-millimeter (12-inch) wafers. Any given chip can be made much less expensively in such a fab facility because the smaller line widths allow many more chips to be packed on a wafer, and the larger wafers cost little more to handle than the smaller ones.

Therefore, in order to stay cost competitive, companies must build and equip these factories. They have no choice because they need to keep improving productivity.

But the sources of productivity growth are changing. This table tells the tale:

	Last 10 Years	Next 10 Years
Equipment productivity:		
Yield	3 x	1.1 x
Feature Size	4 x	4 x
Wafer Size	4 x	2.3 x
Utilization	1.5 x	1.1 x
Total Gain	72 x	11 x
Capital Productivity:		
Equipment Cost	− 3 x	− 3 x
Equipment Throughput	− 1.3 x	+ 5 x
Total Loss/Gain	− 4 x	+ 1.7 x
Net Productivity	18 x	+ 19 x

Average yields, or the percentage of good chips, tripled over the last ten years as equipment got better and better and chip makers learned the recipe. But they cannot do better than perfect, so during the next ten years yields will account for only a 10 percent improvement—about all that is left.

Feature size shrank by a factor of 4x, creating a 4x improvement, and will continue to shrink at that rate, which is good news. But wafer size, which increased 4x over the last ten years, will increase only 2.3x over the next ten years. As wafers get larger, it gets harder and harder to keep the yields up.

Equipment utilization improved 50 percent or 1.5x over the last ten years; but again, companies cannot work more than three shifts, and equipment cannot have more than 100 percent uptime. Considering the remaining room for improvement, we envision only a 10 percent gain—or 1.1x—over the next ten years.

So, for the last ten years, the industry multiplied a 3x improvement in yields by a 4x improvement in feature size by a 4x improvement in wafer size by a 1.5x improvement in equipment utilization, for an overall 72x improvement in the production process.

In terms of dollars, though, the equipment tripled in price (–3x) and throughput fell by about 30 percent (–1.3x). Ten years ago, the industry used batch-processing systems that handled many wafers at once, but suffered from a relatively wide range of results depending on where the wafer was located in the batch. So manufacturers moved to newer single-wafer systems, which solved the process-control problem, but are very slow and compromise throughput.

With prices increased 3x and throughput 30 percent worse, capital productivity fell by a factor of 4x during the last ten years. Dividing the 72x gain in physical productivity by the 4x loss in capital productivity, we end up with net productivity per dollar of semiconductor-equipment spending increasing 18x over the last ten years. That's why chip prices continued to fall and the computer and communications business boomed.

Now look at the next ten years. Physical productivity will increase only 1.1x from yield times 4x from feature size times 2.3x from wafer size times 1.1x from utilization, or about 11x overall. That's much lower than the 72x of the last ten years.

Equipment will continue to get more expensive at a 3x rate. Obviously, if throughput doesn't change, overall productivity for the next ten years will be only 11 divided by 3, or about 3.6x compared to the last ten years' 18x. The cost of semiconductors would continue to fall, but much slower than in the past. The growth rate of the entire electronics industry would be in danger.

For chip manufacturers, productivity during the next ten years is crucially dependent on throughput. Fortunately, there are new technologies that can share a single set of robotics (the mechanical systems that handle a wafer) while processing multiple wafers at once. Our research indicates that throughput will reverse its decline and grow 5x during the next ten years. That allows the productivity of capital to rise 70 percent (1.7x) instead of falling 4x as in the past. And 1.7 multiplied by 11 means that net productivity will rise 19x over the next ten years. The rate of improvement will stay about the same as that of the last ten years, guaranteeing that the cost of semiconductors will continue to fall 50 percent every 18 months and that the world really will be wired.

## CHAPTER SIX

Semiconductors

The semiconductor industry is the eye of the hurricane of change moving through the world economy. No matter what happens in computing devices, communications, the Internet, multimedia, robotic assembly, and even biotechnology, it seems to be driven by powerful new semiconductors. The percentage of semiconductor value in electronic systems continues to rise as more and more features are moved into silicon, but consumers get good value for this investment because of the constantly declining price per semiconductor function. You can see the benefits in your CD player, home fax machine, cell phone, auto engine and emission controls, food processor, and multimedia PC.

Most nontechnology U.S. companies boost earnings by raising prices, stealing market share from one another, or (while they can) downsizing operations to cut costs. By contrast, every year semiconductor companies simply increase the value of their products by lowering the cost of calculating or storing information. This reliable deflation creates its own demand for new products. Complex products and applications, formerly available only on centralized mini- and mainframe computers, become available on desktop machines costing under $10,000, and then under $5,000. Older products and applications can be found on computers costing less than $2,500, and eventually less than $1,000.

At that price, electronic productivity can be spread widely in high volume. Microcontrollers with some memory, costing under $10, can be justified in cars and major appliances. The car that remembers everyone's settings for the driver's seat is already a reality.

While the semiconductor-equipment companies enable the production of ever-faster, ever-smaller, ever-cheaper chips, the chip makers themselves have taken advantage of the trend. In sharp contrast to, say, the automobile industry from 1915 to 1930, as this industry grows, more and more companies spring up, not fewer and fewer. Almost all the original companies are still in the business—Texas Instruments, National Semiconductor, Intel, Advanced Micro Devices—even Fairchild, which bounced around from being a public company to a subsidiary of Schlumberger to a subsidiary of National Semiconductor, and back to a public company as National completes a spin-off to its shareholders.

At the same time, a flock of new companies have been started—not just in Silicon Valley or elsewhere in California, but near universities with strong electrical-engineering departments in the United States, Israel, Taiwan, and around the world. Some make a different kind of chip, such as the programmable logic device that remembers your car-seat adjustment, instead of fixed-function chips. Others use an entirely different, faster wafer—gallium arsenide instead of silicon. Many use a "fabless" strategy; while they design and sell the chips, they contract with outside manufacturers for actual production of their products. Several focus on analog chips instead of digital chips, or limit themselves to specific markets such as communications chips. There are many different strategies that seem to work.

All these companies compete not just in the U.S. market, but in a world market. As leaders in consumer electronics in the 1960s and 1970s, Japanese companies realized that they needed to build millions of cheap chips to keep their costs low. These "jellybean" factories were extremely good at making a very limited number of products. Traditional Japanese worker loyalty meant low employee turnover; so as a new chip came into production, there was a learning curve that showed reliably lower costs related directly to the cumulative number of chips produced. These processes for mass-producing cheap chips were perfectly suited for production of DRAMs; and as the personal computer industry took off in the late 1970s, Japanese manufacturers were fierce competitors in both DRAMs and another high-volume, specialty-memory chip, the electronically programmable read-only memory, or EPROM.

By the early 1980s, U.S. manufacturers of DRAMs and EPROMs were not happy with Japan's growing share of the semiconductor market. They took their case to Congress, launched an astute public-relations campaign to fan the flames of public opinion against the Japanese, and by 1984, had convinced most people that the Japanese dominated the semiconductor industry.

But it was all a lie, and even worse than a lie or a damned lie—it was a statistic. The Japanese did indeed control about 70 percent of the DRAM market and more than half the EPROM market. Their cost of capital was so much lower than that of U.S. companies that they could afford to build ultramodern fabrication facilities using the newest equipment. So the U.S. companies knew the Japanese had lower costs and were about to clean our clock in these two chip markets.

At the same time, the U.S. manufacturers pointed out that the United States had only 11 percent of the Japanese market. This was an outrage! The United States had a big trade deficit with Japan in semiconductors; clearly, Congress had to act quickly.

What the U.S. manufacturers never mentioned was that the Japanese share of the *total* U.S. semiconductor market was a mere 11 percent—the same as the U.S. share of the Japanese market. The U.S. market was twice as large as the Japanese market because we have twice the population and 1.5 times the GDP, so naturally their 11 percent of our market was larger in dollar terms than our 11 percent of their market. That is why there was a trade deficit.

Focusing on the dollar differences and not mentioning the percentage share the Japanese held of the U.S. market was bad enough. But in a twist guaranteed to make Diogenes of Sinope blow out his lantern, the U.S. semiconductor manufacturers also jiggered the numbers. For Japan, the market was defined as *all* semiconductors produced by *any* company, including captive production for their own products. But for the United States, the market was defined only as semiconductors produced by companies that did *not* have captive production. Huge manufacturers like IBM and AT&T were excluded, even though they bought lots of chips from outside vendors. That made our market look smaller and the Japanese share look bigger.

We have not even gotten to the fact that 39 percent of the Japanese semiconductor market was for cheap "jellybean" chips that U.S. manufacturers had no interest in making.

However, Congress bought into the semiconductor-industry lobby's spin on the facts and approved a restrictive semiconductor trade agreement in 1986. Under the U.S.–Japan Semiconductor Agreement, tariffs and quotas were imposed on Japanese DRAM and EPROM manufacturers. Basically, Congress took a very firm stand with the Japanese: "Now that you have 85 percent of the DRAM market, we insist that you raise your prices!"

After they finished laughing, the Japanese manufacturers complied. Personal-computer prices rose to reflect the increased cost of DRAMs. During the first two years of the act, we noticed the following effects:

- About $3 billion in excess cost was transferred from U.S. personal-computer buyers to Japanese DRAM manufacturers.
- Japanese manufacturers used the torrent of cash to build huge, very advanced fabs that lowered their production costs so much

that they wiped out virtually all the remaining U.S. DRAM and EPROM manufacturers and became even stronger competitors against the rest of the U.S. semiconductor industry.

- Korean companies took advantage of the pricing umbrella to invest billions in semiconductor fabs, creating a second fierce competitor for U.S. semiconductor companies where only one had existed before.
- Intel, which had begged to have its EPROM business protected, took advantage of the window of higher chip prices to completely exit the EPROM business at a profit and redeploy its assets into microprocessor manufacturing.

To this day, Congress thinks the program was a success, probably because nobody actually died. Congress will not pass another version of the quotas because leaders in the personal-computer industry now realize how much the whole episode hurt them and would lobby fiercely against it. But the trade negotiators continue to pressure the Japanese to guarantee—even if off the record—a 30 percent market share for U.S. manufacturers. The Japanese share of the total U.S. market has increased slightly to 14 percent, with which they seem content.

Chart 6.1 shows the long-term trend of DRAM prices, which is a good barometer of the long-term trend of many other chip prices. DRAMs are a technology driver; the manufacturers tend to use the absolute latest technology and learn to get high production yields while running flat out. They then transfer this knowledge to the production of other chips, keeping the whole industry in compliance with Moore's Law.

How Fast Is This Industry Growing?

From 1988 to 1997, the semiconductor industry grew at a compound annual rate of 17.6 percent to $150 billion. The growth rate in dollars is all the more impressive when you remember that *prices per bit were falling* at a compound annual rate of 28 percent throughout this period.

At the end of the last chapter, we reviewed the underlying drivers of the decline in semiconductor prices and concluded that there is no reason to expect Moore's Law to change during the next ten years. Falling prices create their own demand, so until everyone in the world has all the computing and communications power they can use, we see no reason for the demand for semiconductors to slow down. The world will not be saturated in the next ten years; so on an overall basis, the semiconductor industry should continue to grow at a rate of 18 percent compounded. It

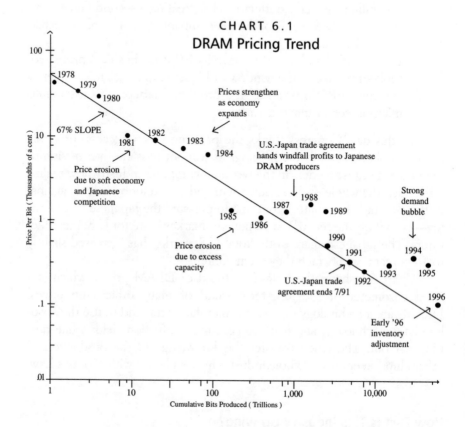

CHART 6.1
DRAM Pricing Trend

Price Per Bit (Thousandths of a cent)

Cumulative Bits Produced (Trillions)

1978
1979
1980
67% SLOPE
1981
1982
1983
1984
1985
1986
1987
1988
1989
1990
1991
1992
1993
1994
1995
1996

Price erosion
due to soft economy
and Japanese
competition

Prices strengthen
as economy
expands

U.S.-Japan trade agreement
hands windfall profits to Japanese
DRAM producers

Strong
demand
bubble

Price erosion
due to excess
capacity

U.S.-Japan trade
agreement ends 7/91

Early '96
inventory
adjustment

is awe-inspiring to think how big some of the current companies will be in ten years, not to mention how many new companies will succeeed.

What Drives the Growth Cycles?

While the trendline growth in semiconductor manufacturing is strong, the industry experiences significant cycles within the overall trend.

Bob Throop, the founder of chip distributor Anthem Electronics, watched the interaction between chip manufacturers (his suppliers) and chip users (his customers) for many years. He explained the semiconductor-industry cycle to us. At the bottom of a recession, no user wanted to hold any inventory, as it only decreased in value. Each morning a buyer would pick up only the quantity of the chips required for that day's production.

But as the recession ended and business picked up, the buyers grew more willing to build a few extra products each day, just in case they got a rush order. So they would buy a few extra chips, or maybe start buying for three days at a time instead of one day at a time. As everyone else started to do the same thing, sooner or later some chip or another would get a little tight on supply. No big deal, but Anthem might be able to fill only half the order for that chip, with a promise to get the rest in a couple of days.

So the next time buyers came in, they would get a week's worth of those chips, just to be sure to have had enough inventory to keep production humming. As end-customer demand continued to improve from the recession, spot shortages would hit other chips. Anthem's buyers again increased orders, and finally the semiconductor manufacturers would add a shift or open a mothballed production line to increase supply.

This process continued until buyers had all the chip inventory they wanted and the chip manufacturers were producing at high levels and making lots of money. Bob used to say that this magic moment, when supply and demand balanced, often occurred on a Friday afternoon and lasted for about an hour.

But the next Monday, orders increased again and there was no more supply. So lead times stretched out from "I'll have it for you today" to "I'll get it for you in a couple of days" to "How about two weeks?" Buyers, nervous that they might completely run out of some crucial chip and be responsible for shutting down the production lines (not to mention their own careers), started double-ordering. Why not put in an order with Anthem and another with Bell, and whoever gets the chips delivered first gets the business? Unfortunately, to the chip manufacturers this looks like an upsurge in orders, so they stretch lead times out further, creating at first additional concern—and later panic—among the buyers.

Of course, chip prices stop declining at their usual rate and prices on the chips most in shortage may rise. The upsurge in DRAM prices in 1995 is a recent example.

Now the semiconductor companies are really in the driver's seat. Production is at high levels, so the cost per chip is low. Prices are high and maybe going higher. Profits are exploding.

There is a sure sign of when this cycle has topped out. Some Wall Street analyst will publish a think piece saying that the semiconductor industry is no longer cyclical. He will be quoted in *The Wall Street Journal* and feted on CNBC. Amateur investors will rush into these now-inexpensive-looking stocks. After all, 20x earnings for a cyclical stock at the top of its cycle is a lot, but 20x earnings for a growth stock compounding at 30 percent a year is cheap.

Alas, what is really happening is that chips are being hoarded in inventories all over the world. To keep up this high level of production and sales, manufacturers must generate a constantly increasing fresh in-flow of new buyers. Sooner or later, there is a pause. Semiconductor manufacturers see that demand has flattened for some hot chips, so they trim prices a little to spur demand. The buyers realize that prices have started to fall, which means now their inventories are losing value. So they trim orders and try to use up their expensive chips as fast as possible.

Now semiconductor manufacturers see demand falling! With chip production high, there's only one choice: significant price cuts. Buyers realize that they have a problem, and some of them will sell off excess inventory in the gray market before it declines further in value. Now they are competing with the manufacturer, prices go into a tailspin, inventories are liquidated, profits vanish, and an embarrassed brokerage firm lets the "no-longer-cyclical" publication go out of print.

Notice that end-user demand did not have to decline at all to have the whole process play out. The entire cycle is caused by an inventory cycle—a buildup followed by a liquidation. This is exactly what happened in 1995 and 1996. Excitement over the impending introduction of Micro-soft's Windows 95 on August 24, 1995, led personal-computer and pe-ripheral manufacturers to build large inventories. No one wanted to be the company that could not ship enough products and grab its share of an exploding market because it did not stockpile enough chips.

We sold most of the personal-computer–related stocks in the early summer of 1995, for the simple reason that there has never been a case of a new operating system replacing an older standard rapidly. Changing operating systems is a painful process full of pitfalls; new software almost always has "undocumented features"—also known as bugs. There was no way Corporate America was going to adopt the new operating system overnight. We thought that even individuals would move slowly because most of them were happy with their computers as they were. Also, it cost about $1,000 to upgrade the hardware and applications software of an older computer, if it was upgradable at all. In practical terms, the vast installed base of Intel 286 and 386 microprocessor-based computers could not be upgraded at a reasonable price.

By the end of September 1995, the third-bestselling software for Windows 95 was a *de*installer. Corporations were just beginning their six-month evaluation periods. In advance of the Windows 95 introduction, Packard Bell decided to build a $1 *billion* inventory of PCs, but guessed wrong on the configuration. They had ordered $500 million worth of motherboards from Intel (which builds half the motherboards in the United States) and couldn't pay for them. Intel had to extend credit. One of Intel's biggest suppliers for those motherboards was Cirrus Logic, but Intel now had all the Cirrus Logic inventory it would need for a long time. As the inventory liquidation and collapse in DRAM chip prices ricocheted around the industry, numerous companies reported losses. Cirrus's stock was cut in half, from $60 to $28, where we bought it before it was cut in half again, to $14. Even those of us who had seen the disaster coming underestimated its magnitude.

Investors must remember that when semiconductor sales are booming and stock prices are high, customers are probably building inventory and setting the scene for a decline. When sales are soft and the headlines are full of moaning and groaning about the death of the semiconductor industry, customers are probably buying chips hand-to-mouth and creating the bottom of the cycle. Stock prices are likely to be near their lows; if you keep your head and remember that the industry cycles around a very attractive 18 percent growth rate, you can pick up some bargains.

How Profitable Is It?

There are three different business models in the semiconductor industry, serving three different business strategies.

Strategy 1: Own your own fab.

First, there are companies that own their own fabrication facilities. This has its ups and downs: Semiconductor fabs are expensive, so semiconductor manufacturers are almost the only technology companies that have substantial depreciation expenses. Because it takes so much capital to own their own means of production, their return on investment can look low even though profit margins are high. They also have to divert part of their R&D spending to continually upgrade the production process rather than just design great new chips.

On the other hand, they should have lower costs of production than companies that use an outside manufacturer, and better control over the schedule of which products are built when. If a new chip design takes off unexpectedly, they can convert production to that chip quickly; by contrast, dealing with an outside supplier might require weeks of negotiation and months to actually shift to production of the new design.

It costs a lot to build a chip-fabrication plant—typically well over $1 billion today—which makes for high operating leverage. Operating leverage means that low wafer volumes or low yields cannot cover the depreciation and operating expenses, leading to outsized losses. But once the plant is up to breakeven, as much as 90 percent of the sales over breakeven can go right to the profit line. That's high operating leverage.

Three companies that own their own facilities are Texas Instruments, LSI Logic, and Cypress Semiconductor. Their average gross profit is 39 percent; a large chunk of this goes for R&D, which averages 14 percent of sales. They also tend to spend another large chunk on SG&A, which averages 13 percent, because they need to communicate with hundreds of thousands of engineers all over the world in order to get their chips designed into new products. That leaves them with average operating profits of 12 percent.

This financial model is typical for companies that own their factories, with the main variation being the level of gross profit, depending on how unique or hot their chip designs are. When you are evaluating a semiconductor company that owns its fab, look first at the gross profit margin (the higher the better), and then be sure the rest of its business model is in line with the average ratios of these three companies. Ask the investor-relations person about anything that seems substantially out of line.

Strategy 2: "Fabless" design.

The second business model is the "fabless" company that does not own a factory. This became a popular model beginning in the late 1980s, because it took advantage of inexpensive excess fabrication capacity in Asia and allowed venture capitalists to build successful companies without laying out the extra capital for a fab. The fabless company focuses instead on design and marketing.

When the business is going well, gross profits can be as high as 70 percent. But when fabrication capacity is tight, as it was in 1994 and early 1995, fabless companies had to pay extra or pay in advance to get their chips manufactured on a timely schedule. That hurt gross profits.

Three successful fabless companies are Xilinx, Altera, and PMC Sierra. Considering good times and tight times, their average gross profit is 49 percent—ten percentage points higher than the companies that own their fabs. They also spend a lot on R&D to develop new designs, averaging 11 percent. They spend an average of 19 percent on SG&A, a high ratio militated by several factors:

- They need to communicate with hundreds of thousands of engineers all over the world.
- They are often introducing very new products and concepts that require explanation and exposure before design engineers will adopt them.
- They have a smaller average size than fab-owning companies, with lower revenues to support the basic expenses of running a public company. (Complying with SEC regulations alone adds about $350,000 a year to general and administrative expenses.)

The average operating profits of these three companies is 19 percent, typical for the fabless industry. Because each company's business is different, there is no one ideal business model that fits all situations, but any fabless company that measures up to these averages is doing well.

Interestingly, there appears to be a practical revenue ceiling around $600–$700 million on the size of a pure fabless company. Above that, the company becomes a large customer of too many different suppliers and is vulnerable to a problem at any one of them. In the late 1980s, Cirrus Logic was the largest consumer of merchant fabrication services in the world, with more than ten different suppliers running dozens of designs. The company struck a deal with IBM to form a joint venture to operate one of IBM's advanced semiconductor fabs, with each company bearing half the costs and entitled to half the output. Although this arrangement hurt Cirrus financially in the industry downturn in 1996 and 1997, in the long run, it is one way to get past the billion-dollar revenue barrier and continue to grow rapidly.

Strategy 3: An unbeatable patent.

The third business model is to have a patented product that absolutely everybody wants. It should have many different functions, thus capturing lots of value and justifying a high price. It should have a clear migration path to becoming faster and cheaper, reducing manufacturing costs while forcing customers to upgrade to the latest version lest they fall behind their competitors.

This business model produces gross profit margins of 55 percent. The fortunate company need spend only 9 percent on R&D to maintain its lead. Because customers must use the chip, sales and marketing expenses can be relatively low. While the company may not have to run lean and mean, there is no reason to waste a lot of money on general and administrative expenses—17 percent should cover SG&A. That leaves whopping operating profits of 28 percent, far above the average for the other two business models. Of course, there is only one product that produces this level of profitability, and only one company that enjoys this model: the microprocessor, and Intel.

Who Are the Customers?

The customers for semiconductors are system-design engineers. These are the people designing products to be sold to system-assembly companies or to end users—manufacturers of computers, add-on boards, disk drives, communications gear, instruments, automobiles, appliances, video game consoles, and so forth. The company they work for may sell direct to end users, like Compaq Computer, or may manufacture an intermediate product like disk drives to sell to Compaq. In either case, the design engineer works with marketing to develop the specifications for a product and then chooses the semiconductors that will meet those specifications. Thus it is crucial for a semiconductor company to be in the running during this "design-in" phase. Once the design is set, the winning chips are likely to be in that product throughout its life. Product cycles are so short that it is not worth redesigning a successful product to lower costs by substituting other chips. It makes more sense to spend that design time working on the replacement product, which undoubtedly will be bigger, faster, and cheaper than the one it replaces.

Semiconductor companies find these customers in a number of ways. They publish data sheets on each new chip and try to get them into engineers' hands. They compete for the cover story in the major electronics magazines, knowing that such an imprimatur will help them rise above the noise level and perhaps come to the attention of someone just starting to design an appropriate product. Of course, they work closely with their major customers to find out what new chips are needed for the next generation of products, and then develop a standard chip that will do the job for many different companies.

What Competitive Strategies Win?

The two key strategies in the semiconductor business are (1) to make chips smaller, and therefore faster yet lower-powered, and (2) to continually integrate more and more functions onto a single chip. For any given function, the smaller the chip, the less real estate it occupies on the silicon wafer. The less real estate it occupies, the more chips that can be squeezed onto a single wafer. Because the cost of processing a wafer is about the same no matter how many chips are on it, the cost per chip falls as the chip gets smaller.

Smaller chips usually run faster because the electrons do not have to travel as far to get from one transistor to another. Also, because the distances are shorter and there are some other power-saving modifications built in, the smaller chip often can run on lower power. This means that in a device like a laptop computer, the batteries will last longer. That is a strong selling point for the computer-systems assembler. Lower-power chips also emit less heat, which makes the system more reliable and may obviate the need for a noisy, energy-draining fan.

The other key strategy is to integrate more and more functions on a single chip. Graphics accelerators began as add-on boards with fifty or more chips. Chip designers then began combining functions—three chips here turned into one, four chips there redesigned into one. Each new generation of graphics boards offered more power with fewer chips, and therefore more power at a lower cost.

Ultimately, the original graphics functions are reduced to one or two chips, and these can be placed right on the motherboard, eliminating the add-on board entirely. Of course, in the real world, as functions like two-dimensional graphics and user-interface accelerators are incorporated onto the motherboard, add-on board companies move on to higher-level functions like three-dimensional graphics and video.

Someday a "fourth-socket" chip that does almost everything will be introduced. The four-chip PC will have a microprocessor (probably made by Intel), a memory chip (probably made by a Japanese or Korean company, or Micron Technology), a glue-logic chip to hold everything together (most likely from Intel, VLSI Technology, Texas Instruments, or OPTI), and the fourth-socket chip. That is the chip that puts color on the screen, accelerates 2-D and 3-D graphics, acts as a modem or fax modem, decodes video, plays high-end stereo sound, and handles anything else that people think up.

The most likely companies to win the race to the fourth socket are Intel, Cirrus Logic or Conexant, but no one has all the neceessary technologies in one place yet. Certainly, companies like S3, Creative Technology, C-Cube Microsystems, and Trident Microsystems all have a shot at the gold ring.

It is interesting that glue-logic companies like OPTI envision a three-chip PC, with all the fourth-socket functions integrated into their glue logic. DRAM companies dream about a two-chip PC, with all the fourth-socket functions and the glue logic integrated right onto the DRAM chip. NeoMagic Corp. already sells a single-chip graphics accelerator integrated with DRAM for the laptop market. Through clever design, their DRAM partners can build the accelerator logic, typically a twenty-five-step–process, on a normal fifteen-step DRAM production line.

Of course, when you talk to Intel, you can just guess who they think is going to supply the single-chip PC of the future!

How Will the Internet Affect It?

The Internet is going to have a major positive impact on many smaller semiconductor companies by helping them overcome two big challenges: getting designed into new products, and finding a way to distribute chips to customers.

The biggest problem all semiconductor companies have is getting their data sheets in front of system designers in time to be considered for a new project. Smaller companies, which are less well known, have a particularly difficult time.

The second problem is that most semiconductors go through two-step distribution, from manufacturer to distributor and from distributor to customer. This is especially true in the early stages of design and production, when the customer is buying onesies and twosies to build prototypes rather than worrying about production levels. Distributors limit the number of firms they represent (the "line card") in order to be trained and up to date on the products they do carry. But that is frustrating both to the customer, who may want something no nearby distributor carries, and to the small firm that cannot get on a major distributor's line card.

Enter the Internet. The Internet's greatest power lies in its potential for disintermediation of the manufacturer-customer relationship. Intermediaries, in the traditional sense, can be bypassed completely. There may be a need for a Web site, like Amazon.com for books, where the customers could search for chips that would perfectly fit their design specifications. Like Amazon.com, the company offering the Web site might choose to stock the most popular chips for immediate shipment, but that would not really be necessary. Between Federal Express, Airborne Express, and UPS, mail-order software companies have gotten one-day delivery down to a science. Chip companies could do the same.

What kinds of information would be on this Web site? Data sheets, for starters. Also a powerful industry-specific search engine that would let the engineer list a chip and find all other chips like it; describe a function and find all the chips that will perform it; download industry reviews, chip comparisons, and even bills of materials for similar products. Cadis, a private company, has started down this road; others will follow.

Imagine the advantages to a company like Information Storage Devices, which makes chips that store a recorded voice, just like a tape recorder. Anyone looking for that specific chip would be able to find it, whether under the current system or in a future Internet-based system. But in an Internet system, ISD could associate its part number with other parts that typically go into consumer devices. If a design engineer specifies something as mundane as a pushbutton, ISD might want its data sheet to download to that person with the headline: "Have You Considered Adding Voice Input?"

Right at the conceptual-design phase of a new project, then, forward-thinking companies would plant seeds of their own alternatives into someone's fertile imagination. Now, *that's* targeted marketing.

What Is the Next Big Change?

Many changes are coming into the semiconductor industry as the standard circuit width drops from 0.25 microns to 0.18 in 2000 and to 0.15 in 2001 or 2002. Each of those reductions produces a sharp drop in costs and much higher integration. In 2001, a microcontroller that costs $2.50 and has as much power as a technical workstation circa 1989 will be able to be embedded in your toaster. Judging by the way this industry has developed, not only will there be a full range of brilliant uses for such a toaster, but people will quickly start demanding even more powerful toasters.

Incidentally, if IBM made toasters there would be only fifty toaster centers in the whole country. You would submit your bread one day, pick up your toast a week later, and no one would ever get fired for specifying an IBM toaster.

If Microsoft made toasters, it would disable all the other toasters, and then secretly query the rest of the kitchen appliances to see what other features it could copy.

If Xerox made toasters, they would toast on one side or two sides; but as you used them, the toast would get lighter and lighter, and eventually the bread would jam the toaster.

If Silicon Graphics made toasters, they would cost $14 million each, but would make the fastest toast in the world.

And if Novell made toasters, eventually people would stop eating toast altogether!

My pick for the single biggest change coming in the semiconductor arena is the close integration of digital and analog chips—the "mixed-signal" devices. Digital chips deal with ones and zeros, the language of the imaginary world of binary mathematics. Analog chips deal with pressure, temperature, sound, color—the real world. Most consumer products have a high analog content; so as the electronics industry continues its shift toward more and more consumer products, mixed-signal semiconductors will become a pivotal technology. These chips will grow much more complex than they are today, enabling the production of dramatically new products that consumers will buy in very high volumes.

## CHAPTER SEVEN

Large Computers

When I first started following technology stocks in 1970, I spent most of my time on IBM and the BUNCH—Burroughs, Unisys, NCR, Control Data, and Honeywell. The mainframe industry was growing 15 percent a year in an environment of very low inflation, as Fortune 500 and major foreign multinational companies computerized their basic recordkeeping and accounting functions.

Each mainframe computer company had a captive semiconductor operation that designed and manufactured proprietary central-processor and support chips. Each company wrote its own operating system and most of its basic, horizontal software like databases, telecommunications, and general-ledger accounting. Customers were expected to write their own specialized applications software, so buying a mainframe meant hiring anywhere from one to a thousand or more programmers and systems analysts—the job I started in at American Express in the late 1960s.

Mainframe computing was and is expensive. The manufacturers know that once customers have committed all the resources to write their applications software under a proprietary operating system running on a proprietary central processor, it is very painful to switch the entire company's computer operations from one proprietary system to another. Not surprisingly, the mainframe companies charge high prices for their equipment. But, to be fair, the mainframe companies' cost of researching, developing, and manufacturing new silicon chips, computers, and operating systems has to be spread over a relatively small number of customers and computers, which contributes to high prices.

The minicomputer "revolution" of the 1970s was really an evolution to a smaller, less expensive box with a simpler operating system. The central processing unit still was proprietary, as was the operating system. Most of the initial customers were scientists or engineers willing to take on a much larger share of the work in creating applications programs. Because a good portion of their work was funded by government grants, lots of "freeware" was shared between universities and computer scientists.

But Digital Equipment, the leading minicomputer company, and its competitors like Data General and Systems Engineering Laboratories, still showed high profit margins, based in large part on the proprietary nature of their systems. It was not much easier to change a program from Digital Equipment to Data General than it was to change from Burroughs to IBM.

In 1969 AT&T, a major customer of several computer companies and a builder of its own dedicated telecommunications computers, developed the one-size-fits-all UNIX operating system as a way to unify different manufacturers' hardware under a common software platform. Other companies admired AT&T's success with UNIX and asked to license the operating system. By the late 1970s, customers were demanding UNIX, at least as an option. But even after most computer manufacturers licensed and began offering the UNIX operating system as a second choice to their proprietary operating system, customers learned there are "flavors" of UNIX. Although it was no longer unthinkable to change computer vendors, it still was no picnic.

Then customers saw the promised land. If they adopted UNIX as a reference operating system, they could insist that the hardware vendors certify an ability to run generic UNIX. That meant all of their existing applications software would run on any new hardware they bought. Suddenly they could pit one hardware vendor against another. The balance of power in the industry shifted to the customer, putting the squeeze on hardware profit margins.

Enter the microprocessor. Around 1984, new companies like Sequent Computer realized that they could build fast, inexpensive computers to run generic UNIX if they combined several standard Intel microprocessors, high-capacity Seagate disk drives, and the like. That put additional profit-margin pressure on the proprietary mainframe and minicomputer manufacturers. For example, at equal levels of performance in a commercial application, Sequent's price often is only 20 percent or 25 percent of the price of the comparable Digital Equipment solution.

How Fast Is This Industry Growing?

On a trendline basis, the proprietary large-computer industry is growing less than 5 percent a year. As standard microprocessors get more and more powerful, inexpensive UNIX-based computers can handle larger and larger tasks. Ultimately, proprietary hardware will disappear, consigned to the scrap heap as an uneconomic alternative in any application; however, that will take decades. One of the key signposts along the road will be the first airline-reservation system that comes off proprietary hardware onto standards-based hardware. These gigantic reservation systems have long been beacons in the industry to other management-information-systems managers dealing with large data-intensive applications. Other major signposts of the declining mainframe market will be the first ATM-card-network defection and credit-card authorization. You will know the process has run its course when—some sad day—even the IRS figures it out. That will be the day the open-systems vendors can declare total victory.

The minicomputer industry has evolved into the "server" industry, as in client/server computing, described on the following pages. While the traditional minicomputer industry is also locked into 5 percent or lower growth, "servers" are growing 20 percent a year and will continue to do so for the next five or more years.

What Drives the Growth Cycles?

Proprietary computing has both an economic cycle and a product cycle; these can either accentuate each other or cancel each other out, smoothing the growth path. Because large computers are major expenditures, typically in the $250,000 to $5 million range, they must go through a company's capital-budgeting process. Capital expenditures for plant and equipment (these being for equipment) are a lagging indicator of the broad economy. That is, in a good economy, companies tend to expand capital spending to increase capacity, gain market share, or introduce new products. When the economy turns down, these large projects cannot be turned off immediately, so capital spending tends to stay strong even after the broad economy weakens. As a recession drags on, companies scale back or cancel capital-spending programs, and eventually capital spending follows the economy down. When the economy hits bottom and turns back up, at first companies are very cautious about boosting capital spending until they are sure the economic cycle has bottomed out and is poised for a rebound. Even after they decide to expand capacity, the process of designing a new system, evaluating vendors, and planning the installation takes time. Capital spending usually turns up well after the broad economy has begun to recover.

The second cycle is a product cycle, driven by the pace of introductions of new hardware. This cycle was much stronger in the 1960s and

1970s than it is today because today's product introductions tend to be incremental rather than revolutionary. I started programming on an IBM 1401 with punched cards. Each line of code was punched onto a computer card; then huge decks of cards were assembled and read into the computer. If someone made a keypunch error or a card fell out of sequence, the program had to be debugged—painfully. Logical errors had to be corrected with new cards of code, which often affected other cards in unexpected ways.

When the IBM 360 series was introduced in 1964, it marked a revolution. Programs were written in logical blocks and translated onto computer tape. Lines of code could be changed and logical blocks rearranged; the computer kept track of the correct order of the things. But committing to upgrade to a System 360 meant committing to rewriting or replacing all your software over a period of several years.

In 1970, at the bottom of the economic cycle, IBM introduced the 370 series. While not as revolutionary as the 360 in terms of requiring a complete rewrite of everything, the 370 offered a compelling price/performance proposition and fueled a continued expansion in IBM's revenues, even as overall capital spending was in the doldrums. In the early years of the IBM 370 product cycle, even in the recession, IBM's sales grew 13 percent a year—about the same as the company's 15 percent trendline. Today, the capital-spending cycle far outweighs the product cycle. IBM, Digital Equipment, Hewlett-Packard, and other vendors of proprietary hardware get a nice kick coming out of a recession, whether in the United States or Europe. That is one reason why Hewlett-Packard's sales grew 13 percent in 1992 and 24 percent in 1993, as the U.S. economy recovered, and then 23 percent in 1994 and 26 percent in 1995, as the European economies came out of their recession. However, some Wall Street analysts still mistake an upswing in the capital-spending cycle for a more fundamental improvement in the proprietary large-computer business. The truth is that in each cycle the highs are lower, the lows are lower, and the long-term growth trendline is still falling toward a flat, no-growth state.

How Profitable Is It?

Profitability was severely compromised in the 1980s by the move to open-system UNIX computers and industry-standard microprocessors. Proprietary vendors scrambled to cut costs, but both IBM and Digital Equipment briefly ran losses. Now that costs have been reduced, the average gross-profit margins as a percentage of sales of IBM, Digital Equipment, and Data General are about 35 percent. They still spend a

significant amount on R&D, an average of 7 percent, and a lot on SG&
A, 22 percent. Although that is less than they used to spend, even in the
open-system UNIX world, expensive one-on-one customer contact and
assistance is required. That leaves them with average operating profits of
just 6 percent.

That's only 25 percent of the profitability of IBM's glory days of the
1970s. Worse, this financial model is under constant pressure as new
companies using inexpensive technology go after the remaining highly
profitable niches, such as proprietary disk drives. IBM used to make 25
percent of its net profits from disk drives alone.

Finally, like UNIX, Microsoft's Windows 2000 is a server operating
system, meant to have many desktop computers attached to it. Desktop
operating systems like Windows 98 or even DOS can be forced to manage other computers on a network, but they are not robust enough to do
a good job. They are best left to run a single desktop computer—and
they still crash too often. Although it is behind UNIX in terms of reliabil-
ity and scalability, Microsoft's Windows 2000 operating system is poised
to climb the ladder of performance to compete with UNIX. In 1998 the
federal government agreed to accept Windows 2000 (then called Windows NT) as an alternative operating system to UNIX. The future is
clear: Customers will have a choice of two alternatives to proprietary
mainframe operating systems. This can only hurt the mainframes.

Who Are the Customers?

The customers for these big systems expanded beyond the Fortune
500 and government agencies to include many medium-sized and smaller
companies during the 1970s and early 1980s. In the 1990s, however, the
customer base contracted back to those very large organizations. Only
the very largest applications cannot be run on open-system computers,
meaning that only the very largest customers still require proprietary
hardware. However, even those customers try to offload as much processing as possible onto less expensive systems. No one is a Big Blue shop
anymore, exclusively using IBM equipment. Big and small companies
alike have a mixed, heterogeneous environment, with several manufacturers' computers interoperating, often without any mainframe systems. So
there is constant pressure on the large computer manufacturers to lower
prices, open up their interfaces to interoperate with other manufacturers,
and provide much more power per dollar to close the gap with the open-
system, standard-processor folks.

What Competitive Strategies Win?

IBM executives should be required to have a brass plate installed in their limos, mounted on their office doors, and possibly placed inside every stall in the executive washroom, proclaiming: "The Truth Is With Hewlett-Packard."

Like Digital Equipment, H-P was a vendor of proprietary minicomputers. But H-P was quick to accept UNIX as a market reality. As a result, early on H-P produced two lines of computers: one proprietary, one running UNIX. If customers wanted to upgrade their computer performance, but were not ready to rewrite all their software—fine. H-P would sell them a new proprietary system. If customers were ready to move to UNIX—fine, too. H-P was there with competitive hardware and the same service, support, and relationships the customer was used to. If a new company requested a quote for UNIX computers—fine. H-P was in there competing for the business. H-P let the customer base and the market decide how fast the transition from proprietary to UNIX computing would go.

Beyond that, very few people seem to know about a crucial change in the industry landscape coming in 2000. Intel will no longer be the sole developer of the microprocessors used to build everything from personal computers to mainframe-size UNIX computers.

Intel developed the Pentium, code-named the P5, and the Pentium II, code-named the P6, by itself. There was one more extension of the PII, the PIII, but the IA-64, scheduled to ship in volume in 2000, and all future microprocessors are being developed in a joint venture with none other than Hewlett-Packard. It is a certainty that H-P is developing computer architectures optimized for new features in the IA-64. When the chip, code-named Merced, is introduced in 2000, H-P should have a significant performance and time-to-market advantage over the rest of the UNIX computer industry, plus an opportunity to enter the high-end Windows 2000 server industry with the most technically advanced product.

Although this joint-venture development agreement is rarely mentioned in analysts' reports and seems to have little impact on H-P's stock price, it probably will go down in H-P's history as the single most important decision made by president Lewis Platt. It secures the future of the company for at least a decade, probably more.

Large computers are evolving into on-line transaction processing servers. In client/server computing, the clients are the personal computers sitting on everyone's desktops. The servers are the central database repositories that also manage the on-line network. Think of a reservation system for a multinational hotel chain. The reservations agent uses a client computer to check on room availability while a customer is on the phone. The customer may be eligible for different potential discounts, some of which are stored in the client computer (AAA, frequent flier, AARP) and others that need to be queried from the server (corporate rates). Only after the customer selects a room and a discount is a message sent to the server, thus minimizing expensive server time. In fact, before the message is sent, the customer's credit card may be verified by an entirely different server owned by the credit-card company, with only the authorization code sent to the reservations server. In the same phone call, the customer may reserve a rental car, which again uses none of the reservation server's more expensive computing cycles.

Client/server computing allows an organization to offer on-line, real-time service to its customers. It can evolve to Internet computing, where all data and processing reside on the server and the clients can be as small as cellphones. It can completely change the way a company does business, altering its cost structure and giving it the opportunity to beat the competition with a product or service closer to what the customer really wants. Of course, that forces the competition to adopt client/server computing. This is why large, proprietary, batch-processing computing is doomed.

For companies to adopt a winning competitive strategy, they must recognize that the only role for large computers is as powerful servers in an open-system, UNIX– and Windows 2000–based, client/server computing world. Seventy percent of corporate data still resides on the mainframes, but to keep it there requires realigning the cost structure of the large computer company to compete in a lower-margin environment. That does not mean simply downsizing by laying people off; it means rethinking all the business processes of the large computer company to succeed in the new environment. Hewlett-Packard has done that. But IBM and Digital Equipment (now owned by Compaq) have a long way to go.

Even simple downsizing is not easy. When IBM began its rapid downsizing in 1991, it offered a lucrative early-retirement plan to everyone, rather than making the hard decisions on who should stay, who was deadwood, and what functions had to be scaled back. Of the 375,000 employees before downsizing began, only 25,000 were rated internally as Fast Trackers. These were the best and the brightest. Over half the Fast Trackers took early retirement and left the company, significantly depleting IBM's corps of top talent. Why not? The Fast Trackers were the ones who could land other jobs easily. Those without bright career prospects stayed on. This program was widely praised on Wall Street, and the management that implemented it wound up on the covers of major business magazines. It certainly makes us realize why we get constant opportunities to buy great companies cheaply and sell troubled stocks at high prices.

How Will the Internet Affect It?

For the large computer company, the Internet stands as both a major opportunity and a major threat. It presents an opportunity because with every person and business destined to be on-line in the twenty-first century, not to mention the incipient merger of computing and communications, it will take a huge annual increase in computing power for many years into the future to run the Internet on a worldwide basis. Although much of this computing power will be distributed in small to medium-sized servers, many databases and much computing capacity will be concerned with very large nodes.

The Internet is a major threat because the client computer does not care what brand of server it is talking to. Everything communicates through the standard Internet Protocol. The last vestiges of proprietary computing systems will be stripped away; it will all come down to price, performance, and customer service.

The world of computing is undergoing a period of rapid change, and change always threatens the industry leader. At best, IBM can update and respond to change rapidly enough to hold its position. Any other outcome will mean a smaller market share and continued, periodic profitability problems.

What Is the Next Big Change?

The next big changes in large computing are:

- the abandonment of proprietary hardware in order to reduce costs;
- support for Microsoft's Windows 2000 operating system in parallel with the UNIX operating system, as a way to offer an upgrade path for companies committed to Windows on the desktop client;
- wholesale recognition that products optimized for the Internet are also the products companies will buy for their internal operations (private "intranets").

These are big, risky upheavals for an industry that traditionally moves slowly to accept change. With the exception of Hewlett-Packard, it is riskier than usual to buy any of these companies' stocks until they have negotiated this tricky period successfully.

## CHAPTER EIGHT

Personal Computers

The personal-computer industry grew from $0 to $180 billion in twenty years, with most of that growth starting in 1981. In that year, IBM made the decision to introduce a PC with a microprocessor it did not make and an operating system it did not design, in order to get to market faster. Little did IBM know it was setting an industry standard that would quickly obsolete the then-most-popular operating system, CP/M, eventually squeeze Apple's proprietary operating system into a small niche of the market, and give Microsoft and Intel the keys to the kingdom.

Today the PC industry is the fastest-growing large industry in the world. There are about 430 million personal computers in use today, and that number would more than double overnight if everyone who currently has the income and education to buy and use a PC did so. With incomes in developing countries rising and new types of inexpensive PCs coming out, we have no doubt that there will be six times as many PCs—2.4 billion—installed by 2007.

The growth in personal computing will not slow down until, as George Gilder says, all people, anywhere in the world can walk up to a box, speak to it in any language, and get any computation or piece of data they want instantly. That extraordinary day will not come to pass in the next ten years, so we can be sure that, well into the twenty-first century, personal computing will continue to drive electronics technology.

But those computers may not be sitting on desktops and certainly will be available in a broader range of prices. The main use of computing devices in the year 2010 will be to connect people to information and to each other. That means the Internet will continue to grow extremely rapidly. It is the cost-efficient, standardized, open-communications channel through which the free market can work most quickly to grow and improve connectivity.

The computing devices connected to the Internet will include desktop computers running at 1,000 MHz (also known as "one gigahertz"). Voice input will be common; the keyboard will be on its way out. Large, high-resolution color screens will be the entry-level technology, and video teleconferencing will be built into the microprocessor.

Travelers will carry very powerful personal digital assistants. Voice input, the natural technology for a hand-held device, will dominate, and wireless connectivity will be as readily available as today's cellular-telephone service.

Today, seven of the ten largest PC companies are based in the United States, including all of the top four (Compaq, IBM, Dell, and Hewlett-Packard). U.S. companies design and manufacture the microprocessor, the operating system, much of the applications software, and most of the specialty logic chips and disk drives. The personal-computer industry holds the key to a golden age of American exports, similar to the international export strength enjoyed by Britain in the 1800s. That may be the reason baby boomers stand to win their bet that when this huge demographic wave hits retirement age, the country will be wealthy enough to support them.

How Fast Is This Industry Growing?

On a worldwide basis, for the last five years the PC industry has grown at a compound annual rate of 19.4 percent. In contrast to many Wall Street analysts, we see no reason for it to slow down during the next five to ten years. With one billion people in Russia and China joining the capitalist workforce, the Internet growing at more than 100 percent a year, and the price of entry-level, PC-like devices falling below $500, the growth rate might even accelerate.

Within the PC industry, certain subsectors are growing even faster. Today the disk-drive industry ships about 1.8 disk drives for every PC shipped. Some PCs are sold with more than one disk drive, some drives are sold as replacements or upgrades, and some are sold for non-PC applications like instruments or communications devices.

Sales of high-speed modems are also growing faster than PC sales, driven by a combination of Internet growth and the trend toward telecommuting.

In addition, multimedia add-on boards are being widely adopted to handle the increasing multimedia content on the Internet and to enable desktop videoconferencing as a way to cut the travel cost and wasted time of physical meetings.

With the $180 billion personal-computer industry growing nearly 20 percent a year overall, it comes as no surprise that these and other large related niches are growing two, three, or five times as fast.

What Drives the Growth Cycles?

Within the PC industry's overall 19.4 percent trendline growth rate, there are two cyclical forces that accelerate or slow down growth: new microprocessors and new operating systems. These do not affect the same buyers in the same way.

New microprocessors always reduce the cost of current computing and may enable significant advances in software. The individual PC market responds to the cost reductions. The corporate PC market responds to the new software.

Each generation of microprocessors forces down the price of the previous generation, allowing PC manufacturers to reduce prices. In addition, the new microprocessor enables new applications software, even if the operating system does not change. At the end of 1994, PC manufacturers introduced multimedia computers with CD-ROMs and fast 486 microprocessors for $1,800 or less. Individuals responded so strongly that it was a "Computer Christmas"; other retail products actually suffered because so much buying power was diverted to PCs. Parents saw an opportunity to buy a computer that would play games (still 45 percent of all home use) and help their kids with their homework (a searchable CD encyclopedia), while providing the adults with a way to bring work home from the office and do personal financial planning.

This story was repeated for Christmas 1995, as the new Pentium Pro forced prices of Pentium-based computers into the $1,800 range. The additional functionality of the chip plus the promise of compatibility with future software written for the new Windows 95 operating system convinced consumers to dig deep again for "Son of Computer Christmas."

Interestingly, Christmas 1996 did not bring with it another generation of microprocessors for computers at the $1,800 price point, nor multimedia computers at a much lower price point. As a result, it was a slow season for home-computer sales, with numerous disappointments at retail companies like CompUSA, Best Buy, and Circuit City.

In early 1997, Intel introduced the Pentium MMX chip, which adds multimedia extensions to the basic Pentium instruction set. This chip allows PC companies to build full-featured multimedia computers in the $1,000 to $1,200 range. That accelerated home-computer sales again, as a new layer of potential customers responded to the lower price point. There is also the Celeron processor for sub-$1,000 systems, which offers enough extra performance to convince some of those 1994 buyers of 486 computers to upgrade.

In contrast to individual PC buyers, corporations are more interested in functionality than in price points. Every additional employee is going to get a computer whether it costs $1,500 or $2,500. Not only is the payback rapid in either case, but employees simply cannot function in today's company without a networked computer.

But corporations will not upgrade computers until they have to do it in order to run compelling new software. The 286-, 386-, and 486-based PCs all were 16-bit microprocessors and therefore ran a 16-bit operating system (DOS, Windows 3.0) and 16-bit applications software like Lotus 1-2-3, Excel, Word, WordPerfect, and so on.

Intel's Pentium, introduced in 1993, is a 32-bit microprocessor, but corporations saw no reason to upgrade until Windows 95, a 32-bit operating system, was introduced in August 1995. Even then, they waited until a substantial amount of 32-bit applications software was available before beginning the upgrade cycle. In early 1996, the installed base of corporate computers included 44 percent 486-based computers and 23 percent 386- or older computers. Two-thirds of corporate computers could not be upgraded to 32-bit software economically. It was obvious that after the usual four- to six-month evaluation period, a massive upgrade cycle of corporate computers would begin. It took until the middle of 1999 to get to the peak shipment rates of this upgrade cycle, and probably until 2001 to complete the transition.

How Profitable Is It?

Companies that sell computer systems to end users, whether corporate or home buyers, tend to have low gross profit margins. Looking at Compaq, Dell Computer, and Micron Electronics, the average gross profit is only 20 percent. They spend very little on R&D, relying on their suppliers to carry the burden of advancing technology. These three companies spend an average of just 1 percent on R&D.

They spend much more on SG&A—11 percent—which is not surprising, considering that they are essentially assembly and distribution businesses. That leaves them with average operating profits of 8 percent. This financial model is typical for the system assemblers.

Companies that build major subsystems, such as disk drives, have a different financial model. These companies sell to the systems assemblers or to distributors for resale through computer stores to end users. They do not sell directly to the end customer. Consequently, they also have low gross profit margins. Seagate, Quantum Corp., and Western Digital average only 15 percent gross profits.

At that low level, they also cannot spend a large percentage of their sales on R&D. They depend on their suppliers—the disk and recording-head manufacturers like Komag, HMT, Read-Rite, and Applied Magnetics—to push the technology to new heights. Seagate, Quantum, and Western Digital average 5 percent on R&D.

With relatively few, easily targeted customers, these companies also run lean—if not skinny—on sales, general, and administrative expenses with an average SG&A of 6 percent. So even starting with low gross profit margins of 15 percent, they are able to bring 4 percent down to pretax income.

Who Are the Customers?

Obviously, the end-user customers are either individuals or organizations. Individuals buy personal computers one at a time, through retail outlets or mail-order suppliers. Organizations may buy a few computers at a time through retail or mail order, but they also buy from system integrators as part of a large project such as a new client/server installation; sometimes they buy directly from manufacturers. American Airlines once ordered 50,000 personal computers all at one time.

At the next step removed, the systems assemblers like Compaq are the customers for manufacturers of keyboards, disk drives, CD-ROMs, add-on graphics boards, modems, motherboards, monitors, and all the other parts that make up today's personal computer.

The industry has developed very efficient distribution methods to get subsystems to assemblers and finished computers to both the corporate and individual buyers. The annual COMDEX personal-computer trade show, usually held in November in Las Vegas, now attracts 200,000 attendees from over 100 countries to over 2,000 exhibitors with more than 10,000 new products spread across two convention centers and four hotels. News and analyses of new products, problems, contracts, and prices spread rapidly around the world.

What Competitive Strategies Win?

For the systems assemblers, the key strategy seems to be just-in-time manufacturing, or building to the customer's order. In addition to the financial benefits of carrying lower inventories, building to order gets the manufacturer out of the business of trying to predict what the customer will want to buy—now known as the Packard Bell Cul-de-Sac, after that company's disastrous attempt to guess what configuration Windows 95 buyers would go for. Because Windows 95 runs so poorly in 16 megabytes of DRAM, in the summer of 1995, Packard Bell figured that buyers would choose 32 megabytes of DRAM and economize by using a 90-megahertz Pentium microprocessor. After all, the processor could be upgraded later.

Instead, users went for the 133-MHz processor and suffered with 16 megabytes of DRAM until DRAM prices collapsed a few months later, then added more memory.

Dell, Gateway, and other companies that build to order quickly realized that (a) demand was not as strong as industry pundits had predicted, because corporations were waiting to finish their evaluations before upgrading to Windows 95, and (b) nobody wanted the slow processor in their new computer. When a logical argument could be made for either of two choices, the only wrong strategy was to bet your company on just one of them.

For companies that sell to the systems assemblers, the key strategy—in fact, the only strategy—is price/performance. Even at the very highest end of any product family, such as the largest disk drives or the fastest graphics processors, customers will pay only a reasonable premium over the next largest or fastest product. In the "sweet spot" of the market—that middle ground where the bulk of the unit sales and dollar volume are being generated—customers are absolutely fierce about paying as little as possible for the functions they need.

Producing good performance means spending money on R&D and, preferably, being the first to introduce new products, even if they are pricey for a while. Offering lower prices requires high-volume, high-yield manufacturing. There are different models to achieve this goal, all valid.

Seagate builds not only its own disk drives, but every component in the disk drive. It does buy some recording heads and disk platters from outside, secondary sources, but it manufactures the bulk of its own requirements.

Quantum has a contract to build all its drives with MKE, a subsidiary of Matsushita. MKE is free to buy components or make its own, as long as it delivers drives to Quantum with the agreed-upon specifications at the contracted price.

Western Digital buys all its components from outside, in the belief that it benefits from other companies' R&D and the competition between suppliers on both price and performance. But it assembles all its drives itself, in the belief that it needs to control its own destiny and can capture the manufacturing profit that Quantum cedes to MKE.

Three very different strategies: all valid, all successful, and all designed to cope with the low-margin, high-volume business environment.

How Will the Internet Affect It?

The earliest users of the Internet were computer professionals and hobbyists. Not surprisingly, the first products sold over the Internet were computer-related—everything from complete systems to very specialized repair parts. Because the Internet eliminates the distribution and retail channel, it can make computers available at lower prices. The parallels to a mail-order operation are obvious, with the added advantage of much lower advertising costs. It costs almost nothing to put an extensive color catalog on the World Wide Web, compared to hundreds of thousands or millions of dollars to mail the same catalog to potential buyers. Gateway and Dell, as well as many other companies, already have extensive Web sites that make suggestions about features, let a customer configure a computer, price it, order it, charge it, and provide a tracking number for an overnight-delivery service. Customers can track delivery of their computers on the Web until they arrive. Dell Computer already sells more than $1 billion worth of personal computers a year over the Internet.

The Internet also gives access to numerous newsgroups with frank discussions about the advantages and disadvantages of various models, sources of help for problems, and suggestions to improve performance and system administration. These days, it is very hard for a shoddy supplier to hide.

What Is the Next Big Change?

For all of you who have struggled through the upgrade to Windows 95 and 98, our condolences. We think it is a dead end. Microsoft's bid to create a rock-stable, serious operating system seems to have shifted to Windows 2000.

Windows 2000 incorporates a lot more system resources—more memory, a bigger disk drive, a faster processor for enhanced performance. It is primarily a server operating system meant to run on beefed-up, somewhat expensive PCs. But the cost of those resources falls reliably every year, and by 2001 a system capable of running Windows 2000 effectively will cost no more than a 1999 system to run Windows 98. So the handwriting is on the wall. For those who think that Microsoft will not abandon a user interface like Windows, we have one word: Bob.

(If you have already forgotten Bob, that's the point. Microsoft introduced Bob to make computers easier to use; the strategy flopped, and Microsoft abandoned it faster than a politician forgets an election promise.)

## CHAPTER NINE

Software

In the early days of computing, hardware manufacturers backed up a big truck to the customer's loading dock, unloaded a huge computer with a very rudimentary operating system, and handed over a programming instruction manual. Each company wrote its own software to run applications like payroll or inventory accounting. A really customer-friendly supplier like IBM might offer a few basic, cross-industry programs like databases, but the customer had to hire systems analysts and programmers—lots of them—to get any value out of the new machine. Still, it did not take long to realize that there was no reason for 500 companies to each write a separate accounts-payable and accounts-receivable program. So manufacturers began offering a few widely used applications packages.

In 1968, IBM signed an antitrust consent decree with the Department of Justice that required it to open its system to third-party software suppliers. The first wave of independent mainframe software companies included Applied Data Research, Cullinet, and Boole & Babbage (all now acquired by other companies). For the next decade, this new software industry catered to Fortune 500 companies and government agencies exclusively, developing mainframe software packages for databases, accounting, payroll, inventory control, computer-performance measurement, and configuration management. The customers still wrote much of their own software, including programs for specialized applications like airline-reservations systems, securities trading and settlement, seismic exploration, weather forecasting, and so on.

Another group of companies, which did not supply software packages, sprang up to offer custom software- and facilities-management services for mainframe users tired of skyrocketing costs with limited results. These new companies included Computer Sciences, EDS (Electronic Data Systems, started by Ross Perot), Planning Research, and University Computing. The problem with these companies was their economic model. Basically, they hired programmers and marked their salaries up 15 percent to 20 percent in order to bid on contracts. Because they were not selling packaged software, they never achieved any meaningful economies of scale.

The advent of the commercial minicomputer in the 1960s generated a much greater unit volume of computers and, therefore, a much larger market for packaged software. Even as the mainframe computer manufacturers were guarding their turf jealously against the independent packaged-software companies, the minicomputer manufacturers welcomed any new software package that made it easier to sell a minicomputer alternative to the mainframe. While a customer who spends $500,000 or more on a mainframe computer could justify hiring a full complement of programmers, a $30,000 minicomputer was often sold to customers too small to hire more full-time help.

And who were these minicomputer customers? In the beginning, most minicomputers were sold to scientists and engineers who could program the machines themselves. But as minicomputers spread into commercial applications, software-package sales to small and medium-sized businesses became—and still remain—a large, fast-growing market. Digital Equipment, the largest minicomputer manufacturer, realized early on that the more software packages there were, the more hardware DEC could sell. In a departure from the adversarial relationship that IBM had with third-party software houses, DEC never tried to write software for all the cross-industry applications. Instead, the DEC salesperson would often call in the sales forces of other companies—accounting packages, manufacturing shop-floor control, human resources—to convince the customer that a minicomputer could do a mainframe's job at substantially lower cost.

The basic applications program is the database. Even though DEC had its own package, it was neutral, at worst, toward other vendors like Oracle, Informix, Sybase, and Ingres (now owned by Computer Associates). Many contracts were lured away from IBM by a combined bid of DEC hardware and one of these relational database vendors.

With a much larger number of installations than mainframes, minicomputers enabled many software companies to build entire businesses based on one or two applications areas:

Marcam—discrete manufacturing
PeopleSoft—human resources

Ross Systems—accounting, human resources, process
    manufacturing
SAP—enterprise resource planning
Walker Interactive—accounting
Baan—enterprise resource planning

The success of the personal computer in the consumer market took the minicomputer-software model to another level, but with a twist. The first personal computers were programmed by their engineer/hobbyist owners, similar to the first minicomputers. But with a price point of $3,000 instead of $30,000, unit volumes of personal computers soared quickly. The only way to create software for personal computers at a reasonable price point was to write a standard package that could be run unmodified by any user, even one without a degree in computer science. Where the minicomputer package often requires some customization and tweaking when it is installed, there was never enough profit margin or customer skill available in the personal-computer business to do anything but install it and run it. Right from the beginning of the PC business, software has had to be "shrink-wrapped."

The low price of shrink-wrapped software required a different sales and distribution model, because there are not enough profit-margin dollars to support a sales force calling on customers. Minicomputer software is generally sold face to face, responding to customers' requests for bids. It takes some time to understand the customers' problems and assist with the installation until the customer accepts the software and writes a check.

The twist on the minicomputer model is that personal-computer software generally is sold through retail stores or by mail. The two exceptions are (1) site licenses, where a company like Microsoft can afford to call directly on a company like Ford and sell thousands of licenses for a package like Microsoft Office, and (2) value-added resellers (VARs), which assemble a complete hardware and software solution for a specific customer's needs, and aggregate all the small profits on the pieces of the solution to a meaningful profit on the whole job.

Distribution by retail and mail order, in turn, creates a channel for any small company that wants to get into the software business. With no need for a sales force, the company's limited resources can be concentrated on developing the package and advertising. A scant 100 independent software suppliers operated during the mainframe era, twenty times as many (2,000) made their mark in the minicomputer era, and ten times as many again (a whopping 20,000) launched businesses once personal computers were developed. Most of these companies are tiny and will never succeed, let alone go public. But the explosion in opportunity created a parallel explosion in publicly traded software stocks.

How Fast Is This Industry Growing?

The mainframe computer software industry is growing very slowly, if at all, but the minicomputer sector of the industry has been revitalized by client/server computing, where the minicomputer is the server. Server-based software includes the traditional database, accounting, human resources, and manufacturing packages plus a wide range of new applications: Internet servers, help desk, sales-force automation, automated call management, order entry, and inventory control.

Database software followed its own technology cycle. Flat files, where every record had to be defined completely in advance, were popular during the mainframe era. But defining every record in advance poses problems when a company wants to do something new, or collect and retain new information, or merge its data with the database of an acquired company.

For example, the Year 2000 problem is caused by flat-file databases that used only the last two digits for the year; it assumed the first two digits were "19." The cost of redefining all those flat-file records to cope with a four-digit year code will be in the billions of dollars.

Hierarchical databases, which came into fashion about the same time as the minicomputer, organize data in groups. The actual components of an "Employee Basic Data" group might be name, street address, city, state, zip code, and telephone number. When other programs need to access any of this data, they call for Employee Basic Data instead of, say, zip code. Then, when the day comes that the government requires everyone to use nine-digit instead of five-digit zip codes, the Employee Basic Data has to be reprogrammed, but not all the programs that use that group.

Later in the minicomputer era, relational databases were invented. In a relational database, everything is stored in tables with a common index. Each table contains only two columns: the index and the data item. When a program is run, it accesses all the tables it needs to pull in and assemble just the data required. An entirely new data item can be created simply by creating another table, with no need to rewrite any of the existing software (unless it would be advantageous to use the new table).

Through 1995, relational databases could effectively manage only six data types: letters, numbers, floating-point numbers, monetary values, time-related values, and dates. Other data types, such as video, sound, and computer-aided designs and color, were handled very awkwardly outside the optimized primary database engine. Then Illustra Information Technology (later purchased by Informix) introduced object-relational databases that can cope with any existing or future data type through plug-in "data blades"—software programs that describe the data type and integrate it into the main database engine.

The relational-database software business is growing at 20 percent per year. Between the spread of client/server computing, the advent of the Internet, and the extra kicker of object-relational technology, it should grow at this rate for the next five to ten years.

Other client/server applications software for minicomputers is growing at a rate of over 40 percent a year. Driven by the spread of fast relational databases, more and more business processes can be changed to on-line, real-time events. For example, customers used to phone or mail in orders. The order taker would transfer the order to a paper form and send it to the credit department for approval. Credit would send it on to shipping, which would check the inventory only to discover that the item was out of stock. Shipping would notify production, which would schedule another run of the out-of-stock item. After the item was back in stock, production would notify shipping and the order would be shipped.

With an on-line client/server application, the order taker is listening on the telephone and typing the order into a personal computer (the client). Software immediately queries the server for the customer's credit status and the availability of each product. Products in stock are shipped by overnight carrier the same day. Out-of-stock products are back-ordered with a firm shipping date because the inventory system automatically notifies manufacturing to schedule another run, and when the products are manufactured, they will be shipped to the customer automatically. All shipments can be tracked real-time on the overnight carrier's client/server system, which may use the Internet to connect client to server.

Dell Computer takes this model one step further. Personal computers are not assembled in advance. Each customer's order is scheduled for assembly and shipment the following day. Dell takes little inventory risk because it can have the component parts arrive every day or two. As component costs fall, Dell has the advantage of always using the cheapest components, staying on the competitive edge, and passing savings along to customers immediately. As customers change what they want—Pentium II versus Pentium III versus Celeron—Dell will not get caught with a large inventory of finished computers that have the wrong processor. The real-time, on-line system lets Dell's production adjust automatically to its customers' orders.

Virtually all new client/server applications software offers similar opportunities to make fundamental changes in the way a business deals with its suppliers, customers, and employees. Our 40 percent revenue-growth-rate estimate probably will turn out to be low, because it is for existing applications only.

In the personal-computer software industry, according to Jeffrey Tartar's *SoftLetter,* the largest 100 companies have grown at a 25 percent rate over the last five years. There is no reason for this pace to abate. The growth of the installed base of personal computers from 350 million today to at least six times as many—2.4 billion—by 2007 is equal to a unit growth rate of 25.9 percent. Although many of the additional machines will be smaller, less-powerful Internet access devices, they will all need software. In truth; with so many computers available, the personal-computer software companies will come up with terrific new applications we cannot even imagine today. (If we could, we all would start software companies and make hundreds of millions of dollars.)

The huge installed base of computers and the wide variety of people using them mean that a software company does not have to address the whole market to be successful. The broad, horizontal applications like word processing, spreadsheets, presentations, and databases are and may remain the province of major companies like Microsoft. But look at any specialized area—there are at least a half-dozen companies selling scriptwriting software, for instance. You can write a film script in Word, but it is much easier if the software provides the proper formatting, keeps track of characters' names, and automatically excerpts each character's lines for rehearsals.

The personal-computer software business promises to continue growing at a rate of 25 percent a year. As slower-growing mainframe software becomes a smaller and smaller portion of the total software industry, and faster-growing personal-computer software becomes ever more dominant, the growth rate of the entire software industry is approaching 18 percent to 22 percent per year.

What Drives the Growth Cycles?

There are two primary growth drivers in software: *new hardware* and *new applications.* Usually, "new hardware" means a new generation of microprocessors. The original Intel 8088 microprocessor was an eight-bit chip, able to process only one character at a time (eight bits equals one byte equals one character). The 286, 386, and 486 processors all were sixteen-bit chips, able to process two characters at a time. That enabled much more powerful software, and Intel's steady speed improvements made what was theoretically possible on a 286 commonplace on the 486.

But sixteen-bit processors need a lot of help to cope with multimedia data like sound and video. Expensive add-on boards with supplemental processors allowed the sixteen-bit processors to handle this complex data fairly well.

Intel's Pentium family of processors feature thirty-two bits and are able to process four characters at a time. Pentiums can process sound and video without assistance, which slashes the price point for multimedia computers. A thirty-two-bit processor can also handle much more data. Ganging many of them together creates a parallel-processing computer as powerful as most mainframes at 10 percent to 20 percent of the cost. The forthcoming IA-64 ("Merced") is a sixty-four-bit processor, expected to run initially at 500 million instructions a second.

Consequently, as each generation of microprocessors is introduced, there is a spurt in software sales. More applications can be moved off expensive mainframes and minicomputers to microcomputers. Software that previously sold in the hundreds of units for large computers now sells in the tens of thousands of units for personal computers. New companies start up to write client/server applications that replace the old batch-processing applications. The progression can be seen very clearly in spreadsheets. VisiCalc ruled the eight-bit world and, along with Word-Star, made the Apple II a business computer.

When sixteen-bit microprocessors were introduced, Lotus 1-2-3 was written to take advantage of the extra processing power. The 286-based IBM PC XT made 1-2-3 possible, and 1-2-3 made the XT a runaway success in corporations.

Thanks to faster sixteen-bit microprocessors and careful competitive analysis, Microsoft entered the market with a similar, but more advanced, program called Excel. By the time thirty-two-bit processors were introduced, Microsoft was ready with thirty-two-bit operating systems (Windows 95 and Windows 2000) and a thirty-two-bit version of Excel, which allowed it to cement the leading position in spreadsheets.

The second growth driver is new applications. Not only does each new generation of microprocessors allow software to migrate from mainframes to minicomputers to microcomputers, but software companies think up interesting new things for computers to do. My favorite recent new area is digital photography. You can buy a small scanner that fits in a floppy-drive slot. You insert a photo just like inserting a floppy disk; it is scanned onto the hard drive and pops back out. Photo software that comes with the scanner lets you crop, change, enhance, and print the electronic picture. Or it can be pasted into a document or presentation, or sent over the Internet to a doting grandparent. Of course, digital photography will create an upgrade cycle in printers. Scanned photos printed on glossy photographic paper with the newest 1,800-dots-per-inch ink-jet printers are hard to tell from the original.

Once consumers get used to scanning their shoeboxes full of photos, creating on-line photo albums, and sharing pictures over the Net, they will decide to eliminate the middleman and buy a digital camera. As digital cameras spread, other software opportunities will arise. Some company will introduce e-mail software that integrates a typed message, a digital photo, and a voice attachment to replace greeting cards with a highly personalized happy-birthday-merry-Christmas-wish-you-were-here-get-well-soon. Another use might be a cheap security system that points a digital camera at your front door, snaps a picture every minute, and transmits it automatically to a central monitoring station. Or perhaps transmits an image only if there has been a change since the last photograph.

How Profitable Is It?

What does it cost to deliver software? For mainframes and minicomputers, software ships on a tape that costs $25. For personal computers, a $2 CD-ROM or a few floppy disks do the job. It costs more to print the user's manual than to produce the software—one reason that most vendors now provide on-line manuals right on the CD-ROM.

As a result, the gross profit margins—sales minus direct cost of goods sold—are the highest in the technology business. Gross profit margins often run over 90 percent. That leaves lots of room for heavy spending on R&D to stay ahead of competitors, as well as heavy spending on sales and marketing. Software companies must advertise directly to consumers, provide dealer-incentive programs and co-op advertising money, and pay for basic technical support to keep their customers happy. Even after all those costs, the typical software company can place 20 cents of every dollar of sales in the net-profits column. One reason that Wall Street loves a software winner is the gusher of free cash flow a successful program creates, even after funding heavy R&D spending to maintain a competitive lead.

Our three sample companies in this area are Microsoft, Adobe Systems, and Autodesk. They have average gross profits of 85 percent. Out of that they spend heavily on R&D, an average of 18 percent. They spend 38 percent on SG&A, which funds their extensive consumer advertising campaigns, leaving them with average operating profits of 29 percent. This financial model is typical for successful software companies and explains why this highly profitable industry is one of Wall Street's darlings.

Who Are the Customers?

The customers for mainframe software are the roughly 25,000 mainframe installations at 8,000 major organizations around the world. That number is very stable, and everyone knows exactly where the computers are, what the configuration is, and who the software customers are.

The minicomputer world includes most mainframe installations plus another layer of smaller accounts that, again, are known by location, machine type, and the person to contact. It is entirely practical to sell to either mainframe or minicomputer customers by telemarketing or face-to-face sales calls.

But personal computer customers are everywhere. One way software companies try to find them is by selling low-priced versions of the software to be preloaded on new computers. Personal-computer manufacturers hope that the free software will attract customers; the software company hopes that the customer will send in the registration card and become a target for upgrades and add-ons.

As personal computers spread around the world, worldwide distribution, language translation, and technical support become major problems. Software companies cannot ignore worldwide growth, both because that is where much of the future growth in the entire industry will come from, and because if they do not provide a software package to do a job, someone else will. And ultimately that someone else could use a large installed base overseas to attack the U.S. domestic market.

What Competitive Strategies Win?

One key to building a big software company is to be first to market with a new application, and then reinvest profits in R&D to make sure that you never lose your lead. Autodesk is a great example of this strategy. I used to jog most mornings along an old railroad right-of-way that ran from Mill Valley to Sausalito, California, past a nondescript low-rent office building. Inside, a few software engineers were working on several different projects in hopes that one would become big enough to create a company. They were not taking salaries. They put their names on the office doors in masking tape so they could save a few bucks anytime they changed offices. The project they thought would win was an automated desktop manager called Autodesk, so they named the company after it. Another project was an automated drafting package, AutoCAD. At an early West Coast Computer Faire, I was walking by one of the smaller booths when Mike Ford, the dynamic sales V.P. of Autodesk, practically snagged me into the booth with a hook. He had seen my press badge, and he was not going to let any opportunity for good P.R. get away.

At that time, architects and construction engineers drew and redrew plans by hand on huge sheets of vellum, then printed them on blueprint paper. It was not uncommon on the job site to make a change to a wall, then—weeks later—discover that the piping diagram ran right through the changed wall.

AutoCAD started as a modest program to simply automate the drawing process. It developed quickly into a program that could rescale an entire structure automatically; check for conflicts between walls, plumbing, and electrical; substitute materials and calculate engineering loads; and, eventually, form the basis of a 3-D rendering so customers could take a virtual walk-through of the proposed building. AutoCAD's file formats became a standard in the architecture, engineering, and construction industry; before long, an architect had to have AutoCAD to submit drawings for bids or exchange information with other companies working on a project.

Today Autodesk has over 3,000 other companies that support its standard, doing AutoCAD training and consulting, writing plug-ins for AutoCAD, or selling the software in a vertical market package. It dominates the market because it was first with a great package.

Another way to win is to get lots of people using your software by giving it away free, then sell upgrades or related products. Eudora is a popular e-mail program available free over the Internet. Qualcomm Corporation bought the rights to Eudora and came out with Eudora Pro, a compatible but much more robust program that most serious Eudora users will upgrade to ultimately.

Network Associates (formerly McAfee Associates) built an entire company by giving away virus-detection software over the Internet. The company knew that early Internet users were computer-savvy, but some were irresistibly tempted to mess with others' computers by infiltrating a benign virus as a prank. Others were downright malicious, sending out viruses that erased hard disks, corrupted files, or made applications software inoperable.

Network Associates put a powerful virus-detection program on the Internet; not as freeware, but as shareware. The difference is that no one expects to get paid for freeware, but users are supposed to try the shareware and, if they like it and intend to keep using it, send a small amount of money to the author on the honor system. Of course, very few people ever send any money, but enough will pony up to support a programmer or two.

But Network Associates had bigger plans. It never really expected the computer whizzes downloading virus protection for personal use to pay much. But it knew that if those people loved the program, they would take it into the corporations, schools, and organizations where they worked. After a series of high-profile cases in the 1980s by the Software Publishers Association against companies that duplicated copyrighted software, Network Associates knew that major organizations had procedures in place to be sure they paid for or licensed all the software they used. So Network Associates was able to find its customers at no cost over the Internet, deliver the product at no cost over the Internet, let the user bring the software into an organization at no cost to Network Associates, and simply negotiate an annual license fee when the organization called.

Of course, Network Associates also offered frequent updates for new viruses and technical hand-holding that made the annual license more valuable. Good customer service also helped the renewal rate; unlike those of most software companies, the Network Associates license has to be renewed every year for an additional payment.

In a way, both of these winning strategies—being first to market or giving an introductory package away free—are parts of the larger winning strategy: Build a big customer base. New software requires installation, learning new commands, and learning how to integrate it or its output with other programs. Once customers have made an investment in time and training, they will not change to a different package lightly. So once a customer is on board, the company simply needs to keep its technology up-to-date and provide decent technical support and customer service to ensure that the customer buys upgrades and remains a user for a long time.

The real power of an installed base shows up when a company does not follow through. WordStar, the first major word-processing program, quickly became a favorite of professional writers everywhere. In spite of kludgy commands, awkward formatting, notoriously bad customer support, and few upgrades, over years of neglect the user base dwindled only slowly. Twenty years after its introduction, WordStar is still being used by thousands of people just because it is not worth their effort to learn a new system.

How Will the Internet Affect It?

The Internet is already having a huge effect on software companies, especially personal-computer software. Although most shrink-wrapped software goes through a two-step distribution process—from manufacturer to distributor to retailer (for ultimate purchase by the customer)— neither the distributor nor the retailer does anything meaningful to attract new customers. That is the job of the manufacturers, which is why their sales and marketing expenses are so high. Some specialty packages, such as screenwriting software, can be targeted through specialty magazines. But most software is used by a wide range of individuals and companies, and it is incredibly expensive to advertise enough to rise above the noise level and establish a brand identity. *PC World* and *MacWorld* were instant successes because advertisers grasped the opportunity to focus on people interested enough in their computers to subscribe to a magazine about them.

As the Eudora and Network Associates models attest, the Internet allows even the smallest company to:

- find customers free through Web sites that will show up in potential customers' search engines; e-mail marketing programs; or chat groups;
- deliver advertising literature free;
- provide a demonstration copy over the Net free;
- offer an electronic user's manual free; this is better than a printed manual because it can be searched by keywords to allow users to solve more of their problems themselves;
- provide technical support for no cost other than the technicians' time;
- collect license fees by credit card from customers who want to keep the software;
- create on-line registration cards for future bug fixes and eventually identify paying customers for upgrades and collateral programs; and
- track which customers do not convert the demonstration copy to a paid-up license, and pursue them in future marketing campaigns.

The primary problem with delivering software to customers over the Internet today is that the software is getting bigger faster than the communications pipe into the customer's computer. Corporations with high-speed connections to the Internet have already solved this problem, but individuals poking along at 33.6 megabits per second find it daunting when they start to download even the simplest software and a message like "28 minutes remaining" pops up. Fortunately, today's Internet users seem willing to schedule program downloads for periods when they have something else to do, and tomorrow's users will have much faster cable modems and direct digital connections to speed the delivery of even the largest software packages. It seems inevitable that the Internet will dominate software sales and distribution eventually.

Yet, in one key respect, the current industry leaders may suffer from the expansion of the Internet. Instead of buying today's multi-megabyte, general-purpose programs, users will be able to download information from the Internet that contains "applets" to do specific tasks. For example, mortgage brokers might post the best available loans on their Web site. The user could download the information, plug in specific loan information, and get a detailed analysis of whether or not to refinance—with no need to buy a spreadsheet program. This could even happen on a set-top box provided by a cable TV company. Applets are small generic programs, often written in the Java language, that will not carry large profit margins. In most cases, they will be free to the end user; the mortgage brokers in this example might pay a few thousand dollars for the original code. Java is catching on so fast that in 1999 well over half the Global 2000 corporations deployed mission-critical systems—applications that go to the heart of their businesses—written in Java.

What Is the Next Big Change?

The next big change in personal-computer software is highly integrated multimedia that also allows for voice input in every package. If personal computing is to spread from 430 million to 2.4 billion machines, the keyboard must go. The newest voice-recognition systems from private companies like Dragon Dictate (normal speaking-speed dictation) and Nuance (application-specific but speaker-independent normal-speaking speed) can already manage most of a computer's input. Voice recognition is also crucial for small hand-held computing/communications devices that do not have enough room for a keyboard.

Highly integrated multimedia in every software package becomes possible with the newest multimedia microprocessors and becomes necessary as the Internet becomes the standard method to connect and communicate, even inside an organization (the "intranet"). Think of what even the lowly spreadsheet could do as a communications tool if it were easy to animate, attach voice or video, and share over a network with more than one person able to work on it. Word processing and desktop publishing are naturals for the richer communications experience that multimedia provides.

## CHAPTER TEN

Communications

Data communications deals with computer-to-computer data over local- and wide-area networks (LANs and WANs). Telecommunications deals with voice traffic and the telephone network. It includes data sent over the switched telephone network, but the customers and growth rates for telecommunications and data communications equipment are different.

Data is digital—a series of 1s and 0s that represent bits turned either on or off. Voice is analog, varying over a range of pitch and intensity. The U.S. telephone system used to be completely analog, converting voice to its equivalent analog electrical signal, sending and switching the signal to its final destination, and then using the analog signal to drive a speaker in the handset of a telephone.

Modems convert digital data to analog signals and vice versa. "Modem" is short for **mo**dulator/**dem**odulator. At first, computers had to adapt to the existing analog telephone system in order to communicate.

But the telephone companies quickly realized that a varying analog signal occupies a wide path on the wire. They had some luck multiplexing voices on a single line, fitting one conversation into the spaces in another conversation, and then sorting the whole thing out at the receiving office before the various conversations were switched on to their intended destinations. But obviously it was wasteful to take an inherently narrowband signal like a stream of 1s and 0s and then allocate most of a wideband analog channel to transmitting it. The solution? By building digital lines for computer data, they could transmit many more digital "conversations" on a single line, sharing the cost among multiple users while making more profit for themselves.

At the same time, the phone companies realized that if they converted analog voice data to digital, it also could share the digital lines at much lower cost than the existing copper infrastructure. So they built high-speed lines, first using copper, now fiber-optic cable, that have changed the economics of the telecommunications industry radically.

With the traditional telephone industry going digital, the telecommunications world and the data-communications world are rapidly converging. In a few years, advanced technologies like ATM (Asynchronous Transfer Mode) and high-speed Ethernet will switch voice, video, or data from anywhere to anywhere—telephone to telephone, digital cellular phone to computer, Internet server to desktop computer, home-security system to laptop computer, and so on.

One of the crucial events that accelerated the convergence of telephony and data communications was the breakup of AT&T in 1984. Until then, AT&T was closely regulated in terms of its return on investment. As a monopoly, it was allowed to set rates to achieve a 12.75 percent return on its investment in capital equipment. Therefore, AT&T had an incentive to invest as much as possible in capital equipment (central offices, copper cables, switches, customer-premises telephones) and depreciate it as slowly as possible. As its costs increased, it simply applied for rate increases to maintain its 12.75 percent return.

Of course, AT&T argued vociferously that its investment in capital equipment was not overstated, because if it had to show a smaller investment, it would have earned less money at the 12.75 percent rate. At the time of the breakup, it had a whopping $20.3 billion in plant and equipment on its balance sheet, net of depreciation, and a total book value of $11.92 per share.

Within four years of the breakup, AT&T had written off $6.7 billion of this supposedly up-to-date equipment as obsolete, including much of its copper infrastructure. After more multibillion-dollar write-offs in 1993, book value fell to $8.65 per share. Of course, in 1993, AT&T reported $4.7 billion in earnings on that lower, more realistic book value—an incredible 35 percent return on investment. Only a few of the former regulators realized how much they had been conned all along.

The breakup was great news for the telecommunications and data-communications industries. First, it created a huge customer, AT&T, finally willing to buy the latest equipment from outside suppliers instead of building everything itself at Western Electric. Second, it created the Baby Bells—the Regional Bell Operating Companies, or RBOCs—eager to throw off the yoke of both AT&T and Western Electric. For many years, the people running the regional companies were treated like second-class citizens by the people running the mother ship. The RBOCs were pretty much forced to buy from Western Electric, which many regarded as a supplier of top-quality, overpriced, last-generation products. As one RBOC executive told me when the breakup was finalized: "It's payback time."

The RBOCs are big companies and, like any big corporations, they move slowly and sometimes in mysterious ways. But at least they move. For example, the idea for the Integrated Services Digital Network—ISDN—was floated in the early 1980s, with the first installation in June 1987, at McDonald's headquarters. It was slow to catch on. By the early 1990s, ISDN was being ridiculed as standing for "I Still Don't Know" or "It Still Doesn't Network."

But someone forgot to tell the RBOCs. They had been proceeding at their stately evaluation pace for many years, testing equipment and designing a service. I will never forget Joe Schoendorf of Accel Partners standing up from the audience at one of Dick Shaffer's Technologic Partners conferences on networking to ask a panel if it would make any difference to their forecasts if they knew that Pacific Bell was about to tariff ISDN to any house in California, no matter how remote, for a flat monthly rate of $28, with no installation charge.

People were stunned. Overnight, the new service not only made ISDN a leading contender for digital access to the Internet, it turned a faltering company named Ascend Communications into a telecom investment darling. Ascend was the only company that had an inexpensive ISDN connection device ready for both the home and the Internet service providers. The stock went from $1^{29}/$_{64}$ to $78^3/$_4$ in less than three years.

We think the RBOCs will continue to be the eight-hundred-pound gorillas of the telecom business. They will defend their franchise in local calling aggressively, while competing in cellular, long-distance, and data communications. Ultimately, they will all provide Internet access, home-security services, video on demand, paging, and any other telecommunications or data-communications service. They must offer everything to maintain that all-important account control. AT&T will be free to compete with the RBOCs nationwide in all these areas, including local calling. Both the RBOCs and AT&T will be major customers for outside equipment.

In addition, new carriers and services in long-distance telephony, audio and video conferencing, private telephone systems for colleges and prisons, integrated paging networks, truck positioning and communications, cellular pay phones, and a host of other specialized services will add to the demand for telecommunications equipment.

In fact, the entire communications infrastructure must be replaced over the next few decades because, close to 100 years ago, people decided that personal communications should go over a wire, while broadcast communications should go over the air. They got it exactly backward. With about 70 percent of the country now wired with cable, broadcast communications have a new path.

Almost fifty years ago, a second poor decision was made in establishing the Windows 2000SC standard for color television. The purpose of the standard was to preserve the receiving equipment and the option to receive future TV in black-and-white. Boy, there was some courageous thinking. Digital, high-definition television obsoletes the existing broadcast infrastructure and is ideally suited for a combination of cable and satellite transmission.

There needs to be an effort to free up the rest of the broadcast spectrum for personal communications. There aren't enough frequencies on the spectrum to transmit wireless video from person to person, but there are probably enough to transmit everything else. Also, broadcast happens to occupy a segment of the spectrum that won't fry your brains. There's no reason every cellular call should be the equivalent of putting your head in a microwave oven; cellular could move into the freed-up broadcast spectrum.

Meanwhile, the data communications business is also booming. Most business computers are connected to a local-area network (LAN). Even portable computers, especially those used by field sales and service forces, have gateway connections to the LAN. Local-area networks are interconnected with intelligent switches. Building and campus LANs are, in turn, interconnected with geographically distant LANs over a wide-area network (WAN). Originally these connections were made with bridges, which created a point-to-point connection over a fixed path whenever it was necessary to transmit data. Today they are made with routers, which are programmed to choose the most cost-effective available path at the exact time data, voice, or video is ready to be transmitted. Cisco Systems rode the router from a startup to a company with more than a $50-billion market capitalization in ten years.

An interesting sidelight on the way Silicon Valley works: NetFRAME Systems was founded to make high-performance servers for Novell local-area networks. The business plan was to replace unreliable, heavily loaded personal computers with a small but robust server offering mainframe-class redundancy, data backup, network administration, and the like. The company quickly found venture funding and was a modest success, racking up nearly $89 million in sales before Novell began to run into competitive problems.

Carlton Amdahl, son of the famous Gene Amdahl of IBM and then Amdahl Corp., is a well-known computer designer in his own right who designed the NetFRAME server. Earlier, he was visiting some professors at Stanford University and tossed out his idea for a smart bridge, one that could evaluate which communication paths were available at any given moment and move data to the one offering the best combination of high speed and low cost.

The NetFRAME server he had in mind sat on the office or factory floor and was sold to the data-communications manager as a better way to manage a LAN. This smart bridge would sit in the telephone closet and be sold to the telecommunications manager. It was not an appropriate product for NetFRAME.

The rest is history. The professors refined his idea, obtained venture capital from Sequoia Capital and others, and Cisco Systems was born. Within two years of its initial public offering in 1990, Cisco had a market capitalization 34 times as large as NetFRAME. In late 1997, NetFRAME was acquired by Micron Electronics for $1 a share.

How Fast Is This Industry Growing?

After many years of slow, steady 5 percent to 7 percent growth, the breakup of AT&T and the onset of new communications technologies and services are prompting a revolution in telecommunications. The industry's growth rate has accelerated to over 10 percent a year. This revolution will take a long time to complete; not only because the RBOC infrastructure moves with deliberate speed, but because its scope extends worldwide. Multinational corporations in the United States need to have the same telecommunications technology everywhere in order to connect immediately to production facilities, sales offices, and customers in other lands. We think the telecom-equipment suppliers can continue to grow at 10 percent a year for the next ten years.

Data communications is growing even faster. Personal computers are often bought one by one for small businesses and personal use. Very quickly, though, the benefits of connecting personal computers together with a LAN become clear. The cost is low; about $25 per computer for Macintoshes or $150 per computer for Wintel (Windows/Intel) machines. Wintel LANs of any significant size also need a dedicated server for another $2,000 or so.

Local-area networking is growing about 30 percent a year and will continue at that rate as LANs spread around the world. Intelligent switching to connect LANs is growing rapidly, too, in the 40 percent area.

Thanks to the boom in Internet traffic, wide-area networking is on a very high growth path. Our best estimate is in the range of 40 percent to 50 percent, but the explosive growth of intranets in the United States and Internet connections in the developing countries makes it hard to know exactly how fast things are actually moving.

Altogether, the converging communications industry is growing at about a 20 percent rate—an astonishing pace for an industry with $200 billion in equipment spending and a whopping $1 trillion in spending on services.

What Drives the Growth Cycles?

So far, there is no cycle in communications spending. The data-communications equipment industry grew over 30 percent per year right through the last recession, has grown at that rate ever since, and probably will not slow down through the next recession, thanks to the liftoff in worldwide spending.

There also has been no cycle in telecommunications spending, just an acceleration from the 5 percent growth track to today's 10 percent growth track.

No one foresees a serious downturn until most of the 2.4 billion personal computers anticipated for worldwide use are installed and connected together—a good ten years from now.

How Profitable Is It?

Three typical manufacturers of telecommunications equipment are Lucent Technologies, spun out of AT&T, Newbridge Networks, and Tellabs. They have average gross profits of 54 percent, and out of that they spend an average of 11 percent on R&D. Another 25 percent goes to SG&A, which is reasonable in light of the relatively small number of large customers. These three companies have average operating profits of 18 percent. This financial model has been stable for the telecommunications industry for many years.

In the more dynamic data-communications industry, three typical manufacturers are Cisco Systems, 3Com, and Premisys. They have higher average gross profits of 61 percent, due primarily to the higher software content in their products. They spend about the same on R&D, an average of 10 percent, and also on SG&A, averaging 24 percent. Within SG&A, they tilt more toward selling expenses because their customers are much more numerous and diverse.

The higher gross profits carry through to the bottom line, resulting in excellent average operating profits of 27 percent. This financial model is not yet stable because the data-communications industry, big as it is, is still in its infancy. Yet we expect the datacom industry to be more profitable than the telecom industry for many years to come.

Who Are the Customers?

One reason the data communications and telecommunications industries are converging is that the *customers* are converging. The traditional telecommunications customer was the telephone company, which owned the equipment even at the customers' sites. After the *Carterfone vs. AT&T* decision in 1968, AT&T's customers were allowed to connect their own equipment to the phone lines, if it was certified. That opened the door for companies to sell customer-premises equipment directly to end users. At first, most of the action was in PBX phone systems and handsets. But now that customers build private data networks, interconnect LANs, and mix voice, data, and video traffic over the same leased lines, many products are sold to both telephone companies and large customers, to handle both data and voice.

Octel Communications, the leader in voice-mail systems, exemplifies this kind of convergence. Octel sells systems to the telephone companies, which then offer voice mail as a service to their individual and small-business customers. Octel also sells to private voice-mail companies that compete with the telephone companies, offering the service to the same customers. Finally, Octel sells to medium-size and large businesses that can afford their own voice-mail systems. Lucent Technologies bought the company for $1.6 billion in 1997.

Today the primary customers for telecommunications equipment are the telephone companies and the Fortune 2000. Individuals and small businesses typically buy only handsets and cellular phones, and depend on Centrex or similar services to provide features like voice mail, conference calling, and call forwarding.

The primary customers for most data-communications equipment are organizations with multiple locations. The exceptions are LANs and modems or other Internet-access devices. LANs are everywhere in businesses of all sizes, and Internet-access devices are sold to every market from the largest corporation to the individual at home.

What Competitive Strategies Win?

More than any other technology business, communications is driven by standards. Standards are like languages; you cannot understand someone speaking a language you do not know. You may not be able to understand someone speaking a language you do know if they do not follow basic rules of usage and sentence construction.

The communications industry adopts new standards when they meet a new need, such as sending video. The industry also adopts new standards as new levels of speed become available at a reasonable cost. Each step in modem speed for the last ten years, from 800 bits per second to 2400 bits, 9600 bits, 14.4 kilobits, 28.8 kilobits, 33.6 kilobits, and now 56 kilobits, was codified in a different standard by the International Telecommunications Union and the CCITT, the international standards bodies.

One winning competitive strategy is creating a new standard. Generally, standards bodies will insist that the inventor contribute the standard to the public domain by publishing the specifications and not charging royalties. The advantage of creating a new standard is that the company that invents it usually has the best understanding of it and is well down the product-development path by the time the standard is adopted. As long as that company produces the hottest box to run the open standard, it should be able to maintain a leadership position.

Companies that follow this strategy are under constant pressure to innovate, and experience periodic profit-margin pressure as other companies introduce competitive products. It always looks tempting to keep part of the standard proprietary, either to ensure a competitive advantage, or to be the sole manufacturer of semiconductors required to implement the standard, or to get royalties. We do not invest in companies that succumb to the proprietary temptation because it almost never works.

A good example of a company that fell into this trap is U.S. Robotics, one of many modem competitors at the 2400-bit level. It began to distinguish itself at the 9600-bit level by excellent dealer relationships and garnered a large share of the retail modem market. But it really started to dominate when its 14.4-kilobit modem was one of the first solid products in the market. Unlike previous modem leaders, which never had been able to dominate two modem generations in a row, U.S. Robotics' 28.8-kilobit modem was also early to market. It garnered rave reviews. The transition to 33.6 kilobits was relatively easy, and the company retained its leadership position.

But the modem market was and is brutally price competitive. For the next generation of 56-kilobit modems (actually up to 53 kilobits downloading to the personal computer, but only 33.6 kilobits uploading), U.S. Robotics was seduced by the potentially better profit margins of a proprietary product. While the entire modem industry lined up behind Rockwell's 56-kilobit standard and chip sets, U.S. Robotics tried to leverage its market leadership by cramming down its own standard, called X2. Beginning in late 1996 and for several months thereafter, a heavy television advertising campaign featuring Steve Wozniak, the inventor of the Apple II, tried to convince Internet service providers and personal-computer owners that X2 was the only way to go. But at heart the communications industry knows proprietary standards are expensive and stagnate the technology, and X2 was rejected in early 1998 in favor of a blend of the Rockwell and X2 features. Fortunately for U.S. Robotics shareholders, 3Com bought the company in 1997.

Another successful competitive strategy is to be a broad-line supplier, able to solve most or all of the customer's problems. Cisco Systems, 3Com, and Bay Networks (now a subsidiary of NorTel) all pursue this "one-stop shopping" strategy. They offer products they do not invent themselves through a joint venture with a specialty company, or they simply buy one of the manufacturers. When Cisco realized that the intelligent switch was a new niche product and potentially competitive to its router sales, it bought not one but two intelligent-switch companies. When it began to look as if the "frame-relay" standard was attracting substantial customers, Cisco paid $4.6 billion for Stratacom. As companies were moving from Ethernet LANs that ran at 10 megabits per second to those running at 100 megabits per second, engineers began talking about gigabit-per-second Ethernet networks. Andy Bechtolsheim, a founder of Sun Microsystems, left Sun to start Granite Systems to develop gigabit Ethernet. Cisco bought the company for $200 million before it even had a product. Clearly, Cisco is determined to offer any data-communications product that a customer might want.

In general, every new standard and every major increase in speed creates a window for new companies to succeed. When these new companies go public, they often have sensational valuations—over 100x earnings or 10x sales—that reflect the large, fast-growing market in which they participate. If you wait patiently, you usually get a chance to buy these companies after the market has matured somewhat, when it is easier to sort out the winners and losers, at a fraction of those valuations. These are the sorts of stocks that report earnings up 70 percent year-over-year and promptly drop 30 percent in value because the momentum investors were looking for 75 percent growth.

How Will the Internet Affect It?

The major impact of the Internet in the near term is on the communications-hardware companies because their gear is required to build the Internet's infrastructure. Software-infrastructure companies like Netscape Communications (now a subsidiary of American Online) and Spyglass battle to see if the customers will pay for their products. Content suppliers are trying both subscription and advertiser-supported business models to see if anything will make a profit. But datacom-equipment manufacturers are booking profits today.

Beyond the Internet, the corporate intranets—the private networks based on Internet technology—are a market three to five times as large as the Internet. Intranets require the same routers, switches, interconnect devices, and communications networks as the Internet. We expect the Internet and intranets to set the worldwide standard for data communications for the next ten years. That is the primary driver of our 30 percent datacom growth forecast.

The Internet also is useful as a place for a small company to garner "mind share." News of a hot product or a unique technology twist travels fast, because the customers for datacom gear are some of the heaviest users of the Net. New products can be introduced free, reviewed on the discussion boards, ordered and paid for by e-mail, and shipped by overnight parcel delivery.

What Is the Next Big Change?

The next big change in telecommunications is digital cellular-telephone systems, in both the developed and developing world. There are two competing standards: time-division multiple-access (TDMA) and code-division multiple-access (CDMA). Although proponents of each of the two standards will claim higher numbers than the other, each new standard offers about a 5x improvement over current analog cellular systems in the number of calls that can be carried in a given amount of bandwidth. TDMA is an open standard with hundreds of suppliers driving costs down. It has been accepted as the standard in Europe, Japan and most of the Pacific Rim, South America, and half the United States.

CDMA is a closed standard with royalties paid to Qualcomm. It has been accepted as the standard in Korea, where the Ministry of Telecommunications mysteriously outlawed all other digital cellular standards. It may be accepted as a standard in India, again as a cram-down by some government bureaucrat. It has three large customers in the United States trying to implement it: PCS Primeco, which is a consortium of four RBOCs building one of the new personal-communications systems; Sprint for its PCS system, and GTE for the same application. CDMA system deployment is behind schedule due to performance and software problems. It appears it takes more cellular base stations, not fewer (as CDMA proponents claim), and therefore is a more costly system. Voice quality was very poor, but has improved to TDMA levels. However, CDMA systems still seem to drop calls easily when a phone is in motion, as in a car. Most CDMA phones are sold with a dual-mode switch to flip back to the analog network when necessary.

The next generation of cellular telephones will use a combination of the TDMA and CDMA standards, based on CDMA. It probably will evolve to an open standard, with royalties payable to no one.

The advantage of digital cellular in the near term is lower cost per call and, therefore, lower prices. In Europe, young people do not even get a home telephone number anymore. They get a TDMA cell phone and a personal number that they keep with them, wherever they move or travel. The cost is about the same as a fixed phone, so why not?

The longer-term promise of digital cellular is the ability to expand the handset to be a personal communicator that can send and receive faxes, surf the Net, and connect to a home computer or office LAN. Once enough personal communicators are in use, companies will invent new applications that make the devices indispensable.

The next big change in data communications is a convergence on two major standards: ATM and gigabit Ethernet. Asynchronous Transfer Mode is the most advanced data-communications protocol today, and the only one that can reliably carry voice, video, and data from mainframe to desktop. Video is especially difficult because the data travel in small packets that are switched around the country (or world) to their destination. One packet might travel a longer route than the next, but ATM will sort out the arrival times and put them in the right order to play continuous video. We think ATM will have a significant share of the backbone—the interstate highways of data communications that go from one location to another.

Gigabit Ethernet is a less expensive technology and should win the LAN market—data communications inside the building. But these technologies overlap more than many people realize. Several companies are working on ATM to the desktop, reducing the cost by reducing the speed from 155 megabits per second to 25 megabits per second. Their theory is that videoconferencing will be the next great application, reducing travel costs and keeping widely separated teams in multinational companies working in harmony.

At the same time, other engineers are just starting to explore the possibility of using gigabit Ethernet on the backbone. It is a cheaper technology and, given equal performance, cheaper always wins. There are difficult technical issues in handling video, but once inventors realize something might be possible, it usually turns out to get invented. We suspect gigabit Ethernet will win a large share of the backbone.

So our forecast is that ATM and gigabit Ethernet share the backbone, gigabit Ethernet wins on the LAN, and ultimately one of them displaces the other—but it is too early to tell which.

## CHAPTER ELEVEN

The Internet

The Internet is a pervasive force affecting virtually all technology companies, as you can tell by the separate "How Will the Internet Affect It?" sections in each of the previous industry chapters. Investors need to adapt to the new opportunities the Internet provides—and, in some cases, the dangers it poses—to high-tech stocks. But what about investing in Internet stocks themselves?

It is a tribute to how rapidly the Internet is growing that this chapter was added for the second edition of this book. Many Internet stocks went public after Netscape's debut in August 1995. Some, apparently operating in what the industry wryly refers to as "Web-time," already have cycled from promising initial public offering to total collapse and impending bankruptcy as their vision of the Internet industry turned out to be wrong. Many others have managed to build real, albeit small, revenue bases and are struggling in the Land of the Living Dead, trying to figure out what part of the Internet will pay off next and how they can wrench their businesses from here to there. A few, like Yahoo and Amazon.com, have seen sensational revenue growth, even if profitability remains small or elusive.

There is no doubt that the Internet will reshape our lives, our economy, and our society in many fundamental ways, rapidly driving down the costs of research, distribution, and communications. We were the second investment adviser on the World Wide Web (John Westergaard beat us by a few weeks) and we are on the Web every day for work and play. I have been buying stuff over the Web for more than three years, from books and vitamins to our electric land-speed-record car and a tractor. I belong to several discussion groups, focusing on topics as diverse as electric vehicles, permaculture, and our local Coastside community. I get numerous e-mail publications, including *Conspiracy Nation* ("Jim Jones, Paula Jones, Jonesboro High School Murders: What's the Connection?").

In short, I am a believer that great fortunes will be made as we move into this next stage of the Information Economy. Like any emerging investment opportunity, though, the Internet's potential risks tend to be downplayed while the envisioned rewards become the fodder of weekly news-magazine covers.

By 1999, with the frenzy in certain of these stocks reaching new heights almost daily, it seemed tempting to jump on the bandwagon. After all, how could so many investors, analysts, brokers, and pundits be wrong? Tulip bulbs and the Nifty Fifty went to the moon, so why not Net plays as well?

Unfortunately, euphoria in an emerging investment area almost always signals a classic blowoff top. The momentum investing crowd becomes frantic searching for anything that promises to go up in the face of declining growth rates. Wall Street is happy to comply, fueling the fire with second-rate initial public offerings and promotional stock recommendations that make biotech new issues look like seasoned companies.

This chapter offers a framework for investing in the Internet. Some pundits would say that "investing" and "Internet" should not appear in the same sentence, but I can give you some value criteria that will screen out at least the most overhyped, hopeless prospects. (That's "hopeless" from the investor's point of view; a company may do well while its overpriced stock is declining.)

The Internet constitutes a three-part investment opportunity. The first part—the *hardware infrastructure* companies—are building out the Net; most of these are profitable, but many sell at rather rich valuations. These companies were covered in the last chapter. The second part—the *software infrastructure* companies—provide Internet access, server software, browsers, firewalls, search engines, directories, Web-site management, and a host of specialty products to create and enhance the Web experience. The third part—the *content* companies—offer information, goods, and services over the Internet. The latter two groups are what most people think of as "Internet stocks."

The software infrastructure companies have some very serious problems. Many of them are unprofitable, with business models based on unproved propositions like advertising banners as a major source of income. Others have a "product" that will eventually wind up as a feature of someone else's product. For example, in five years your word processor probably will have a firewall and maybe a Web browser built right in.

Most of these companies face terrific price pressure because they are competing with every computer-science graduate student in the world who wants to give away great new software free on the Internet, get noticed by the venture capitalists, raise a lot of money, and become the next Marc Andreessen (co-founder of Netscape at the age of 24; multi-millionaire at 25). Even the underlying technologies are not stable; there are many ways to program a search engine, as you can see when you try a few and discover they return totally different answers. (It is truly written: "Give a man a fish and you feed him for a day; teach him about search engines and he won't bother you for weeks.") Perhaps they should use their own technologies to search for a profitable business model.

In the long run, the real money on the Internet will be made by content companies. The cost of acquiring a customer is much higher than what a company can charge for basic Internet access and e-mail (due, again, to intense competition), so companies must generate extra revenues by charging those customers for extra services and products. Because the Internet can reduce so many of the costs of advertising and fulfillment, suppliers of goods and services can operate on much slimmer profit margins. That is why an online bookseller can discount almost every book in its catalog more than any retail store, or Shopping.com can provide a wider range of merchandise at discounts larger than Wal-Mart's.

The Internet has certain unique attributes that color the investment opportunity. First, it is an *information utility.* Beginning in the United States and Europe, and then spreading around the world, virtually every person, device, household, business, and institution will be able to reach the Internet. Most will enjoy multiple access options, including telephone, cable, wireless, and even the electric power system.

Like any utility, the Internet will always be available. The cost of providing bandwidth, whether digital subscriber line (DSL), cable, wireless access, or backbone transportation, is plummeting. As a consequence, devices can remain attached, instantly ready to reach out or respond to queries.

Connecting to and using the Internet requires the use of Internet Protocol (IP), a defined standard of bits and bytes that is the electronic language of the Net. With IP as a least common denominator, everything connected to the Internet can count on a minimum level of intercommunication.

Standards like IP drive the development of semiconductors to implement the standard, and, as we saw in Chapter 6, semiconductors advance by lowering costs through higher and higher levels of integration. With convergence on a few physical interfaces and IP as the primary data and network interface, one or two chips can hold the intelligence to connect a device to the Internet. That means a huge variety of low-cost Internet access platforms can be created, appealing to a wide range of tastes and technical sophistication. Moreover, non-Internet devices can inexpensively add the intelligence to connect to the Web, enabling remote control of appliances, heating systems, and the like.

A second attribute of the Internet is *high fixed costs but low variable costs.* Providing access and transporting information require a large up-front investment in fiber-optic and copper cables, repeaters, line conditioners, computer servers, and networking software. Once the bandwidth is in place to carry traffic, though, the true incremental costs of carrying the next few bytes of data are virtually nil (just a bit of power to propel the traffic along).

Not only are most Internet costs fixed, but the user's investment to get started is minimal. Almost any business or individual can establish a presence on the Internet for less than $2,000. From there, your functionality and "reach" is determined by how much you spend on additional capacity and marketing.

With a mostly fixed-cost model, size matters. The cost of doing one additional transaction is almost zero, so Internet participants who come up with the right marketing mix should be able to grow substantially.

A third unique and very interesting attribute of the Internet is *payment*—who pays who for what, and how much. Consumers will pay monthly Internet access charges, but many will switch service providers to save money and some may be willing to put up with advertising if they can get access free. To a limited extent, consumers are opting to pay very low subscription fees for just a smattering of sites or so-called "premium channels." *The Wall Street Journal* provides a tremendous amount of information yet charges only $59 a year for www.wsj.com ($29 for print subscribers). *Silicon Investor* runs chat groups on hundreds of stocks and asks $120 for an annual membership. Yahoo, a competitor, provides the same investment chat groups for free.

Consumers are just getting used to the idea of paying small, per-item charges to trusted sources (magazines, newspapers, research firms) and a small markup on each product (like books) or service (like airline tickets) they buy on the Net. Generally speaking, these markups are smaller than their real-world equivalents (and can be driven down to very minuscule levels if consumers are willing to shop hard).

On the flip side, future consumers could conceivably receive payments for allowing firms to collect information on them.

Businesses will pay for information about potential customers, either directly or through media-placement agencies. They will also pay for the message that is delivered to the customer, which brings us to the fourth novel attribute—*advertising.*

Classical advertising is defined as nonpersonal communications using paid media with clear sponsorship. As such, mass-message "spamvertising" on the Internet will almost surely cease to exist. Forrester Research estimates that advertising on the Internet will grow to only modest levels, from less than $1 billion in 1997 to around $2.5 billion in 2002. That is a far cry from the $80 billion spent in 1997 on TV and print advertising.

Distinct from advertising, money *will* be spent on direct marketing. The Internet gives businesses an unprecedented ability to collect and process data on individuals, and to use that information to target product offerings and infomercial messages directly to interested prospects. But the technology is also available to make consumers' Web sessions more productive by refining the results of search queries, for example, so Internet users will still feel as if they're in control. Eventually, the influence of direct marketing on the Web experience will be unnoticeable.

A major controversy is brewing over how to measure use of the Net, the size of the audience, and the impact of Web ads. "Clickthrough rates" are falling out of favor because advertisers have not seen an impact on their bottom line, which should be apparent immediately because of Web-time feedback loops.

A half-dozen startups and crossovers from traditional media are all trying to measure Internet traffic and impact. With no established "Nielsen," advertisers and placement agencies don't know what to trust. So far, ad dollars have flowed to larger portal sites like America Online and Yahoo. But soon we should see a rapid shift to Web-site mega-sponsorships—as Chrysler-Benz strives to compete with Rolls-Wagen (or is that Volks-Royce?)—and to smaller, specialized sites as the technology for targeting improves. Coming to the realization that advertising on the Net was *not* going to explode, Yahoo, Lycos, and Netscape suddenly decided that it made better business sense to abandon their advertising-supported search-engine models and compete with America Online instead.

A fifth salient attribute of the Internet is the importance of *controlling eyeballs,* or the Web-portal strategy. Following America Online's example, everyone now wants to be the Net users' preferred entryway to the Internet, controlling what they see, collecting information about their preferences, selling that information to direct marketers, and taking a slice out of what they buy on-line.

This concept actually might have some merit. Most consumers use the Net primarily for shopping and entertainment, with some educational uses by the kids and some day-to-day activities (checking Johnny's grades, getting the local theater schedule) thrown in. They will get locked into a particular pattern of use, identify with a few brands, and develop loyalty to those brand names. They are not likely to search far and wide for the absolutely best deal or the precise answer, unless it is very easy or it is something about which they are very knowledgeable or passionately concerned.

To whom will people turn for the few sites they visit?

- familiar names and trusted brands like Disney and *The New York Times*
- membership clubs like Cendant or, perhaps, AAA or AARP
- "metabrands" like a "Good Housekeeping Seal" or "Underwriter's Laboratory"
- "microbrands" for specific passions, like *CTSL* for technology investing

Obviously, the Web portals like America Online and Yahoo are striving to become trusted Internet brands. A few will succeed; others will survive by partnering with the telephone companies and cable companies that control the "pipes" to the consumer. The real question is whether, given the Internet's propensity to disintermediate, the Web portals can take enough of the revenue pie to justify the valuations Wall Street is placing on their stocks. One has to make some pretty wild assumptions about the growth of on-line advertising and the share flowing to the portals, the volume of business-to-consumer e-commerce and the share flowing to the portals, overall growth of Internet access fees, and the ultimate price/earnings multiple Wall Street will be willing to assign to these "new media" companies.

The trouble is that the Internet is all about *disintermediation*—getting rid of the middleman and connecting the producer directly with the consumer. Because the Internet reaches everyone, a diligent consumer should be able to find the lowest-cost provider of anything. Disintermediation will depress profit margins for all Internet commerce, as it pressures vendors to find ways to keep customers loyal and "hooked."

Total disintermediation isn't a given, because many people for most purposes are unlikely to search exhaustively for the cheapest and the best. But the cheapest and the best will be there if they want to find it, and the nature of the Internet ensures that much of the middleman profit will be squeezed out of many transactions.

Yet many of the current crop of content and portal companies are trying to be intermediaries, inserting themselves back into the transaction, like Amazon.com. In 1997 I speculated in print that someone somewhere was working on a software program that would let readers connect directly to publishers and search across all publishers' Web sites for books on a particular topic or by a particular author. The publishers then would sell the book on-line at a bigger discount than Amazon.com, yet would still keep a larger percentage of the list price by cutting out Amazon, the new middleman.

Within a few days I received a call from an irate reader who said: "First, who are you? Second, how did you get hold of my business plan?

Third, how dare you break the confidentiality agreement and publish this?"

I explained that I had never heard of his company and had not seen the business plan, but rather had made up the example as the next logical step in Web commerce. He immediately said: "Wait a minute. Have you seen someone else's business plan? Is there someone competing with me?"

I reassured him I had not seen anyone's business plan, at which point he grumbled something about how I should not have published the information anyway, and hung up.

Whether at the hands of my irate caller or some other group, the re-intermediators are in some trouble. Each new medium encompasses the prior content. An electronic bookstore still is a bookstore—a comfortable idea, easy to grasp, with numerous successful examples in the physical world. Why not just put it in cyberspace?

Because cyberspace creates a whole new way to relate to customers and connect customers to content suppliers. It has occurred to me, for example, that printed investment newsletters might be on their way out. E-mailing a newsletter is just putting the old content in the new medium. But this new medium enables an entirely different kind of service that may be much better for customers. I could offer to make a recommendation and follow a stock for a low flat fee, because it does not cost anything to e-mail updates for years, if necessary. The "subscriber" gets an e-mail only *when* something noteworthy happens, rather than having to read a printed newsletter every two weeks to find out *if* anything happened. Likewise, readers may not want to browse through an on-line bookstore if they could consult an on-line librarian who knew their interests and could suggest appropriate books, perhaps reviewed and ranked according to relevance. Those "books" might exist only as computer files, with the publisher or author getting paid depending on how much of the file is downloaded.

Companies that work on a slim profit margin may be able to re-intermediate if they provide added value, although slim margins usually do not go hand in hand with high profitability. For example, on-line travel agencies work on about a 4 percent markup. It costs an airline 5 percent of revenues to write and handle a ticket, so the airline has no incentive to get rid of the on-line travel agency that is actually saving the carrier money. Traditional travel agents work on about an 8 percent profit margin, so the airline would rather write a ticket itself than lose those extra profits. Of course, the airline would much prefer the on-line agent's 4 percent cut to the traditional travel agent's 8 percent cut.

At the same time, traditional travel agents are working for a small dollar amount per ticket, so after a ticket is written they cannot justify spending a lot of time calling and following up to see if any new fares are more attractive. The on-line agent's computers can take advantage of night downtime to search for any new fares that might make a ticket switch worth it, thus providing a higher level of customer service for a lower profit margin.

Of course, the online travel agents will be pressuring each others' profit margins, just as the music sites do. I received a glossy catalog from a music club with a ten-CD boxed set I was interested in at $129.97 plus $4 shipping. I hopped on the Web and went to CDNow.com, where the set was available for $90.98 plus $2.99 shipping. I then checked Musicboulevard.com, where the CDs were $90.99 plus $2.99 shipping. So I bought it from CDNow because it was one cent less.

Does this sound like a great business to you?

How Fast Is This Industry Growing?

The number of new users of the Internet in the United States is growing 30 percent per year. In 1999 about 65 million U.S. adults, or 38 percent of the adult population, used the Internet. That leaves lots of room for continued double-digit growth. The number of users in the rest of the world is more than doubling each year. The amount of traffic on the Net is doubling *every 100 days.* Obviously, that cannot continue forever, or even much longer; everyone in the world would be spending all their waking moments connected to the Net.

However, this growth rate should hold for the next two or three years. After that, worldwide growth will start to slow to "only" 50 percent a year, as the rest of the world catches up to the United States. By 2003 there will be upwards of 300 million consumers connected to the Internet, plus virtually every business including the local hardware store.

As a group, the Internet software infrastructure companies grow mainly with new connections, which are increasing about 50 percent a year. The content companies sell to both new and existing users, and their potential growth rates are extremely high as they take market share from older media and distribution chains.

What Drives the Growth Cycles?

So far there has not been a down-cycle in the Internet. The most likely source for a downturn would be if usage outgrows bandwidth, so the whole Internet slows down or even comes to an occasional halt ("brownout"). In that event, new users might shy away and existing users pull back until capacity expands. At that point they might return in droves and eventually again overwhelm bandwidth, sparking another cycle. It has not happened yet, and many large companies and organizations are determined to keep bandwidth growing faster than usage, to make sure it never happens. Of course, a private network can easily be overwhelmed, as America Online was when they introduced flat monthly pricing.

A significant portion of business-to-business traffic will flow over special "business-only" Internet bypasses to reduce the impact of a brownout. Taking a separate route won't avoid problems like AT&T's frame-relay outage in the spring of 1998, caused by bugs in Cisco's frame-relay switches. But by overpaying for capacity, businesses will be able to ensure that their mission-critical data doesn't get stalled by 100 million "Happy Mother's Day" messages.

How Profitable Is It?

Most of the software infrastructure and content companies are barely profitable or not at all. Three infrastructure companies that are profitable to some extent are America Online, Yahoo, and Check Point Software. They have average gross profit margins of 71 percent and spend 9 percent on R&D and 39 percent on SG&A. That leaves 23 percent operating profit, for which in the middle of 1998 Wall Street would like you to pay 176x estimated 2000 earnings. By contrast, the price tag for Microsoft, which earns 51 percent operating profit, was a mere 61x 2000 earnings. For double the profitability, MSFT gets one-third of the multiple?

The content companies are not profitable. Amazon.com, SportsLine, and Preview Travel average 34 percent gross margins. They spend just 8 percent on R&D, but a whopping 68 percent on SG&A (42 percent on Sales & Marketing alone). That leaves them losing forty-two cents on each dollar of revenues—maybe they hope to make it up on volume!

The question of profitability leads to the issue of stock valuation. Many Internet companies invest far more in marketing than they do in R&D, so on a growth-flow basis they always will look terribly overvalued. Most of them are losing money and could be classified as development-stage companies, but the M Score valuation approach described in Chapter 15 will not work because of low R&D spending.

There are two reasonable ways to value Internet stocks. First, it is very difficult for any software/service company to sell consistently for more than 45x forward earnings—the earnings per share expected for the next twelve months. If you take the average Wall Street forecast for forward earnings and apply the 45x multiple, you probably will be shocked by how low the target price is compared to the current price of the stock.

I have found that you can take 45x the most positive estimate for the year *following* the next twelve months and often the stocks still are overpriced.

The other way to get a handle on some reasonable value is to look at the ratio of price to revenues. The price-revenues ratio, or PRR, has been used for decades to value private companies that, for tax reasons, chose to understate their earnings as much as was legally possible. A PRR of 1.0, or $1 of market capitalization for every $1 of revenues, was commonly thought of as fair value.

But these are technology companies, which commonly trade at a PRR of 3.0 to 6.0. In fact, these are more like software than hardware companies and might reasonably trade at even higher PRRs—5.0 to 8.0. Microsoft, the king of the software stocks, sells for a PRR of about 20.0. It seems logical to think that Internet stocks should not sell for PRRs of more than 15.0 to 20.0. Unfortunately, many do, as you can see from the forty companies listed in Table 11.1. It will be very difficult for shareholders in the overvalued companies to make any money, even if those companies achieve their business objectives. PRRs over 20.0 and price/forward earnings ratios over 45x have spelled investment disaster in the past.

Who Are the Customers?

Everyone. That is why investors are so excited about the Internet. Internet businesses can be segmented by who is dealing with whom:

Consumer to Consumer includes mostly personal correspondence. Today that largely constitutes e-mail and file transfers, but tomorrow it will probably include telephoning and video conferencing over the Internet. This traffic will essentially serve as an alternative to telephone use.

Consumer to Noncommercial includes queries to the library, Department of Motor Vehicles, university records, the IRS, and the like. As in the first category, this traffic will resemble today's telephone access, and the bulk of the content will be free.

Consumer to Business is a big unknown—what will consumers buy and how will they pay for it? Forrester Research estimates the value of on-line shopping at $9.2 billion in 1999, and projects it to reach $100 billion by 2002. For the same period, Jupiter Communications estimates $10.8 billion in 1999 on-line sales growing to $125 billion in 2002. In terms of household income, the largest group of users in the U.S. (32.5 percent) are in the $75,000 to $150,000 category—a very attractive demographic. While 68 percent of current users of the Internet are men, 50 percent of new users are women. About half of all users are aged 35 to 54.

Table 11.1
Selected Internet Software Stocks

SYMBOL	NAME	6/30/99 PRICE	PRICE/ REVENUES	2000 P/E	BUSINESS
ATHM	@ Home	47.313	180.0	946.3	Internet access via cable TV
AMZN	Amazon.com	99.750	9.2	1,995.0	Books
AOL	America Online	105.125	9.3	122.2	Internet access + community
AXNT	AXEWindows 2000	30.625	9.1	30.3	Security/Firewalls
BVSN	Broadvision	23.875	16.2	54.3	Software for e-commerce
CDNW	CD Now	20.125	9.5	NM	Music CDs
CKFR	Checkfree	29.438	7.2	98.1	Electronic payment
CHKPF	Check Point	32.750	9.7	18.4	Security/Firewalls
CMGI	CMG Info Svc	70.750	21.0	277.3	Internet services
CNWK	CNET	68.250	23.8	113.7	TV + Web + community
CNCX	Concentric NW	30.313	6.5	NM	Internet access
CYCH	Cybercash	12.188	18.0	9.8	Electronic payment
CYSP	Cybershop	11.250	40.6	NM	General merchandise
CYLK	Cylink	12.000	5.5	16.2	Security/Firewalls
DCLK	Doubleclick	49.688	15.2	NM	Advertising management
EGRP	E*Trade	22.938	4.2	25.5	Stock broker
ELNK	Earthlink	38.375	30.1	89.2	Internet access
XCIT	Excite	46.750	22.4	101.6	Search engine
FVHI	First Virtual Hldgs	3.063	22.7	NM	Banking via the Internet
GNET	go2net	29.500	55.3	NM	Search engine + games + stocks
HRBC	Harbinger	24.188	6.5	28.3	Software for e-commerce
SEEK	Infoseek	35.875	19.4	128.1	Search engine
LCOS	Lycos	75.375	23.3	443.4	Search engine
MSPG	Mindspring	34.297	13.6	66.0	Internet access
NTKI	N2K	19.625	8.5	NM	Music CDs
NTBK	Net.B@nk	29.500	34.9	30.1	Banking via the Internet
NSCP	Netscape	27.063	5.3	71.2	Browser + community
NSOL	Network Solutions	45.000	3.0	53.6	Domain name registration
ONSL	Onsale	24.750	2.9	176.8	General merchandise, auction format
OMKT	Open Market	18.825	9.9	57.2	Software for e-commerce
PPOD	Peapod	6.000	1.4	NM	Groceries
PTVL	Preview Travel	34.375	24.4	NM	Online travel

SYMBOL	NAME	6/30/98 PRICE	PRICE/ REVENUES	1999 P/E	BUSINESS
PSIX	PSINet	13.000	3.7	NM	Internet access
RNWK	RealNetworks	37.313	4.6	NM	Audio/video delivery over the Net
SDTI	Security Dynamics	18.063	4.6	18.3	Security
IBUY	Shopping.com	24.750	82.5	NM	General merchandise
SPLN	SportsLine	36.353	21.7	NM	Sports info and merchandise
SE	Sterling Comm.	48.500	10.3	30.3	Software for e-commerce
VRSN	Verisign	37.375	47.1	1,868.8	Digital Certificates
YHOO	Yahoo	78.750	59.8	225.0	Search engine + community

Business to Business transactions should constitute a significant portion, if not the majority, of Internet traffic. Electronic data interchange (EDI) has long been important to a few large firms. But most businesses have found EDI inconvenient to use because the software was hard to integrate into existing business processes, most trading partners were not using EDI, and connections went through proprietary wide-area networks. Now the Internet provides a common network, small companies are installing enterprise resource-planning systems and supply-chain management software, and the common (Internet-based) communications hooks are in place.

Interactive Data Corporation projects the value of on-line business to business commerce to grow from $44 billion in 1999 to $338 billion in 2002. EDI reduces expenses, can improve revenues, and makes outsourcing practical. One study on the insurance industry found $670 billion in annual premium cash flow. For each $1 of premiums, sixteen cents goes to overhead (commissions and administration). Half of that, or $54 billion, could be saved through Internet-based distribution and back-office efficiencies.

What Competitive Strategies Will Win?

FIRST MOVER The people doing Baby.com, Garden.com, and Health.com have a meaningful lead over whoever is second into the area. It's a long way from a guarantee of success, but it is an advantage.

KEY PARTNERS Locking up the big portal companies like America Online and Netscape as strategic partners means the next person into the business has to settle for the number-two portal—or worse.

THE DIRTY LITTLE SECRET OF SEARCH ENGINES

When you run a search engine, do you expect to get a list of potential sites in response to your question, ranked in order of how likely they are to fit the bill?

Or do you expect to get a list of sites that have paid the search-engine company to be listed first anytime a search term includes one of dozens or hundreds of key-words?

Alan Freed, the Cleveland disk jockey who invented the phrase "rock 'n' roll," destroyed his career by taking money to play certain records. It's called payola. Many search-engine companies are taking money to push you toward Web sites you might not even care about. One will even sell off search-hit slots.

How many of your search results are infomercials? When search-engine results are biased by how much is paid to search-engine companies, I have a name for it: payola.

MASS CUSTOMIZATION Software already exists to track preferences and present users with ads and Web pages targeted to their needs. There's no reason for this trend to abate.

RAPID EVOLUTION Things happen in "Web Time." With virtually instant information exchange, new Internet business models and technologies can be tested quickly. Because size matters, established players will have to watch competitors and upstarts closely, lest a great new idea make them obsolete.

What Is the Next Big Change?

Accurately predicting the next big change in a fast-moving new technology that is already changing in every direction at once borders on the impossible. But, as John Maynard Keynes once said: "I answer not because I know, but because I was asked."

I think the next big change will be micropayments for information content. If Internet sites and services cannot be supported by advertising (not enough to go around, low impact) or subscriptions (ethos against paying upfront), on-line companies will try charging micropayments for specific information and services. Users may pay five cents for a search guaranteed to turn up relevant information—if you don't click through, you don't pay. They may pay fifty cents for an archived newspaper article that is summarized right on the screen in front of them and answers a major question or solves a major problem. They may pay five dollars to get a recommendation on an Internet stock (we did not specify "long" or "short"). Someone will aggregate all the micropayments for a month in a single bill, collect payment, and divide the revenue among the various contributors.

To maintain a viable business, companies will need to cultivate and maintain customer loyalty to generate return sales. Developing the techniques and raising the capital to do this will be formidable challenges for Internet businesses.

Some content companies will succeed, but the foregoing profitability anaysis convinces me that it's too early to call the winning business models. Be very careful about investing in emerging software infrastructure companies—their capabilities stand to be absorbed into a few large players like Microsoft, and the one or two likely survivors (AOL, Yahoo) tend to be perpetually overvalued.

## CHAPTER TWELVE

Medical Technology

Medical technology, including both biotechnology and medical devices, is at the beginning of a thirty-year advance, characterized by substantial scientific progress, rapid growth, and the opportunity to build the multinational pharmaceutical companies of the future. In a very real sense, semiconductor and computer technology have propelled medical technology. Many medical devices depend on low-power microcontrollers. Laparoscopic surgery, performed through a narrow tube inserted through a small opening in the skin instead of a massive incision, requires modern X-ray and ultrasound imaging systems, tiny sensors, and a host of other modern electronic devices. The breakthroughs in biotechnology could not have happened without scanning electron microscopes, computerized genetic sequencing, and automated chemistry.

Conventional chemical drugs seem to have hit a wall when it comes to treating the causes of the chronic diseases of aging. Although there are many fine conventional drugs to treat symptoms, cures are still elusive for heart disease, cancer, diabetes, arthritis, macular degeneration, osteoporosis, and many other chronic diseases. Chronic illnesses are very expensive to treat; about half of all the money people spend on medical care in their entire lives is spent in the last two years. For example, poorly controlled diabetes causes foot ulcers, which are responsible for half of all amputations in the United States each year. Most are partial amputations, usually of the toes or half the foot. The patient goes through a long rehabilitation process to learn to walk again. Within two years, many diabetics are back with another round of untreatable wounds, requiring an additional amputation of the remaining foot and further rehab. The whole process is difficult and painful for the patient, extremely expensive for the health-care system, and usually doomed to failure because most patients will die within five to seven years.

Biotechnology holds the promise of drugs that heal wounds, acting quickly to close foot ulcers before gangrene sets in. Biotech companies are already finding ways to better control insulin and glucose levels with drugs (Amylin Pharmaceuticals) or devices (Cygnus Therapeutics' GlucoWatch monitors glucose levels through the skin). Gene-sequencing companies eventually will identify the gene that governs insulin production. Cell-signaling companies may develop ways to control insulin production at the genetic level. Gene-therapy companies could pioneer repair of a defective insulin gene and stop diabetes before it starts.

The best thing about medicine as a business is that virtually any market you can think of is huge because there are so many people in the world. The worst thing about medicine as a business is that the process of getting a drug approved takes a long time and costs a lot of money. A major pharmaceutical company developing a new chemically based drug will spend up to $300 million over twelve to fifteen years of clinical development. A biotechnology-based drug costs $100 million plus, and takes about eight to ten years from invention to approval. If the drug is for cancer or an untreatable disease, it might get fast-track approval in six to eight years for less than $100 million. Medical devices that work inside the body also take six to eight years, but can be developed for well under $100 million. Devices that are not invasive but work in a laboratory or hospital setting can take as little as five years and cost less than $50 million to get to approval—but that is still a big bet on a product that might never get to market.

Fortunately, investors are systematically undervaluing the biotechnology industry, which improves the odds of investment success when these big bets pay off. Compare the entire public U.S. biotechnology industry to Merck, as of mid-1999:

	290 U.S. Biotech Companies	Merck
Market Capitalization	$110.0 Billion	$171.7 Billion
Total Revenues	$27.0 Billion	$26.9 Billion
R&D Spending	$12.0 Billion	$1.8 Billion

Although the biotech industry is roughly comparable to Merck in terms of revenues, it spends over five times as much on R&D. When that R&D turns into approved drugs, the market capitalization will be many times the size of Merck instead of smaller—as will the investment returns for those who buy in now.

The U.S. Food and Drug Administration (FDA) has a clear procedure to obtain approval. A new drug is invented in the laboratory and goes through tests to see if it has any obvious toxicity and if it appears to do any good. Investors should realize that these tests mean almost nothing in terms of ultimate drug approval. Many chemical and biological reactions that work in a lab never even make it to human trials. For example, an unscrupulous company could announce that in laboratory tests, a proprietary mixture of sodium hydroxide, sodium nitrate, and aluminum killed 100 percent of HIV in a test tube, as it would. Hot-money investors might run the stock up, not realizing those are the ingredients in Drano—a substance not likely to be injected into people.

Drugs that show good efficacy and low toxicity in the test tube go into preclinical trials to make sure they are basically safe. These trials are conducted in animals. The company usually also collects efficacy data but, again, investors should not extrapolate from animal results to humans. Bitter experience teaches that in many areas, human and animal bodies just do not react the same way.

If a drug survives preclinical trials, the company applies to the FDA for an IND—Investigational New Drug status. The FDA will review the laboratory and animal data, and usually approve the IND to let the drug proceed into Phase I clinical trials.

There are three phases of clinical trials: Phase I for safety, Phase II for efficacy, and Phase III to show both appropriate doses and significantly better results than a placebo. Each level of trials requires a trial design approved in advance by the FDA. The trial design specifies the number of participants, the specific rules for accepting people for the trials, the dosages and length of time they will be on medication, and the outcomes or end points that will define success or failure. Companies often carry out several trials at each phase, and sometimes combine phases.

A typical Phase I safety trial will involve a small number of volunteers—typically up to twenty-five. Often, these are healthy volunteers, sometimes prisoners who get good-time credit on their sentences and some spending money in exchange for their participation. For drugs targeting terminal diseases, the volunteers can be people near death who—God bless them!—take one more risk of pain or harmful side effects so others might live.

A pure Phase I trial would look only at the safety and side effects of a new drug, including earlier death than usual. But many companies now perform a combined Phase I/II trial, in which they give several different dosage levels and follow up on patients to spot early indications that the drug does some good against the disease. Some companies go so far as to carry out more complex and expensive placebo-controlled Phase I/II trials, on the premise that the earlier they abandon a drug that ultimately will be proven ineffective, the less money it costs overall.

A pure Phase I trial might include fourteen to twenty-five people; a Phase I/II trial rarely uses more than one hundred people. These trials usually can be completed in a few weeks or months, although analyzing the data, designing a follow-up Phase II trial, and garnering FDA approval to proceed to the next step can easily take a year. Companies often do more than one Phase I trial if they want to segment the target population, say, into those at different stages of the disease, or those who have failed to respond to existing treatment regimens.

Phase II trials test efficacy. The typical Phase II trial design includes a number of dosage levels, or steadily increased doses, and different intervals of administration. The goals are twofold: to find out how much of the drug can be given on what schedule without making the patient sicker, and to measure the response of the illness or condition to various levels of the drug. Some companies use a Phase IIa trial to home in on a dosage level, followed by a Phase IIb trial to identify the optimal frequency or timing for administering the drug. Others use a combined Phase II/III trial with a placebo group.

These dose-ranging studies take several months to a year or more, depending on the length of patient follow-up. Phase II trials can be as small as one hundred people for a rare or terminal disease with no current treatment, or can involve thousands of patients over several years. Analysis of the data and design of the Phase II trial can absorb another year.

Typically, Phase II is the crucial stage for a new drug. Drugs may work against a disease in the lab, seem safe in Phase I, and totally flop in Phase II. That is because your body does an excellent job of defending you against foreign substances. Large-molecule drugs generally cannot be given orally because the stomach and intestines will tear them apart before they can get into the bloodstream. Infusing drugs into the bloodstream by injection immediately mobilizes the body's defenses to neutralize the drug, disassemble it, and transport the inactivated pieces to the liver or kidneys to be excreted. Some drugs can be cleared from the bloodstream in two minutes or less.

Recall the septic-shock disaster of the early 1990s, epitomized by the collapse of Synergen's stock. Septic shock is a difficult disease with multiple causes and pathways. Synergen had a drug that seemed to show efficacy, at least against some of the causes. But while reading their Phase III clinical-trial plan, we discovered that doctors were infusing a whopping ten grams of drug. This meant that either the patients' immune systems were destroying the drug so rapidly that Synergen had to go to extraordinary lengths to get any of the drug to the site of the problem, or the drug was affecting only part of the problem and Synergen hoped massive amounts would somehow compensate. It was amazing that patients did not get sick from so much drug; the most common story in Phase II is that the efficacious dose is larger than the dose that makes people sicker, so the drug fails. Synergen's drug was not even efficacious.

Phase III trials are placebo-controlled, randomized, and double-blind. Placebo-controlled means that the drug is tested against a placebo or against the current standard of care. The mind is a powerful thing; about 10 percent to 40 percent of a sick population will get better from any treatment, including sugar pills. The FDA wants to remove this placebo effect from the real benefit of the new drug. In the case of an existing standard of care, the FDA does not want to confuse doctors by approving a new treatment that is no better than—or even worse than—current treatments.

The standard of care question can be crucial. Telios Pharmaceuticals was a biotech company with a promising treatment for diabetic foot ulcers. In Phase II trials, the drug Argidene Gel healed about 41 percent of foot ulcers that had not responded to treatment for at least nine months. It is these intractable foot ulcers that lead to partial amputations. The placebo, an inert gel, healed only 8 percent of the ulcers. With those good results, the company went into Phase III.

Phase III results for Argidene showed continued good results, healing 42 percent of all intractable ulcers. But—unexpectedly—the placebo healed 40 percent. There was no statistically significant difference between the two courses of treatment, so the FDA would never approve the drug. The company voluntarily returned an infusion of capital it had received just before the results were announced and then went into Chapter 11 bankruptcy.

The standard of care for foot ulcers was frequent cleaning, antiseptics, and changing bandages. Why would ulcers that had not responded to this care for nine months suddenly respond during the Phase III trial? The only explanation we could come up with was that the Phase III trial must have focused extra attention on the need for constant cleaning and rebandaging, resulting in a higher level of care than the "normal" standard of care.

When there is an existing effective standard of care, an old trick is to use something else as the comparison. For example, venous stasis leg ulcers used to be treated with Una's boot. This device put pressure on the wound, helping it heal. But in the mid-1970s Una's boot was discarded in favor of pressure bandages, which put equal pressure on the wound and promoted faster healing.

Two companies, Advanced Tissue Sciences and Organogenesis, were

locked in a race to get an artificial-skin product on the market. Organogenesis did its Phase III trial comparing pressure bandages with its product AppliGraf, not against pressure bandages without AppliGraf, but
against Una's boot. Of course, it was much easier to show statistical improvement against a therapy that had been discarded twenty years earlier.
Although Organogenesis was granted fast-track review, there was no
word from the FDA for much longer than normal—almost three years.
Advanced Tissue Sciences, the competitor that filed for approval after
Organogenesis, received FDA approval in December 1996. This was a
clear warning to investors that something was seriously wrong with the
Organogenesis clinical trial. After additional unannounced clinical trials,
the FDA finally approved the product in May 1998. By then, however, it
was too late for any competitive advantage, and the product has not been
a success.

In addition to placebo control, the FDA wants a randomized trial.
That means patients will be assigned randomly to the drug-receiving
group or the placebo-receiving group. The patient population can be defined very tightly, but a fair test requires random assignment in order to
get statistically meaningful results.

In the early days of the HIV panic, ICN Pharmaceuticals dusted off
an old drug that had been promoted periodically as a cure for everything
from colds to cancer. The company announced that it was effective
against HIV and went into a Phase III trial. I heard the results at a Hambrecht & Quist Life Sciences Conference. Milan Panic, the chief executive officer, described a startling success: the death rate of HIV-infected
patients on the drug was much lower than the mortality rate of those on
the placebo. The trouble was that the death rate on the placebo was much
higher than the death rate in the average population. A hostile, skeptical
crowd peppered Mr. Panic with questions.

Several months later, ICN signed a consent decree with the SEC.
The SEC said the company had assigned the sickest patients to the placebo group, keeping the healthiest to try the drug. Of course, that completely skewed the statistical results to make the drug look better. The
FDA was not amused.

"Double-blind" means that neither the patients nor the doctors
know who is getting the drug and who is getting the placebo. Obviously,
if patients know they are getting a placebo, they are not likely to show
the normal "placebo effect." If doctors know, they may act differently
toward drug and placebo patients, perhaps expressing surprise that a placebo patient is getting better. People are not stupid, especially people
with a serious illness that has become the focus of their lives. They will
figure it out.

One of the biggest failures to maintain a double-blind trial was the original trial for AZT against HIV. AZT is a chain terminator of DNA; it stops DNA replication, period. Naturally, HIV stops replicating. But so does every other cell; essentially, the patient dies slowly. The drug originally was developed by the National Institutes of Health as a possible cancer treatment, but the side effects were so horrendous that it was put back on the shelf.

Then along came AIDS, with high-risk groups like gay men agitating for the government to do something—anything—to treat the disease. AZT was licensed to Burroughs-Wellcome (later acquired by Glaxo) and went into a Phase III trial in Florida. Of course, those taking AZT immediately started to get sick, while those taking the placebo did not react. But the close-knit gay community believed that AZT was their only hope for survival, and that their friends taking the placebo were doomed. So those getting the drug began sharing it with their friends who supposedly were getting the placebo. Now, even on the lower dose, everyone got sick. So Burroughs-Wellcome began treating those patients known to be on the drug with blood transfusions, massage, and other helpful supplemental treatment. Those supposedly on the placebo had to tough it out.

At the end of the "trial," AZT was declared a great success. Those on the drug showed a statistically better quality of life than those on the placebo. No mention was made of the transfusions and supplemental treatment that warped the statistics. Worse, no mention was made of the fact that because the drug was being shared, the actual average dose was far below the prescribed dose. AZT was rushed to approval.

Predictably, the results were disastrous. Doctors began administering AZT in the dose supposedly used in the trial. Patients got sick and died. But many doctors and gay men at first ascribed the deaths to AIDS, not to the drug. Even children who tested HIV-positive but showed no sign of AIDS were given the drug. Many died. Others were taken off the drug by parents who could not stand to watch the side effects; many of those lived. Word spread through the gay community that AZT was a killer, and doctors began lowering the dosage. Today, AZT is used at only 20 percent of the original dosage level. Of course, the tainted trial spawned numerous lawsuits against Glaxo for endangerment and wrongful death. We expect these to be consolidated into a class-action lawsuit with as much impact on Glaxo as the asbestos lawsuit had on Johns Manville or the silicone-implant suit had on Dow-Corning.

Companies file for FDA approval for drugs that get through Phase III. This filing can be an NDA (New Drug Application) for a chemical-based drug, a BLA (Biologic License Application) for a biotech drug, or a PLA (Product License Application) for a medical device. The applications and supporting documentation take tens of thousands of pages. After review, the FDA may decide to accept the application and start the formal approval process. At that point, the company's manufacturing facilities undergo an extensive examination called a GMP (Good Manufacturing Practices) audit. The FDA virtually always comes up with a list of problems that must be corrected. Meanwhile, the application is reviewed by an FDA examiner or team. Ultimately, one of the FDA advisory panels will meet to review the application. The FDA examiners make their recommendation, and the company presents its case. The advisory panel votes to recommend or not recommend approval. Although FDA officials do not have to follow the advisory panel's recommendation, they usually do. Formal FDA approval can take from a few weeks to several months after the advisory panel meeting.

After approval, the drug or device may be launched for sale in the United States. It must still get on the reimbursement lists of third-party, health-care payers like Blue Cross or HMOs. It also needs a Medicare code to qualify for reimbursement. Parallel to or following approval in the United States, a similar but shorter process must be pursued in Europe. In Japan, companies need only prove safety in order to get to market.

Many in the industry believe that the FDA should adopt the Japanese model, certifying only safety and leaving the decision on efficacy up to the doctor and patient. Pharmaceutical companies that want to pursue the entire three-phase clinical-trial regimen could obtain an additional FDA certification for efficacy. Doctors unwilling to experiment would then use only FDA-efficacy-certified drugs, while others might use drugs certified for safety, but not efficacy. Under today's rules, if a drug cannot be patented (such as a natural substance or a compound widely used for many years), no company can afford to take it through the full three-phase process. Certification for safety only might permit more of those time-tested cures to reach the market.

How Fast Is This Industry Growing?

During the ten years that ended in 1994, thirty biotechnology-based drugs were approved, an average of three per year. In 1995 six were approved. In 1996 seventeen were approved, in 1997, twenty-seven, and in 1998, fifty-two. In 1999 close to eighty should make the grade. The biotech industry has hit the hockey stick in terms of drug approvals, meaning that numerous companies will make the transition in the next ten years from R&D project to functioning pharmaceutical company.

Total biotech industry product sales were $19 billion in 1999 and are growing about 28 percent a year. (In addition to product sales, the industry received about $9 billion from R&D payments.) With many development programs ending, approvals of new drugs will continue to accelerate. I forecast revenue to grow at 30 percent compounded for the next twenty years.

The medical-device industry is larger, but growing more slowly. The total U.S. market was $27.3 billion in 1999, with the world market about twice that size. The industry is growing 20 percent a year and should continue at that rate for the next five to ten years. Drug delivery, which is regulated as a device, is in a rapid development period and will maintain a 20 percent growth rate.

What Drives the Growth Cycles?

Health care is insensitive to economic cycles. Growth cycles—such as they are—are driven by technology breakthroughs. Recent advances in gene sequencing, rational drug design, combinatorial chemistry, and "inside-the-cell" technologies like cell signaling, antisense, and gene therapy are pushing a growth cycle that should last for at least a decade, probably much longer.

Growth cycles are also affected by the aging of the population. Europe, the United States, Japan, and China all have increasing average ages due to low birth rates. The chronic diseases of aging differ in the West and in Asia; but wherever the burden of medical costs of an aging population falls on a relatively smaller group of working-age people, the demand for less expensive, better treatments will be substantial. That is good news for spending on new health-care technologies, which can replace expensive operations or hospitalizations with a pill.

How Profitable Is It?

The average stock-market capitalization of an early-stage, research-level biotechnology company is about $100 million. By the time a company is in late-stage research, such as Phase III clinical trials, the average market capitalization is $300 million. Investors can triple their money by successfully identifying early-stage companies that will make it to Phase III.

The markup from Phase III to functioning pharmaceutical company with approved products is even larger. These companies have an average market capitalization of $3 billion. So investors average a 10-to-1 return from Phase III to an approved, successful drug.

The two reasons the markup is so large are, first, because there are many investors who will not or, by prospectus, cannot buy development-stage, unprofitable companies. They jump on when the profits start to flow. Second, the pharmaceutical business is extremely profitable and not cyclical.

Take Amgen, Genentech, and Genzyme. Their average gross profit is 77 percent. They continue to spend a lot on R&D, an average of 30 percent. They spend 26 percent on SG&A, because it is expensive to introduce new drugs and hold doctors' hands, leaving them with average operating profits of 21 percent. This financial model is typical for a successful biotech company. Merck, the class act in the traditional pharmaceutical industry, shows lower gross profits of 65 percent, much lower R&D spending of 8 percent, and the same SG&A ratio of 26 percent. Operating profits average 31 percent of sales. All biotech companies expect to reach that same financial model eventually, as their portfolio of approved drugs grows larger relative to their ongoing R&D effort.

Profitable medical-device companies have a similar, healthy bottom line. St. Jude Medical, Biomet, and Boston Scientific average gross profits of 70 percent, with only 7 percent spent on R&D, and 33 percent on SG&A, leaving operating profits averaging 30 percent of sales.

Who Are the Customers?

The easy answer is "everybody"; but, like many easy answers, it is wrong. The customer is the one who pays the bill: primarily Medicare, HMOs, insurance companies, and other third-party payers. Some of these will pay any bill a doctor submits for an approved drug. But many drugs are used "off-label"—approved for one purpose, but used widely for another purpose. For example, every drug used for non-Hodgkin's lymphoma was used off-label until the 1997 approval of IDEC Pharmaceuticals' Rituxan. Third-party payers might question off-label use until it is so widespread that it becomes accepted as a conventional treatment. They are even tougher on experimental treatments or drugs in clinical trials.

Consequently, the biotech and drug companies now collect economic as well as medical data from their clinical trials. A drug that cuts days off a hospital stay, precludes the need for surgery, turns a chronic disease into a curable disease, or prevents the onset of expensive additional complications can cost-justify its price. In Europe, many countries formally set drug prices, especially where government medical plans pay close to 100 percent of their citizens' drug bills. Good pharmacoeconomic data can make all the difference between a very profitable drug and a so-so return on the development investment.

What Competitive Strategies Win?

Again, there seems to be an easy answer: Develop a successful drug. While it does come down to that, some strategies work better than others.

The first is to use technologies that promise the highest specificity. Imagine a large hotel with several wings, several floors on each wing, and many rooms on each floor. Each room is a disease.

Drugs are like keys to the rooms. The master key for the whole hotel is like aspirin. In low doses, it does a little good for a lot of diseases—it unlocks all the rooms. But in higher doses, it will kill the patient. A more specific key—or drug—would unlock only a few floors, or perhaps just a small block of rooms on one floor. A totally specific drug would unlock just one room.

Conventional chemical drugs are at approximately the one-floor level. They help treat the disease, but they also affect a lot of healthy processes—they open a lot of other rooms. These other rooms are side effects. Pharmaceutical companies are constantly balancing the efficacy of the drug against the side effects, or tinkering with the chemical structure to try to find a more specific version. Many early biotechnology drugs were at the same one-floor level, or worse. But the better new biotech drugs, based on human proteins, seem to be at the small-block-of-rooms level, and genetic sequencing promises to lead to drugs so specific that they affect only the disease—the single room.

Another common gambit is to focus a drug that may have wide applicability on a small subset of problems that afflict a small number of people for whom there is no effective current therapy. It is easier to manage clinical trials at a small number of centers that specialize in a particular disease. Patients are likely to be referred to such centers by their community doctors and clinics, so it's easy to find patients for the trial. For a very small indication, a company can get an Orphan Drug designation, which protects it from competition for seven years after approval. The FDA and its advisory panels are more likely to approve a drug that shows safety and any efficacy if there is no other treatment.

Once a drug is approved for a small indication, the company can launch additional Phase II and Phase III trials for broader indications. Word will spread rapidly if the drug shows efficacy against these other diseases. Due to a change in the law in late 1997, companies now can provide information on a drug for an off-label indication if they have a clinical trial under way for that use. Sales of the drug will increase, and the profits can be used to fund FDA filings to expand approval to these new areas.

Another strategy is to balance near-term and longer-term technologies in a particular area. Wall Street loves companies that focus. For example, a company working with monoclonal antibodies could look for a number of diseases responsive to that technology, make terrific progress in several different clinical trials, and then be blown away by newer technologies like human proteins, cell signaling, gene therapy, or combinatorial chemistry. It would be better to focus on a disease or disease area and then pursue all the new technologies as they come along for applicability to that specialty. Thoroughly understanding a disease makes for more intelligent R&D spending. At the same time, it is practical to build a focused sales force that can start selling in-licensed, chemically based drugs even before a company has any biotech drugs approved. When the biotech drugs come out, the sales force will be up and running, ready to go. As new technologies point the way to new drugs, the company can obsolete its own products while leveraging the focused sales force. This strategy works best when the sales force can be small because the disease is treated in a few hundred specialty centers or by clearly defined specialists such as urologists or radiologists.

A third strategy is to fund drug discovery internally, but partner out the drug-development process. Preclinical lab work is tedious but does not absorb a lot of money. Phase I safety trials can be small and inexpensive, and preliminary efficacy data can be collected at little additional cost. Large Phase II trials involve hundreds of patients and cost tens of millions of dollars to complete. Phase III trials may require thousands of patients over several years and cost close to $100 million.

A biotech drug that has a successful Phase I trial behind it is valuable. Biotech companies take the data to a big pharmaceutical partner to cut a deal that often involves an equity investment, an up-front payment for the technology, milestone payments based on clinical progress, funding of all clinical trials, and, ultimately, royalties on sales of an approved drug. Especially strong data puts the biotech company in the driver's seat. It can retain manufacturing or co-manufacturing rights and co-promotion rights in the United States or worldwide. Sometimes company officials strike a deal with one partner for Europe, another for Japan and the Pacific Rim, and retain all U.S. rights. Axys Pharmaceuticals and Neurocrine Biosciences are stellar examples of biotech companies that utilize this strategy; every one of their development programs is funded by another company. Keeping their burn rate (expenses) low eliminates the need to continually dilute current shareholders' equity by selling new stock to fund operations.

As a variant of this strategy, some very focused Phase II trials, especially those targeting solid-tumor cancers, can be completed with less than 100 patients for a few million dollars. Biotech companies in that fortunate position with a strong belief in the efficacy of the drug can sharply increase the value of the technology before seeking a partner by completing a Phase II trial on their own. The risk is higher; the potential reward is much higher.

How Will the Internet Affect It?

The Internet was developed originally so that scientists could exchange information easily. It has had a substantial effect in two scientific areas. First, research news spreads faster. Although the crucial test of research is still publication of results that can be duplicated in a peer-reviewed scientific journal, the Internet allows informal exchange and discussion during the publication process, which can take six to twelve months. Peer-reviewed Internet journals are imminent.

Second, in many areas, such as sequencing the human genome, companies use "Web crawlers" to track down newly discovered sequences posted on the Internet so they can update and expand their internal databases. With many university labs sequencing genes, it would be easy to have lots of wasteful duplicative effort going on while various papers are wending their way through the publication process. The Internet enables instant publishing, sharply reducing unnecessary research.

But the really big impact of the Internet will be on individual patients. Virtually every disease now has an on-line discussion group, with patients sharing information about treatments, clinical trials, alternative medicine, success rates at different treatment centers, and so on. There are large, searchable Web sites covering specific diseases or general health-care topics. Individual patients now have much more information to take into discussions with their doctors and other health-care providers. Quack cures make little headway when the early customers report on-line that the therapy does no good. Patients in promising clinical trials post the details to a discussion group, and that trial quickly gets all the patients it needs to complete a Phase II or Phase III study.

Internet pharmacies already match patients to approved overseas drugs and streamline the importing process. Although it is not widely known, most drugs approved overseas can be imported by an individual for personal use under a doctor's supervision. A letter to the overseas pharmacy, to be returned with your shipment and the required FDA information (your name, your doctor's name, and so forth), will get the drug through customs, with a very few exceptions. That means hundreds of drugs approved in Japan are now available to U.S. consumers, even though they never will be approved in the United States because of a patent position or the expense of clinical trials. Drugs are often available in Europe two to four years before they earn FDA approval, because of a streamlined approval process put in place for the European Union.

What Is the Next Big Change?

Although biotechnology is a young industry, it already has moved through three important stages. The earliest companies developed products based on recombinant DNA, fermentation technology, and mono-clonal antibodies. Toxicity and low efficacy accounted for many clinical failures.

The second wave worked with human proteins, either focusing research on one lead product or concentrating on a technology based on a receptor or other underlying mechanism that could generate many products. Human proteins were tolerated more easily in clinical trials. Many of the drug approvals coming in the next couple of years stem from this generation of research.

Third-wave companies are working inside the cell, close to or directly on DNA itself. By blocking or stimulating the production of proteins at the source, rather than trying to cope with them after they are circulating in the body, these companies expect to develop highly potent drugs with very specific activity and, therefore, few side effects.

Inside-the-cell companies working in such areas as gene sequencing, gene therapy, antisense, cell signaling, and ribozymes (a catalytic enzyme that destroys messenger RNA) are likely to make the big breakthroughs against the chronic diseases of aging like cancer and heart disease that are so burdensome for the health-care system today and will only get worse as the baby boomers age. Because these are very early-stage companies, most investment managers and Wall Street analysts have little interest in their stocks. Yet, under the newest FDA standards for cancer drugs, approval can be gained merely by showing tumor shrinkage rather than the more rigorous standard of increased life expectancy. That change cuts up to two years off the development time for many inside-the-cell drugs. Stocks can be bought today in low double digits that should sell for well over $100 a share once they get a drug approved, of which there will be many in the next ten years.

The next big change will build on the work of the inside-the-cell companies to develop small-molecule chemical drugs. A synthesis of biotechnology and chemistry may seem like a step back from research on human proteins, but protein-based medications are large-molecule drugs that have to be given by injection. Small-molecule drugs, by contrast, can usually be taken orally, making them less costly and more likely to be taken by patients with chronic diseases.

This interplay of biotechnology and chemistry is generating an exciting synergy in the biotech field. *Gene sequencing* is shedding light on disease and helps identify targets for intervention. *Rational-drug design* creates highly specific small molecules that have fewer side effects because of their specificity. *Combinatorial chemistry* produces hundreds or thousands of variants on a molecule, and rapid screening allows selection of the most active, specific molecule for clinical development. This group of new technologies forms a drug-discovery machine that produces new compounds by the dozens instead of by ones and twos.

In the protein area, the next big change will be predicting protein folding directly from genetic-sequence information. The way a protein folds defines its activity as a drug or receptor. When companies like Molecular Applications Group can predict protein folding, they will be able to compare the projected shape of a protein from a healthy gene to that same protein produced by a defective gene. The folded protein may serve as a receptor for a drug, so if a drug can be designed to dock only with the protein from the defective gene, it will be highly specific for that genetic disease. High specificity is the Holy Grail of medical technology because it means higher efficacy and lower side effects.

## PART III

Picking
Technology Stocks

NOW that you understand

the economics and business models of the eight major technology industries, you will learn to select and manage the specific stocks and mutual funds that should produce high investment returns for the next decade and more. Your crucial advantage is "growth flow"—a way to look at companies that lets you spot cheap stocks before Wall Street, which is fixated on earnings. When you know how to calculate and compare growth-flow opportunities, you can make the value decision: Is this the right price to invest in this company?

Then you will learn how to tell if there is any price at which you want to own a stock. There are a few extraordinarily successful companies that apply R&D to basic technology to create products people really want and need. The Great Growth-Flow model makes it easy to limit your investments to these great companies, while avoiding second-rate companies, hyped-up stocks, and outright frauds.

Picking development-stage stocks requires a different approach, so next we introduce the M Score. This simple technique will let you sort through opportunities in biotechnology and medical-technology stocks quickly, focusing on those Wall Street has overlooked or undervalued relative to their scientific programs.

The potential profit on a stock is only one part of the investment decision. Chapter 16 shows how to calculate the potential downside risk, understand seasonality, use options to protect your portfolio, and make the crucial decision to sell.

Combining stocks into a portfolio is the next step. Diversification, building a portfolio over time, and taking advantage of Wall Street's short-term, momentum thinking are all part of portfolio management.

By 2010, at least half the Dow Jones Industrial Average will be technology stocks. Which ones are likely to make it? In Chapter 18 you will find the top thirty candidates, with the information you need to calculate price to growth-flow ratios and take advantage of opportunities to build a portfolio of these dominant companies as the market knocks them down.

Finally, for investors who need both income and growth, technology convertible bonds and preferred stocks are ideal. You can quickly become an expert in these little-known securities by learning to analyze a convertible versus its underlying common stock and building a portfolio of convertibles to generate monthly income.

## CHAPTER THIRTEEN

How to Pick Winning Technology Stocks: The Growth-Flow Model

Over the eighteen years that I have been publishing the *California Technology Stock Letter*, one factor stands out when it comes to picking winning technology stocks: research and development. The key characteristic of a great technology company is effective R&D spending. From that come new products, dominant market share, high margins, and high rates of growth.

R&D is paramount because it makes a difference in the real world, not just in the rarefied financial world of the stock market. For example, all other things being equal, Japanese companies spend about 50 percent more on R&D than American companies. They then invest about twice as much as we do in getting new products to market. The result: a $50 billion to $70 billion annual trade deficit between the two countries (Chart 12.1).

So far, the Japanese have creamed us in cars and consumer electronics, and they're only turning up the pressure in both those areas. Are you ready for high-definition TV? Flat-screen TVs that hang on your wall? Solid-state tape recorders with no moving parts?

Even outside Japan's traditionally strong areas, everything that the United States has historically had a lock on—from credit cards to jet planes to fast-food hamburgers to agricultural tractors—will be under

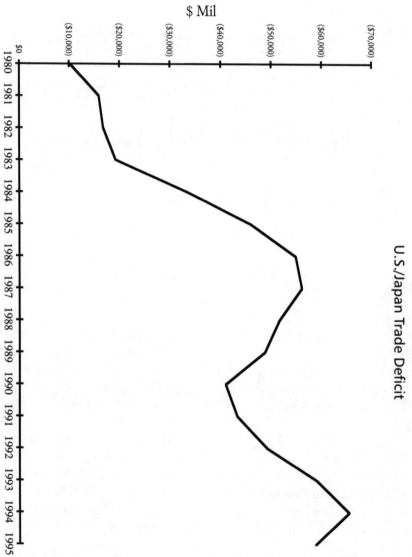

CHART 12.1
U.S./Japan Trade Deficit

attack. The best small-farm tractor you can buy today is the Kubota. The next-best is a Ford—and it is made by Kubota.

U.S. companies must use superior R&D to win in the U.S. market first, then take their superior products out to compete successfully in the rest of the world. We saw this happen in the early 1980s with personal-computer technology. Higher levels of R&D created product opportunities, which, in turn, demanded a higher level of corporate investment. Producing the new, high R&D-content products required better workforce training, and better products were easier to export, even though export-promotion programs got no better. Yet it was received wisdom early in the 1980s that soon the Japanese would enter the U.S. personal-computer market and overwhelm manufacturers of computer systems, hard-disk drives, microprocessors, and logic semiconductors.

It never happened.

U.S. personal-computer manufacturers dominate the United States and the world market, even inside Japan, by producing high-quality, innovative products that require expensive R&D. The rest of the economy—especially consumer electronics, automobiles, and robotics—could take a lesson.

Admittedly, these companies face a dilemma that affects us as investors. Unfortunately, the more a company spends on R&D, the worse its *current* reported earnings will be. Even though R&D is an investment in the future made for the shareholder's benefit, it is accounted for primarily as a direct deduction from current earnings. This is one of the few cases where accountants deviate from their fundamental principle that revenues should be matched to the costs that created them and accounted for in the same period. Appendix D examines this issue in more detail.

In contrast to the treatment of R&D, if a company builds a new plant, it cannot write off all the costs immediately, even if it wants to. It has to depreciate the plant or amortize the cost over a period of years while the plant is in use. Thus, the new plant, which is also an investment for the shareholder's future benefit, doesn't gut current earnings.

Or consider a company that buys another company to get control of a great new product. Most of the costs of the purchase must be capitalized and amortized over a period of years. So our tax and accounting systems discourage in-house innovation, which is subtracted from current earnings, and encourage acquisitions that can be capitalized and then amortized over a period of years!

Because Wall Street looks mainly at earnings in valuing a company, the more a company spends on R&D, the further Wall Street will knock the stock down compared to its competitors *even if that is the only company in the industry investing in the future.*

Look at the income statement of a typical industrial company and ask: "What belongs to the shareholder?" Obviously, bottom-line earnings do. But there's also a noncash charge for "depreciation." For decades many investors, especially in Europe, have added depreciation to earnings to calculate "cash flow." Cash flow can be a better indicator of the true earnings power of some companies that have heavy investments in plant and equipment.

Cash flow was the basis of the leveraged-buyout mania of the 1980s. The theory was that the cash represented by the depreciation charge could be diverted to paying off the bank debt used to take over a company. The leveraged-buyout artists often targeted companies that were doing badly, earning little or nothing on shareholders' equity and ripe for restructuring by a tougher-minded management. All through the 1980s, some of the best-performing stocks were some of the worst companies. Huge amounts of equity capital flowed into leveraged-buyout pools, magnified by even larger amounts of bank debt. While many technology companies were virtually starved for capital in the mid-1980s, traditional U.S. businesses seemed to be writing blank-check golden parachutes for some of the worst managements in America!

During this time, I was in the grip of a white heat to formalize and document the approach to technology stocks I had developed over the previous twenty years. We published three issues of the *California Technology Stock Letter* that laid out, for the first time, our Growth-Flow model and its use in identifying great companies, valuing technology stocks, and even (with a twist) picking our way through the minefield of development-stage companies. Focusing on R&D and using Growth Flow to pick technology stocks—these have been the secret weapons that pushed us to the top of the newsletter ratings over the past fifteen years. It is the key to your opportunity to earn high rates of return and to substantially outperform Wall Street during the next ten years—and it's not hard to do.

Keep in mind that cash flow is not a very useful approach to technology stocks. The income statement of a technology company usually does not show much depreciation, except for semiconductor companies that own their own fabrication factories. As with any other company, bottom-line earnings of a technology company belong to the shareholder. But when you ask what else belongs to the shareholder, the answer is not "depreciation," it is "R&D." The intelligent technology shareholder should be interested in both earnings as reported, representing today's return on investment, and spending on R&D, representing tomorrow's return on investment.

We named this concept "Growth Flow"—meaning after-tax earnings plus R&D, or earnings per share plus R&D per share. This is the true source of wealth for shareholders. Investors who can buy into an innovative, R&D-intensive, high-growth-flow company at an attractive price-to-growth-flow ratio will reap substantial profits over the long run.

Calculating and Using Growth Flow

Just as you look at a stock's price/earnings (P/E) ratio, you can look at its price/growth-flow (P/GF) ratio.

Begin with the earnings actually reported for the last twelve months (four quarters). Then look at how much the company spent on R&D during that same period, and divide R&D spending by the number of shares outstanding. Notice that there is no tax adjustment; R&D is taken as a pretax number.

You have now calculated how much the company spends per share on R&D. Add the R&D spending per share to the last twelve months' reported earnings per share to calculate the **growth flow per share.** That's all there is to it!

Next, divide the current price of the stock by the growth flow per share to calculate P/GF, the price/growth-flow ratio. This is the crucial ratio to identify stocks that may be very cheap on underlying investment value even when reported earnings are depressed temporarily, or when the price looks high based on earnings alone.

The price/growth-flow ratio identifies cheap technology stocks earlier and more accurately than the price/earnings ratio. That is because quarterly R&D spending is more stable than earnings, which can bounce up and down. When earnings are depressed, Wall Street is unsure what to do—the price/earnings ratio usually looks uncomfortably high at any reasonable price, so the stock tends to sink and then sit there until the company gets its earnings growing again.

But R&D spending usually does not drop with earnings. Generally, the level of R&D spending is a function of how many scientists and engineers are on the payroll. Companies hire engineers for $80,000, equip them with $50,000 to $100,000 worth of computers and laboratory equipment, and turn them loose on projects. Each quarter they hire a few more engineers, and R&D increases slowly and steadily.

Because growth flow adds R&D to earnings, it is more stable than earnings alone. When stocks drop due to disappointing earnings, they will look cheap on a price/growth-flow ratio long before they look cheap on a price/earnings ratio. You have an early warning to take a look at the company and decide if and when you want to buy the stock. Later, after the R&D pays off in new products, accelerating revenues, and recovering earnings, Wall Street will bid up the stock for you.

Generally, stocks are fairly priced at a growth-flow ratio of 10x to

14x. Anything under 8x starts to get our attention, and under 5x we really get interested. The P/GF ratio can get astonishingly low—under 2x. That's when we mortgage the ranch!

At the other extreme, we have a tough time holding a stock over 16x; over 20x, we tend to smile politely and excuse ourselves.

An example: In the late 1980s, Tektronix sold for $12 per share. The company's earnings were depressed to about 35¢ per year. Wall Street didn't know what to do with the stock.

At that time, Tektronix management was spending $8 per share on research and development. It could have cut R&D spending in half, saving $4. The tax man would have taken $1 of the savings, so it could have reported an additional $3 per share in earnings. Of course, if it reported $3.35 per share instead of 35¢ per share, Wall Street immediately would have bid the stock up into the mid-$30s.

But Tektronix management *didn't* go for the short-term fix. Instead, it spent the money, developed the products—a family of high-resolution monitors and color printers—and introduced them. The products were successful, TEK's earnings took off, and the stock went over $60. When the stock was $12, the price/earnings ratio was $12/$0.35, or 34.3x. That did not look cheap. But the price/growth-flow ratio was $12/$8.35, or 1.4x. A screaming buy!

Three Rules of Thumb

RULE OF THUMB 1: It is interesting to compare the price/growth-flow ratio to the price/earnings ratio. If the P/GF ratio is a small fraction of the P/E ratio, as it was for Tektronix, it's a tip-off that Wall Street may be badly mispricing a stock, looking too much at current earnings and not enough at the R&D investment being made for the future.

RULE OF THUMB 2: You also can compare the P/E ratio to R&D as a percentage of sales. A company may have a P/E ratio of 13.3x and R&D as a percentage of sales of 19.6 percent. As a general rule, if a company's P/E ratio is below its percentage of sales spent on R&D, the stock is worth a look. As far as we're concerned, that may be a good rule for all U.S. companies—if they think they can compete in an international economy by spending only 2 percent of sales on R&D, maybe you shouldn't buy their stocks at any more than 2x earnings. Too risky in the long run!

RULE OF THUMB 3: In addition to these valuation measures, pay attention to the sheer size of R&D spending. The opportunities one can exploit come in different sizes. While there may be many companies that can spend $3 million trying to bring a new product to market, there are a lot fewer that can commit to $30 million and only a handful that can go to $300 million. With less competition at the rarefied levels, companies that know how to spend big bucks on R&D should have bigger paybacks from these bigger bets. Boeing is the ultimate example of this strategy.

Paying attention to dollar levels also helps you focus on the competitive situation. For example, Intel spends over $2.5 billion a year on R&D. Its main competitor, Advanced Micro Devices, spends only 20 percent as much—around $500 million. Cyrix, the number-three competitor, spent about $33 million—less than 2 percent as much—before it was acquired by National Semiconductor in 1997. Every now and then, a Wall Street analyst or broker would call us up with a story about how Cyrix or AMD was about to catch up to Intel. We had a prerecorded tape that said: "Uh-huh, uh-huh, I see, uh-huh, uh-huh. You don't say! Uh-huh . . . Well, thanks for the call."

The Future of Growth Flow

A key financial trend of the next ten years will be acquisitions by old-line operating companies of newer technology companies—based on growth flow. The old-line companies need new sources of real growth—price increases alone will not cut it in the new economy. Only technology offers the size and growth rates required to make an impact on the parent company's bottom line. Due in part to Wall Street's exclusive focus on reported earnings, the technology stocks are relatively cheap. By recognizing the importance of growth flow, the old-line companies can impact their businesses radically at comparatively modest cost.

If you can anticipate which technology companies the old-line companies will want to buy, you can position yourself for major profits throughout the next ten years. Focus on the Great Growth-Flow companies discussed in the next chapter; they have the market dominance and size the old-economy companies need to have a real impact on net profits.

If you use a high commitment to R&D spending to identify a good company, and a low P/GF ratio to identify a cheap, good company, and then confine yourself to the "Greater Glory of Man" situations described in the next chapter, you will have all the ingredients for long-term successful investment in technology stocks.

## CHAPTER FOURTEEN

How to Spot the Great Growth-Flow Companies

One of the most important things to keep in mind as an investor is this: Investing is a two-step process. The first step, addressed in this chapter, is to identify situations—managements, products, and markets—with which you would like to associate your capital. The second step (discussed in Chapters 13 and 15) is to decide what price you are willing to pay to associate your capital with those situations.

This means that you do not buy bad companies or bad managements at any price. It also means that you do not fall in love with stocks or pay *any* price to buy into an attractive situation. Instead, focus on a small list of superior companies with rapid growth and excellent financial ratios. Then wait for each of them to get knocked down by Wall Street to the point where they are cheap, based on their price/growth-flow ratio.

Beyond the numbers, though, you as a successful high-tech investor need to look for the kinds of companies John Westergaard of Westergaard Research calls "Greater Glory of Man" companies. These are the extraordinarily successful companies that apply R&D to basic technology and create new products people really want and need. These companies are driving an explosive worldwide increase in the standard of living, improving the richness and diversity of life by connecting people together and to the resources that will inform, entertain, and empower them.

These are the companies that put people on the moon, bring new drugs to market to fight cancer, create extremely high-fidelity audio systems, invent inexpensive self-paced educational tools, and take the country from slide rules to 16-bit desktop personal computers in just one decade.

These are the companies that the stock market gets excited about, builds a concept around, and shoots up to very high price/earnings ratios after the R&D pays off. These companies let you answer "yes" to the question: "Is this a company I want to be involved with someday, at some attractive price?"

"Value" investors who focus on simple balance-sheet or income-statement ratios such as a low price-to-book value or a low price-to-revenue ratio often do badly investing in technology because technology stocks fall to very low valuations by making mistakes: They don't spend enough on R&D, or they make a bad forecast on where their technology is going or what their customers want. Their natural reaction is to cut back even further on R&D and lay off people in order to restore profitability.

That's almost always the wrong thing to do. Once a technology company falls off the bus, the only way back on the bus is through R&D. Yet while the company that cuts back and stabilizes earnings in the short term often looks very attractive on a "value" screen, don't be sucked in. A downward spiral is under way that will be difficult to stop. Apple Computer took more value investors to the cleaners than any other technology stock in recent memory; perhaps the new management installed in 1997 will increase R&D spending and continue their turnaround.

"Momentum" investors, on the other hand, will pay any price to buy into an attractive situation. Momentum investing does best in a bull market, and in the long bull market of the 1990s it looked especially good. At least twice a year, The Wall Street Journal quoted some hot money manager explaining why worrying about high price/earnings ratios would just keep you out of the best companies. Identify the good ones, they said, then buy them at any price because as long as the business holds together, the stock will go higher. That's how perfectly decent companies growing at 30 percent a year wound up selling for 100x earnings and 20x revenues.

Of course, the problem is that when a business stumbles, all the momentum investors want to sell at the same time; but the value investors—the people they need to sell to—won't look at the stock until it's down 80 percent to 90 percent. We lived through these kinds of collapses in 1970, 1974, 1984, and 1997, and it is not a pretty sight.

Instead of buying bad companies or high-priced stocks, combine the best parts of the value and momentum philosophies: Buy good growth companies, but only at reasonable prices. If you invest in *growth* stocks with a *value* philosophy, you will do very well with much lower risk.

While it may be practical for investment professionals to follow most of the hundreds of public technology companies, individuals are much better off focusing on a smaller list of situations that they want to own someday. Call them your *universe*. Get to know those companies over a period of time, even if you do not own their stocks. Wait patiently for an opportunity to buy them, perhaps on an earnings report that disappoints Wall Street, perhaps on a general market decline, perhaps on a dip caused by a big-name Wall Street brokerage-firm analyst who turns negative on a group or a stock.

We have a universe of stocks we call the Great Growth-Flow companies. The list includes companies in all the technology industries we covered in Part II. It is small enough to master, yet large enough to provide numerous opportunities throughout the year to buy and sell stocks. The average annual high price of these stocks is about double the average annual low price almost every year; if you are patient and buy them when they are down, you can make as much or more money over time as the most aggressive momentum trader in thinly traded small-cap junk—with a lot less risk.

In selecting candidates for Great Growth-Flow companies, we look at four key factors: Is the business growing? Is it highly profitable? Does it make good use of its invested capital? Is it reinvesting for the future? Based on our research into how high-tech companies have performed over time, and how they are likely to perform in the future, we determined that these were the key factors to look for in identifying Great Growth-Flow companies:

- sales growth of at least 15 percent per year
- pretax profit margins of 15 percent or better
- return on equity of 15 percent or more
- R&D spending of at least 7 percent of sales

Is the Business Growing?

Companies with sales growth of at least 15 percent per year have a real, growing market for their products. In the current low-inflation economy, it is very hard to grow revenues at 15 percent. There just are not very many markets with unit growth (real stuff, out the door) that high.

Growth in sales drives everything else on the income statement and balance sheet. Good top-line growth means that investments in new products are paying off. Companies that meet this standard either are participating in a fast-growing business or are taking market share away from weaker competitors. Either way, they make the first cut.

Generally, a company that passes on the other three factors but fails to pass the sales-growth screen is not worth pursuing. Spending a lot of money on R&D doesn't make much sense if customers don't buy the products. Having high pretax margins and low sales growth usually means the company's prices are too high. If it cuts prices to get the sales growing, it will probably start failing the profit-margin test.

Is the Business Highly Profitable?

Pretax profit margins of 15 percent or better show that the company can deliver its products at a substantial profit, usually because it has a proprietary edge. If a business gives things away, it is easy to show good sales growth. However, without strong profits to pay for R&D, finance expansion, and leave a good return for the shareholders, a business is unlikely to maintain its competitive advantage.

There are two levels of profits to look at: *Gross profits* are sales minus the direct cost of sales—the labor and materials it took to make the product. As you saw in Chapters 4 through 12, gross profits vary widely, depending on industry sectors. For example, a software company sells a few floppy disks and a manual for hundreds of dollars to an end-user customer. Its gross profits would be very high compared to a disk-drive company that sells a complex electromechanical product to a personal-computer manufacturer.

Pretax profits are gross profits minus all the indirect costs— marketing, administrative, R&D, and so forth. That software company probably spends a fortune on advertising, customer hand-holding, and dealer education. The disk-drive company has only a few potential major customers that can be called on in person. So the pretax profits of the two companies might be similar, even though the gross profits are vastly different.

Obviously, companies that can deliver 15 percent pretax profits are not giving their products away to create sales growth (a problem with many Internet software and service suppliers). Our economy is so competitive that the only way to maintain a 15 percent pretax margin is to have some special edge, either through important patents, a wonderful market position, a loyal customer base, or very productive R&D. Companies with that kind of edge make the second cut.

Does the Business Make Good Use of Invested Capital?

Return on equity is after-tax profits divided by shareholders' equity, or earnings per share divided by book value per share. A return on equity of 15 percent or more indicates that the company can finance its own growth internally, without resorting to Wall Street for constant financings that dilute earnings.

"0" or
Low Debt   In the long run, companies can finance internal growth at the same rate as their return on equity. But faster growth has to be financed by taking on debt—a process that can't go on forever and creates its own set of problems—or selling more stock to the public.

Normally, that is not a big problem; Wall Street usually can underwrite a stock financing for a growing, profitable company. The problem comes when the stock market is *not* normal, either in a bear market, or during a period when traders take a temporarily negative view of the industry in which a company operates.

Because you cannot always count on the market's normalcy, a company's return on equity ultimately determines its growth rate. If a company can't earn at least 15 percent on its shareholders' equity, it can't grow fast enough to merit designation as a Great Growth-Flow company. While this is the least important of our four criteria, the ability to self-finance is required to make the third cut.

Return on equity is most important in a capital-intensive industry like semiconductor manufacturing. With capital expensive in the United States, the need to renew and expand a huge base of physical plant can be a real impediment to the nimbleness required to succeed in a technology business.

Is the Business Reinvesting for the Future?

Finally, spending at least 7 percent of sales on R&D shows the management is determined to invest in the future, even at the cost of current earnings, and still deliver high profit margins and returns on equity. A company that invests less than 7 percent of sales in R&D either is not committed to the Virtuous Circle growth model, or is operating in an industry that is so price-competitive there aren't enough profits to accelerate R&D. An example of the former is Apple Computer, where R&D spending fell below 7 percent of sales in its 1993 fiscal year, presaging its rapid fall in market share for personal computers. An example of the latter is Seagate Technology, the premier company in the disk-drive industry, with R&D spending under 5 percent of sales. Seagate's managers are acquiring and building up software companies in an effort to get into higher-margin, less-competitive businesses that might allow them to slowly increase the percentage of sales they spend on R&D. But for now, much as we like that company, it does not make the fourth cut for the Great Growth-Flow universe.

Some companies like Seagate are "getting the word," but if they go straight from R&D spending at, say, the 4 percent level to the 8 percent level, they will wipe out their earnings growth, and Wall Street will butcher the stock. One can understand their problem; so if a company otherwise qualifies as a Great Growth-Flow company, be willing to consider it if R&D as a percentage of sales is below 7 percent but is increasing every year. Since well-spent R&D generates new products that will improve profitability and accelerate growth, if a company spends just 1 percent more of sales on R&D every year, in two or three years it will be selling the fruits of that spending, and the extra profits generated by those sales can be reinvested in more R&D. In other words, after a two- or three-year transition period, in a sense, the R&D program can fund itself. Like investments to create higher-quality products, we believe that the true cost of increasing R&D spending is $0. Over even a fairly short five-year time horizon, increased R&D will pay for itself and generate extra profits.

What About Stocks That Fail the Screen?

We certainly think some non–Great Growth-Flow stocks can be bought and held, especially if you know the company or industry really well. Seagate, for example, sells disk drives to OEMs (Original Equipment Manufacturers). Its gross profit margins are in the 20 percent to 25 percent range, about half of what we think of as good end-user margins. However, OEM sales have much lower selling costs, so the net margins aren't as bad as you might think. Still, when you start with 20 percent gross margins it's hard to do much better than 10 percent to 12 percent pretax, so Seagate doesn't qualify as a Great Growth-Flow company.

Does this mean that Seagate is not a growth company? No. We can look at other factors, such as the high quality of the management, its dominant market position, its large investment in low-cost production facilities, and its attractive acquisition and investment program, and say with some confidence that SEG should be in our universe. But it might not belong in yours.

What the lower margins tell us is that Seagate will always be a more volatile situation, subject to wider swings in results than companies in higher-margin businesses, and requiring very close monitoring on a quarter-by-quarter basis. We also can expect Wall Street to take the stock to more extreme highs in good times and more extreme lows in bad times, and adjust our investment strategy accordingly. For example, we pay more attention to insider-trading reports filed with the SEC by Seagate officers than we do for a high-margin company like Adobe Systems.

In the *California Technology Stock Letter*, we recommend several non–GGF companies each year, but we label them as "Trading Ideas." You have to be pickier about when and where you buy them and be ready to sell them when others are enthusiastic and move prices up. They simply are a lot more work than buying and owning a portfolio of Great Growth-Flow companies.

Where Can I Find Great Growth-Flow Companies?

In addition to the companies you can identify for your Growth-Flow portfolio using the four tests above, we list some Great Growth-Flow companies in Appendix A. A few years ago, we had a similar list analyzed by an outside research service specializing in cash-flow analysis to predict improving and declining corporate performance several quarters before it hits the income statement. Their response was, "What a wonderful group of companies—strong and growing cash flow, high incremental returns on investment, tight expense controls."

If a Great Growth-Flow company has one or a few quarters of subpar growth in sales or depressed profitability, we do not knock it off the list immediately. If the problem seems transitory—a delayed product, a difficult-to-swallow acquisition, an industrywide temporary slow-down—we will keep the company in the universe. Whether or not we buy the stock is a separate question.

If a Great Growth-Flow company develops a more permanent problem, perhaps stemming from a change in the market or the competitive arena, we drop it from our universe. Of course, we review the initial public offerings of new companies constantly to find candidates to add to the universe. Dropping a few and adding a few each year keeps our universe fresh and in line with changing technologies and markets.

## CHAPTER FIFTEEN

What About the Little Guys? Finding Opportunities in Development-Stage Companies (and Avoiding the Dogs)

The classic Growth-Flow company is earning money but deliberately sacrificing some current earnings to invest in R&D. So how do you value a development-stage company that is spending large amounts of money on R&D, has low or no sales, and is racking up big losses? Calculating the growth flow won't work with these companies; their losses often approach their R&D spending, generating a zero-growth flow.

You may even wonder whether investing in development-stage companies is worth the effort. In the computer, electronics, software, and communications industries, there is little need to buy development-stage companies. Most "real" companies go through a well-understood process of two or three rounds of venture-capital funding, developing and introducing their products, accelerating sales, and turning profitable before they go public. Marginal companies that either cannot get financed by professional venture capitalists, or are operating in small markets or with "me-too" products, try to short-circuit this program and go public early. Usually, too early.

We all know that the risks of investing in stocks are high enough without buying into a company with no history of profitability, an untested business model, or even a product that doesn't quite work yet. One look at the penny-stock market will tell you that most development-stage companies wind up in Chapter 11 bankruptcy.

On the other hand, when a carefully purchased, development-stage company hits pay dirt, you can get a truly spectacular return on a small investment. The leading edges of science—genetic engineering, superconductivity, three-dimensional solids modeling—are available for public investment in development-stage form. There's nothing wrong with being early if you can find the right company to bet on for the future.

To value these development-stage companies, we developed the "M Score." The M Score is a hype-buster. It will not tell you whose scientific effort will bear the most commercial fruit, but it will tell you when you are being asked to pay too much to get into the game. This is crucial, because in development-stage investing, preserving capital is about 75 percent of the battle for long-term profits.

Before we discuss the M Score, you should know some of the risks and tricks you will face when looking at development-stage companies, so you can avoid getting trapped in a bad deal.

What to Look Out For

Development-stage investing is like venture-capital investing with some huge handicaps: You often can't get a detailed review of the scientific progress, and you can't change management if they start to blow it.

Valuing development-stage companies is difficult. By definition, these companies have no real revenues. They may have some interest income coming in on the cash they have raised, but investors are perfectly able to earn interest on their own cash without handing it over to the management of a development-stage company to do the same thing.

Valuing such a company becomes harder when the company takes advantage of a popular accounting fake-out and shows their research and development expenses as revenues. In this legal (unfortunately) maneuver, the company raises a separate R&D partnership. The partnership contracts with the company to conduct research on a particular problem and develop a solution. The company books the money from this contract as revenues.

Voilà! Research expenses have been turned into revenues. Later, if the product is successful, the company buys out the R&D partnership for cash or stock and books a huge loss—but it's presented as a one-time, nonrecurring item. For example, in 1987, Genentech reported $134 million in sales and $13 million in earnings *before* a one-time writeoff of $365 million to buy out an R&D partnership. Do you think anyone went back and adjusted GNE's past income statements to allocate that R&D partnership–related loss against revenues and profits previously reported from the same partnership? Not a chance.

With no real revenues, there's no way to value the company in relationship to current sales. And because the company shows no earnings other than from interest income or R&D contracts, the price/earnings multiple is equally useless. Book value usually approximates the amount of money raised minus the losses to date. It tends to be small relative to the stock price and declines because of continuing losses.

Because these companies spend almost every nickel of earnings on R&D, the growth flow—earnings (or, in this case, losses) plus R&D—typically hovers around zero or in the negative zone.

In other words, traditional valuation measures will tell you that a development-stage company is worthless. While that often turns out to be true in the long run—most development-stage companies fail to become successful businesses—there are two reasons it's important to have *some* way to sort through these companies:

- Many development-stage companies will make it into production, and an early investment in them can bring tremendous profits; and
- Most development-stage companies are terribly overhyped; their stock price and total market capitalization are so high that even if the company is successful, your *investment* may earn a tiny return relative to the risk you took.

Venture capitalists face this problem every day. Their approach to valuing development-stage companies makes sense, but is very complex and time-consuming. They estimate the size of the market opportunity for several years into the future, using their knowledge base and the best consultants they can find. Then they estimate a company's possible market share, based on both their projection of what the market structure and the competition will look like and the company's goals (usually adjusted with a skeptical eye—even in the venture-capital process, a considerable amount of hyping goes on).

Next, they use their experience in similar businesses to develop a pro forma income statement and balance sheet several years into the future. Finally, they estimate the future value of the company based on its projected earnings stream and growth rate, then use their required rate of investment return to discount that future value back to a fair value today.

The problems with applying this process to public development-stage companies are obvious. First, by choosing to go public too early instead of going through the venture-capital process, a company is choosing to deal with less-sophisticated investors and provide them with less information. The opportunities for hype artists are manifold, and they know it. Therefore, the investor is far more likely to be conned in a development-stage investment than in any other. (We admit that managers are often fooling themselves as well as the public investors.)

Second, companies don't supply nearly as much information as needed for individual investors to form intelligent estimates of future sales and earnings. Venture capitalists demand business plans with market-research projections, detailed five-year company projections, and extensive personal references. The public development-stage company typically provides few projections, due to fears of lawsuits, although the promoters may whisper about incredible markets, mythical joint ventures, impending takeovers, and so on.

Third, it takes a lot of time and resources to check out a company's technology and people, to cross-check market projections, to build a model of the company's financial statements, and to come up with an intelligent estimate of the current value of a future stream of earnings. We know, because that's what we do as professional security analysts.

Finally, the most glowing stories that you hear often are those that are being hyped the hardest. By the time you get the news, you're being set up to take stock off the promoters' hands at exorbitant prices.

We also publish a short-selling newsletter, the *Overpriced Stock Service,* that loves to uncover these hyped-up stories at high market capitalizations with little substance. We call them the "Hot-Air Balloons"—they have about that much substance, and they're about that much fun. Cardio-Pet, one of our favorites, was a company with a $60 million market capitalization that performed electrocardiograms on dogs over the telephone.

In 1985, Dento-Med ran up to a $70 million market capitalization based on a miracle product that started as a better way to hold false teeth and wound up as a better mouthwash. At the time the company was worth $70 million, it had total revenues of less than $250,000, and three employees—the president, his wife, and a receptionist. Lots of dentists bought the stock, although none of them wanted to use the product.

CopyTele has a $96 million market capitalization today, with thirty-four employees working in a Long Island lab on flat-panel displays using magnetically charged ink. After seventeen years in business, the company has never made a sale, booked any earnings, or presented a technical paper at a professional conference.

In most areas of the stock market, you simply should ignore development-stage companies. These penny- and dollar-stock deals, often coming out of Denver, Salt Lake City, or the Vancouver Stock Exchange, simply aren't worth the time it takes to sort through the trash for the occasional gem. Many of them aren't really companies, they're an alternative to buying a lottery ticket—with somewhat lower odds of collecting anything.

Except Biotechnology

In biotechnology, bringing development-stage companies public is acceptable. It takes $100 million to $300 million to develop a drug, and five to ten years to get it through the Food and Drug Administration approval process. The venture capitalists can't carry so large a load that long, so they take the companies public early.

The good news is that individuals have an opportunity to buy legitimate development-stage companies and get paid venture capital–level returns. The better news is that of all the industries you would like to invest in early, biotechnology should lead the list. The market for almost any successful major drug is well over $100 million, simply because there are so many people in the world. And the stock market certainly pays for success; Amgen reached a $16 billion market capitalization based on only two successful drugs (Epogen and Neupogen).

The bad news is that if you want to participate directly in biotech companies developing drugs, you probably have to buy them at the development stage. By the time a company's first drug is approved, the stock has often tripled or more from its offering price. That means you must learn how to value these stocks.

The M Score—Your Key to Development-Stage Profits

The M Score will keep you out of the most overhyped development-stage stocks and point you toward those that are overlooked or out of favor with Wall Street. When combined with a simple test of financial viability, the M Score can at least focus you on a group of stocks that will generate decent investment returns for you *if* their research is successful—and they will not go broke while you are waiting for product announcements.

Development-stage companies have no dividends, no earnings, and little depreciation. But they have R&D spending—boy, do they ever. If we believe, for example, that biotech is a huge opportunity, with hundreds of potential products serving hundreds of very large markets, then, as a first cut, we can assume that all R&D dollars are equally well spent. Most of these companies have top scientists working on leading-edge problems, and information and breakthroughs tend to travel very quickly throughout the industry. In good Adam Smith style, R&D spending ought to be a very efficient market.

So, if we assume that all R&D dollars are roughly equally well spent, then the current value of a development-stage biotech company ought to bear some relationship to its level of R&D spending.

Add up the total amount of money the company spent on R&D during the last five years. Do not give it any credit for money spent more than five years ago; the technology changes too quickly. Don't give it any credit for money spent on administration, regulation, or manufacturing. Just R&D. That is its investment in its science.

Now calculate the total market capitalization of the company today—the stock price times the number of shares outstanding. That is what you are being asked to pay to buy into their science.

The M Score equals the total market capitalization of the company divided by its total R&D spending for the last five years (or the price per share divided by the last five years of R&D per share—same thing).

Instead of a price/sales ratio, a price/earnings ratio, or a price/growth-flow ratio, the M Score is a price/cumulative R&D ratio. Like those traditional ratios, a lower number is better. Companies hyped all out of proportion to the level of research effort they can maintain will have high ratios, while companies on which Wall Street is too negative will have low ratios. Admittedly, we investors will have to sort through the low-ratio group to throw out the companies that are wasting their R&D on trivial pursuits or me-too work in overcrowded areas. You can't buy development-stage stocks on their M Score alone, but you can use the M Score to sort through a big pile of names, evaluate a tip quickly, or develop a useful core group of companies to follow for the long haul.

M Scores range all over the map, from under 1x, where you are buying into the technology for much less than the venture capitalists spent to create it, to 40x or more. Like growth-flow multiples, M Scores in the 10x to 12x range are typical. Under 8x is interesting, under 5x is compelling, and under 3x—there are many of them around these days—means that if the science works you will make *lots* of money. At under 3x, you often pay less for the stock than the venture capitalists paid in the last round of private financing. Check the company's initial public offering prospectus under "Certain Transactions" to see what the venture capitalists paid.

At the other end of the scale, buying a development-stage company at 40x the amount it has invested in its science during the last five years is a very dubious proposition. Even if you agree that its drug will work, you are being asked to pay an excessive multiple of the money it has invested in its science. The research would have to pay off in a huge ratio of product sales to R&D dollars invested in order for you to make any money. That's possible, but it's just not likely.

The other important question with any development-stage company is this: Can it survive financially long enough to achieve its research objectives? Companies report a Statement of Changes in Financial Condition every quarter, either in their quarterly report to shareholders or in their 10-Q filing with the Securities and Exchange Commission. Look at how much cash a company uses in the quarter, and then divide that number (the "burn rate") into the cash and short-term securities it has left on the balance sheet.

The ratio of cash to burn rate tells you how many quarters it can survive at the current level of operations without further external financing. Anything less than two years of cash is worth a discussion with the chief financial officer. If it has less than one year of cash—watch out! A potentially dilutive financing is probably coming.

You may want to adjust your view of a particular company after further analysis, taking into consideration, for example, future funds promised from a joint-venture agreement or a warrant conversion. But the burn rate is the key to estimating the financial viability of a development-stage company.

From M Score to Growth Flow

When a company like Genentech finally makes the transition to a real company with sales and earnings, when should you stop using the M Score and start looking at the price/growth-flow ratio?

Use the method that provides the *highest* valuation for a company. When a development-stage company introduces products and starts generating earnings, the initial price/earnings ratios can look terribly high. Often the stock moves *down* as the story finally comes to fruition, to the great dismay of all the faithful investors who have believed and held on through the tough times. That can be the very best time to buy a development-stage company; much of the product development or FDA approval risk is behind the company, yet the price is lower than it was before products were approved and sales were made.

By paying attention to an attractive M Score, you can scoop up these companies and hold them until more products are introduced and more earnings are generated to support higher stock prices. Eventually, the company will be worth more using the price/growth-flow ratio or traditional valuation measures like P/E ratios than by using the M Score—and that tells you when to switch from development-stage valuation to operating-company valuation.

## CHAPTER SIXTEEN

Controlling the Risk in Technology Stocks

It is easy to say tech stocks and mutual funds are "risky," but what does that mean? They certainly have more short-term volatility than blue-chip stocks. The price of the typical technology stock varies 100 percent from low to high almost every year. Some years the lows come before the highs, technology investors are happy, subscriptions to our newsletter go up, CNBC calls every other week, and everyone thinks I'm brilliant. Other years, the highs come before the lows and subscriptions fall, the phone is silent, and as for brilliant . . .

If you are on the Internet and type "Michael Murphy + technology," you will find lots of references to stocks we follow and opinions we've offered. In years when the lows come after the highs, try typing "Michael Murphy + idiot," and you'll get a good measure of the pain level among technology investors. Someone should start keeping the "MMI" index; it would be a great contrary indicator.

If risk equaled short-term volatility, stocks whose prices double or drop 50 percent in a year certainly would be risky. But do you care about short-term volatility? Unlike the mutual-fund and pension-fund managers, no one is holding your feet to the fire every quarter, or every month, or even every week to produce short-term performance. As an individual, you want to make investments in great companies that you can hold for several years, adding to your positions when the stocks are knocked down and selling only when they either get grossly overvalued or the fundamentals change.

Which brings us to a more important point: In technology, things change. IBM went from the overwhelming force in the computer industry in 1970 to a loss-plagued dinosaur fifteen years later. The efficient, popular CP/M operating system ran most non-Apple personal computers in 1978 but virtually vanished by 1985. Digital Equipment soared to $1 billion in revenues making minicomputers that IBM sneered at as toys compared to Big Blue's mainframes. Then Digital sneered at personal computers as toys compared to DEC's minicomputers—and paid the inevitable price when it had to sell out to Compaq.

As a technology-stock investor, you must be willing to spend a little time thinking about the big picture. There are always new technologies that supposedly threaten the established companies, but the vast majority of these scare stories never come to fruition. Those that do often produce two or three new leaders, some or all of which are acquired by the established companies. So do not pay a lot of attention to technologies, but do pay attention to those few new companies that grow rapidly to a substantial size. They really have something—their size and growth rate prove it—and it is worth your time to think about how their technology might affect your current investments. You probably will have identified these companies as new entrants in the Great Growth-Flow universe, and you may even have already had a chance to buy them.

Stratacom went public in July 1992, when its sales for the prior twelve months were $46.3 million. Over the next four years, the company grew 78 percent compounded to a run rate ten times as large—$463.2 million, annualizing its June 1996 quarter. Stratacom specialized in a new data-communications protocol called "frame relay." It sold a variety of equipment to build large-frame relay networks, and buyers started to realize that if they bought Stratacom gear and then leased a high-speed backbone data channel, they might not need to keep buying so many Cisco Systems routers. At the time, Cisco was a $3.7 billion sales company, annualizing its June 1996 quarter, and a stock-market darling with a total market capitalization of $38.0 billion. It also was (and is) a Great Growth-Flow company, albeit not a cheap stock. As investors, we started worrying that the Stratacom threat to Cisco might be real and certainly required close monitoring. Apparently Cisco agreed, because in July 1996, it bought Stratacom for $4.6 billion in stock.

During Cisco's long growth period, various Wall Street analysts and industry pundits pronounced numerous different technologies potential threats to Cisco. But you would have been wrong to sell your stock for that reason because none of them except Stratacom panned out.

By focusing on a successful *implementer* of the technology instead of the underlying technology itself, you would have been spared hours of learning and agonizing over issues that turned out to have no investment relevance. However, once you identified Stratacom as a potential threat, should you have sold Cisco stock?

No. Not until the potential threat became an actual problem. Stratacom's rapid growth never *did* impact Cisco's growth rate. The data-communications market is huge and is growing at over 30 percent a year, with a worldwide customer base. There was plenty of business for both Cisco and Stratacom.

Ultimately, the two companies would have collided, and perhaps Cisco would have reported a surprisingly bad quarter. The stock would then have dipped, bounced back, and gone into a churning, toppy period. That's when you would have sold, because you were monitoring the situation but waiting for real impact before abandoning your Cisco. Of course, Cisco saw the same thing coming and put an end to the problem by acquiring Stratacom.

Sun Microsystems presented a similar situation. *CTSL* had a long history with Sun, having recommended its initial public offering in an interview in *Business Week* in 1986. Later, during a product transition that led to a soft quarter, we were able to recommend the stock at $13⅝₆ in November 1993. We held happily for a couple of years and had no intention of selling. But then Microsoft introduced the Windows 2000 operating system, and we started hearing remarkably positive reviews of the new package from sophisticated technical people. Still, we did not sell our Sun. Positive reviews don't always make for a successful product, and it looked as if Microsoft was confusing the market with several flavors of Windows, including 3.1, 95, and now Windows 2000.

But in the March quarter of 1996, Windows 2000 sold more units than Sun's UNIX operating system. Windows 2000 was on a steep acceptance ramp, and we realized that as good as Sun was as a company, it was going into a head-to-head war with Microsoft. That's not good ground for an investor to stand on—witness the smoking carcasses of Digital Research, Lotus, Novell, Borland, and many others. So we sold Sun for $53—nearly quadrupling our investment in less than three years—and walked away for now. We still follow the company closely, but we'll wait to see who wins the war before we repurchase the stock.

Managing Risk Within Your Portfolio

Your first technology-investment goal should be to build a ten-stock portfolio. You do not have to buy them all at once; by picking up Great Growth-Flow stocks when Wall Street knocks them down, you should end up with ten stocks within two years or less.

When ten to twenty stocks are assembled into a portfolio, much of the *specific risk* of the individual companies is diversified away. Sun might have a problem with Microsoft just as Cisco is acquiring your Stratacom; good specific-company news offsets bad specific-company news, and vice versa.

In addition to specific-company risk, there is *industry risk*. The FDA turns down Synergen's septic-shock drug, and the whole biotechnology industry takes a hit on fears that the FDA is getting extra tough on bio-technology drugs. Personal-computer sales take off because Intel introduces a new, cheaper microprocessor, and the stocks of all the systems manufacturers, disk-drive companies, and manufacturers of electronic components, semiconductors, and even semiconductor equipment rise in tandem.

In 1970 there was only one technology industry. The customers were the Fortune 500 companies and the Department of Defense. In an economic slowdown, capital spending sneezed, and the whole industry caught a cold.

Today there are many technology "industries." Biotechnology has little correlation to personal computers. Data-communications growth is determined by very different economic drivers than computer retailers. Semiconductor companies have cycles, and so do software companies, but the cycles are barely related.

As you are building your ten-stock portfolio, by deliberately picking stocks from different industries, you can offset a substantial portion of the industry risk while you are hedging the specific-company risk. This takes a little willpower, because Wall Street tends to dump entire industries at once, and all the Great Growth-Flow companies in that industry will look cheap simultaneously.

For example, in late 1995 and the first half of 1996, the semiconductor stocks dropped 50 percent because of an inventory correction in the personal-computer channel. End-user sales of personal computers did not decline, but manufacturers had ordered and double-ordered too many chips. When Wall Street realized this, it smashed Great Growth-Flow semiconductor stocks: Intel went from $73 to $50; Xilinx fell from $54 to $25; Altera, a competitor, fared even worse as it dropped from $39 to $14; LSI Logic plummeted 71 percent from its high of $60 to $17⅝; the two largest static random-access-memory producers, Cypress Semiconductor and Integrated Device Technology, dropped 65 percent and 78 percent, respectively.

You could have built an entire ten-stock portfolio out of semiconductor stocks. You would have hedged a lot of the specific-company risk, but the industry risk would have depressed your investment results for many months. Better to cherry-pick the three best companies and move on to another industry.

In addition to specific risk and industry risk, there is *sector risk*. Technology as a sector sometimes shoots up or takes a tumble. Technology stocks are about half again as risky as the broad market averages (often described as their having a beta of 1.5). For example, when the Fed increases interest rates, growth stocks are hurt more than value stocks. (That's because more of the current value of growth stocks depends on future earnings, which will be much greater than they are today, but have to be discounted back to a current value using the general level of interest rates.) Technology stocks are growth stocks.

On the other hand, when the economy weakens and the old mass-production, consumer companies (or the even older industrial companies) are having earnings problems, technology stocks often shine because they are the only place to find earnings growth. Investment capital flows out of old-economy stocks into technology stocks.

As a technology investor, the only way to lower sector risk is to reduce the percentage you allocate to technology. But that is not desirable when the investment returns on technology stocks are substantially higher than they are on other investments, as they will be for the next five to ten years. Our best advice is to invest 100 percent minus your age in the technology sector and diversify the remainder in nontechnology stocks: international, value, energy, or elsewhere. By definition, as a technology investor, you are going to have to accept more sector risk than the average diversified investor.

This is true even for the technology *mutual-fund* investor. A single technology mutual fund hedges a lot of specific risk. A small group of funds also offsets industry risk, but you still will have sector risk on the percentage of your assets invested in technology. Be comforted by the knowledge that, over the medium and long term, your returns on both individual technology stocks and mutual funds should be much higher than the index averages, especially on technology investments made in the next few years. Why? Internet growth is powering computer and communications stocks, and biotechnology companies are poised to obtain a host of FDA approvals.

Finally, there is *market risk*—the risk of loss from being in any equity investment, regardless of sector. You take on market risk when you decide to take money out of savings, where a return of your capital is guaranteed—but not its purchasing power, and the only question is what interest rate you will earn—and invest it where return of your capital is not guaranteed. Fortunately, while the risk of loss in any one-year period is high (the market declines in about one out of three years), the risk drops sharply as stocks are held for three, five, or seven years. If you can hold stocks for ten years, the risk of loss is very low, and at fifteen to twenty years, it approaches the nonexistent.

Market risk is a problem only for those who will need the money in the near future or for professional money managers, who have a three-month time horizon due to performance pressures. Individual investors, beholden to no one but themselves, can turn short-term market volatility to their advantage by using dips to increase their portfolio holdings.

How Low Can It Go?: Downside Risk Value

Even though specific risk can be offset, to a large extent, it is always important to have an idea in advance of how much risk you are taking with each individual stock you buy. In a ten-stock portfolio, there will always be a stock or two that underperforms due to unanticipated problems. If 10 percent or 20 percent of your portfolio is lagging or even declining a few percentage points, it is annoying, but not painfully debilitating to your investment returns. It is the individual stock that plunges 80 percent unexpectedly that damages your investment return and your psyche. To avoid these, we use a proprietary risk measure: the Downside Risk Value.

The Downside Risk Value, or DRV, is the average of three estimates of how low a stock can go if everything goes to hell. We make separate estimates based on sales per share, book value per share, and the price/earnings ratio. These are lowball estimates meant to give you—and us—pause before we pull the trigger and buy a stock. For that one-in-ten case where everything does go to hell, the DRV can give you some comfort that a reasonable bottom is in sight. Many investors ride a bad stock down and then sell it in dismay because they have no way to tell how much worse it can get. Often they sell it near the DRV; the stock stops declining, builds a base, and rallies back without them. If you go through the effort to understand the company, wait patiently for a chance to buy the stock, and then suffer the pain of a sharp decline, the last thing you need is to be panicked out at the bottom.

How to Determine Your Stock's Downside Risk

The first estimate we make for the DRV is on sales per share, because this is a longstanding way to value private businesses when they are sold. Entrepreneurs often want to show the lowest possible profits to avoid taxes. Sharpies might want to show unsustainably high profits to sucker in a buyer at a high price. Profits are what the accountant says they are, but sales are sales.

In the old economy, stocks can be bought at half of sales per share and less. That does not happen often in the new economy. We have found that one times sales per share offers support for a declining stock. Many technology companies sell at two or three times sales per share, with very successful companies like Microsoft up at ten times sales or more. If and when a technology stock drops to one times sales, things have gotten pretty bad, and the value hunters will start paying attention.

We may be the last technology analysts in America who pay any attention to book value, but when all else fails, assets still count for something and they are the basis of our second estimate for the DRV. Most of the real assets of a technology company are their people, patents, know-how, strategic and marketing relationships, and customer base—none of which appear on the balance sheet. Excepting semiconductor companies, which sometimes own huge, expensive fabrication facilities, most technology companies have relatively little plant and equipment. But when it comes to evaluating risk, we think that is more of a reason to look at book value, not less. A technology company that looks cheap based merely on its physical assets probably is very cheap based on its less tangible, but more important, people/patents/customer-base assets.

Portfolio managers who rely on price-to-book value measures in the old economy generally try to buy stocks at less than book value per share. But, like sales per share, it is unrealistic to think that technology stocks will sell for valuations as low as some old-economy stocks do. We use 1.5x book value—a 50 percent premium to hard assets—as a reasonable floor for a stock based on its physical assets.

Finally, for our third estimate of the DRV, we look at Wall Street's favorite valuation measure: the price/earnings ratio. We use a very tough standard. Depressed stocks almost always have depressed earnings, so right off the bat, we know that this measure is going to point to a low price per share as a potential bottom. But the reality is that most institutional investors follow price/earnings ratios blindly, and those are the people we need to see buying the stock to establish a floor.

Traditionally, technology investors think a fairly priced stock sells at a price/earnings ratio equal to its growth rate. That is, if a company is growing at 20 percent a year it should sell for 20 times earnings, 30 percent a year is worth 30 times earnings, and so forth. One of the reasons hot stocks look so overvalued is that a hot company growing at, say, 90 percent a year will sell for a whopping 90 times earnings. We all know that 90 percent growth is not likely to be sustainable. New competition will come into the market, or the company will skim the cream of potential customers in its niche, or as the company grows, the law of large numbers will force down its growth rate.

But many portfolio managers, especially those who rely on earnings momentum, willingly pay up to 90 times earnings, as if the growth rate was going to last forever. They are afraid that if they don't buy the stock, their competitors will; if the company continues to compound earnings at 90 percent for a few years and the price/earnings ratio holds up, they will have missed out on a great stock their competitors caught. Secretly, they all believe they'll be the first to sell if the growth rate slows below 90 percent.

If a price/earnings ratio equal to the growth rate is "fair," we want to use a ratio low enough to believe that the stock will attract some institutional investors if the stock falls that low. So we use a price/earnings ratio equal to only one-third of the growth rate for the last three years times the last four quarters of earnings. In other words, a company growing 30 percent a year would be cheap only at a price/earnings ratio of 10. A 20 percent grower would be worth only seven times earnings. Multiplying those low P/E ratios by earnings that are probably depressed will result in low target prices, indeed. But there is no reason to kid yourself; when companies get into trouble, stocks can go to surprisingly low levels. The only slack we cut them is if they are reporting losses. We don't use a negative number—we arbitrarily set the value based on the price/earnings ratio to zero.

After we calculate the three target DRV prices—one based on sales, one based on assets, and one based on earnings—we simply calculate their average to obtain the Downside Risk Value. For example, in early 1997, Microsoft was a high-flying company, loved and held by almost all technology-portfolio managers, and widely regarded as the dominant company in personal computing. Apple Computer was in the doldrums with falling market share, reporting losses, and undergoing seemingly endless reorganizations. What would the Downside Risk Value say about these two stocks?

DRV Factor	Microsoft	Apple Computer
Last 12 months' sales	$9.435 B	$8.814 B
Number of shares	1.203 M	124.7 M
1. Sales per share	$7.84	$70.68
Book value per share	$7.23	$15.59
2. Book value × 1.5	$10.85	$23.39
Last 12 months' earnings	$1.92	−$7.01
Last 3 years' growth rate	36.3%	9.3%
3. ⅓ of growth rate times EPS	$23.23	$0.00
Average 1, 2, 3 = DRV	$13.97	$31.36

At the time we made this calculation, Microsoft was trading for $97 and Apple for $17. You can calculate the percentage change from the current price to the Downside Risk Value to find out how much money you are likely to lose if things go wrong for Microsoft or get even worse than they are for Apple. In this case, the percentage changes were –85.6 percent for Microsoft and a *gain* of 84.5 percent for Apple.

Obviously, we like to see the percentage risk as low as possible. In Great Growth-Flow companies like Microsoft, we consider ourselves fortunate to get a buying opportunity with only 25 percent risk to the DRV; 50 percent risk is more common. You will be buying these stocks after they have been knocked down by Wall Street for some transitory reason like a shortfall in quarterly earnings; but even so, you will still be taking the risks of equity ownership. However, the 85 percent risk in Microsoft is too much for our blood.

In a turnaround situation, like Apple's, we like to see the stock trading at or even under its DRV, as Apple was. George Miller, my first boss in the investment business, told me the way most turnaround investments work out. A man comes into your office, puts your money in his pocket, turns around and walks out the door, and that's the last you ever see of it. There's a lot of truth in his dictum. Stocks of companies that rise from the ashes can be tremendous winners, but you take a lot of specific risk based on their ability to turn around. Buying the stock when it is at or under the DRV gives us some comfort that if things don't work out, there may be a corporate buyer at or near our cost.

The Seven Rules of Seasonality

There is a seasonal pattern to technology-stock prices. It occurs in most years, but not all years. Some years it is very strong; others, barely discernible. It should not drive your investment decisions, but it is well worth understanding to fine-tune the timing of the decisions you make for more fundamental reasons.

Let us start not with the beginning of the year, but in October. Given that mutual funds must recognize capital gains and losses by October 31, a whole new ballgame starts on November 1.

Most companies have fiscal years that end in December, so they report quarterly earnings for a March first quarter, a June second quarter, a September third quarter, and then the December fourth quarter. Companies that don't end their fiscal year in December usually end it in June (second most popular), March (third choice), or September (fourth). Only a few companies have oddball months ending their fiscal years, like Micron Technology (August) and Adobe Systems (November).

Typically, companies report quarterly earnings two to four weeks after the quarter ends, unless it is their audited fourth quarter, which can take an extra week or two. So in the second half of October, most companies are reporting their September quarter results, generally the third fiscal quarter of the current December year or possibly their first fiscal quarter of the coming June fiscal year.

All year long, analysts worry about earnings for the current year. Some companies do well; others badly. But after the September third quarter is reported, the die is pretty much cast for the current year. Leaders are unlikely to blow the December quarter hopelessly; laggards are unlikely to make up enough ground to turn a bad year into a good one.

At this point, analysts turn their attention away from the current year to the coming year. Being analysts, they want to find reasons that customers should buy a stock and generate a commission. So they ask: "If things go right next year, what could this company earn?"

They might mean "if things continue to go right," or "if things get better," or even "if you get this horrible mess straightened out"—it doesn't matter. They are addressing the management of the company. Guess what the answer will be?

Entreprenial ventures are like second marriages: the triumph of hope over experience. In fact, we have never been surprised by how many entrepreneurs are in their second (or third) marriages. They always believe that with a few small changes, their current products will sell better, their market share will improve, their earnings will grow, and, hey, don't forget that R&D is promising a breakthrough product real soon now!

Naturally, they feed back to the analysts estimates on sales growth and profitability that are on the enthusiastic side. But with the beginning of the new fiscal year still a couple of months away, who is the analyst to be a total wet blanket? Analysts may tone down some of the more outrageous assumptions, but after they have cranked through their financial models for the company, they will almost always conclude that:

- next year's earnings will be much better than this year's, and
- based on next year's earnings, the stock looks pretty cheap.

Consider a stock growing at 30 percent a year, earning $2.00 per share this year and selling for $60. The analyst has gotten used to the 30x price/earnings ratio and is focused mainly on whether the earnings are going to hit $2.00. After the September quarter, results are reported and the analyst breathes a big sigh of relief. They'll make the $2.00. Now the analyst looks hard at the coming year and—no surprise—earnings are going to grow 30 percent to $2.60. Suddenly our $60 stock has a price/earnings ratio of only 23x. Wow! Cheap! When it gets back to 30x, it will be at $78—a substantial gain from $60. So the analyst changes his recommendation from "Buy" to "Aggressive Buy."

Now imagine this process happening for not one but dozens and even hundreds of stocks, all at about the same time. Is it any surprise that:

Seasonality Rule 1: Technology stocks tend to rally beginning at the end of October.

There is another impetus to this rally. Since 1971, the American Electronics Association has held a conference for financial analysts at the end of October or early November. That first year, 30 companies presented their story to 60 technology analysts and portfolio managers. The format grew so popular that in 1996, the last year the conference was held in Monterey, California, representatives of 380 companies spoke and 1,200 financial types showed up. Having outgrown Monterey, the AEA moved the conference to San Diego beginning in November 1997.

This intense focus on the technology sector, coming just as or after September-quarter earnings are reported, also tends to kick-start technology stocks. With hundreds of analysts focused on any company that seems the slightest bit underpriced, and the ability to talk to many companies' suppliers, competitors, or customers just by walking down the hall, stocks start to move. Thus the corollary to Seasonality Rule 1: **Buy 'em at the AEA.**

Fast-forward to December 18—a crucial day for technology investors. The technology rally has been under way for six weeks. Individual money is flowing into technology mutual funds. The investment bankers are taking advantage of the inflow to bring public every respectable deal they have that couldn't go public during the summer doldrums. They've waited to include in the prospectus the companies' September quarter and now the companies each have spent about $300,000 on auditors' fees, legal fees, prospectus printing, and the black hole called nonaccountable underwriters' expense allowance ("I was thinking about your road show while driving my Porsche when something went wrong with first gear—that's why my new transmission counts as an expense of this deal!").

The initial public offerings are soaking up some or all of the fresh money coming into the sector, but on December 18, all that will end. The investment bankers have to get to their ski condos in Aspen or Sun Valley, or their beach house on Aruba, lest their long-suffering families divorce or disown them. And there's no point in trying to do deals after that anyway, because the institutional buyers are gone, too—Telluride, Snowbird, or Belize are popular destinations. So the initial public offerings stop, but the big inflows of cash into mutual funds continue. Individual investors, who may be planning an exciting trip across town to the brother's place for Christmas dinner or cleaning up the spare bedroom for Mom to fly in from Florida, have plenty of time to think about jumping on board the technology-stock rally. In fact, since they'll never get the spare bedroom clean enough for Mom anyway, it may be a relief to retreat to the old personal computer and calculate how much richer they have become since the September 30 statement.

Consequently, the technology-stock rally accelerates and starts to focus on the smaller stocks—the ones typically bought by portfolio managers who play the initial public offering game.

"But wait," you say. "If they're in Snowbird, who's buying the stocks?"

They are. They call in every morning to find out how much cash flowed into the fund, then tell the traders to buy more of what they already own. This has two great advantages: It requires little time and thought, because they already understand the companies they own, and it may boost the price of those stocks—and therefore the performance of the fund—before the December 31 cutoff date. They can head for the slopes while the traders put the money to work. Traders are not allowed to go on vacation if the market is open.

So now we have . . .

Seasonality Rule 2: Technology stocks—especially smaller stocks—tend to accelerate their rally into a new year.

Coincident with the rally in electronics and computer stocks, biotechnology stocks usually give a good account of themselves during this period for somewhat different reasons. Biotech stocks tend to move on news of drug approvals, clinical-trial results, new patents granted, major collaborations signed, and so forth. Most years, the Food and Drug Administration has a substantial backlog of pending approvals as they come to the end of the year. They have two choices.

One is to continue to review applications at a leisurely pace, approving drugs only when the complete process ends. If FDA officials do that, they will get severely criticized by Congress for sitting on drugs that could save lives. Their statistics on the number of drugs approved may look worse than the year before. They will go into the new federal budgeting process facing peeved members of Congress and defending bad stats.

Or they can say, "What the hell?," approve anything that looks like it doesn't kill people, and raise their budget requests to the now-smiling Congress folks, backed by excellent statistics on the number of new drugs approved before the end of the calendar year.

Which is a bureaucrat likely to choose?

Exactly.

One reason the biotechs tend to rally at year-end is an acceleration in FDA approvals. It does not happen every year, but it happens often enough to make a difference.

Another event that gets the Wall Street bulls running every year is the Hambrecht & Quist Life Sciences Conference, which begins the first or second Monday after New Year's Day and runs for most of the week. Like the AEA October conference for electronics and computer companies, the H&Q Life Sciences Conference is the granddaddy of these events. At the 1999 Conference, about 300 companies made presentations to over 3,000 health-care and biotechnology security analysts and portfolio managers. Needless to add, stocks moved.

This leads to . . .

Seasonality Rule 3: Biotech stocks do well beginning early in December.

By the end of January, things are starting to change for both electronics/computer and biotech stocks. Refreshed by slopes or surf, the investment bankers start another class of initial public offerings on their road shows early in the month. A few weeks later, they are ready to bring those companies public. Much of the year-end cash has flowed into mutual funds for IRA, Keogh, and 401K accounts, and has been put to work. The halo effect of the Hambrecht & Quist Life Sciences Conference is starting to dim.

Worse, analysts realize that business in January just isn't as strong as it was in December. Every year they seem surprised that sales in a month with no Christmas are sequentially lower than sales in a month with Christmas. Nervousness—not a lot, but a little—about the strength of the March quarter sets in. Technology stocks often go into a high-level churning or consolidation pattern until the middle of April. Cash inflows to mutual funds continue at a reasonable clip right up to the April 15 tax deadline for many retirement-plan contributions, but the investment bankers do their best to divert that cash to initial public offerings (typical commission: 70¢ per share) from already public stocks (typical commission: 6¢ per share).

Seasonality Rule 4: Do not be surprised if technology stocks stall in February and March.

This is a good time to sell stocks that have benefited from the year-end rally but do not make your cut as continuing holdings.

Mid-April starts the March-quarter earnings reports. Like the mid-October earnings reports, small disappointments might be overlooked, this time because the company still has three more quarters to make up a shortfall and hit the estimate for the full year. As always, big disappointments will cause a sharp drop in the stock. Yet these stocks often recover quickly based on the same three-quarters-still-to-go theory. And all technology stocks benefit from another impending conference, the longest-running brokerage-firm effort, the Hambrecht & Quist Technology Stock Conference starting the last Monday in April for a five-day run.

Hambrecht & Quist is a San Francisco–based brokerage firm that started in the late 1960s as a partnership with many venture capitalists as limited partners. Its goal: to provide research and underwriting services for Silicon Valley companies. Many other brokerage firms, some larger, hold technology-stock conferences these days, but this was the first and traditionally is one of the biggest. Good March-quarter earnings results or a strong presentation by a previously little-known new company can move a stock up sharply.

Seasonality Rule 5: Expect a good rally into and through the Hambrecht & Quist Conference, usually extending into mid-May.

Because we started in October, so far the seasonality rules have dealt with a technology market generally in an uptrend. Unfortunately, the corollary to Seasonality Rule 5 is: **Sell 'em at the H&Q.** Putting the two corollaries together—**buy 'em at the AEA, sell 'em at the H&Q**—seems to work more years than not. You capture most of the good times in technology stocks while being in the market only six months a year. Some years the stocks continue to rally after the H&Q Conference, as in 1995, when the excitement over the introduction of Windows 95 kept the ball rolling into September. Unfortunately, that was followed by a substantial decline in the group in the first half of 1996, AEA Conference or no AEA Conference.

Another event normally prompts tech stocks to top out in May, and, strangely enough, this one often seems to come as a surprise to portfolio managers: Summer happens. In the summer, business slows down. Corporate evaluations take more time because people are on vacation. Europe, an important market for U.S. technology companies, virtually shuts down in August.

Even companies that put together a decent June quarter have to report it in the last half of July, when no one seems to care. Report a good number, and little happens. Your company is on track to make its earnings estimate for the year, so what's new? Report a bad number, and your stock gets clobbered. Portfolio managers are on vacation, or thinking about it, and, anyway, who wants to catch a falling knife when the September quarter is likely to be equally weak? Mutual-fund inflows are lower as individuals worry more about paying for the beach house than stuffing a little more money into a mutual fund that is probably stagnating.

Seasonality Rule 6: Expect a mild decline up to Labor Day, with substantial volatility on a stock-by-stock basis.

The day after Labor Day is another crucial point for technology stocks. Portfolio managers come back from the beach with eight months of the year gone. In the next four months, they have to improve their performance sharply to beat the competition and earn the large bonus to which they have become accustomed, if not entitled. A quick call to each of their investee companies reveals that business was soft everywhere because it was summer. Little was sold in July and August. The company will have to make its entire earnings estimate for the third quarter during the month of September. Can it succeed? Managers and analysts call weekly to get an update. Stocks may be quite volatile as the rumors fly—interest is strong, orders are weak, an unexpected large order arrives for immediate shipment, another big contract looks like it will be delayed until the December quarter, they made it, they didn't—until finally the month and the quarter end.

Seasonality Rule 7: Technology stocks tend to be very volatile from Labor Day through mid-October, and may offer excellent buying opportunities.

Now we all wait for the September-quarter results to be reported in mid-October—and, say, isn't that the American Electronics Association Conference coming right at us again?

To summarize the seasonality rules:

1. Technology stocks tend to rally beginning at the end of October. Corollary: Buy 'em at the AEA.
2. Technology stocks—especially smaller stocks—tend to accelerate their rally into a new year.
3. Biotech stocks do well beginning early in December.
4. Do not be surprised if technology stocks stall in February and March.
5. Expect a good rally into and through the Hambrecht & Quist Conference, usually extending into mid-May. Corollary: Sell 'em at the H&Q.
6. Expect a mild decline up to Labor Day, with substantial volatility on a stock-by-stock basis.
7. Technology stocks tend to be very volatile from Labor Day through mid-October and may offer excellent buying opportunities.

As a long-term investor in Great Growth-Flow companies, you should not sell stocks you like fundamentally just because it is mid-May. But that is a good time to sell stocks you no longer want to hold. Rather than put the proceeds to work right away, you might want to keep some powder dry for opportunities in the dog days of August, when you might be the only buyer, or even in late September, when panic over third-quarter earnings estimates reaches its highest pitch.

Protecting Your Portfolio

Without selling your best stocks or even raising any cash, there are things you can do to protect against the summer slump. Most people think of options as racy, dangerous, somewhat mysterious financial instruments best left to professionals. But options are a tool, like hammers. You can use them to build churches, or you can use them to kill people. If you don't know how to use them, you'll probably hit your thumb.

Options can be used to speculate and add leverage to your portfolio, but we do not advocate buying them for long-term technology investing. If that is your game, you can use the tools in this book to pick stocks to buy and then get a good options book (and start slowly) to learn to speculate.

Options also can be used like insurance, to protect your portfolio. Like fire insurance, you pay a premium and hope you never have to collect on the policy. But if you do, you will be mighty glad to have it.

We use options for two strategies. First, you may have an individual stock position that you are not yet ready to sell, but you are worried about its fundamental position in the current quarter. Perhaps the company has a new product coming that is late, which caused it to miss an earnings estimate, which caused the stock to decline, which is why you bought it in the first place. But now you are thinking it may get the new product out too late in the current quarter, or miss the quarter entirely, and suffer another leg down on the stock price. You could buy a protective put option on the stock, an option that expires after the earnings will be reported.

A put option gives you the right to sell a stock to someone else at a fixed price—the "strike price"—for a fixed period of time, after which the put expires worthless, unless the stock goes down enough before expiration to make it worthwhile to exercise the option and put the stock to someone else. You do not have to give up your stock because you can sell a put that has value after a stock has dropped. What you pay for the put option is the "premium." If the stock drops, your profit on the put option will offset part or all of your losses on the stock. If the stock goes up, the put option will expire and you will lose the premium you paid.

Put options on individual stocks with a strike price at or near the current price of the stock are expensive, often carrying premiums of about 3 percent per month. An option bought just after the middle of a quarter, say on May 21 of the June period, that expires just after the earnings will be reported—say, July 19—would cost about 6 percent. If you are right that the company misses the quarter, but the stock drops only 5 percent or so, the insurance will have saved you nothing. If the stock doesn't drop at all or even goes up, your put will expire worthless, and the 6 percent cost will reduce your rate of return. The first 6 percent the stock goes up just makes you even.

A good alternative for an individual stock is to buy an out-of-the-money put. For a $30 stock, a two-month put contract at a $30 strike price might cost the full 6 percent. But if you were willing to accept some risk, you could buy a put with a $25 strike price for about half of that, or 3 percent. Another step down would take you to a $20 strike price and a cost of about 1.5 percent, but that truly is disaster insurance. What are the chances your stock will drop more than 33 percent in two months? Not likely.

Another possibility is to buy the $25 strike price, but go out an extra month to three months. That probably will cost you 4 percent; but after the earnings are reported, the put will have a month of life left and therefore some residual value. If the stock falls a lot, you will have some protection. If it falls less, you still may get your premium back. If the stock goes up, you can sell the option for the remaining time value to recapture part of the cost.

A third possibility is to wait until a few days before the earnings are reported, buy a put option with a strike price near the current price, and sell it quickly after earnings are reported. Much of the cost of an option relates to the amount of time you hold it; a shorter holding period means a lower cost. You often can get this kind of insurance for 1 percent or so, during the most vulnerable period that you are holding the stock.

We buy puts on individual stocks only rarely, due to the expense.

The second way to use put options is more interesting: to protect the entire portfolio. In addition to buying puts on stocks, you can buy puts on entire indices, such as the Standard & Poor's 500, the Standard & Poor's 100 (the "OEX"), the Wilshire 2000 Small Cap, and others. Index puts cost less than stock puts, usually as little as 1 percent a month. They are most useful when you are worried about the whole technology group, as during the seasonally weak summer period, or when you think the broad-market, old-economy stocks are overpriced and might fall, dragging down your technology portfolio—as in 1997.

On August 28, 1987, we published an issue of the *California Technology Stock Letter* with the headline: "1000 (Gulp!) Down?" Although many people have claimed in retrospect to have predicted the Crash of October 19, 1987, ask them for written proof. Most of them will say they were afraid to commit their sentiments to paper, out of fear they would knock the market down due to their powerful impact. Right.

We were worried that the broad-market, old-economy stocks had gotten hopelessly overvalued. But at the same time, the technology sector was in a strong upswing from a nasty downturn in 1984 and early 1985. We didn't want to sell our tech stocks, but we didn't want to be blindsided by a broad market decline, either.

This was an ideal situation to buy Standard & Poor's 100 (OEX) puts. The OEX is made up of the largest 100 companies by market capitalization. These are mostly old-economy stocks, held by large institutions. If the market is going to crack, these stocks have to go down.

At this writing the OEX index is around 720. Each option contract covers 100 units, so each contract will protect about $72,000 of portfolio value. You can divide the total value of your portfolio by $72,000 to figure out how many contracts you need to protect the total amount.

Contracts are quoted per unit, so an option price of, say, $7½ means that each contract will cost $750. In this example, for $750 you can protect $72,000 of portfolio value for one month—a cost, or insurance premium, of 1.4 percent.

Puts also can be bought on technology indices or small-stock indices like the Wilshire 2000, the NASDAQ 100, the Pacific Stock Exchange High-Tech Index, or the Philadelphia Semiconductor Index. The percentage cost usually will be a little higher and liquidity not quite as good. But looking back at the seasonality rules, it often makes sense to buy protective puts on a technology index around the end of June that are set to expire in mid-September. If a 4 percent or 5 percent premium is what it takes to give you the comfort to stay fully invested in great companies growing 20 percent to 30 percent a year, it's worth it.

## CHAPTER SEVENTEEN

Managing Your Technology Portfolio

The most important principle in managing a portfolio of technology stocks is to move deliberately. Day traders, hedge-fund managers, and momentum mutual funds and investors are in a frenetic race for short-term performance. It is a loser's game; don't play it. Instead, build a portfolio of great companies over time.

The day you decide to commit more of your assets to technology industries is not necessarily the day you need to buy the stocks. Managing a portfolio is like batting in baseball, except no one is calling balls and strikes. You can stand there as long as you want to, waiting for the perfect pitch. If a few good ones get by you, so what? Others will come along.

You know from Chapter 14 that the investment decision should be divided into two steps: First, is this a company you want to own someday? Second, are you willing to pay the current price for the stock? The portfolio-management decision requires a third step: Does this stock fit well into your portfolio?

When you find a Great Growth-Flow company selling at a low price/growth-flow ratio, you still must consider the impact on your total portfolio position if you proceed with a purchase. Related stocks tend to get cheap or expensive together. For example, when semiconductor-equipment orders started slowing down in early 1996, all the semiconductor-equipment stocks tumbled. Several large Great Growth-Flow companies, like Applied Materials, Lam Research, and Novellus, plunged to two- or three-year lows. The stock of smaller, newer companies like Mattson Technology and GaSonics also plummeted. You could have built an entire portfolio of attractively priced, high-quality, semiconductor-equipment stocks.

But that would have been a major mistake. Industry stock prices came down with the chip-makers' stocks; but when the semiconductor group rallied in the fall, only the largest semiconductor equipment stocks followed suit. The rest languished until their earnings, which always lag behind the chip makers', turned up in mid-1997. You would have missed good performance in stocks of chip makers, disk-drive manufacturers, component suppliers, and major personal-computer manufacturers, even though you correctly spotted the major trend: burgeoning personal-computer sales.

Diversification: Mixing and Matching Stocks for Higher Returns

Diversification is the key to avoiding this mistake. Twenty years ago, all technology stocks pretty much moved in sync. Today the sector is so diversified that it is worth the effort to avoid overconcentration in any one subsector. Software and biotechnology do not move together most of the time. Communications stocks and personal-computer stocks almost seemed negatively correlated in 1996 and early 1997. Client/server software and personal-computer software companies have entirely different economic drivers. Sometimes the stocks move together; sometimes they do not.

New investors should try to start with at least four stocks: two Great Growth-Flow companies in electronics and computers, and two development-stage companies in medical technology. One of the electronics stocks might be a large, established name and the other smaller and newer. If one is in hardware, try to choose the other from the software sector. If you also find a promising communications stock and a strong computing stock, buy them as well in the drive to diversify.

In the medical area, look for a broadly based, late-stage company like Chiron and an early-stage, inside-the-cell company like Vical or Ligand. Or choose one biotech and one medical-device company.

In any case, we generally advise newcomers to buy equal dollar amounts of all four stocks. With a one-hundred-share minimum trade, you can assemble a four-stock portfolio with as little as $5,000.

Once you have your four-stock portfolio, set a goal of ten stocks: five in electronics/computers and five in medical/biotech. Instead of adding to your four stocks, continue to watch for buying opportunities in other Great Growth-Flow or quality medical companies. If you buy your fifth name in the medical area, buy your sixth in electronics and computers.

Always try to diversify further with each stock purchase—diversification adds extra value to your purchase. By the time you get to ten stocks, you will own different-size companies in a variety of industries that respond to many different business and economic drivers.

We stay at ten to twelve stocks for portfolios as large as $250,000 to $300,000. Once you get to ten stocks, simply add new funds proportionately to your holdings, or put a little bit more into positions where the stock price is lagging behind the fundamental progress of the company. If a new stock gets so cheap that you cannot resist buying it, consider selling your least-attractive holding (even if it also looks cheap) in order to maintain portfolio focus. As your portfolio grows to over $300,000, slowly increase the number of positions to a maximum of twenty. It is very difficult for an individual investor to track more than twenty positions. Again, if a new stock opportunity becomes available, use the "pigs at a trough" philosophy. I grew up on a farm, and I noticed early on that when a new pig forces its way up to the trough, another pig drops out. A firm twenty-stock limit forces you to keep your portfolio fresh.

Seasonality: Don't Forget the Seven Rules

Chapter 16 covered the seven rules of seasonality. While not 100 percent reliable, there is enough seasonality to technology-stock prices that it is worth considering in managing your portfolio. For example, if in mid-May you are planning to sell a semiconductor stock that has reached your objectives, you might wait until Labor Day to reinvest the money in a replacement chip stock. Odds are that any stock you are considering will be in the same range or lower, and some other stocks might unexpectedly get beaten down during the normally weak summer period, giving you a broader range of choices.

Timing Buys: Taking Advantage of Unpopular Stocks

Investors cannot create opportunities; they simply react to opportunities the market presents. Wall Street is dominated by a short-term focus on quarterly earnings. Companies that announce or preannounce a disappointing quarter usually watch their stocks get clobbered. Wall Street analysts cut estimates and move stocks from "buy" to "hold" or "strong buy" to "buy" after the bad news is out. They will not turn positive again until the company actually reports a good quarter. (One exception is usually the underwriter, which often maintains a buy rating in written material while downplaying the stock in sales calls.)

Momentum investors are even worse. Not only do they want to see quarterly earnings growing, they generally consider only companies with earnings growth rates in the top 25 percent, or even the top 10 percent. Furthermore, they will not buy even a top 10 percent stock until the stock price starts to move up. They are afraid they will reduce their rate of return if they buy a "dead" stock one quarter too early. Many momentum investors say they would rather buy an $8 stock at $15 on its way to $25 than buy an $8 stock that just sits there or goes to $6 before it goes to $25.

Individuals can take advantage of these short-term investors. Somebody has to own the stock while it is going from $8 to $15. If the risk is that it goes to $6 first or does not do much for six months, so be it. By taking a long-term view, individuals can refuse to play Wall Street's game and instead play the game they are best at. Buying stocks after they have been downgraded and only at low price/growth-flow ratios is the best way to build long-term wealth—and keep it.

Wall Street follows a well-worn pattern: Stocks decline on bad news, establish a base, lift off the base, advance, and eventually top out. We like to buy stocks that are establishing a base; that is when they look attractive on a price/growth-flow analysis. In April and May 1997, Informix announced an unexpectedly bad March quarter, and the stock fell sharply, down about 75 percent from its 1996 high. Right at the bottom of the Informix skid, *The Wall Street Journal* ran a story saying that of thirty-five analysts following the stock, only one—yours truly—rated it a buy. I immediately got a call from a local reporter who said earnestly, "Mr. Murphy, if thirty-four analysts think this stock should be sold, what on earth makes you think it is a buy?"

I replied, "The fact that thirty-four analysts think it should be sold. Who is left to sell it? If nobody is left to sell it, how risky can it be?"

Needless to say, that was within $1 of the stock's absolute bottom during that period.

When to Sell: Spotting the Warning Signs in Your Stocks

One of the key portfolio-management decisions is when to sell. You can make a *relative* decision using the pigs-at-the-trough approach. Sell a stock when you have a better stock to buy. A big winner in a quality company is hard to sell; Wall Street has probably turned positive, and your friends think you were prescient to buy it when it was down. We do not sell stocks just because they have gone up; cutting your losses and letting your profits run is a basic strategy for superior long-term performance.

But if your research turns up another quality company at a low price/ growth-flow ratio, the expected future rate of return on the new idea is almost certainly substantially higher than the expected future return on the comfortable current investment. Selling one to buy the other will improve the future rate of return on your portfolio and keep you in tune with the most attractive areas. Imagine how prescient your friends will think you are when your new idea also works out!

You can also make an *absolute* decision that a stock needs to be sold, even if you do not have another immediate use for the proceeds. Sometimes you will be selling winners. If the price/growth-flow ratio gets as high as the growth rate, sell. Everyone who wants to own that stock already owns it.

We do not advocate selling half a position if a stock doubles—stocks do not know where you bought them. But if a stock grows to be more than one-third of a ten-stock portfolio, trim it back and reinvest the proceeds in one or more of the most-attractive other holdings.

Sometimes, unfortunately, you will be selling losers. Never make the mistake of saying, "I can't afford to take the loss." You already took the loss when the stock went down. You just have not converted the loss to a tax savings; to do that, you have to sell.

We do not sell stocks just because they go down. We don't buy stocks and immediately put on a stop-loss point. If a stock is attractive on a price/growth-flow analysis, then it is more attractive at a lower price.

But we do sell stocks that do not meet our fundamental expectations. For example, stocks often get depressed when a product is late. We may buy it after the decline, but we want to see management execute their plan and get the product out on the revised schedule. If they have a second miss, we evaluate the new, undoubtedly lower price of the stock in light of the twice-delayed schedule. You simply have to forget you have lost money in the stock, or even own it. You have to ask, "If I were looking at this stock for the first time today, would I buy it?" If not, sell it.

If management lies to you, sell the stock. If the chief financial officer quits just before earnings are due to come out, sell or buy a protective put. If the chief executive officer suddenly resigns without a replacement identified, sell. The new CEO is certain to reorganize and write off everything he can blame on the old management. If the auditors resign due to accounting disagreements with management, sell.

As of the fifteenth of each month, the major exchanges collect short-interest data. Short-interest data for stocks on the New York Stock Exchange and the American Stock Exchange are published about the twenty-second of each month. NASDAQ short-sale data comes out about the twenty-fifth.

The ratio of a stock's short interest to its average daily trading volume is the short-interest ratio. It is the number of days of volume that would have to be bought to cover the entire short interest. A typical short-interest ratio is 6.0, or short interest equal to six days of average volume. When the short-interest ratio gets over 12 or 15 days, something is up. If the company is involved in a takeover or has a large convertible bond, the high short interest may be harmless arbitrage. But if you see the short-interest ratio climbing to over 15, 20, 25 days without any obvious explanation, sell. Somebody has a strong reason to believe your stock is headed for trouble.

Bulls on the stock will tell you that high short interest is a positive, because it represents stock that has to be bought back and a source of future demand for the stock. Do not believe them. Academic research shows that short sellers do their homework. Heavily shorted stocks tend to underperform other stocks, as the bad news short sellers anticipated starts to come out.

Sources of Information

If you do business with a full-service broker, get a copy of its coverage list for technology stocks. Wall Street provides good industry research; request a few copies of industry studies. Large wirehouses like Merrill Lynch can bury you in useful paper.

If you need more extensive information, consider opening a second account with a brokerage firm that specializes in technology, like Hambrecht & Quist or DB Alex. Brown. Big-ticket retail accounts are welcome at some primarily institutional firms like Nationsbank Montgomery Securities; BancBoston Robertson, Stephens & Co.; Goldman Sachs; and Morgan Stanley Dean Witter. Some smaller firms like L. H. Alton & Co. and First Security Van Kasper are primarily retail and emphasize technology stocks.

If you use a discount broker, you need your own research sources. Most important is the investor-relations person at any company you take an interest in. Companies know exactly how to get to institutional investors. They call a few brokerage-firm analysts, schedule management lunches, host analyst conference calls, and maintain a fax list of interested buy-side analysts. But they do not have a clue how to get to individuals. Yet they like individual holders, who tend to have a longer-term outlook and are less likely to act like sheep if one analyst cuts an estimate ten cents per share. Investor-relations people are hired to help you. In fact, if you do not call, they might get fired. You wouldn't want that to happen!

Companies will send you background literature, copies of brokerage-firm reports (giving you an idea where you could open an account if you want close coverage), management presentations, and so on. They can tell you which trade publications do the best job of covering their industry, if you want to do some in-depth reading. Of course, most companies have good Web sites filled with press releases, technical papers, and product information.

In addition to the resources listed in Chapter 3, the technology pages in *The Wall Street Journal* and *Investor's Business Daily* are excellent. The Tuesday science page in *The San Jose Mercury News* is useful, and the Sunday edition covers computing in some detail.

There is a tremendous amount of information available on the Internet, both on the World Wide Web and in the Usenet discussion groups. There are several technology-stock discussion groups. Almost every stock has a separate discussion thread, and while most of the postings are not useful, a surprising number of professionals, sophisticated outsiders, customers, and suppliers contribute valuable tidbits.

You also will find discussion groups on the macroeconomic issues that can affect your portfolio: interest-rate increases, the economic outlook, mutual-fund cash flows, and the like. The very technology we invest in is making our job easier every day—and you can now manage your money effectively from any vacation spot in the world.

## CHAPTER EIGHTEEN

Blue Chips 2010

In 1939, Dow Jones & Co., the keepers of the Dow Jones Industrial Average, decided to drop one company from the DJIA and replace it with another, on the grounds that the dropped company seemed to have a niche market and was not representative of U.S. industry. The dropped company was International Business Machines. By the time Dow Jones & Co. put Big Blue back in the blue-chip index in 1979, forty years later, the DJIA would have been almost twice as high if it never had been taken out.

The thirty stocks in the DJIA are the best guess of a small group of people on where American industry is trending. In 1997, the keepers of the flame dropped Bethlehem Steel, Texaco, Westinghouse, and Woolworth in favor of Travelers, Wal-Mart, Johnson & Johnson, and Hewlett-Packard. Five technology companies in all—Johnson & Johnson, Merck, Hewlett-Packard, IBM and, arguably, AT&T—comprise the full tech complement in the Dow Jones, just 16.7 percent of the thirty DJIA stocks.

By the year 2010, we think half or more of the Dow Jones Average will be technology stocks. This chapter examines thirty stocks our research indicates will be blue chips in 2010; at least ten of these should be added to the Dow by then. Of the Great Growth-Flow stocks, these are the greatest, yet even these get cheap enough to buy from time to time.

For each stock, the upper-left box includes the name, symbol, address, and contact information, including a Web site, if any. You should "bookmark" the Web site of any company you are interested in or own; Web sites are one of the best new resources available to individual investors. We have also listed the chief executive officer and the investor-relations contact.

Never hesitate to pick up the phone and give those nice investor relations folks a call about any question you have or information you need. They are paid to help you.

The business description in the upper-right box summarizes the company's major activities and position in relation to its competitors. To build a diversified portfolio, buy stocks in companies in unrelated businesses during periods when they are out of favor on Wall Street.

Next, we show a five-year price and volume chart. This details where the stock has traded and, looking at periods of high volume, at about what price many current holders may have bought the stock. Stocks that are below a high-volume point often run into resistance as they climb back from a lower point because current holders may sell when they break even. Conversely, stocks that are above a high-volume point usually find some support if they subsequently decline back to that point. Investors who bought some of the stock may double up; others who missed it entirely will take advantage of their second opportunity.

The next table, covering the last five years' financial results, has the data you need to identify and track a Great Growth-Flow company. The sales history includes the compound annual growth rate (CAGR) over the period, which should be 15 percent or better. R&D is shown in dollars, to get a feel for the size of the research effort, and as a percentage of sales: 7 percent is a minimum.

Net income is shown in dollars, as a compound-growth rate and as a percentage of sales. This figure should be over 15 percent.

In addition to annual earnings per share, we have shown the crucial annual growth flow per share, adding R&D per share to earnings. Below the stock's annual high, low, and close we have calculated the price/growth flow ratio (P/GF) at those prices.

Book value can be important in periods of stock-price weakness. The return on equity should be above 15 percent to qualify the company as a Great Growth-Flow candidate. The number of employees is a useful indication of the size of the enterprise.

In the lower left of each table are a variety of risk measures, including the Downside Risk Value described in Chapter 16. The balance-sheet information in the lower right includes the company's

- current ratio, or current assets divided by current liabilities, a measure of liquidity;
- debt/equity ratio, a measure of financial stability;
- cash and cash per share; and
- the number of days of sales that are in accounts receivable, a measure of how quickly customers are paying their bills.

Adaptec

(ADPT - OTC)
Address: 691 S. Milpitas Blvd.
Milpitas, CA 95035
Phone: (408) 945-8600
Fax: (408) 262-2533
Web: www.adaptec.com
CEO: Robert Stephens
Inv. Relations: Sandra O'Halloran

Business

Fabless semiconductor supplier of high-performance disk drive and other input/output controllers. SCSI (Small Computer Systems Interface) specialist. Also sells controller boards and networking interfaces. Competes with QLogic and LSI Logic.

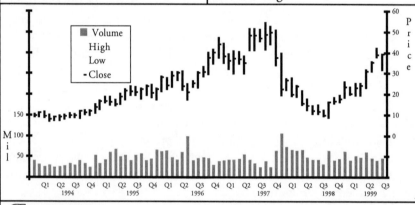

ⓒ adaptec

Recent Results (Fiscal Year : Mar)

	2000 Q1	1999	1998	1997	1996	CAGR%
Sales ($M)	192.4	692.4	1,007.3	933.9	659.4	3.9%
R & D ($M)	24.5	146.2	172.5	128.5	87.6	
R & D % of Sales	12.7%	21.1%	17.1%	13.8%	13.3%	
Pretax Income ($M)	66.7	20.9	236.3	171.8	138.0	17.9%
Pretax % of Sales	34.7%	3.0%	23.5%	18.4%	20.9%	
Earnings Per Share	0.44	-0.12	1.46	0.93	0.94	
Growth Flow Per Share	0.66	1.21	2.92	2.05	1.74	11.1%
Stock High	35.63	25.88	53.19	41.13	24.19	
Low	19.75	8.69	19.63	17.50	10.88	
Close	35.31	22.81	19.63	40.00	20.50	
P/GF High	53.7	21.4	18.2	20.1	13.9	
Low	29.8	7.2	6.7	8.5	6.2	
Book Value	6.74	7.18	7.94	6.17	4.69	
Return On Equity	9.0%	2.6%	26.1%	25.0%	27.0%	
Employees	2,200	2,123	3,500	2,794	2,211	

Risk Measures

Price / Sales Ratio : 5.0x
Price / Book Ratio : 5.2x
# of Employees : 2,200
Market Cap. / Employee : $1.8 M
Sales / Employee : $175,000

L12M Low : $7 7/8
% To Low : -77.7%
Downside Risk Value : $6.21
% Chg. to DRV : -82.4%
Insider Buy / Sell : 1 / 8

Balance Sheet

Current Ratio : 5.8x
Debt / Equity : 20%
Cash : $733.7M
Cash / Share : $6.69
Days Sales Outstanding : 53

Adobe Systems

(ADBE - OTC)

Address: 345 Park Avenue
San Jose, CA 95110
Phone: (408) 536-6000
Fax: (408) 537-6000
Web: www.adobe.com
CEO: John E. Warnock
Inv. Relations: Mike Saviage

Business

Computer software. Leader in desktop publishing (PageMaker, InDesign) and graphics arts (Illustrator, PhotoShop). Also a power in multimedia (Premier) and on the Internet (PageMill, SiteMill, Acrobat). Competes with Quark and Microsoft in publishing, Macromedia in multimedia.

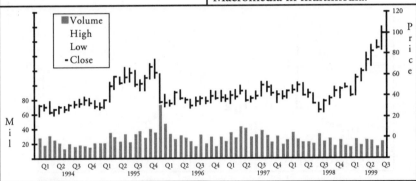

Recent Results

(Fiscal Year : Nov)

	1999 H1	1998	1997	1996	1995	CAGR%
Sales ($M)	472.8	894.8	911.9	786.6	762.3	5.5%
R & D ($M)	92.5	207.3	170.9	152.9	138.6	
R & D % of Sales	19.6%	23.2%	18.7%	19.4%	18.2%	
Pretax Income ($M)	131.1	167.7	296.1	244.8	163.9	12.5%
Pretax % of Sales	27.7%	18.7%	32.5%	31.1%	21.5%	
Earnings Per Share	1.30	1.55	2.52	2.04	1.26	
Growth Flow Per Share	2.75	4.60	4.82	4.08	3.13	15.2%
Stock High	80.25	50.75	51.98	64.50	74.14	
Low	37.38	24.44	32.83	28.50	27.25	
Close	74.13	44.75	42.00	37.38	62.00	
P/GF High	29.2	11.0	10.8	15.8	23.7	
Low	13.6	5.3	6.8	7.0	8.7	
Book Value	9.00	7.60	10.40	9.41	9.41	
Return On Equity	14.4%	20.4%	24.2%	21.7%	13.4%	
Employees	2,400	2,664	2,702	2,266	2,322	

Risk Measures

Price / Sales Ratio : 5.0x
Price / Book Ratio : 8.2x
# of Employees (1996) : 2,400
Market Cap. / Employee : $2.0M
Sales / Employee : $394,000

L12M Low : $28
% To Low : -62.2%
Downside Risk Value : $10.93
% Chg. to DRV : -85.3%
Insider Buy / Sell : 0 / 16

Balance Sheet

Current Ratio : 1.1x
Debt / Equity : 0.0%
Cash : $326.5M
Cash / Share : $5.11
Days Sales Outstanding : 55

Altera

(ALTR - OTC)

Address: 101 Innovation Drive
San Jose, CA 95134-2020
Phone: (408) 544-7000
Fax: (408) 428-0463
Web: www.altera.com
CEO: Rodney Smith
Investor Relations: Lance Lissner

Business

Fabless semiconductor manufacturer of programmable-logic circuits and related circuit-design software for rapid prototyping and shorter time to market. Sells to computer, communications, military. Competes with Xilinx, Lattice Semiconductor, and QuickLogic.

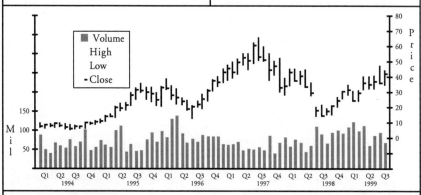

Recent Results (Fiscal Year: Dec)

	1999 H1	1998	1997	1996	1995	CAGR%
Sales ($M)	384.2	654.3	631.1	497.3	401.6	17.6%
R & D ($M)	36.9	59.9	54.4	49.5	33.9	
R & D % of Sales	9.6%	9.1%	8.6%	10.0%	8.4%	
Pretax Income ($M)	150.4	233.7	229.6	169.1	137.9	21.5%
Pretax % of Sales	39.2%	35.7%	36.4%	34.0%	34.3%	
Earnings Per Share	0.48	0.82	0.77	0.58	0.48	
Growth Flow Per Share	0.66	1.11	1.04	0.83	0.67	18.6%
Stock High	40.31	30.44	32.44	19.44	17.44	
Low	24.31	14.41	15.28	7.00	5.06	
Close	36.81	30.44	16.81	18.19	12.44	
P/GF High	61.2	27.3	31.3	23.5	26.2	
Low	36.9	12.9	14.8	8.5	7.6	
Book Value	4.97	4.34	2.62	1.84	1.40	
Return On Equity	9.7%	18.9%	29.4%	31.6%	34.3%	
Employees	1,108	1,151	1,086	918	881	

Risk Measures

Price / Sales Ratio : 9.9x
Price / Book Ratio : 7.4x
# of Employees : 1,108
Market Cap. / Employee : $6.8 M
Sales / Employee : $693,000

L12M Low : $14 3/4
% To Low : -59.9%
Downside Risk Value : $5.67
% Chg. to DRV : -84.6%
Insider Buy / Sell : 0 / 11

Balance Sheet

Current Ratio : 4.5x
Debt / Equity : 0.0%
Cash : $675.8M
Cash / Share : $3.28
Days Sales Outstanding : 31.0

America Online

(AOL - NYSE)

Address: 22000 AOL Way
Dulles, VA 20166
Phone: (703) 448-8700
Fax: (703) 265-2384
Web: www.aol.com
CEO: Steve Case
Inv. Relations: Michael Broder

Business

Leading online service providing interactive communications, online communities and Internet access to nearly twenty million paying customers. Now expanding overseas and providing access to the AOL portal via the Internet at reduced rates.

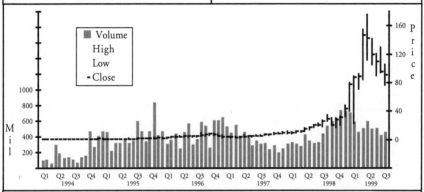

Last Five Years   (Fiscal Year : Jun)

	1999	1998	1997	1996	1995	CAGR%
Sales ($M)	4,777.0	3,091.0	1,685.2	1,093.9	394.3	86.6%
R & D ($M)	286.0	239.0	58.2	43.2	63.2	
R & D % of Sales	6.0%	7.7%	3.5%	3.9%	16.0%	
Pretax Income ($M)	1,096.0	-90.0	-499.4	62.3	-20.6	160.0%
Pretax % of Sales	22.9%	-2.9%	-29.6%	5.7%	-5.2%	
Earnings Per Share	0.73	-0.09	-0.65	0.04	-0.06	
Growth Flow Per Share	0.95	0.17	-0.57	0.09	0.06	103.0%
Stock High	167.50	27.02	7.63	8.75	2.91	
Low	20.48	7.81	2.84	2.77	0.87	
Close	102.81	26.94	6.81	5.47	2.75	
P/GF High	175.6	160.4	-13.3	97.3	51.7	
Low	21.5	46.4	-5.0	30.8	15.5	
Book Value	2.38	1.08	0.17	0.59	0.40	
Return On Equity	30.7%	-8.4%	-380.4%	6.7%	-15.0%	
Employees	12,100	8,500	7,371	5,828	2,481	

Risk Measures

Price / Sales Ratio : 27.5x
Price / Book Ratio : 43.2x
# of Employees : 12,100
Market Cap. / Employee : $10.9 M
Sales / Employee : $395,000

L12M Low : $20 5/8
% To Low : -79.9%
Downside Risk Value : $6.23
% Chg. to DRV : -93.9%
Insider Buy / Sell : 0 / 14

Balance Sheet

Current Ratio : 1.2x
Debt / Equity : 11.5%
Cash : $887.0 M
Cash / Share : $0.69
Days Sales Outstanding : 19.7

Amgen

(AMGN - OTC)

Address: One Amgen Center Drive
Thousand Oaks, CA 91320
Phone: (805) 447-1000
Fax: (805) 447-1010
Web: www.amgen.com
CEO: Gordon Binder
Inv. Relations: Cary Rosansky

Business

Leading biotechnology firm focused on secreted protein and small molecule therapeutics for neuroscience and cancer. Epogen and Neupogen are their primary approved drugs, with numerous research programs, some joint ventured, in a wide range of diseases.

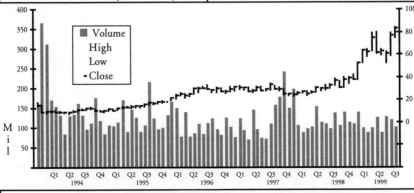

Last Five Years

(Fiscal Year : Dec)

	1999 H1	1998	1997	1996	1995	CAGR%
Sales ($M)	1,566.0	2,718.2	2,401.0	2,239.8	1,939.9	12.7%
R & D ($M)	382.1	663.3	630.8	528.3	451.7	
R & D % of Sales	24.4%	24.4%	26.3%	23.6%	23.3%	
Pretax Income ($M)	728.1	1224.4	861.4	962.3	794.4	14.8%
Pretax % of Sales	46.5%	45.0%	35.9%	43.0%	41.0%	
Earnings Per Share	0.96	1.63	1.17	1.21	0.96	
Growth Flow Per Share	1.67	2.88	2.32	2.15	1.76	17.3%
Stock High	80.00	33.38	34.19	32.75	20.11	
Low	52.31	22.97	25.75	19.63	10.81	
Close	60.88	32.50	29.72	27.00	20.11	
P/GF High	47.9	11.6	14.7	15.2	11.4	
Low	31.3	8.0	11.1	9.1	6.1	
Book Value	5.17	4.85	3.89	3.40	2.98	
Return On Equity	18.6%	33.6%	30.0%	35.6%	32.2%	
Employees	5,494	5,500	5,308	4,646	4,046	

Risk Measures

Price / Sales Ratio : 10.5x
Price / Book Ratio : 11.8x
# of Employees : 5,494
Market Cap. / Employee : $6.0 M
Sales / Employee : $570,000

L12M Low : $33 1/16
% To Low : -45.7%
Downside Risk Value : $7.10
% Chg. to DRV : -88.3%
Insider Buy / Sell : 1 / 18

Balance Sheet

Current Ratio : 2.3x
Debt / Equity : 11.6%
Cash : $1,368.3 M
Cash / Share : $2.54
Days Sales Outstanding : 40

Applied Materials
(AMAT - OTC)
Address: 3050 Bowers Ave.
Santa Clara, CA 95054
Phone: (408) 727-5555
Fax: (408) 748-9943
Web: www.appliedmaterials.com
CEO: James C. Morgan
Inv. Relations: Caroline Schwartz

Business

Largest manufacturer of semiconductor equipment for wafer fabrication, usually #1 or #2 in each niche. Sells and services globally. Competes with entire industry, especially Japanese companies, Lam Research, and Novellus.

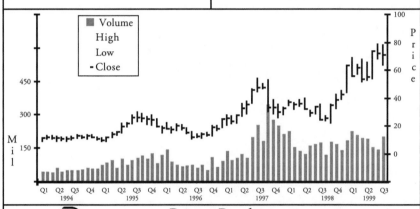

Recent Results (Fiscal Year : Oct)

APPLIED MATERIALS®

	1999 9M	1998	1997	1996	1995	CAGR%
Sales ($M)	3,293.6	4,041.7	4,074.3	4,144.8	3,061.9	9.4%
R & D ($M)	478.5	643.9	567.6	481.4	329.7	
R & D % of Sales	14.5%	15.9%	13.9%	11.6%	10.8%	
Pretax Income ($M)	636.1	437.8	799.0	922.4	698.5	5.0%
Pretax % of Sales	19.3%	10.8%	19.6%	22.3%	22.8%	
Earnings Per Share	1.11	0.61	1.32	1.635	1.28	
Growth Flow Per Share	2.32	2.31	2.82	2.95	2.21	8.8%
Stock High	68.69	39.50	54.00	22.38	29.94	
Low	32.75	22.38	13.06	10.88	9.25	
Close	55.00	34.69	33.38	17.97	19.69	
P/GF High	29.6	17.1	19.1	7.6	13.6	
Low	14.1	9.7	4.6	3.7	4.2	
Book Value	9.30	8.24	7.79	6.45	5.03	
Return On Equity	11.9%	7.4%	17.0%	25.3%	25.5%	
Employees	13,000	12,060	13,924	11,403	10,537	

Risk Measures

Price / Sales Ratio : 4.9x
Price / Book Ratio : 5.9x
# of Employees : 13,000
Market Cap. / Employee : $1.7 M
Sales / Employee : $338,000

L12M Low : $21 9/16
% To Low : -60.8%
Downside Risk Value : $9.57
% Chg. to DRV : -82.6%
Insider Buy / Sell : 0 / 12

Balance Sheet

Current Ratio : 3.2x
Debt / Equity : 18.6%
Cash : $1,764 M
Cash / Share : $4.47
Days Sales Outstanding : 85

Cadence Design Systems

(CDN - NYSE)

Address: 555 River Oaks Pkwy
San Jose, CA 95134
Phone: (408) 943-1234
Fax: (408) 943-0513
Web: www.cadence.com
CEO: Raymond Bingham
Investor Relations: Lisa Eubank

Business

Electronic design automation software. Used by chip and systems designers to create and test new products before committing to silicon. Several packages cover each major step needed by designers. Competes with Mentor Graphics, Synopsys and Avant!.

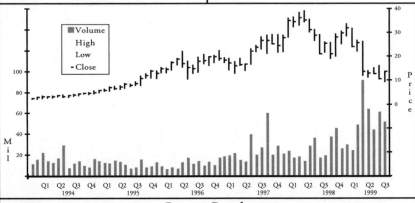

CĀDENCE — Recent Results (Fiscal Year : Dec)

	1999 H1	1998	1997	1996	1995	CAGR%
Sales ($M)	599.4	1,216.1	915.9	741.5	548.4	21.6%
R & D ($M)	101.2	179.4	140.4	115.3	88.6	
R & D % of Sales	16.9%	14.8%	15.3%	15.6%	16.2%	
Pretax Income ($M)	73.3	-21.9	247.4	93.5	136.4	16.2%
Pretax % of Sales	12.2%	-1.8%	27.0%	12.6%	24.9%	
Earnings Per Share	0.19	-0.47	0.77	0.16	0.52	
Growth Flow Per Share	0.58	0.38	1.41	0.79	1.00	3.8%
Stock High	33.50	38.00	28.75	22.19	14.13	
Low	11.31	19.19	13.38	10.69	4.28	
Close	12.63	29.75	24.50	19.75	14.00	
P/GF High	57.8	101.0	20.4	28.2	14.1	
Low	19.5	51.0	9.5	13.6	4.3	
Book Value	4.03	3.42	3.31	2.30	0.79	
Return On Equity	4.7%	-13.7%	23.2%	7.0%	65.8%	
Employees	4,000	4,200	3,945	3,190	3,028	

Risk Measures

Price / Sales Ratio : 2.7x
Price / Book Ratio : 3.1x
# of Employees : 4,000
Market Cap. / Employee : $0.8 M
Sales / Employee : $300,000

L12M Low : $9 3/16
% To Low : -27.3%
Downside Risk Value : $5.98
% Chg. to DRV : -52.7%
Insider Buy / Sell : 2 / 4

Balance Sheet

Current Ratio : 1.6x
Debt / Equity : 0.3%
Cash : $226.0 M
Cash / Share : $0.87
Days Sales Outstanding : 72

Cisco Systems

(CSCO - OTC)

Address: 170 W. Tasman Dr.
San Jose, CA 95134
Phone: (408) 526-4000
Fax: (408) 526-4100
Web: www.cisco.com
CEO: John Chambers
Inv. Relations: Mary Thurber

Business

Leading router manufacturer for networks; also sells intelligent switches and a broad range of connectivity solutions, covering most major protocols. Largest company in the center of the network. Competes with Lucent, Nortel, 3Com, Newbridge.

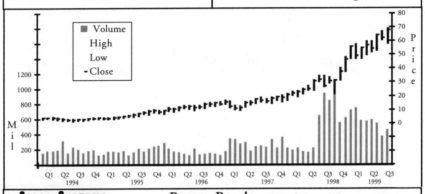

CISCO SYSTEMS	Recent Results	(Fiscal Year : Jul)				
	1999	**1998**	**1997**	**1996**	**1995**	**CAGR%**
Sales ($M)	12,154.0	8,458.8	6,440.2	4,096.0	2,232.7	52.7%
R & D ($M)	1,594.0	1,020.4	698.2	399.3	210.8	
R & D % of Sales	13.1%	12.1%	10.8%	9.7%	9.4%	
Pretax Income ($M)	3,803.0	2,890.8	1,888.9	1,464.8	738.4	50.6%
Pretax % of Sales	31.3%	34.2%	29.3%	35.8%	33.1%	
Earnings Per Share	0.75	0.58	0.46	0.30	0.19	
Growth Flow Per Share	1.22	1.54	1.14	0.70	0.41	31.1%
Stock High	67.06	34.39	60.58	46.08	29.80	
Low	21.94	45.50	30.17	21.30	10.80	
Close	62.13	31.92	55.75	42.42	24.88	
P/GF High	55.0	22.4	53.4	65.6	72.2	
Low	18.0	29.6	26.6	30.3	26.2	
Book Value	3.44	6.63	4.15	2.86	1.69	
Return On Equity	21.8%	8.8%	11.1%	10.6%	11.2%	
Employees	18,700	15,000	11,000	8,782	4,086	

Risk Measures

Price / Sales Ratio : 17.4x
Price / Book Ratio : 18.1x
# of Employees : 18,700
Market Cap. / Employee : $11.3 M
Sales / Employee : $650,000

L12M Low : $20 9/16
% To Low : -66.9%
Downside Risk Value : $7.31
% Chg. to DRV : -88.2%
Insider Buy / Sell : 1 / 12

Balance Sheet

Current Ratio : 1.8x
Debt / Equity : 0.0%
Cash : $2,016.0M
Cash / Share : $0.59
Days Sales Outstanding : 53

Cypress Semiconductor	Business
(CY - NYSE)	Semiconductor manufacturer; owns
Address: 3901 N. First St.	its fabrication facilities. About 1/3
San Jose, CA 95134	SRAM, mostly high-speed, and 2/3
Phone: (408) 943-2600	logic, including programmable logic
Fax: (408) 943-2796	and microcontrollers. Also fast
Web: www.cypress.com	EPROMs and communications
CEO: T. J. Rogers	chips. Competes with Integrated
Inv. Relations: Joe McCarthy	Device Technology and Altera.

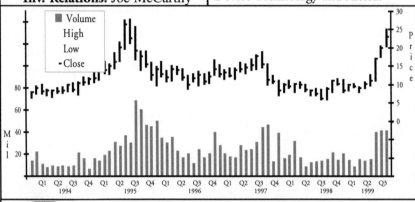

Recent Results (Fiscal Year : Dec)

	1999 H1	1998	1997	1996	1995	CAGR%
Sales ($M)	313.1	486.8	544.4	528.4	596.1	1.2%
R & D ($M)	63.3	99.5	93.8	84.3	71.7	
R & D % of Sales	20.2%	20.4%	17.2%	16.0%	12.0%	
Pretax Income ($M)	18.1	-125.6	24.0	83.5	161.4	NM
Pretax % of Sales	5.8%	-25.8%	4.4%	15.8%	27.1%	
Earnings Per Share	0.17	-1.24	0.21	0.62	1.09	
Growth Flow Per Share	0.77	-0.13	1.20	1.54	1.82	NM
Stock High	17.13	11.63	18.56	16.06	27.75	
Low	8.06	6.06	7.75	9.50	10.75	
Close	17.13	8.31	8.38	14.13	12.63	
P/GF High	22.2	-92.0	15.4	10.4	15.2	
Low	10.4	-48.0	6.5	6.2	5.9	
Book Value	5.42	5.47	6.80	5.58	4.84	
Return On Equity	3.1%	-22.7%	3.1%	11.1%	22.5%	
Employees	2,500	2,901	2,770	1,859	1,423	

Risk Measures		Balance Sheet
Price / Sales Ratio : 2.9x	L12M Low : $7 3/8	Current Ratio : 2.6x
Price / Book Ratio : 3.2x	% To Low : -56.9%	Debt / Equity : 28.1%
# of Employees : 2,500	Downside Risk Value : $4.71	Cash : $168.4 M
Market Cap. / Employee : $0.7 M	% Chg. to DRV : -72.5%	Cash / Share : $1.60
Sales / Employee : $250,000	Insider Buy / Sell : 0 / 4	Days Sales Outstanding : 47

Hewlett-Packard

(HWP - NYSE)

Address: 3000 Hanover St.
Palo Alto, CA 94304
Phone: (650) 857-1501
Fax: (650) 857-3258
Web: www.hp.com
CEO: Cara Fiorina
Inv. Relations: Marlene Somsak

Business

Second largest U.S. computer company with UNIX and NT products from mainframe to desktop. Large peripherals business, especially printers and fax/copiers. Competes with IBM, Digital Equipment, Sun. Intel's partner on future microprocessors.

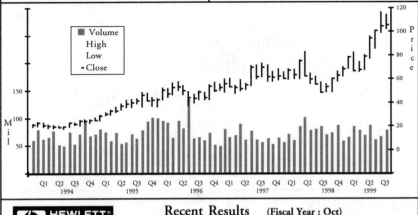

Recent Results (Fiscal Year : Oct)

	1999 9M	1998	1997	1996	1995	CAGR%
Sales ($M)	36,590.0	47,061.0	42,895.0	38,420.0	31,519.0	11.5%
R & D ($M)	2,533.0	3,355.0	3,078.0	2,718.0	2,302.0	
R & D % of Sales	6.9%	7.1%	7.2%	7.1%	7.3%	
Pretax Income ($M)	3,741.0	4,091.0	4,455.0	3,694.0	3,632.0	8.2%
Pretax % of Sales	10.2%	8.7%	10.4%	9.6%	11.5%	
Earnings Per Share	2.61	2.77	2.95	2.46	2.32	
Growth Flow Per Share	5.01	5.90	5.86	5.04	4.51	10.3%
Stock High	116.25	81.63	71.56	57.69	48.31	
Low	57.81	48.56	43.13	36.81	24.50	
Close	112.25	60.25	61.63	50.25	41.88	
P/GF High	23.2	13.8	12.2	11.4	10.7	
Low	11.5	8.2	7.4	7.3	5.4	
Book Value	18.04	15.78	15.28	12.77	11.25	
Return On Equity	14.5%	17.6%	19.3%	19.3%	20.6%	
Employees	123,000	124,600	121,900	112,000	102,300	

Risk Measures

Price / Sales Ratio : 2.4x
Price / Book Ratio : 6.2x
# of Employees : 123,000
Market Cap. / Employee : $1.0 M
Sales / Employee : $397,000

L12M Low : $37 7/16
% To Low : -66.6%
Downside Risk Value : $28.83
% Chg. to DRV : -74.3%
Insider Buy / Sell : 1 / 24

Balance Sheet

Current Ratio : 3.2x
Debt / Equity : 3.1%
Cash : $6,106 M
Cash / Share : $5.79
Days Sales Outstanding : 48

Informix	Business
(IFMX - OTC) **Address:** 4100 Bohannon Drive Menlo Park, CA 94025 **Phone:** (650) 926-6300 **Fax:** (650) 926-6593 **Web:** www.informix.com **CEO:** Jean-Yves Dexmier **Inv. Relations:** Kate Patterson	Second largest relational database-management software producer for personal, mini and mainframe computers. Most advanced object-relational and data warehousing packages. Competes with industry leader Oracle, IBM, Sybase, Microsoft and Object Design.

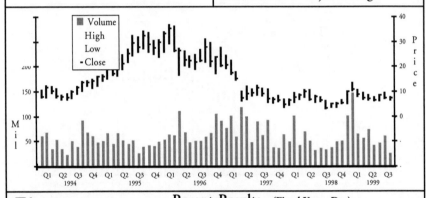

INFORMIX

Recent Results (Fiscal Year : Dec)

	1999 H1	1998	1997	1996	1995	CAGR%
Sales ($M)	403.4	735.0	663.9	727.9	632.8	6.3%
R & D ($M)	79.3	146.3	139.3	120.2	85.6	
R & D % of Sales	19.7%	19.9%	21.0%	16.5%	13.5%	
Pretax Income ($M)	29.8	62.1	-349.1	-61.0	70.7	15.1%
Pretax % of Sales	7.4%	8.5%	-52.6%	-8.4%	11.2%	
Earnings Per Share	0.13	0.30	-2.32	-0.48	0.03	
Growth Flow Per Share	0.54	1.14	-1.40	0.29	0.65	37.2%
Stock High	13.38	10.06	24.00	36.75	34.38	
Low	6.50	3.50	4.06	16.88	14.56	
Close	8.53	9.88	4.75	20.38	30.00	
P/GF High	24.8	8.8	NM	125.6	53.2	
Low	12.1	3.1	NM	57.7	22.5	
Book Value	1.23	1.20	0.39	2.09	2.58	
Return On Equity	12.5%	29.9%	NM	NM	19.8%	
Employees	3,950	3,984	3,489	4,491	3,219	

Risk Measures	Balance Sheet
Price / Sales Ratio : 2.1x Price / Book Ratio : 6.9x # of Employees : 3,950 Market Cap. / Employee : $0.4 M Sales / Employee : $204,000	L12M Low : $3 3/4 % To Low : -56.0% Downside Risk Value : $2.27 % Chg. to DRV : -73.4% Insider Buy / Sell : 2 / 2	Current Ratio : 1.2x Debt / Equity : 0.0% Cash : $205.8 M Cash / Share : $1.06 Days Sales Outstanding : 82

Intel

(INTC - OTC)

Address: 2200 Mission College
Santa Clara, CA 94088
Phone: (408) 765-8080
Fax: (408) 765-1821
Web: www.intel.com
CEO: Craig Barrett
Investor Relations: Lisa Ansilio

Business

The leading microprocessor producer with a large business in assembling motherboards. Also produces microcontrollers, network and communication hardware, and parallel supercomputers. Competes with Motorola, Sun, Advanced Micro Devices, and Via (Taiwan).

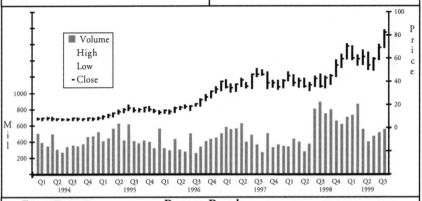

intel.   Recent Results   (Fiscal Year: Dec)

	1999 H1	1998	1997	1996	1995	CAGR%
Sales ($M)	13,849.0	26,273.0	25,070.0	20,847.0	16,202.0	14.3%
R & D ($M)	1,394.0	2,509.0	2,347.0	1,808.0	1,296.0	
R & D % of Sales	10.1%	9.5%	9.4%	8.7%	8.0%	
Pretax Income ($M)	5,594.0	9,137.0	10,659.0	7,934.0	5,638.0	18.7%
Pretax % of Sales	40.4%	34.8%	42.5%	38.1%	34.8%	
Earnings Per Share	1.08	1.73	1.93	1.45	1.01	
Growth Flow Per Share	1.48	2.44	2.58	1.96	1.38	21.1%
Stock High	70.47	62.50	51.00	35.38	19.59	
Low	50.50	32.97	31.44	12.46	7.88	
Close	59.50	59.28	35.13	32.74	14.38	
P/GF High	47.5	25.6	19.7	18.1	14.2	
Low	34.1	13.5	12.2	6.4	5.7	
Book Value	7.36	6.63	5.37	4.75	3.43	
Return On Equity	22.0%	39.2%	55.2%	47.0%	46.4%	
Employees	65,300	64,500	63,700	48,500	41,600	

Risk Measures

Price / Sales Ratio : 7.4x
Price / Book Ratio : 8.1x
# of Employees : 65,300
Market Cap. / Employee : $3.2 M
Sales / Employee : $424,000

L12M Low : $37 7/8
% To Low : -36.3%
Downside Risk Value : $9.72
% Chg. to DRV : -83.7%
Insider Buy / Sell : 1 / 13

Balance Sheet

Current Ratio : 3.2x
Debt / Equity : 3.1%
Cash : $10,609 B
Cash / Share : $3.06
Days Sales Outstanding : 48

Lam Research

(LRCX - OTC)

Address: 4650 Cushing Pkwy
Fremont, CA 94538
Phone: (510) 659-0200
Fax: (510) 572-6454
Web: www.lamrc.com
CEO: James W. Bagley
Investor Relations: Kathleen Bela

Business

Manufacturer of semiconductor equipment, specializing in depositing chemical films, etching chips, cleaning, chemical mechanical polishing. Sells and supports worldwide. Competes with Applied Materials, Tokyo Electron, Novellus, Mattson and Speedfam.

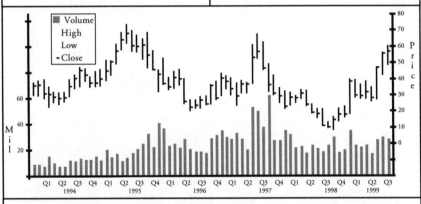

Recent Results (Fiscal Year: Jun)

Lam RESEARCH	1999	1998	1997	1996	1995	CAGR%
Sales ($M)	648.0	1,050.5	1,073.2	1,276.9	810.6	-5.4%
R & D ($M)	142.5	206.5	192.3	173.0	127.8	
R & D % of Sales	22.0%	19.7%	17.9%	13.5%	15.8%	
Pretax Income ($M)	-112.9	-179.1	-51.7	209.0	127.4	#NUM!
Pretax % of Sales	-17.4%	-17.1%	-4.8%	16.4%	15.7%	
Earnings Per Share	-2.93	-3.08	-0.83	4.92	3.27	
Growth Flow Per Share	0.77	2.34	4.38	10.51	7.49	-43.3%
Stock High	46.69	66.31	41.38	52.50	73.38	
Low	8.81	19.13	20.75	20.00	35.25	
Close	46.69	19.13	37.06	28.13	45.75	
P/GF High	60.5	28.3	9.5	5.0	9.8	
Low	11.4	8.2	4.7	1.9	4.7	
Book Value	10.62	13.74	17.54	19.71	13.05	
Return On Equity	-27.6%	-22.4%	-4.7%	25.0%	25.1%	
Employees	2,700	3,300	4,500	4,500	3,600	

Risk Measures

Price / Sales Ratio : 2.8x
Price / Book Ratio : 4.4x
# of Employees : 3,600
Market Cap. / Employee : $0.7 M
Sales / Employee : $240,000

L12M Low : $8 3/8
% To Low : -82.1%
Downside Risk Value : $10.42
% Chg. to DRV : -76.6%
Insider Buy / Sell : 0 / 1

Balance Sheet

Current Ratio : 3.4x
Debt / Equity : 87.2%
Cash : $372.2 M
Cash / Share : $9.67
Days Sales Outstanding : 71

Linear Technology

(LLTC - OTC)

Address: 1630 McCarthy Blvd.
Milpitas, Ca 95035
Phone: (408) 432-1900
Fax: (408) 434-0507
Web: www.linear-tech.com
CEO: Robert Swanson
Investor Relations: Paul Coghlan

Business

Fabless semiconductor producer specializing in linear or analog applications that interface with the real world: sound, temperature, pressure, power management. Competes with Analog Devices, Maxim, Burr-Brown and Exar.

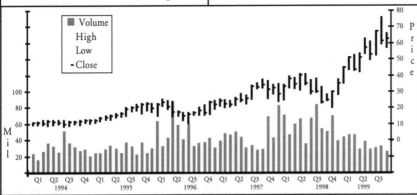

Recent Results (Fiscal Year : Jun)

	1999	1998	1997	1996	1995	CAGR%
Sales ($M)	506.7	484.8	379.3	377.8	265.0	17.6%
R & D ($M)	53.2	46.2	34.1	31.1	23.9	
R & D % of Sales	10.5%	9.5%	9.0%	8.2%	9.0%	
Pretax Income ($M)	285.7	271.3	204.5	203.9	128.5	22.1%
Pretax % of Sales	56.4%	56.0%	53.9%	54.0%	48.5%	
Earnings Per Share	1.22	1.13	0.86	0.86	0.56	
Growth Flow Per Share	1.56	1.42	1.07	1.06	0.71	21.6%
Stock High	67.25	20.13	28.13	25.13	22.82	
Low	20.50	12.94	21.13	10.88	11.50	
Close	67.25	15.08	25.88	21.94	19.63	
P/GF High	43.2	14.2	26.2	23.7	32.1	
Low	13.2	9.1	19.7	10.3	16.2	
Book Value	5.29	4.73	3.75	2.83	2.02	
Return On Equity	46.2%	23.9%	45.6%	30.4%	27.5%	
Employees	2,155	2,155	1,638	1,638	1,350	

Risk Measures

Price / Sales Ratio : 21.1x
Price / Book Ratio : 12.7
# of Employees : 2,155
Market Cap. / Employee : $5.0 M
Sales / Employee : $235,000

L12M Low : $19 9/16
% To Low : -85.8%
Downside Risk Value : $6.11
% Chg. to DRV : -90.9%
Insider Buy / Sell : 0 / 13

Balance Sheet

Current Ratio : 7.6x
Debt / Equity : 0.0%
Cash : $695.3 M
Cash / Share : $4.37
Days Sales Outstanding : 50

LSI Logic

(LSI - NYSE)

Address: 1551 McCarthy Blvd.
Milpitas, CA 95035
Phone: (408) 433-8000
Fax: (408) 954-3773
Web: www.lsilogic.com
CEO: Wilf Corrigan
Investor Relations: Diana Matley

Business

High-capacity custom semiconductors designed with high-density library functions. Owns fabrication facilities. Offers application-specific and standard parts to customers designing personal computers, medical instruments, and data communications. Competes with Motorola in system-on-a-chip and several Japanese manufacturers.

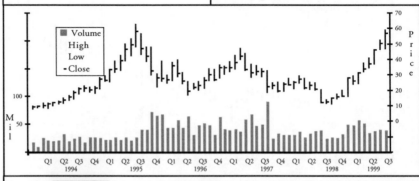

Recent Results (Fiscal Year : Dec)

LSI LOGIC

	1999 H1	1998	1997	1996	1995	CAGR%
Sales ($M)	964.6	1,490.7	1,290.3	1,238.7	1,267.7	11.1%
R & D ($M)	151.6	286.0	226.2	184.5	123.9	
R & D % of Sales	15.7%	19.2%	17.5%	14.9%	9.8%	
Pretax Income ($M)	23.0	-198.8	224.2	205.1	334.9	-39.1%
Pretax % of Sales	2.4%	-13.3%	17.4%	16.6%	26.4%	
Earnings Per Share	0.10	-1.47	1.11	1.07	1.75	
Growth Flow Per Share	1.11	0.56	2.68	2.36	2.64	-4.1%
Stock High	46.19	29.00	46.88	39.63	62.50	
Low	16.13	11.13	18.63	17.00	18.25	
Close	46.13	16.13	19.63	26.75	32.75	
P/GF High	41.5	51.6	17.5	16.8	23.7	
Low	14.5	19.8	6.9	7.2	6.9	
Book Value	9.93	10.19	11.17	9.24	8.75	
Return On Equity	1.0%	-14.4%	9.9%	11.6%	20.0%	
Employees	5,500	6,420	4,443	3,912	3,870	

Risk Measures

Price / Sales Ratio : 3.6x
Price / Book Ratio : 4.6x
# of Employees : 5,500
Market Cap. / Employee : $1.3 M
Sales / Employee : $351,000

L12M Low : $10 1/2
% To Low : -77.2%
Downside Risk Value : $10.00
% Chg. to DRV : -78.3%
Insider Buy / Sell : 0 / 0

Balance Sheet

Current Ratio : 2.1x
Debt / Equity : 59.1%
Cash : $345.2 M
Cash / Share : $2.31
Days Sales Outstanding : 56

Macromedia

(MACR - OTC)

Address: 600 Townsend Street
San Francisco, CA 94103
Phone: (415) 252-2000
Fax: (415) 626-0554
Web: www.macromedia.com
CEO: Robert K. Burgess
Investor Relations: Kimberly Leo

Business

A leader in multimedia presentation software to create and publish on the World Wide Web. Director, AuthorWare, Deck and other programs run on Macintosh or Windows. Developer of Shockwave standard for the Internet. Competes with Adobe Systems and Autodesk.

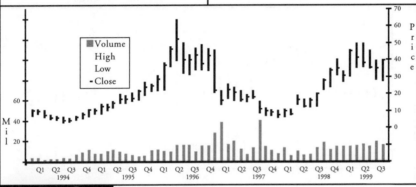

Recent Results (Fiscal Year : Mar)

macromedia	2000 Q1	1999	1998	1997	1996	CAGR%
Sales ($M)	48.9	149.9	113.1	107.4	116.7	13.8%
R & D ($M)	11.3	35.6	32.2	30.0	20.0	
R & D % of Sales	23.0%	23.8%	28.5%	28.0%	17.2%	
Pretax Income ($M)	9.7	27.4	-6.9	-9.4	31.8	5.1%
Pretax % of Sales	19.8%	18.3%	-6.1%	-8.8%	27.2%	
Earnings Per Share	0.15	0.44	-0.16	-0.16	0.59	
Growth Flow Per Share	0.39	1.25	0.69	0.64	1.10	8.9%
Stock High	49.63	45.69	15.00	16.00	53.75	
Low	35.25	12.56	6.50	6.80	14.13	
Close	35.25	45.31	14.88	8.63	18.00	
P/GF High	128.1	36.5	21.9	25.0	48.7	
Low	91.0	10.0	9.5	10.6	12.8	
Book Value	3.41	3.57	3.37	3.52	3.41	
Return On Equity	8.8%	24.7%	-9.5%	-9.1%	17.3%	
Employees	553	553	491	455	396	

Risk Measures

Price / Sales Ratio : 8.5x
Price / Book Ratio : 10.3x
# of Employees : 553
Market Cap. / Employee : $3.0 M
Sales / Employee : $354,000

L12M Low : $12 5/8
% To Low : -64.2%
Downside Risk Value : $3.90
% Chg. to DRV : -89.0%
Insider Buy / Sell : 0 / 11

Balance Sheet

Current Ratio : 3.8x
Debt / Equity : 0.0%
Cash : $112.6 M
Cash / Share : $2.39
Days Sales Outstanding : 25

Mattson Technology

(MTSN - OTC)

Address: 3550 W. Warren Ave.
Fremont, CA 94538
Phone: (510) 657-5900
Fax: (510) 657-0165
Web: www.mattson.com
CEO: Brad Mattson
Investor Relations: Lindsey Mitobe

Business

Semiconductor equipment company with unique robotics platform offering four times the throughput of a single wafer system. Various products in etch, deposition, rapid thermal processing. Competes with Gasonics, Applied Materials, Lam Research, and Novellus.

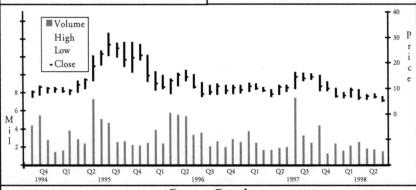

Recent Results (Fiscal Year: Dec)

	1998 H1	1997	1996	1995	1994	CAGR%
Sales ($M)	35.9	76.7	73.3	55.3	19.6	38.4%
R & D ($M)	8.3	14.7	11.5	6.3	2.3	
R & D % of Sales	23.0%	19.2%	15.7%	11.4%	11.8%	
Pretax Income ($M)	-3.4	1.9	9.7	14.5	3.2	-49.1%
Pretax % of Sales	-9.4%	2.5%	13.2%	26.3%	16.6%	
Earnings Per Share	-0.17	0.09	0.42	0.71	0.29	
Growth Flow Per Share	0.41	1.05	1.17	1.14	0.51	36.0%
Stock High	10.00	17.00	17.00	31.63	10.88	
Low	5.13	6.94	7.25	8.00	6.88	
Close	5.25	7.00	9.50	15.00	9.63	
P/GF High	24.6	16.2	14.5	27.8	21.2	
Low	12.6	6.6	6.2	7.0	13.4	
Book Value	4.52	4.45	4.53	4.11	2.74	
Return On Equity	-7.5%	2.0%	9.3%	17.3%	10.6%	
Employees	372	372	298	198	97	

Risk Measures

Price / Sales Ratio : 1.1x
Price / Book Ratio : 0.8x
# of Employees : 372
Market Cap. / Employee : $0.2 M
Sales / Employee : $193,000

L12M Low : $5 1/8
% To Low : -2.4%
Downside Risk Value : $3.93
% Chg. to DRV : -25.2%
Insider Buy / Sell : 0 / 1

Balance Sheet

Current Ratio : 4.5x
Debt / Equity : 0.0%
Cash : $16.2 M
Cash / Share : $1.13
Days Sales Outstanding : 73

Maxim Integrated Products

(MXIM - OTC)

Address: 120 San Gabriel Drive
Sunnyvale, CA 94086
Phone: (408) 737-7600
Fax: (408) 737-7194
Web: www.mxim.com
CEO: Jack F. Gifford
Investor Relations: Richard Slater

Business

Fabless semiconductor producer specializing in linear or analog applications that interface with the real world: sound, temperature, pressure, power management. Competes with Analog Devices, Linear Technology, Burr-Brown, and Exar.

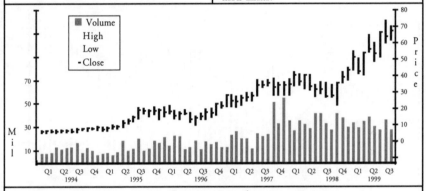

Recent Results (Fiscal Year: Jun)

MAXIM

	1999	1998	1997	1996	1995	CAGR%
Sales ($M)	607.0	560.2	433.7	421.6	250.8	24.7%
R & D ($M)	88.2	72.2	51.3	47.5	42.4	
R & D % of Sales	14.5%	12.9%	11.8%	11.3%	16.9%	
Pretax Income ($M)	297.2	269.9	207.5	190.5	59.9	49.3%
Pretax % of Sales	49.0%	48.2%	47.8%	45.2%	23.9%	
Earnings Per Share	1.29	1.18	0.94	0.87	0.29	
Growth Flow Per Share	1.87	1.66	1.29	1.21	0.61	32.4%
Stock High	66.50	41.63	37.31	24.13	20.94	
Low	22.56	27.63	14.13	10.32	7.07	
Close	66.50	32.00	34.31	21.63	19.25	
P/GF High	35.6	25.1	28.9	20.0	34.4	
Low	12.1	16.6	10.9	8.6	11.6	
Book Value	5.78	4.19	3.19	2.29	1.34	
Return On Equity	29.7%	37.5%	29.4%	37.9%	21.6%	
Employees	3,066	3,066	2,444	1,987	1,552	

Risk Measures

Price / Sales Ratio : 16.7x
Price / Book Ratio : 11.5x
# of Employees : 3,066
Market Cap. / Employee : $3.3 M
Sales / Employee : $198,000

L12M Low : $22 5/16
% To Low : -66.4%
Downside Risk Value : $7.77
% Chg. to DRV : -88.3%
Insider Buy / Sell : 0 / 16

Balance Sheet

Current Ratio : 5.9x
Debt / Equity : 0.0%
Cash : $514.7 M
Cash / Share : $3.38
Days Sales Outstanding : 63

Microchip Technology

(MCHP - OTC)

Address: 2355 W. Chandler Blvd.
Chandler, AZ 85224
Phone: (602) 786-7200
Fax: (602) 899-9210
Web: www.microchip.com
CEO: Steve Sanghi
Inv. Relations: Philip Chapman

Business

Semiconductor manufacturer specializing in 8-bit microcontrollers for embedded control applications. Sells to automotive, computer, communications, industrial, and consumer markets. Competes with National Semiconductor, Motorola, Intel, and Advanced Micro Devices.

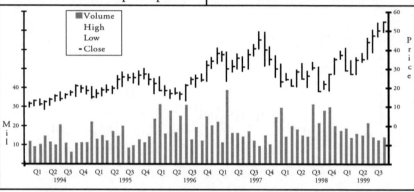

Recent Results (Fiscal Year: Mar)

	2000 Q1	1999	1998	1997	1996	CAGR%
Sales ($M)	107.7	406.5	396.9	334.3	285.9	10.8%
R & D ($M)	10.3	40.8	38.4	32.1	27.5	
R & D % of Sales	9.6%	10.0%	9.7%	9.6%	9.6%	
Pretax Income ($M)	27.7	68.6	88.2	69.5	59.9	16.6%
Pretax % of Sales	25.7%	16.9%	22.2%	20.8%	21.0%	
Earnings Per Share	0.38	1.33	1.14	1.04	0.80	
Growth Flow Per Share	0.57	2.09	1.82	1.63	1.30	15.0%
Stock High	50.44	40.88	45.88	39.50	35.75	
Low	33.69	18.31	32.44	25.00	13.17	
Close	47.38	34.63	21.00	29.75	33.92	
P/GF High	88.3	19.5	25.2	24.3	27.4	
Low	59.0	8.8	17.8	15.4	10.1	
Book Value	7.21	6.71	6.52	5.79	4.03	
Return On Equity	5.3%	19.8%	17.5%	18.0%	19.9%	
Employees	2,200	1,977	1,879	1,879	1,665	

Risk Measures

Price / Sales Ratio : 5.9x
Price / Book Ratio : 6.6x
# of Employees : 2,200
Market Cap. / Employee : $1.2 M
Sales / Employee : $196,000

L12M Low : $17
% To Low : -64.1%
Downside Risk Value : $7.97
% Chg. to DRV : -83.2%
Insider Buy / Sell : 0 / 7

Balance Sheet

Current Ratio : 2.0x
Debt / Equity : 4.2%
Cash : $44.2 M
Cash / Share : $0.82
Days Sales Outstanding : 53

Micron Technology

(MU - NYSE)

Address: 8000 S. Federal Way
Boise, ID 83707
Phone: (208) 368-4000
Fax: (208) 368-2536
Web: www.micron.com
CEO: Steve Appleton
Investor Relations: Kipp Bedard

Business

Second largest worldwide DRAM producer (behind Samsung). Also makes SRAM, motherboards, and majority holder of Micron Electronics, a PC-by-mail company. Competes with Cypress, Integrated Device Technology, and large Korean and Japanese DRAM manufacturers.

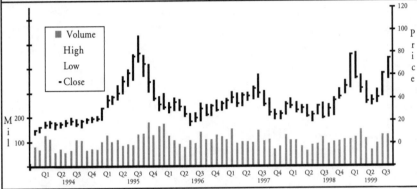

Recent Results (Fiscal Year : Aug)

	1999 9M	1998	1997	1996	1995	CAGR%
Sales ($M)	2,683.2	3,011.9	2,569.3	3,653.8	2,952.7	4.9%
R & D ($M)	234.7	271.8	146.6	191.9	128.8	
R & D % of Sales	8.7%	9.0%	5.7%	5.3%	4.4%	
Pretax Income ($M)	-71.6	-335.2	490.1	958.8	1362.0	NM
Pretax % of Sales	-2.7%	-11.1%	19.1%	26.2%	46.1%	
Earnings Per Share	-0.20	-1.10	1.20	2.76	3.90	
Growth Flow Per Share	0.71	0.18	1.88	3.65	4.50	NM
Stock High	79.50	45.31	45.25	44.00	94.75	
Low	23.63	20.13	37.38	16.63	21.25	
Close	37.88	22.75	40.00	29.13	39.63	
P/GF High	112.5	250.5	24.1	12.0	21.1	
Low	33.4	111.3	19.9	4.6	4.7	
Book Value	15.17	12.69	12.87	11.89	8.77	
Return On Equity	-1.7%	-8.7%	12.1%	23.2%	44.5%	
Employees	16,000	11,400	9,900	9,900	8,080	

Risk Measures

Price / Sales Ratio : 2.7x
Price / Book Ratio : 2.5x
# of Employees : 16,000
Market Cap. / Employee : $0.6 M
Sales / Employee : $224,000

L12M Low : $23 7/16
% To Low : -38.1%
Downside Risk Value : $12.19
% Chg. to DRV : -67.8%
Insider Buy / Sell : 1 / 7

Balance Sheet

Current Ratio : 3.5x
Debt / Equity : 42.3%
Cash : $1,660.5 M
Cash / Share : $6.42
Days Sales Outstanding : 54

Microsoft	Business
(MSFT - OTC) **Address:** One Microsoft Way Redmond, WA 98052 **Phone:** (425) 882-8080 **Fax:** (425) 936-8000 **Web:** www.microsoft.com **CEO:** William H. Gates, III **Investor Relations:** Carla Lewis	Dominates desktop computer operating systems; largest market share in basic business applications. Major thrust on the Internet with Explorer and Microsoft Network. Building a content-based media business. Competes with Sun, Oracle, IBM, Apple, and AOL.

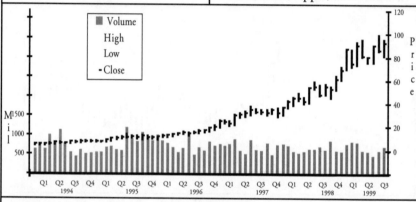

Microsoft — Recent Results (Fiscal Year : Jun)

	1999	1998	1997	1996	1995	CAGR%
Sales ($B)	19,747.0	15,262.0	11,358.0	8,671.0	5,937.0	35.0%
R & D ($B)	2,970.0	2,601.0	1,925.0	1,432.0	860.0	
R & D % of Sales	15.0%	17.0%	16.9%	16.5%	14.5%	
Pretax Income ($M)	11,891.0	7,117.0	5,314.0	3,379.0	2,167.0	53.1%
Pretax % of Sales	60.2%	46.6%	46.8%	39.0%	36.5%	
Earnings Per Share	1.42	0.84	0.66	0.43	0.29	
Growth Flow Per Share	1.96	1.33	1.02	0.71	0.46	43.6%
Stock High	94.94	54.19	33.55	21.53	13.66	
Low	45.59	29.73	20.41	9.99	7.28	
Close	90.19	54.19	31.60	20.66	10.97	
P/GF High	48.4	40.8	32.8	30.3	29.6	
Low	23.2	22.4	19.9	14.1	15.8	
Book Value	5.19	3.11	2.05	1.37	1.09	
Return On Equity	27.4%	27.0%	32.0%	31.3%	26.7%	
Employees	31,575	27,055	22,232	20,561	17,801	

Risk Measures

Price / Sales Ratio : 25.0x
Price / Book Ratio : 17.4x
# of Employees : 31,575
Market Cap. / Employee : $15.7 M
Sales / Employee : $625,000

L12M Low : $43 7/8
% To Low : -51.4%
Downside Risk Value : $9.25
% Chg. to DRV : -89.8%
Insider Buy / Sell : 1 / 16

Balance Sheet

Current Ratio : 3.1x
Debt / Equity : 0.0%
Cash : $13,927M
Cash / Share : $2.54
Days Sales Outstanding : 31

Motorola

(MOT - NYSE)

Address: 1303 E. Algonquin Rd.
Motorola Ctr.
Schaumburg, IL 60196
Phone: (847) 576-5000
Fax: (847) 576-3258
Web: www.mot.com
CEO: Christopher B. Galvin
Inv. Relations: George Grimsrud

Business

Dominant company in analog cellular is in a market-share fight for digital cellular. Also a semiconductor manufacturer; Apple Computer, a major customer, should not cause future problems. Competes with Ericsson, Nokia, Intel, Microchip, Texas Instruments, AMD, and National Semiconductor.

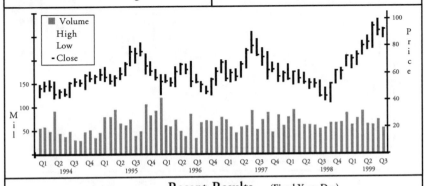

Recent Results (Fiscal Year: Dec)

MOTOROLA

	1999 H1	1998	1997	1996	1995	CAGR%
Sales ($M)	14,745.0	29,398.0	29,794.0	27,973.0	27,037.0	2.2%
R & D ($M)	1,555.0	2,893.0	2,748.0	2,394.0	2,197.0	
R & D % of Sales	10.5%	9.8%	9.2%	8.6%	8.1%	
Pretax Income ($M)	539.0	-1,374.0	1,816.0	1,775.0	2,782.0	-21.1%
Pretax % of Sales	3.7%	-4.7%	6.1%	6.3%	10.3%	
Earnings Per Share	0.61	-1.61	1.94	1.90	2.93	
Growth Flow Per Share	3.12	3.22	6.43	5.83	6.53	-1.1%
Stock High	96.56	64.94	90.50	68.50	82.50	
Low	63.50	38.56	54.00	44.13	51.50	
Close	94.75	61.06	57.19	61.25	57.00	
P/GF High	31.0	20.1	14.1	11.8	12.6	
Low	20.4	12.0	8.4	7.6	7.9	
Book Value	51.22	20.42	22.22	19.35	18.12	
Return On Equity	1.2%	-7.9%	8.7%	9.8%	16.2%	
Employees	133,000	133,000	150,000	139,000	142,000	

Risk Measures

Price / Sales Ratio : 2.0x
Price / Book Ratio : 1.8x
# of Employees : 133,000
Market Cap. / Employee : $0.4 M
Sales / Employee : $222,000

L12M Low : $38 3/8
% To Low : -59.5%
Downside Risk Value : $41.73
% Chg. to DRV : -56.0%
Insider Buy / Sell : 2 / 11

Balance Sheet

Current Ratio : 1.4x
Debt / Equity : 36.5%
Cash : $2,649 M
Cash / Share : $4.27
Days Sales Outstanding : 61

Novellus Systems

(NVLS - OTC)

Address: 4000 N. First Street
San Jose, CA 95134
Phone: (408) 943-9700
Fax: (408) 943-3422
Web: www.novellus.com
CEO: Richard S. Hill
Inv. Relations: Luann Campbell

Business

Semiconductor equipment supplier focused on chemical-vapor deposition. Sells and services worldwide. Made major acquisition of Varian physical-vapor deposition business. Competes with Applied Materials and Japanese companies.

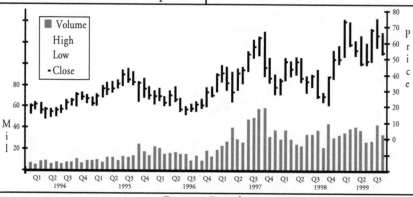

Recent Results (Fiscal Year: Dec)

NOVELLUS SYSTEMS, INC.

	1999 H1	1998	1997	1996	1995	CAGR%
Sales ($M)	246.1	518.8	534.0	461.7	373.7	7.1%
R & D ($M)	56.5	106.5	89.8	53.9	41.0	
R & D % of Sales	23.0%	20.5%	16.8%	11.7%	11.0%	
Pretax Income ($M)	32.6	80.1	-121.1	144.7	125.1	-15.0%
Pretax % of Sales	13.2%	15.4%	-22.7%	31.3%	33.5%	
Earnings Per Share	0.56	1.51	-2.88	2.85	2.41	
Growth Flow Per Share	2.01	4.55	-0.18	4.48	3.61	2.7%
Stock High	74.38	57.94	66.38	32.25	43.63	
Low	47.25	21.94	23.88	15.75	21.38	
Close	68.25	49.50	32.31	27.10	27.00	
P/GF High	37.0	12.7	-370.5	7.2	12.1	
Low	23.5	4.8	-133.3	3.5	5.9	
Book Value	17.17	10.73	9.05	11.31	7.96	
Return On Equity	3.3%	14.1%	-31.8%	25.2%	30.3%	
Employees	1,524	1,524	1,776	1,143	790	

Risk Measures

Price / Sales Ratio : 5.4x
Price / Book Ratio : 4.0x
# of Employees : 1,524
Market Cap. / Employee : $1.7 M
Sales / Employee : $323,000

L12M Low : $20 7/8
% To Low : -69.4%
Downside Risk Value : $13.59
% Chg. to DRV : -80.1%
Insider Buy / Sell : 0 / 9

Balance Sheet

Current Ratio : 5.5x
Debt / Equity : 1.7%
Cash : $345.3 M
Cash / Share : $8.85
Days Sales Outstanding : 108

Oracle Corporation

(ORCL - OTC)

Address: 500 Oracle Parkway
Redwood Shores, CA
94065
Phone: (650) 506-7000
Fax: (650) 506-7107
Web: www.oracle.com
CEO: Larry Ellison
Inv. Relations: Stephanie Aas

Business

The largest relational database vendor. Supplies its own applications programs, as well as supporting the major client/server packages like SAP, PeopleSoft, and Baan. Competes with IBM, Informix, Microsoft, Sybase and Object Design.

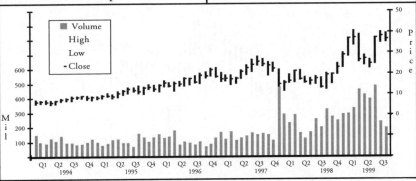

Recent Results (Fiscal Year: May)

ORACLE

	1999	1998	1997	1996	1995	CAGR%
Sales ($M)	8,827.3	7,143.9	5,684.3	4,223.3	2,966.9	31.3%
R & D ($M)	841.4	719.1	555.5	389.1	260.6	
R & D % of Sales	9.5%	10.1%	9.8%	9.2%	8.8%	
Pretax Income ($M)	1,982.1	827.8	1,283.5	919.5	659.0	31.7%
Pretax % of Sales	22.5%	11.6%	22.6%	21.8%	22.2%	
Earnings Per Share	0.87	0.54	0.54	0.40	0.30	
Growth Flow Per Share	1.44	1.26	1.09	0.79	0.56	26.5%
Stock High	40.50	27.42	23.67	22.68	14.45	
Low	12.70	12.04	15.17	11.71	8.05	
Close	24.81	15.75	22.40	18.56	12.56	
P/GF High	28.2	21.8	21.7	28.8	25.7	
Low	8.8	9.6	13.9	14.9	14.3	
Book Value	2.49	2.03	1.57	1.24	0.81	
Return On Equity	34.9%	26.6%	34.5%	32.3%	37.1%	
Employees	44,000	36,802	23,113	23,113	16,882	

Risk Measures

Price / Sales Ratio : 4.2x
Price / Book Ratio : 10.0x
# of Employees : 44,000
Market Cap. / Employee : $0.8 M
Sales / Employee : $201,000

L12M Low : $14 7/8
% To Low : -40.0%
Downside Risk Value : $6.26
% Chg. to DRV : -74.8%
Insider Buy / Sell : 0 / 12

Balance Sheet

Current Ratio : 1.8x
Debt / Equity : 8.3%
Cash : $2,562.8 M
Cash / Share : $1.73
Days Sales Outstanding : 85

PairGain Technologies

(PAIR - OTC)

Address: 14402 Franklin Avenue
Tustin, CA 92780
Phone: (714) 832-9922
Fax: (714) 832-9924
Web: www.pairgain.com
CEO: Charles S. Strauch
Investor Relations: Kim Gower

Business

Communications products using Digital Subscriber Line technology for networking and teleconferencing to the home or via private networks over standard copper wire. Competes with Lucent and Northern Telecom.

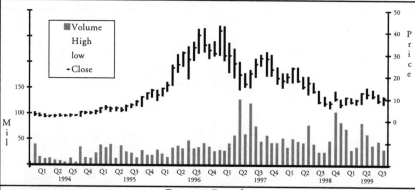

PAIRGAIN

Recent Results (Fiscal Year: Dec)

	1999 H1	1998	1997	1996	1995	CAGR%
Sales ($M)	122.1	283.1	282.3	205.4	107.2	22.8%
R & D ($M)	20.6	37.6	32.0	18.6	10.7	
R & D % of Sales	16.9%	13.3%	11.3%	9.1%	10.0%	
Pretax Income ($M)	8.7	63.1	78.0	56.9	26.1	-9.6%
Pretax % of Sales	7.1%	22.3%	27.6%	27.7%	24.3%	
Earnings Per Share	0.07	0.55	0.63	0.51	0.01	
Growth Flow Per Share	0.34	1.05	1.06	0.77	0.17	42.0%
Stock High	15.06	24.00	43.25	41.88	14.00	
Low	8.00	6.22	14.63	9.75	3.31	
Close	11.50	7.69	19.38	30.44	13.69	
P/GF High	43.7	22.8	41.0	54.5	82.6	
Low	23.2	5.9	13.9	12.7	19.5	
Book Value	4.49	3.73	3.41	2.17	1.40	
Return On Equity	1.6%	14.7%	18.5%	23.5%	0.7%	
Employees	692	692	640	486	375	

Risk Measures

Price / Sales Ratio : 3.5x
Price / Book Ratio : 2.6x
# of Employees : 692
Market Cap. / Employee : $1.2 M
Sales / Employee : $353,000

L12M Low : $6
% To Low : -47.8%
Downside Risk Value : $4.20
% Chg. to DRV : -63.5%
Insider Buy / Sell : 0 / 7

Balance Sheet

Current Ratio : 6.2x
Debt / Equity : 0.6%
Cash : $222.4 M
Cash / Share : $2.96
Days Sales Outstanding : 36

Premisys Communications

(PRMS - OTC)

Address: 48664 Milmont Drive
Fremont, CA 94538
Phone: (510) 353-7600
Fax: (510) 353-7601
Web: www.premisys.com
CEO: Nick Williams
Investor Relations: Scott Smith

Business

Telecommunications hardware; integrated-access devices for service providers and building owners. Uses existing wiring to connect to all modern communications services, such as Centrex, ISDN, and digital wide-area networks. Competes with Lucent.

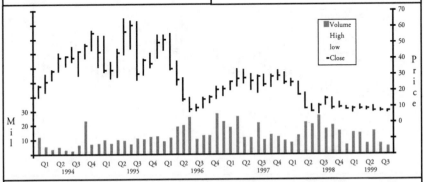

≡Premisys.

Recent Results (Fiscal Year : Jun)

	1999	1998	1997	1996	1995	CAGR%
Sales ($M)	92.4	102.3	78.4	73.9	30.9	31.5%
R & D ($M)	19.8	16.2	10.5	7.5	4.5	
R & D % of Sales	21.4%	15.8%	13.4%	10.1%	14.7%	
Pretax Income ($M)	11.2	21.8	17.9	26.5	5.3	28.4%
Pretax % of Sales	12.1%	21.3%	22.8%	35.8%	17.1%	
Earnings Per Share	0.30	0.50	0.41	0.64	0.18	
Growth Flow Per Share	1.08	1.09	0.81	0.92	0.38	67.7%
Stock High	24.81	33.25	37.25	65.00	57.25	
Low	5.63	15.00	7.13	26.63	15.75	
Close	7.31	24.88	15.75	33.75	56.00	
P/GF High	23.0	30.5	46.3	70.4	149.1	
Low	5.2	13.8	8.8	0.4	0.3	
Book Value	3.91	4.39	3.64	2.94	2.11	
Return On Equity	15.4%	22.8%	22.5%	21.8%	8.5%	
Employees	358	238	183	183	117	

Risk Measures

Price / Sales Ratio : 2.0x
Price / Book Ratio : 1.8x
# of Employees : 358
Market Cap. / Employee : $0.5 M
Sales / Employee : $258,000

L12M Low : $5 3/8
% To Low : -26.5%
Downside Risk Value : $4.22
% Chg. to DRV : -42.3%
Insider Buy / Sell : 0 / 6

Balance Sheet

Current Ratio : 5.5x
Debt / Equity : 0.0%
Cash : $84.4 M
Cash / Share : $3.33
Days Sales Outstanding : 35

Seagate Technology

(SEG - NYSE)

Address: 920 Disc Drive
Scotts Valley, CA 95067
Phone: (831) 438-6550
Fax: (831) 438-2631
Web: www.seagate.com
CEO: Steve Luczo
Investor Relations: Bill Rowley

Business

Largest manufacturer of Winchester disk drives up to 5 1/4" form factor. Especially strong in high-capacity drive market. Builds all its own parts and buys from some second sources. Assembles and sells worldwide. Competes with Quantum, Western Digital, IBM, and Fujitsu.

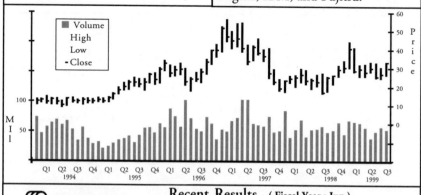

SS Seagate

Recent Results (Fiscal Year : Jun)

	1999	1998	1997	1996	1995	CAGR%
Sales ($M)	6,802.0	6,819.0	8,940.0	8,588.4	7,256.2	-1.6%
R & D ($M)	581.0	585.0	452.4	420.4	353.5	
R & D % of Sales	8.5%	8.6%	5.1%	4.9%	4.9%	
Pretax Income ($M)	1873.0	-704.0	891.3	331.5	487.5	40.0%
Pretax % of Sales	27.5%	-10.3%	10.0%	3.9%	6.7%	
Earnings Per Share	1.40	-2.17	2.61	0.97	1.45	
Growth Flow Per Share	3.79	0.09	4.36	2.75	2.88	7.1%
Stock High	44.00	44.81	54.25	42.75	27.38	
Low	17.13	17.75	33.50	18.06	11.81	
Close	25.63	23.88	35.25	39.50	23.75	
P/GF High	11.6	475.3	12.4	15.5	9.5	
Low	4.5	188.3	7.7	6.6	4.1	
Book Value	14.66	11.37	15.22	10.44	7.83	
Return On Equity	9.6%	-19.1%	17.1%	9.3%	18.5%	
Employees	82,000	87,000	110,000	87,000	77,000	

Risk Measures

Price / Sales Ratio : .0.9x
Price / Book Ratio : 1.7x
# of Employees : 82,000
Market Cap. / Employee : $0.1 M
Sales / Employee : $83,000

L12M Low : $19 13/16
% To Low : -22.7%
Downside Risk Value : $16.41
% Chg. to DRV : -36.0%
Insider Buy / Sell : 0 / 9

Balance Sheet

Current Ratio : 2.2x
Debt / Equity : 19.8%
Cash : $1,623.0 M
Cash / Share : $6.68
Days Sales Outstanding : 45

Sun Microsystems

(SUNW - OTC)

Address: 901 San Antonio Road
Palo Alto, CA 94303
Phone: (650) 960-1300
Fax: (650) 329-7869
Web: www.sun.com
CEO: Scott G. McNealy
Investor Relations: Mark Paisley

Business

A leading manufacturer of technical workstations, file servers and larger computers running the UNIX operating system. Also runs Microsoft NT. Inventor of Java. Competes with Microsoft, IBM, Dell, Compaq, Motorola, Intel and Hewlett-Packard.

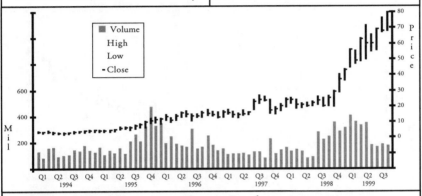

Recent Results (Fiscal Year : Jun)

	1999	1998	1997	1996	1995	CAGR%
Sales ($M)	11,726.3	9,790.8	8,598.3	7,094.8	5,901.9	18.7%
R & D ($M)	1,262.5	1,013.8	826.0	657.1	519.9	
R & D % of Sales	10.8%	10.4%	9.6%	9.3%	8.8%	
Pretax Income ($M)	1,605.7	1,176.2	1,121.2	708.9	523.3	32.4%
Pretax % of Sales	13.7%	12.0%	13.0%	10.0%	8.9%	
Earnings Per Share	1.35	0.97	0.98	0.61	0.45	
Growth Flow Per Share	2.90	2.25	2.04	1.44	1.11	27.1%
Stock High	71.50	26.66	18.78	17.57	12.86	
Low	19.81	15.88	13.16	9.00	3.74	
Close	68.88	21.72	18.61	12.85	11.41	
P/GF High	24.7	11.8	9.2	12.2	11.6	
Low	6.8	7.1	6.4	6.2	3.4	
Book Value	5.91	4.46	3.52	2.86	2.70	
Return On Equity	22.8%	21.7%	27.8%	21.1%	16.7%	
Employees	29,000	21,500	17,400	17,400	14,500	

Risk Measures

Price / Sales Ratio : 4.8x
Price / Book Ratio : 11.7x
# of Employees : 29,000
Market Cap. / Employee : $1.9 M
Sales / Employee : $404,000

L12M Low : $19 1/2
% To Low : -71.7%
Downside Risk Value : $10.56
% Chg. to DRV : -84.7%
Insider Buy / Sell : 1 / 33

Balance Sheet

Current Ratio : 1.9x
Debt / Equity : 0.4%
Cash : $2,665.1 M
Cash / Share : $3.27
Days Sales Outstanding : 65

Vitesse Semiconductor

(VTSS - OTC)

Address: 741 Calle Plano
Camarillo, CA 93012
Phone: (805) 388-3700
Fax: (805) 987-5896
Web: www.vitesse.com
CEO: Louis R. Tomasetta
Investor Relations: Patricia Ito

Industry

Semiconductors based on gallium arsenide, which are faster, more expensive, and harder to make than silicon chips. Sells to military, communications, automated test equipment, and high-speed computing. Competes with TriQuint, Anadigics, Conexant.

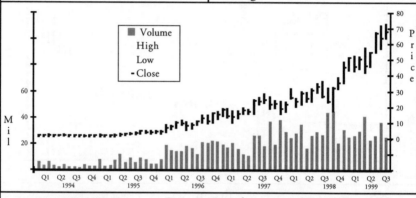

VITESSE
SEMICONDUCTOR CORPORATION

Recent Results (Fiscal Year : Sept)

	1999 9M	1998	1997	1996	1995	CAGR%
Sales ($M)	200.1	175.1	104.9	66.1	42.9	57.8%
R & D ($M)	32.0	27.9	16.8	11.1	8.7	
R & D % of Sales	16.0%	15.9%	16.0%	16.7%	20.3%	
Pretax Income ($M)	78.3	66.0	36.5	14.1	1.6	68.8%
Pretax % of Sales	39.1%	37.7%	34.8%	21.3%	3.7%	
Earnings Per Share	0.64	0.67	0.57	0.14	0.02	
Growth Flow Per Share	1.03	1.02	0.86	0.51	0.35	40.3%
Stock High	67.56	36.31	28.25	17.08	4.88	
Low	42.38	16.44	9.95	3.25	1.42	
Close	67.44	23.63	24.78	15.17	4.25	
P/GF High	65.5	35.5	32.7	33.8	13.7	
Low	41.1	16.1	11.5	6.4	4.0	
Book Value	5.49	3.97	4.63	2.93	0.96	
Return On Equity	11.7%	16.9%	12.3%	4.8%	2.1%	
Employees	590	590	443	293	NA	

Risk Measures

Price / Sales Ratio : 20.6x
Price / Book Ratio : 12.3x
# of Employees : 590
Market Cap. / Employee : $9.3 M
Sales / Employee : $452,000

L12M Low : $17 1/8
% To Low : -74.6%
Downside Risk Value : $9.36
% Chg. to DRV : -86.1%
Insider Buy / Sell : 0 / 10

Balance Sheet

Current Ratio : 11.8x
Debt / Equity : 0.01%
Cash : $199.0 M
Cash / Share : $2.44
Days Sales Outstanding : 63

Xilinx

(XLNX - OTC)

Address: 2100 Logic Drive
San Jose, CA 95124
Phone: (408) 559-7778
Fax: (408) 559-7114
Web: www.xilinx.com
CEO: Willem Roelandts
Investor Relations: Maria Ouillard

Business

The largest fabless semiconductor manufacturer of programmable-logic circuits and related circuit design software for shorter time to market and rapid prototyping. Sells to communications, PC and military industries. Competes with Altera, Lattice, and QuickLogic.

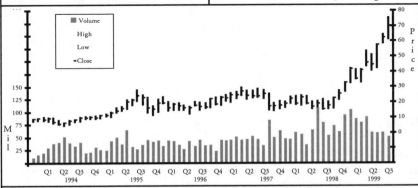

Recent Results (Fiscal Year : Mar)

	2000 Q1	1999	1998	1997	1996	CAGR%
Sales ($M)	211.4	662.0	613.6	568.1	560.8	10.8%
R & D ($M)	26.0	90.9	80.5	71.1	64.6	
R & D % of Sales	12.3%	13.7%	13.1%	12.5%	11.5%	
Pretax Income ($M)	71.8	189.4	183.3	165.8	170.9	13.9%
Pretax % of Sales	34.0%	28.6%	29.9%	29.2%	30.5%	
Earnings Per Share	0.31	0.84	0.79	0.70	0.64	
Growth Flow Per Share	0.46	1.43	1.29	1.14	1.05	15.4%
Stock High	57.25	41.75	28.75	25.44	26.94	
Low	40.56	15.25	14.84	13.31	10.63	
Close	57.25	40.56	18.72	24.38	15.88	
P/GF High	123.3	29.2	22.2	22.3	25.7	
Low	87.3	10.7	11.5	11.7	10.1	
Book Value	5.56	5.70	3.44	3.08	2.33	
Return On Equity	5.6%	14.7%	23.0%	22.6%	27.4%	
Employees	1,491	1,491	1,391	1,277	1,201	

Risk Measures

Price / Sales Ratio : 11.4x
Price / Book Ratio : 10.3x
# of Employees : 1,491
Market Cap. / Employee : $6.5 M
Sales / Employee : $567,000

L12M Low : $15 7/16
% To Low : -73.0%
Downside Risk Value : $5.66
% Chg. to DRV : -90.1%
Insider Buy / Sell : 0 / 8

Balance Sheet

Current Ratio : 4.0x
Debt / Equity : 0.0%
Cash : $480.8 M
Cash / Share : $2.85
Days Sales Outstanding : 37

## CHAPTER NINETEEN

Technology Convertible Bonds and Stocks

At a presentation I made recently at one of the five Money Shows held around the country every year, a white-haired woman stood up and said, "I'm seventy-nine years old, and I believe in all this new technology, but I need income and these stocks are too risky for me."

I said, "Mom, I keep telling you—buy technology convertible bonds."

Using our asset-allocation formula of 100 percent minus your age for investing in technology, it is important to keep a substantial portion of your assets invested in the new economy even after you retire. Technology convertibles offer worthwhile investment opportunities to investors who need current income, yet want to invest in companies that will benefit from the technology revolution. The total convertible-bond market today amounts to about $62 billion—big, but nothing compared to stocks and straight bonds. Convertibles are not well followed, and therefore can offer the extra opportunities and rewards of any less-efficient market.

Where do convertibles fit into the financial world? Companies raise cash to fund their operations in a number of ways. They can borrow from a bank, creating either short-term debt or a long-term loan. They can sell long-term bonds. Or they can sell common stock to shareholders.

We listed these choices in increasing order of financial risk to the investor. If the business goes bad, the bank gets paid off first. Then the bondholders collect, and anything left over at the end goes to the common shareholders.

Convertible bonds fit right between long-term bonds and common stocks. Like bonds, they pay a stated rate of interest (the "coupon") and will be redeemed on a particular day.

However, the convertible bondholder also has the right to exchange or convert the bond into a fixed number of shares of common stock. If the company does very well, the convertible bondholder can convert and enjoy part of the appreciation on the stock. The regular bondholders just get their capital back, and woe unto them if inflation has eroded their purchasing power.

Convertible preferred stock is a similar financial instrument. It fits between convertible bonds and common stock. Like convertible bonds, convertible preferred stock receives a regular distribution—a dividend rather than an interest payment. Unlike convertible bonds, the distribution generally is not guaranteed.

Like convertible bonds, convertible preferred stock can be exchanged or converted into a fixed number of shares of common stock. Unlike the bonds, the stock lives forever or until converted. The investor doesn't get "paid off" on a particular day. For purposes of discussion, though, we treat convertible preferreds as if they were convertible bonds. About two-thirds of the total convertible market today is convertible bonds, and one-third is convertible preferreds.

If the company takes a while to do well, the convertible investor gets paid a good rate of interest for waiting. The stocks of most technology companies pay little or no dividend. Convertibles offered by these companies usually offer attractive yields, plus the opportunity to participate in the appreciation of the underlying growth stock—all at substantially lower risk.

We believe that convertible bonds of technology companies are nearly ideal investments for IRA, Keogh, and pension plans. The high current income can be sheltered from taxes, and the long-term growth potential of the common-stock "kicker" can make a meaningful difference to retirement plans.

For retired investors, convertibles provide required current income while the conversion to common stock protects you against inflation between the time you retire and your hundredth birthday. (You know what "moderate" inflation can do to you over time!) Straight BBB-rated bonds have less than a one percentage point yield advantage over convertibles. By trading your low-rated straight bonds for convertibles, you could give up 1 percent in current yield and get an important equity kicker that the straight bond lacks. Convertible bonds of technology companies provide a safer way than common stock to participate in the technology revolution, which is the main investment theme of our time. Computers, software, bioengineering, specialty materials, electronics: You name the area, and you can probably find a convertible bond to buy.

A few years ago, we compared the performance of the Value Line convertibles index to the Value Line stock index. In sixteen quarters of down markets, the stocks dropped an average of 5.5 percent per quarter, while the convertible bonds fell only 2.9 percent per quarter. Convertibles "participated" in 53 percent of the downswing. You'll certainly sleep better if your converts are only half as risky as common stocks.

Interestingly, over twenty-one quarters of up markets, the stocks averaged an 9.5 percent per-quarter gain, while the convertibles averaged an 8.1 percent gain! Convertibles participated in 85 percent of the upswing. That's not much upside participation to give away, considering the substantial downside protection. And investors often get excited about the underlying conversion rights late in a bull market, giving you an extra premium just when it's time to sell.

The reasons for this skewed behavior can be understood from Chart 19.1.

Convertible bonds have an **investment value** based on their coupon and quality, ignoring the conversion factor. The investment value is their value as a straight bond. Given a structure of market interest rates, the investment value is plotted on the chart as a horizontal line. It does not vary with the price of the common stock.

Convertible bonds also have a **conversion value** based on the number of shares of common stock they can be converted into, and what price the common is selling for. This conversion value is plotted on our chart as a sloping line.

When the conversion value is far *below* the investment value, as at point C, the price of the convertible bond will track more closely to the horizontal investment-value line. Small fluctuations in the common stock will not affect the bond price, but changes in interest rates will.

When the conversion value is far *above* the investment value, as at point B, the price of the bond will track more closely to the sloping conversion-value line. Small fluctuations in interest rates won't affect the bond price as much as changes in the price of the underlying common stock.

At point A, the bond is equally sensitive to changes in interest rates or the underlying common. Bonds selling at or near point A are usually an attractive alternative to the common stock, because the upside/downside leverage of the bond is most favorable at this point.

Does this nice, neat theory work in practice? On October 13, 1989, the DJIA staged a mini-Crash, falling 190 points in one day. That was a decline of 6.9 percent, going into the record book as the second-largest point drop and third-largest percentage drop in history. On that day, the convertible-bond index dropped only 1.8 percent! There was a flight from stocks to fixed income, so interest rates fell sharply and partially sup-

CHART 19.1

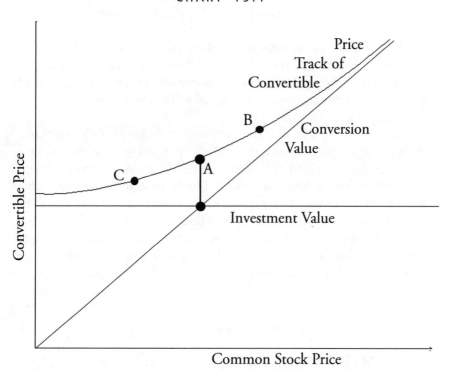

Price Track of Convertible

Conversion Value

B

C   A

Investment Value

Convertible Price

Common Stock Price

ported the prices of convertible bonds. The dual-market characteristics of converts clearly cushioned their price declines.

Picking Convertible Bonds

There's a lot of mumbo-jumbo about convertibles, but we have two simple rules to help you pick a portfolio of convertible bonds that should perform as well as most professionals' picks.

Rule 1: Buy bonds only convertible into attractive stocks.

You may think that should be called *Idiot Simple Rule 1,* but a lot of convertibles are bought and sold "on the numbers" by comparing yields to conversion rates and financial risk, rather than on an evaluation of the underlying stock.

We advocate an entirely different approach: long-term commitment to quality situations that have the ability to pay you interest and the prospects to make you a load of money on the conversion—or an acquisition.

Rule 2: Try to buy convertible bonds in equity accounts when the incremental yield will pay back the premium in less than three years. In a bond account, try for less than seven years.

That requires an explanation; you'll be glad to know it's simpler than it looks. You'll find a Convertibles Worksheet in Appendix C. As an example, we've filled in a worksheet using a mythical company, California Technologies.

CONVERTIBLES WORKSHEET

COMPANY NAME _California Technologies_   STOCK SYMBOL _XXXX_

STOCK PRICE _17⅞_   DIVIDEND, IF ANY _0.00_   EXCHANGE _OTC_

1. CONVERTIBLE INFORMATION

CONVERTIBLE SYMBOL, IF ANY ____NONE____   PRICE ___85.00___

COUPON _____8.0_____ %

YEAR DUE .... _2015_

CONVERSION RATIO .... _33.33_
(How many shares per bond? Divide $1,000 by conversion price per share.)

2. VALUE CALCULATION

CONVERSION VALUE _____59.58_____
(Multiply conversion ratio times price of one common share.)

PREMIUM _____ 42.7% _____
(Percentage convertible price is higher than conversion value.)

CONVERTIBLE YIELD _____ 9.4% _____
(Divide coupon by current convertible price.)

COMMON YIELD _____ 0.0% _____
(Divide dividend, if any, by current common stock price.)

YIELD ADVAWindows 2000AGE _ 9.4% _____
(Subtract common yield from convertible yield.)

PAYBACK PERIOD _____ 4.5 years _____
(Divide premium by yield advantage.)

California Technologies has a convertible bond with an 8.0 percent coupon, due to be redeemed in 2015. An 8.0 percent coupon means that it pays $80.00 per year on every $1,000 bond.

One of the annoying things about bonds is that they are sold in units of $1,000, but the prices are always quoted as a percentage of the face value instead of in real dollars. It's dumb, pointless, traditional, and totally ingrained into the bond world, so there's nothing to do but get used to it.

A typical price of the California Technologies "eights of '15" is 85.00. We know that really means $850.00 per bond.

Next we find out the conversion ratio, which is 33.33. We can exchange each bond for 33.33 shares of California Technologies common stock. Just for fun, you can divide the original price of the bond—$1,000—by 33.33 to see what the *conversion price* is on the stock. In this case, it is $30.

Now we look at the price of the common stock, say $17⅞. That's well below the $30 conversion price, so this bond may not pass Rule 2 for equity accounts.

The conversion value is the number of shares you could convert into, multiplied by the current price per share. If you converted in this example, you'd get 33.33 shares worth $17 7/8 each or $595.77. Owing to the dumb tradition mentioned above, this number is referred to as if it were divided by 10: 59.58.

Now we know two things. We know the bond will cost us 85.00. We also know it is worth only 59.58 if it is converted. So we calculate the *premium* we are paying for the conversion value. We see that 85.00 is 42.7 percent higher than the conversion value of 59.58, so if we buy this bond we'll be paying a 42.7 percent premium.

In general, if the premium is under 40 percent, you can expect the convertible to participate in any appreciation of the common. Bonds bought at higher premiums usually will not move much in the early stages of a stock's surge. Then, as the stock rises and the premium narrows, the bond begins to participate. (Recheck Chart 19.1 if this is not clear to you.)

In order to decide whether a 42.7 percent premium is too high, we need to calculate the *yield advantage* we'll get if we buy the convertible bond instead of the common stock. The current yield of the bond is 9.4 percent. All we did was divide the coupon—$8.00—by the current price of the bond—85.00.

Next we find out the yield on the common stock. Like most technology companies, California Technologies doesn't pay any dividend on its common stock, so the yield is zero.

A crucial number is the yield advantage per year of buying the bond instead of the common stock. To calculate the yield advantage, you simply subtract the yield on the common from the yield on the bond. In this case, with zero yield on the common, the yield advantage of the convertible is the full 9.4 percent.

We already know we'll pay a 42.7 percent premium if we buy the bond. And we know we'll pick up a 9.4 percent yield advantage if we buy the bond.

If we divide the 42.7 percent premium by the 9.4 percent annual yield advantage, we can calculate **how many years of interest payments it will take us to earn back the premium.**

That payback period is 4.5 years. It will take 4.5 years of coupon payments to make up for the 42.7 percent premium. California Technologies does not pass Rule 2 for equity accounts. If we wanted to invest in this company, we would buy the common stock, not the convertible.

But what about in a retirement account, where we are buying the convertible bond instead of a straight bond? The 9.4 percent yield is terrific, and the payback period is less than seven years, so we probably will get an equity kicker some years in the future. We would buy California Technologies converts for this kind of account. In fact, even if the payback period stretched out to eight or nine years, that very high 9.4 percent current yield probably would tempt us to bend Rule 2 and buy the bond anyway.

The Call Provision

The final factor affecting investment in a convertible bond is the call provision. Most convertibles can be redeemed or "called" before the maturity date, at a price usually between 101 and 107. If you pay over 100, the call price theoretically can be below the price you paid for the bond, but companies usually don't really expect to buy back any bonds. They call the bond when the stock is up, forcing conversion of the bonds into common stock because the value of the common stock you will get is higher than the call price.

Normally, companies won't call a convertible bond until the conversion price is 20 percent to 25 percent higher than the call price. Sometimes they'll call it at a somewhat lower percentage if the interest rate on the bond is relatively high. In fact, the higher the coupon on the bond relative to current interest rates, the more likely the bond will be called.

Convertible Underwritings

For the past several years, a number of technology companies have been issuing new convertible bonds. In some cases, their stocks were down so low (in their opinion) that they refused to sell straight common stock. Because the stocks were down because of widely recognized fundamental problems, they've had to offer high coupons in order to attract investors.

On a new underwriting, convertible bonds usually are priced at a 15 percent to 25 percent premium in relation to the common, with a payback period of two to three years—right up our alley. **Buying convertibles on a new underwriting often is the best way to take a position.** We don't buy many common stocks on the initial public offering because they tend to be overpriced. That isn't true of convertibles.

Some Selected Convertibles

For your convenience, we've listed some interesting convertibles in Appendix C. Not all these bonds qualify as good investments under Rules 1 and 2, so be sure to get current prices and fill out a Convertibles Worksheet before you buy any of them.

## PART IV

Choosing High-Tech Mutual Funds

MUTUAL funds have a place

in most investors' portfolios, either as a place to park your technology asset allocation until you have opportunities to pick individual stocks, or as a core holding to be surrounded by individual stocks, or even as a substitute for stocks if you do not have the time to follow individual companies.

After describing how to analyze technology mutual funds and build a diversified portfolio, we present twenty technology funds and seven medical and biotechnology funds as a starting point for your consideration.

## CHAPTER TWENTY

Technology Mutual Funds

Although there has been a tremendous inflow of money into all mutual funds and a large number of new funds opening up, we have been surprised that so few specialize in electronics or medical technology. This is good news for you in two ways: It suggests that technology investing is still an emerging opportunity, and it makes it easier for you to pick good mutual funds. After all, there are only about 90 choices. Rather than be overwhelmed by the 9,000 mutual funds, you can discard the 8,910 that don't focus on the biggest opportunity of our generation: equity investments in technology stocks.

Technology mutual funds fall into three broad categories: electronics/computer, communications, and health care/biotechnology. Category memberships are somewhat subjective, based on a reading of the prospectus and the portfolio makeup from time to time. We screen out a few funds that do not own companies with a heavy component of R&D. Many of the health/biotech funds, in addition to their investments in development-stage biotechnology and medical-device companies, also carry at least a moderate investment in big drug companies and service/delivery firms like HMOs. The communications funds often have substantial exposure to the telephone carriers (that's why they pay larger dividends) as well as equipment companies.

The technology sector largely underperformed through the 1980s, but leaped ahead for the first part of the 1990s. The lead held through 1997, although the broad market began to catch up.

HIGH-TECH FUNDS VS. THE S&P 500

Year	High-Tech Fund Perf.	S&P 500
1984	−9.4%	+5.6%
1985	+18.9	+30.7
1986	+6.7	+18.5
1987	+0.4	+5.4
1988	+4.9	+16.3
1989	+24.0	+31.2
1990	−5.1	−3.1
1991	+44.6	+30.0
1992	+12.6	+7.4
1993	+24.0	+9.9
1994	+10.5	+1.3
1995	+41.1	+37.1
1996	+19.1	+22.6
1997	+13.5	+32.2
1998	+35.4	+6.9
H1:99	+61.8	+30.0

Although they have been slow to recognize the profound changes in our economy, the rest of the investing world is starting to realize that technology is a great place to put your money to work. The number of technology funds increases a little each year, and assets under management have grown from less than $10 billion in the early 1990s to over $50 billion recently. Of course, that's still less than one-fourth the market capitalization of just Intel. We're in no danger of having too many investment dollars chasing too few technology opportunities, even considering that some aggressive growth (read "momentum") and small cap funds buy some technology stocks. In spite of all the press, these stocks— especially the ones with fundamental strength—remain largely ignored by Wall Street. There are exactly five biotechnology mutual funds, of which only two are managed no-load: Dresdner RCM Biotechnology and our Murphy New World Biotechnology. That seems rather amazing, considering that the next revolution in health care will be exclusively based on biotech.

There are many good sources of information on the performance of technology mutual funds. The Morningstar service is available by subscription; most libraries have it. Quarterly performance data provided by Lipper Analytical Services appears in *Barron's* in the issue after each quarter ends. Annual performance data can be found in a number of financial magazines, usually in a January issue. *Business Week* has a good listing, although it doesn't track enough funds. *Forbes* evaluates performance over market swings, not for fixed calendar periods.

We are also interested in finding fund managers who can build wealth during the upturns, and then protect it during the downturns. As value-oriented investors, we get nervous when managers ignore balance sheets and even earnings to focus on the hottest plays in town. One red flag is the average price/earnings ratio of the fund.

With only half of the funds reporting P/Es, it is hard to draw any sweeping conclusions. Nonetheless, when you can get the information it's useful to compare it with the prospectus to see if the investment managers are meeting their stated goals for risk. And remember to look at P/E ratios over time. Some funds might turn in good numbers for several years with a reasonable P/E, and then suddenly shift their strategy toward high momentum, high P/E stocks—especially after a change in portfolio managers.

Management is an important factor to monitor—you used to have to call the fund every six months or so to find out who was the lead portfolio manager. Happily, *Barron's* and the Morningstar mutual-fund service now print that information. A record built by one person is not completely useful for projecting performance after that person leaves, although it isn't completely useless, either. The research organization supporting the departed portfolio manager is still there for the new one. You just have to be more alert to changes in the performance pattern after a change in managers.

The final piece of the puzzle we check is the actual composition of the portfolio. We want to see what stocks the funds own, how much they own of each one, and how fast the portfolio turns over. You can get this information from the fund's semiannual and annual reports or find it in the Morningstar service.

Recommended Mutual Funds

We rate the following funds as Buys, including the funds we manage. For those who don't have the time to build an entire portfolio of stocks, using a few of these funds as a core holding can be a very effective way to participate in the technology revolution. For some sectors, such as global telecommunications, it may be the only practical way.

In general, we recommend buying two or three broad-based computer/electronics funds, a global telecommunications fund, and one or two biotechnology funds. You do not need to own more than five funds to be adequately diversified. If you can stand the volatility, use our formula of 100 minus your age to calculate what percentage of your total assets should be in technology. Whatever portion of that percentage you want to keep in mutual funds, allocate it about equally between the four or five funds you select, unless you want a heavier weighting in biotechnology.

If you are starting with a smaller amount of money, buy a computer/electronics fund first, then a biotech fund, then another computer/electronics fund, then a global telecommunications fund, and then another computer/electronics or biotech fund. Many of these funds have minimums as low as $1,000. Anyone can build a diversified portfolio of technology mutual funds over a short period of time. Make regular monthly additions to your five funds (dollar-cost averaging) and you will build substantial wealth over time. Once a year, review your holdings, checking performance, portfolio-manager continuity, securities held, and the Morningstar ratings (the ★ ratings following are from Morningstar). Make changes slowly, but don't be afraid to swap one for another if you become uncomfortable with the progress an investment is making. It's your money.

Computer/Electronics

★★★★★**Alliance Technology,** a load fund, avoids large losses in down markets, and preserves its impressive gains made in upswings. This is a broadly based fund with investments in everything from semiconductor equipment to chips to computers to networking.

★★★★★**Fidelity Select Software & Computer** is a lower-load fund that also showed strong performance in the 1990–1995 upswing, then preserved capital in the down periods. The managers have a value-oriented investing style. This fund is less exposed to personal-computer and semiconductor stocks than we would like, but carries a well-balanced portfolio of other technology stocks like Microsoft, Oracle, and 3Com.

★★★★**Firsthand Technology Value Fund** (formerly Interactive Investments) is a no-load fund with an impressive four-year history. The fund reflects the industry backgrounds of the two managers in semiconductors and medical devices, but also owns communications equipment and biotechnology stocks.

★★★★**Invesco Strategic Technology** is a broadly-based no-load fund that uses a theme-oriented approach to get in front of important changes and new concepts in technology.

★★★★**T. Rowe Price Science & Technology,** a true no-load fund with a fairly low expense ratio, shows very strong performance, holding up well over all the periods we measure. The managers made some smart calls on PC stocks to sidestep the decline from mid-1995 to mid-1996, and then increased networking exposure going into 1997. This broadly based portfolio includes stocks from chip makers like Maxim, Xilinx, Altera, and Cirrus Logic to software companies like Adobe, Intuit, and Informix.

★★★★**Seligman Communications & Information,** a load fund that managed to more than double in the twelve months through mid-1995, was hit hard in the subsequent decline. It is a more narrowly focused, more volatile fund than the others, but its extra risk should pay off over time.

Communications

★★★**Fidelity Select Developing Communications** is a lower-load fund that has beaten the technology-fund average in every quarter since it began. The portfolio is loaded with communications stocks, including both U.S. and overseas hardware and service suppliers. Typical holdings include DSC Communications, AirTouch, Vodafone, and Nokia. We think this area will show major growth going forward.

★★★**Montgomery Global Communications** is another no-load way to participate in the globalization of telecommunications. Over 80 percent of the portfolio is in foreign stocks, compared to 30 percent for the average global-telecom fund. It gives you a lot of diversification for your dollar. Windows 2000T Data Comm, Global Telesystems, Gilat Satellite Networks, WorldCom, and CPT Telephone of Peru are some major holdings.

Health Care/Biotechnology

Eaton Vance Worldwide Health Sciences (formerly Capstone Medical Research) is an excellent smaller load fund. About 60 percent of the equities are foreign: Altana, Ares-Serono, and Swiss Serum in Europe; Tekoku Hormone in Japan, and so on. The U.S. holdings include Arris, Cytel, and Isis.

★★★**Fidelity Select Biotechnology,** a low-load fund, owned large pharmaceutical stocks to protect the net asset value during the biotech bear market of the early 1990s. Now it is more heavily in biotech: Recently the top ten holdings were Amgen, Biogen, Roche, Genentech,

Schering-Plough, Merck, COR Therapeutics, Protein Design Labs, Genetics Institute, and SmithKline Beecham.

Franklin Biotech Discovery, a relatively new low-load fund, focuses on biotechnology companies with market capitalizations under $1 billion. The manager sells short and buys puts to profit from stocks he expects to decline.

Murphy New World Technology Funds

In late 1996, we assumed responsibility for three funds in the Monterey Mutual Fund group. These funds were converted to no-load status, and their portfolios and objectives were changed with shareholder approval to match the opportunities available in the new economy. These funds are too new to be rated by Morningstar.

Murphy New World Technology Fund, a no-load fund, invests in all sectors of technology, including computer/electronics, communications, except biotechnology. Its goal is to provide broad exposure to the best opportunities in all major fast-growing areas.

Murphy New World Biotechnology Fund, a no-load fund managed by Lissa Morgenthaler, invests primarily in development-stage companies in biotechnology, medical devices, health-care services, bioinformatics (the application of computing to biotechnology), and medical-research support. As we discussed in Chapter 11, we believe that the biotech revolution is just getting under way and will last for several decades.

Murphy New World Technology Convertibles Fund, a no-load fund, buys convertible securities and preferred stocks of technology companies in every sector. As discussed in Chapter 19, technology convertibles are an ideal way to capture most of the upside in technology stocks with less risk, while generating current income. In many situations, current income is important (retirement, life estates with remaindermen), yet investors still need growth for inflation protection.

## CHAPTER TWENTY-ONE

Twenty Technology Mutual Funds

Many of the technology funds not in this group of twenty are excellent investment opportunities or offer diversification into specific industries or geographies that can be very useful in constructing a well-rounded portfolio of funds. The funds chosen for this chapter generally have been in business for a while, are well rated by Morningstar and other rating services, or are expected to perform well in the future, and offer a good starting point for a technology investing program.

For each fund you will find a chart of the quarterly investment returns compared to the S&P 500 for the last five years. The table immediately below each chart shows the net asset value and total percentage return for each year, any income or capital gains distributions, the reported expense ratio and the percentage of the portfolio turned over each year.

Below that, on the left you will find the actual performance quarter-by-quarter. Continuing down, I have listed some investment style parameters: the average price/earnings ratio of the fund, the price/book value ratio, the average earnings growth rate of the portfolio holdings for the last five years, and the median market capitalization. Further down is the asset allocation to cash, stocks, and bonds.

On the right is a portfolio analysis as of June 30, 1999, including the total number of stocks and a list of the top ten holdings with the dollar amount of each position. Below that is an indication of whether the fund can buy private placements, options, or futures.

Across the bottom of each page is contact information, the name of the manager, minimum purchase levels, sales fee (load) if any, management fee, and the Morningstar rating.

Be sure to obtain updated information from the fund's prospectus and interim reports, as well as a recent Morningstar report if available, before investing.

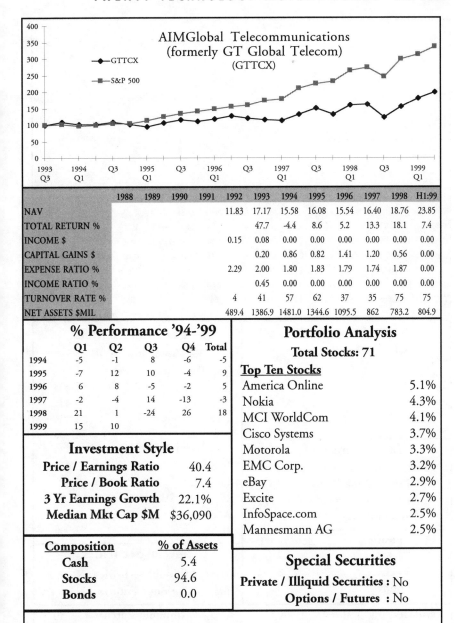

	1988	1989	1990	1991	1992	1993	1994	1995	1996	1997	1998	H1:99
NAV					11.83	17.17	15.58	16.08	15.54	16.40	18.76	23.85
TOTAL RETURN %						47.7	-4.4	8.6	5.2	13.3	18.1	7.4
INCOME $					0.15	0.08	0.00	0.00	0.00	0.00	0.00	0.00
CAPITAL GAINS $						0.20	0.86	0.82	1.41	1.20	0.56	0.00
EXPENSE RATIO %					2.29	2.00	1.80	1.83	1.79	1.74	1.87	0.00
INCOME RATIO %						0.45	0.00	0.00	0.00	0.00	0.00	0.00
TURNOVER RATE %						4	41	57	62	37	35	75	75
NET ASSETS $MIL					489.4	1386.9	1481.0	1344.6	1095.5	862	783.2	804.9

% Performance '94-'99

	Q1	Q2	Q3	Q4	Total
1994	-5	-1	8	-6	-5
1995	-7	12	10	-4	9
1996	6	8	-5	-2	5
1997	-2	-4	14	-13	-3
1998	21	1	-24	26	18
1999	15	10			

Investment Style

Price / Earnings Ratio	40.4
Price / Book Ratio	7.4
3 Yr Earnings Growth	22.1%
Median Mkt Cap $M	$36,090

Composition	% of Assets
Cash	5.4
Stocks	94.6
Bonds	0.0

Portfolio Analysis

Total Stocks: 71

Top Ten Stocks

America Online	5.1%
Nokia	4.3%
MCI WorldCom	4.1%
Cisco Systems	3.7%
Motorola	3.3%
EMC Corp.	3.2%
eBay	2.9%
Excite	2.7%
InfoSpace.com	2.5%
Mannesmann AG	2.5%

Special Securities

Private / Illiquid Securities : No
Options / Futures : No

Address : 50 California St., 27th Floor
San Francisco, CA 94111
Telephone: (800) 824-1580 or (415) 392-6181
Web: www.aimfunds.com
Advisor: Chancellor LGT Asset Mgmt.
Manager: David Barnard & Team
States Avail: All

Minimum Purchase: $500
Add: $100
IRA: $100
Front Load: 4.75%
Management Fee: 0.98%
Expense Ratio: 1.87%
Morningstar Rating: *

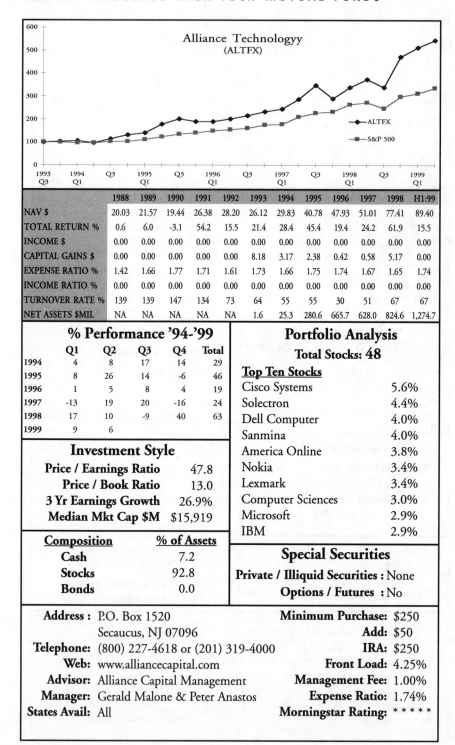

Alliance Technologyy (ALTFX)

	1988	1989	1990	1991	1992	1993	1994	1995	1996	1997	1998	H1:99
NAV $	20.03	21.57	19.44	26.38	28.20	26.12	29.83	40.78	47.93	51.01	77.41	89.40
TOTAL RETURN %	0.6	6.0	-3.1	54.2	15.5	21.4	28.4	45.4	19.4	24.2	61.9	15.5
INCOME $	0.00	0.00	0.00	0.00	0.00	0.00	0.00	0.00	0.00	0.00	0.00	0.00
CAPITAL GAINS $	0.00	0.00	0.00	0.00	0.00	8.18	3.17	2.38	0.42	0.58	5.17	0.00
EXPENSE RATIO %	1.42	1.66	1.77	1.71	1.61	1.73	1.66	1.75	1.74	1.67	1.65	1.74
INCOME RATIO %	0.00	0.00	0.00	0.00	0.00	0.00	0.00	0.00	0.00	0.00	0.00	0.00
TURNOVER RATE %	139	139	147	134	73	64	55	55	30	51	67	67
NET ASSETS $MIL	NA	NA	NA	NA	NA	1.6	25.3	280.6	665.7	628.0	824.6	1,274.7

% Performance '94-'99

	Q1	Q2	Q3	Q4	Total
1994	4	8	17	14	29
1995	8	26	14	-6	46
1996	1	5	8	4	19
1997	-13	19	20	-16	24
1998	17	10	-9	40	63
1999	9	6			

Investment Style

Price / Earnings Ratio	47.8
Price / Book Ratio	13.0
3 Yr Earnings Growth	26.9%
Median Mkt Cap $M	$15,919

Composition	% of Assets
Cash	7.2
Stocks	92.8
Bonds	0.0

Portfolio Analysis

Total Stocks: 48

Top Ten Stocks

Cisco Systems	5.6%
Solectron	4.4%
Dell Computer	4.0%
Sanmina	4.0%
America Online	3.8%
Nokia	3.4%
Lexmark	3.4%
Computer Sciences	3.0%
Microsoft	2.9%
IBM	2.9%

Special Securities

Private / Illiquid Securities : None
Options / Futures : No

Address : P.O. Box 1520
Secaucus, NJ 07096
Telephone: (800) 227-4618 or (201) 319-4000
Web: www.alliancecapital.com
Advisor: Alliance Capital Management
Manager: Gerald Malone & Peter Anastos
States Avail: All

Minimum Purchase: $250
Add: $50
IRA: $250
Front Load: 4.25%
Management Fee: 1.00%
Expense Ratio: 1.74%
Morningstar Rating: ★ ★ ★ ★ ★

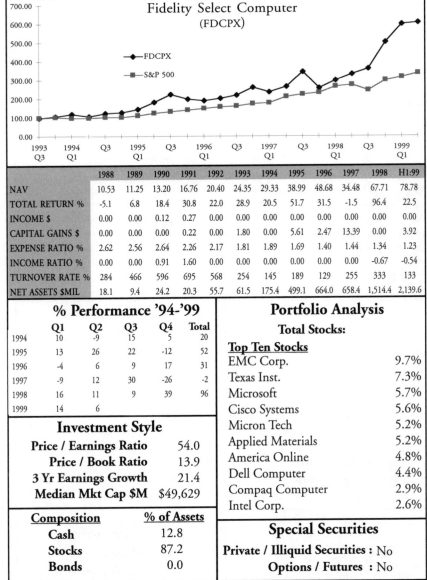

Fidelity Select Computer (FDCPX)

	1988	1989	1990	1991	1992	1993	1994	1995	1996	1997	1998	H1:99
NAV	10.53	11.25	13.20	16.76	20.40	24.35	29.33	38.99	48.68	34.48	67.71	78.78
TOTAL RETURN %	-5.1	6.8	18.4	30.8	22.0	28.9	20.5	51.7	31.5	-1.5	96.4	22.5
INCOME $	0.00	0.00	0.12	0.27	0.00	0.00	0.00	0.00	0.00	0.00	0.00	0.00
CAPITAL GAINS $	0.00	0.00	0.00	0.22	0.00	1.80	0.00	5.61	2.47	13.39	0.00	3.92
EXPENSE RATIO %	2.62	2.56	2.64	2.26	2.17	1.81	1.89	1.69	1.40	1.44	1.34	1.23
INCOME RATIO %	0.00	0.00	0.91	1.60	0.00	0.00	0.00	0.00	0.00	0.00	-0.67	-0.54
TURNOVER RATE %	284	466	596	695	568	254	145	189	129	255	333	133
NET ASSETS $MIL	18.1	9.4	24.2	20.3	55.7	61.5	175.4	499.1	664.0	658.4	1,514.4	2,139.6

% Performance '94-'99

	Q1	Q2	Q3	Q4	Total
1994	10	-9	15	5	20
1995	13	26	22	-12	52
1996	-4	6	9	17	31
1997	-9	12	30	-26	-2
1998	16	11	9	39	96
1999	14	6			

Investment Style

Price / Earnings Ratio	54.0
Price / Book Ratio	13.9
3 Yr Earnings Growth	21.4
Median Mkt Cap $M	$49,629

Composition	% of Assets
Cash	12.8
Stocks	87.2
Bonds	0.0

Portfolio Analysis

Total Stocks:

Top Ten Stocks

EMC Corp.	9.7%
Texas Inst.	7.3%
Microsoft	5.7%
Cisco Systems	5.6%
Micron Tech	5.2%
Applied Materials	5.2%
America Online	4.8%
Dell Computer	4.4%
Compaq Computer	2.9%
Intel Corp.	2.6%

Special Securities

Private / Illiquid Securities : No

Options / Futures : No

Address : 82 Devonshire St.
Boston, MA 02109
Telephone: (800) 544-8888 or (617) 439-1648
Web: www.fidelity.com
Advisor: Fidelity Mgmt. & Research
Manager: Michael Tempero
States Avail: All

Minimum Purchase: $2,500
Add: $250
IRA: $500
Front Load: 3.00%
Management Fee: 0.30%+
Expense Ratio: %
Morningstar Rating: * * *

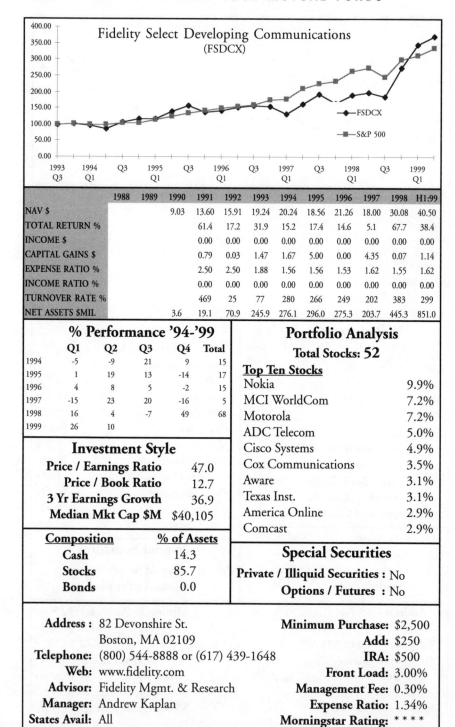

	1988	1989	1990	1991	1992	1993	1994	1995	1996	1997	1998	H1:99
NAV $			9.03	13.60	15.91	19.24	20.24	18.56	21.26	18.00	30.08	40.50
TOTAL RETURN %				61.4	17.2	31.9	15.2	17.4	14.6	5.1	67.7	38.4
INCOME $				0.00	0.00	0.00	0.00	0.00	0.00	0.00	0.00	0.00
CAPITAL GAINS $				0.79	0.03	1.47	1.67	5.00	0.00	4.35	0.07	1.14
EXPENSE RATIO %				2.50	2.50	1.88	1.56	1.56	1.53	1.62	1.55	1.62
INCOME RATIO %				0.00	0.00	0.00	0.00	0.00	0.00	0.00	0.00	0.00
TURNOVER RATE %				469	25	77	280	266	249	202	383	299
NET ASSETS $MIL			3.6	19.1	70.9	245.9	276.1	296.0	275.3	203.7	445.3	851.0

% Performance '94-'99

	Q1	Q2	Q3	Q4	Total
1994	-5	-9	21	9	15
1995	1	19	13	-14	17
1996	4	8	5	-2	15
1997	-15	23	20	-16	5
1998	16	4	-7	49	68
1999	26	10			

Investment Style

Price / Earnings Ratio	47.0
Price / Book Ratio	12.7
3 Yr Earnings Growth	36.9
Median Mkt Cap $M	$40,105

Composition	% of Assets
Cash	14.3
Stocks	85.7
Bonds	0.0

Portfolio Analysis

Total Stocks: 52

Top Ten Stocks

Nokia	9.9%
MCI WorldCom	7.2%
Motorola	7.2%
ADC Telecom	5.0%
Cisco Systems	4.9%
Cox Communications	3.5%
Aware	3.1%
Texas Inst.	3.1%
America Online	2.9%
Comcast	2.9%

Special Securities

Private / Illiquid Securities : No
Options / Futures : No

Address :	82 Devonshire St.	**Minimum Purchase:**	$2,500
	Boston, MA 02109	**Add:**	$250
Telephone:	(800) 544-8888 or (617) 439-1648	**IRA:**	$500
Web:	www.fidelity.com	**Front Load:**	3.00%
Advisor:	Fidelity Mgmt. & Research	**Management Fee:**	0.30%
Manager:	Andrew Kaplan	**Expense Ratio:**	1.34%
States Avail:	All	**Morningstar Rating:**	★ ★ ★ ★

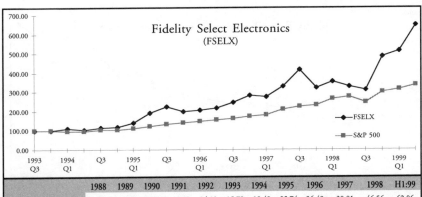

Fidelity Select Electronics (FSELX)

	1988	1989	1990	1991	1992	1993	1994	1995	1996	1997	1998	H1:99
NAV	6.70	7.75	8.19	11.08	14.12	15.78	18.49	25.74	36.48	30.81	46.56	62.06
TOTAL RETURN %	-8.5	15.7	5.8	35.3	27.4	32.1	17.2	69.4	41.7	13.3	51.1	33.3
INCOME $	0.00	0.00	0.01	0.00	0.00	0.00	0.00	0.00	0.00	0.00	0.00	0.00
CAPITAL GAINS $	0.00	0.00	0.00	0.00	0.00	2.75	0.00	5.25	0.00	6.95	0.00	0.00
EXPENSE RATIO %	2.54	2.79	2.57	2.26	2.16	1.69	1.67	1.71	1.22	1.29	1.15	1.29
INCOME RATIO %	0.00	0.00	0.00	0.00	0.00	0.00	0.00	0.00	0.00	0.00	0.00	0.00
TURNOVER RATE %	686	697	378	268	299	293	163	205	366	341	435	160
NET ASSETS $MIL	10.9	5.0	13.4	10.3	53.7	45.6	156.6	892.3	1,565.0	2,603.2	2,772.8	4,224.6

% Performance '94–'99

	Q1	Q2	Q3	Q4	Total
1994	11	-6	9	3	17
1995	18	36	19	-11	69
1996	3	5	13	16	42
1997	-3	20	26	-23	14
1998	10	-8	-6	57	51
1999	6	26			

Investment Style

Price / Earnings Ratio	52.9
Price / Book Ratio	8.2
3 Yr Earnings Growth	4.6
Median Mkt Cap $M	$10,572

Composition	% of Assets
Cash	10.6
Stocks	69.4
Bonds	0.0

Portfolio Analysis

Total Stocks: 66

Top Ten Stocks

Texas Instruments	10.1%
Micron Tech	9.5%
Intel	6.9%
Applied Materials	5.6%
Motorola	5.0%
KLA-Tencor	3.6%
Xilinx	3.2%
Teradyne	3.2%
Lam Research	2.8%
Cadence Design	2.7%

Special Securities

Private / Illiquid Securities : No
Options / Futures : No

Address : 82 Devonshire St.
Boston, MA 02109
Telephone: (800) 544-8888
Web: www.fidelity.com
Advisor: Fidelity Mgmt. & Research
Manager: Matthew Grech
States Avail: All

Minimum Purchase: $2,500
Add: $250
IRA: $500
Front Load: 3.00%
Management Fee: 0.30%+
Expense Ratio: 1.15%
Morningstar Rating: * * * * *

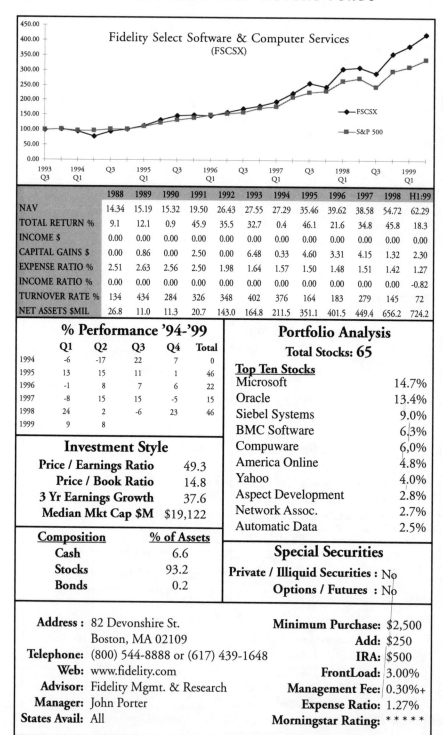

Fidelity Select Software & Computer Services (FSCSX)

	1988	1989	1990	1991	1992	1993	1994	1995	1996	1997	1998	H1:99
NAV	14.34	15.19	15.32	19.50	26.43	27.55	27.29	35.46	39.62	38.58	54.72	62.29
TOTAL RETURN %	9.1	12.1	0.9	45.9	35.5	32.7	0.4	46.1	21.6	34.8	45.8	18.3
INCOME $	0.00	0.00	0.00	0.00	0.00	0.00	0.00	0.00	0.00	0.00	0.00	0.00
CAPITAL GAINS $	0.00	0.86	0.00	2.50	0.00	6.48	0.33	4.60	3.31	4.15	1.32	2.30
EXPENSE RATIO %	2.51	2.63	2.56	2.50	1.98	1.64	1.57	1.50	1.48	1.51	1.42	1.27
INCOME RATIO %	0.00	0.00	0.00	0.00	0.00	0.00	0.00	0.00	0.00	0.00	0.00	-0.82
TURNOVER RATE %	134	434	284	326	348	402	376	164	183	279	145	72
NET ASSETS $MIL	26.8	11.0	11.3	20.7	143.0	164.8	211.5	351.1	401.5	449.4	656.2	724.2

% Performance '94-'99

	Q1	Q2	Q3	Q4	Total
1994	-6	-17	22	7	0
1995	13	15	11	1	46
1996	-1	8	7	6	22
1997	-8	15	15	-5	15
1998	24	2	-6	23	46
1999	9	8			

Investment Style

Price / Earnings Ratio	49.3
Price / Book Ratio	14.8
3 Yr Earnings Growth	37.6
Median Mkt Cap $M	$19,122

Composition	% of Assets
Cash	6.6
Stocks	93.2
Bonds	0.2

Portfolio Analysis

Total Stocks: 65

Top Ten Stocks

Microsoft	14.7%
Oracle	13.4%
Siebel Systems	9.0%
BMC Software	6.3%
Compuware	6.0%
America Online	4.8%
Yahoo	4.0%
Aspect Development	2.8%
Network Assoc.	2.7%
Automatic Data	2.5%

Special Securities

Private / Illiquid Securities : No
Options / Futures : No

Address : 82 Devonshire St.
Boston, MA 02109
Telephone: (800) 544-8888 or (617) 439-1648
Web: www.fidelity.com
Advisor: Fidelity Mgmt. & Research
Manager: John Porter
States Avail: All

Minimum Purchase: $2,500
Add: $250
IRA: $500
FrontLoad: 3.00%
Management Fee: 0.30%+
Expense Ratio: 1.27%
Morningstar Rating: * * * * *

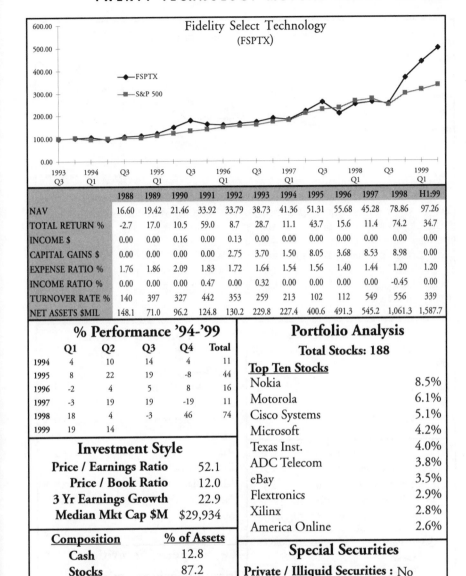

Fidelity Select Technology (FSPTX)

	1988	1989	1990	1991	1992	1993	1994	1995	1996	1997	1998	H1:99
NAV	16.60	19.42	21.46	33.92	33.79	38.73	41.36	51.31	55.68	45.28	78.86	97.26
TOTAL RETURN %	-2.7	17.0	10.5	59.0	8.7	28.7	11.1	43.7	15.6	11.4	74.2	34.7
INCOME $	0.00	0.00	0.16	0.00	0.13	0.00	0.00	0.00	0.00	0.00	0.00	0.00
CAPITAL GAINS $	0.00	0.00	0.00	0.00	2.75	3.70	1.50	8.05	3.68	8.53	8.98	0.00
EXPENSE RATIO %	1.76	1.86	2.09	1.83	1.72	1.64	1.54	1.56	1.40	1.44	1.20	1.20
INCOME RATIO %	0.00	0.00	0.00	0.47	0.00	0.32	0.00	0.00	0.00	0.00	-0.45	0.00
TURNOVER RATE %	140	397	327	442	353	259	213	102	112	549	556	339
NET ASSETS $MIL	148.1	71.0	96.2	124.8	130.2	229.8	227.4	400.6	491.3	545.2	1,061.3	1,587.7

% Performance '94-'99

	Q1	Q2	Q3	Q4	Total
1994	4	10	14	4	11
1995	8	22	19	-8	44
1996	-2	4	5	8	16
1997	-3	19	19	-19	11
1998	18	4	-3	46	74
1999	19	14			

Investment Style

Price / Earnings Ratio	52.1
Price / Book Ratio	12.0
3 Yr Earnings Growth	22.9
Median Mkt Cap $M	$29,934

Composition	% of Assets
Cash	12.8
Stocks	87.2
Bonds	0.0

Portfolio Analysis

Total Stocks: 188

Top Ten Stocks

Nokia	8.5%
Motorola	6.1%
Cisco Systems	5.1%
Microsoft	4.2%
Texas Inst.	4.0%
ADC Telecom	3.8%
eBay	3.5%
Flextronics	2.9%
Xilinx	2.8%
America Online	2.6%

Special Securities

Private / Illiquid Securities : No

Options / Futures : No

Address : 82 Devonshire St.
Boston, MA 02109
Telephone: (800) 544-8888 or (617) 439-1648
Web: www.fidelity.com
Advisor: Fidelity Mgmt. & Research
Manager: Andrew Kaplan
States Avail: All

Minimum Purchase: $2,500
Add: $250
IRA: $500
Front Load: 3.00%
Management Fee: 0.30%+
Expense Ratio: 1.20%
Morningstar Rating: * * * * *

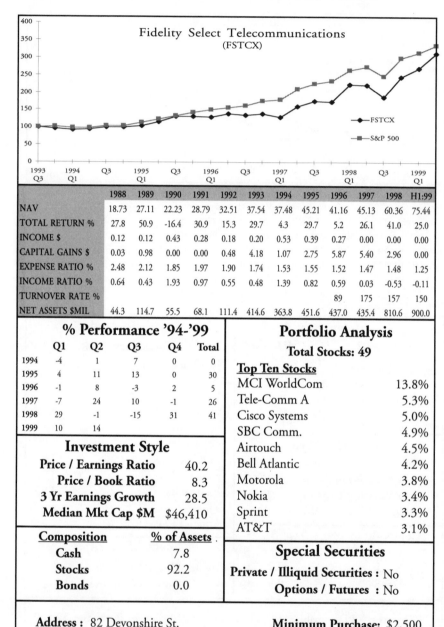

	1988	1989	1990	1991	1992	1993	1994	1995	1996	1997	1998	H1:99
NAV	18.73	27.11	22.23	28.79	32.51	37.54	37.48	45.21	41.16	45.13	60.36	75.44
TOTAL RETURN %	27.8	50.9	-16.4	30.9	15.3	29.7	4.3	29.7	5.2	26.1	41.0	25.0
INCOME $	0.12	0.12	0.43	0.28	0.18	0.20	0.53	0.39	0.27	0.00	0.00	0.00
CAPITAL GAINS $	0.03	0.98	0.00	0.00	0.48	4.18	1.07	2.75	5.87	5.40	2.96	0.00
EXPENSE RATIO %	2.48	2.12	1.85	1.97	1.90	1.74	1.53	1.55	1.52	1.47	1.48	1.25
INCOME RATIO %	0.64	0.43	1.93	0.97	0.55	0.48	1.39	0.82	0.59	0.03	-0.53	-0.11
TURNOVER RATE %									89	175	157	150
NET ASSETS $MIL	44.3	114.7	55.5	68.1	111.4	414.6	363.8	451.6	437.0	435.4	810.6	900.0

% Performance '94-'99

	Q1	Q2	Q3	Q4	Total
1994	-4	1	7	0	0
1995	4	11	13	0	30
1996	-1	8	-3	2	5
1997	-7	24	10	-1	26
1998	29	-1	-15	31	41
1999	10	14			

Investment Style

Price / Earnings Ratio	40.2
Price / Book Ratio	8.3
3 Yr Earnings Growth	28.5
Median Mkt Cap $M	$46,410

Composition	% of Assets
Cash	7.8
Stocks	92.2
Bonds	0.0

Portfolio Analysis

Total Stocks: 49

Top Ten Stocks

MCI WorldCom	13.8%
Tele-Comm A	5.3%
Cisco Systems	5.0%
SBC Comm.	4.9%
Airtouch	4.5%
Bell Atlantic	4.2%
Motorola	3.8%
Nokia	3.4%
Sprint	3.3%
AT&T	3.1%

Special Securities

Private / Illiquid Securities : No

Options / Futures : No

Address : 82 Devonshire St.
Boston, MA 02109
Telephone: (800) 544-8888 or (617) 439-1648
Web: www.fidelity.com
Advisor: Fidelity Mgmt. & Research
Manager: Peter Saperstone
States Avail: All

Minimum Purchase: $2,500
Add: $250
IRA: $500
Front Load: 3.00%
Management Fee: 0.30%
Expense Ratio: 1.25%
Morningstar Rating: ★ ★ ★ ★

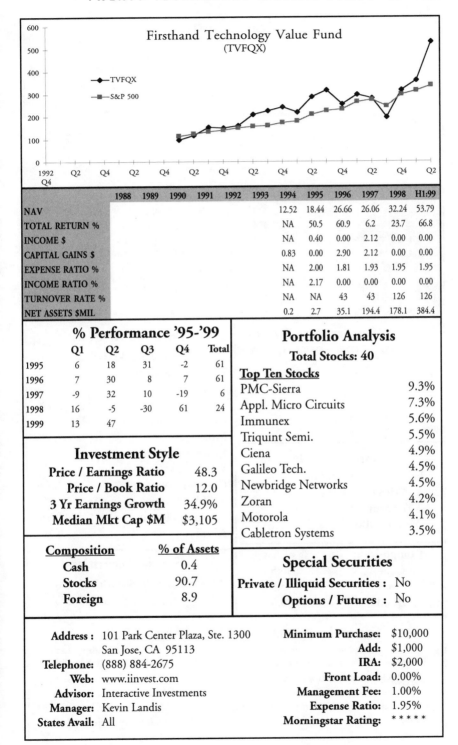

Firsthand Technology Value Fund (TVFQX)

	1988	1989	1990	1991	1992	1993	1994	1995	1996	1997	1998	H1:99
NAV							12.52	18.44	26.66	26.06	32.24	53.79
TOTAL RETURN %							NA	50.5	60.9	6.2	23.7	66.8
INCOME $							NA	0.40	0.00	2.12	0.00	0.00
CAPITAL GAINS $							0.83	0.00	2.90	2.12	0.00	0.00
EXPENSE RATIO %							NA	2.00	1.81	1.93	1.95	1.95
INCOME RATIO %							NA	2.17	0.00	0.00	0.00	0.00
TURNOVER RATE %							NA	NA	43	43	126	126
NET ASSETS $MIL							0.2	2.7	35.1	194.4	178.1	384.4

% Performance '95-'99

	Q1	Q2	Q3	Q4	Total
1995	6	18	31	-2	61
1996	7	30	8	7	61
1997	-9	32	10	-19	6
1998	16	-5	-30	61	24
1999	13	47			

Investment Style

Price / Earnings Ratio	48.3
Price / Book Ratio	12.0
3 Yr Earnings Growth	34.9%
Median Mkt Cap $M	$3,105

Composition	% of Assets
Cash	0.4
Stocks	90.7
Foreign	8.9

Portfolio Analysis

Total Stocks: 40

Top Ten Stocks

PMC-Sierra	9.3%
Appl. Micro Circuits	7.3%
Immunex	5.6%
Triquint Semi.	5.5%
Ciena	4.9%
Galileo Tech.	4.5%
Newbridge Networks	4.5%
Zoran	4.2%
Motorola	4.1%
Cabletron Systems	3.5%

Special Securities

Private / Illiquid Securities : No
Options / Futures : No

Address :	101 Park Center Plaza, Ste. 1300	**Minimum Purchase:**	$10,000
	San Jose, CA 95113	**Add:**	$1,000
Telephone:	(888) 884-2675	**IRA:**	$2,000
Web:	www.iinvest.com	**Front Load:**	0.00%
Advisor:	Interactive Investments	**Management Fee:**	1.00%
Manager:	Kevin Landis	**Expense Ratio:**	1.95%
States Avail:	All	**Morningstar Rating:**	✶ ✶ ✶ ✶ ✶

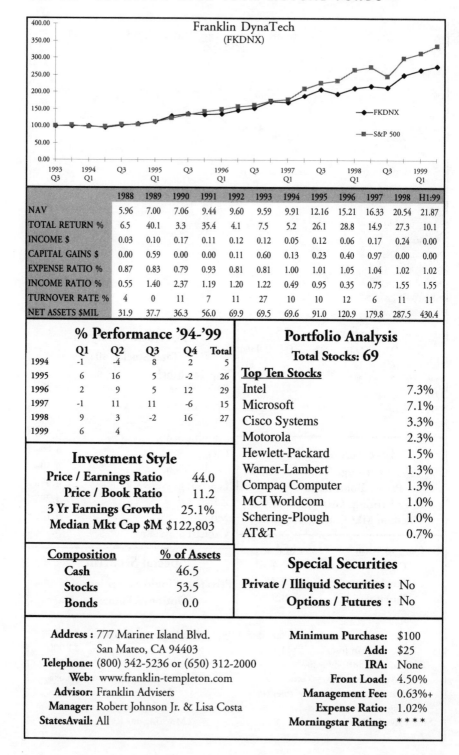

Franklin DynaTech (FKDNX)

	1988	1989	1990	1991	1992	1993	1994	1995	1996	1997	1998	H1:99
NAV	5.96	7.00	7.06	9.44	9.60	9.59	9.91	12.16	15.21	16.33	20.54	21.87
TOTAL RETURN %	6.5	40.1	3.3	35.4	4.1	7.5	5.2	26.1	28.8	14.9	27.3	10.1
INCOME $	0.03	0.10	0.17	0.11	0.12	0.12	0.05	0.12	0.06	0.17	0.24	0.00
CAPITAL GAINS $	0.00	0.59	0.00	0.00	0.11	0.60	0.13	0.23	0.40	0.97	0.00	0.00
EXPENSE RATIO %	0.87	0.83	0.79	0.93	0.81	0.81	1.00	1.01	1.05	1.04	1.02	1.02
INCOME RATIO %	0.55	1.40	2.37	1.19	1.20	1.22	0.49	0.95	0.35	0.75	1.55	1.55
TURNOVER RATE %	4	0	11	7	11	27	10	10	12	6	11	11
NET ASSETS $MIL	31.9	37.7	36.3	56.0	69.9	69.5	69.6	91.0	120.9	179.8	287.5	430.4

% Performance '94-'99

	Q1	Q2	Q3	Q4	Total
1994	-1	-4	8	2	5
1995	6	16	5	-2	26
1996	2	9	5	12	29
1997	-1	11	11	-6	15
1998	9	3	-2	16	27
1999	6	4			

Investment Style

Price / Earnings Ratio	44.0
Price / Book Ratio	11.2
3 Yr Earnings Growth	25.1%
Median Mkt Cap $M	$122,803

Composition	% of Assets
Cash	46.5
Stocks	53.5
Bonds	0.0

Portfolio Analysis

Total Stocks: 69

Top Ten Stocks

Intel	7.3%
Microsoft	7.1%
Cisco Systems	3.3%
Motorola	2.3%
Hewlett-Packard	1.5%
Warner-Lambert	1.3%
Compaq Computer	1.3%
MCI Worldcom	1.0%
Schering-Plough	1.0%
AT&T	0.7%

Special Securities

Private / Illiquid Securities :	No
Options / Futures :	No

Address : 777 Mariner Island Blvd.
San Mateo, CA 94403
Telephone: (800) 342-5236 or (650) 312-2000
Web: www.franklin-templeton.com
Advisor: Franklin Advisers
Manager: Robert Johnson Jr. & Lisa Costa
StatesAvail: All

Minimum Purchase:	$100
Add:	$25
IRA:	None
Front Load:	4.50%
Management Fee:	0.63%+
Expense Ratio:	1.02%
Morningstar Rating:	★ ★ ★ ★

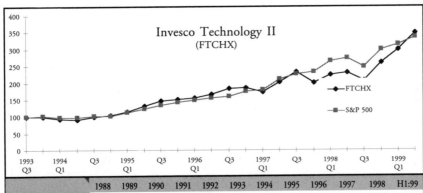

Invesco Technology II
(FTCHX)

	1988	1989	1990	1991	1992	1993	1994	1995	1996	1997	1998	H1:99
NAV	10.45	12.69	13.78	19.62	23.31	23.59	24.04	29.19	30.99	26.89	34.99	46.72
TOTAL RETURN %	14.2	21.4	8.6	76.9	18.8	15.0	5.3	45.8	21.8	8.9	30.1	34.0
INCOME $	0.00	0.00	0.00	0.00	0.00	0.00	0.00	0.00	0.07	0.00	0.00	0.00
CAPITAL GAINS $	0.00	0.00	0.00	4.39	0.00	3.22	0.79	5.86	4.49	6.45	0.00	0.00
EXPENSE RATIO %	1.72	1.59	1.25	1.19	1.12	1.13	1.17	1.12	1.08	1.05	1.17	1.17
INCOME RATIO %	0.00	0.00	0.00	0.00	0.00	0.00	0.00	0.00	0.20	0.41	0.00	0.00
TURNOVER RATE %	356	259	345	307	169	184	145	191	168	237	178	178.00
NET ASSETS $MIL	14.5	10.1	27.0	106.7	256.5	251.6	310.1	576.0	838.5	1,021.3	1,147.7	1,077.8

% Performance '94–'99

	Q1	Q2	Q3	Q4	Total
1994	-4	-4	11	4	5
1995	9	15	12	4	46
1996	3	6	11	1	22
1997	-7	17	15	-14	8
1998	12	4	-10	25	30
1999	15	16			

Investment Style

Price / Earnings Ratio	51.8
Price / Book Ratio	12.5
3 Yr Earnings Growth	33.8%
Median Mkt Cap $M	$7,050

Composition	% of Assets
Cash	5.3
Stocks	94.7
Converts	0.0

Portfolio Analysis

Total Stocks: 90

Top Ten Stocks

Microsoft	2.9%
Cisco Systems	2.8%
Nokia	2.6%
America Online	2.4%
Sun Microsystems	2.2%
CMGI	2.2%
EMC Corp.	2.0%
Gemstar	2.0%
Fiserv	1.9%
Maxim Integrated	1.8%

Special Securities

Private / Illiquid Securities :	Yes
Options / Futures :	Yes

Address : P.O. Box 173706
Denver, CO 80217-3706
Telephone: (800) 525-8085 or (303) 930-6300
Web: www.invesco.com
Advisor: Invesco Funds Group
Manager: Bill Keithler
States Avail: All

Minimum Purchase:	$1,000
Add:	$50
IRA:	$250
Front Load:	0.00%
Management Fee:	0.75%
Expense Ratio:	1.17%
Morningstar Rating:	★ ★ ★ ★ ★

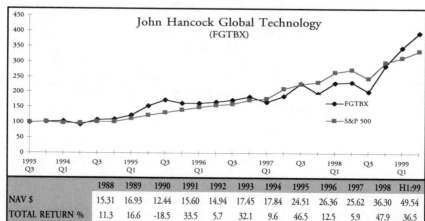

John Hancock Global Technology (FGTBX)

	1988	1989	1990	1991	1992	1993	1994	1995	1996	1997	1998	H1:99
NAV $	15.31	16.93	12.44	15.60	14.94	17.45	17.84	24.51	26.36	25.62	36.30	49.54
TOTAL RETURN %	11.3	16.6	-18.5	33.5	5.7	32.1	9.6	46.5	12.5	5.9	47.9	36.5
INCOME $	0.24	0.13	0.00	0.04	0.00	0.00	0.00	0.00	0.00	0.00	0.00	0.00
CAPITAL GAINS $	0.00	0.78	1.36	0.97	1.51	2.20	1.26	1.64	1.22	2.40	0.25	0.00
EXPENSE RATIO %	1.75	1.90	2.36	2.32	2.05	2.10	2.16	1.67	1.57	2.21	2.41	2.41
INCOME RATIO %	1.57	0.73	0.00	0.23	0.00	0.00	0.00	0.00	0.00	0.00	0.00	0.00
TURNOVER RATE %	NA	NA	NA	NA	NA	NA	NA	NA	64	104	104	104
NET ASSETS $MIL	38.6	40.3	28.9	31.6	32.1	41.7	52.2	155.0	173.1	180.0	246.3	402.7

% Performance '94-'99

	Q1	Q2	Q3	Q4	Total
1994	2	9	15	3	10
1995	11	25	13	-6	47
1996	0	3	3	6	13
1997	-10	12	22	-15	6
1998	18	1	-13	43	49
1999	20	14			

Investment Style

Price / Earnings Ratio	49.8
Price / Book Ratio	14.1
3 Yr Earnings Growth	30.8
Median Mkt Cap $M	$7,229

Composition	% of Assets
Cash	10.6
Stocks	89.3
Bonds, Other	0.1

Portfolio Analysis

Total Stocks: 90

Top Ten Stocks

America Online	7.2%
EMC Corp.	4.0%
Cisco Systems	3.8%
Microsoft	3.4%
Dell Computer	3.0%
Metromedia Fiber	2.6%
Exodus Comm	2.2%
Realnetworks	2.1%
Yahoo	2.1%
Nokia	2.1%

Special Securities

Private / Illiquid Securities : No

Options / Futures : No

Address :	101 Huntington Ave. Boston, MA 02199	**Minimum Purchase:**	$1,000
		Add:	None
Telephone:	(800) 225-5291 or (617) 375-1500	**IRA:**	$250
Web:	www.jhancock.com/funds	**Deferred Load:**	5.00%
Advisor:	John Hancock Advisers	**Management Fee:**	0.82%
Manager:	Marc Klee & Barry Gordon	**Expense Ratio:**	2.41%
States Avail:	All	**Morningstar Rating:**	*

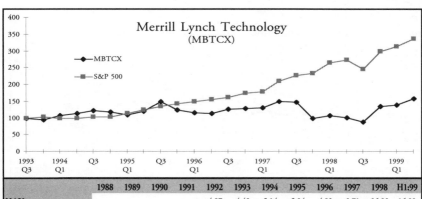

Merrill Lynch Technology (MBTCX)

	1988	1989	1990	1991	1992	1993	1994	1995	1996	1997	1998	H1:99
NAV					4.87	4.43	5.14	5.04	4.82	3.71	36.93	16.30
TOTAL RETURN %					0.4	0.2	0.3	0.0	0.0	-23.0	36.9	16.3
INCOME $					0.34	0.00	0.40	0.00	0.00	1.20	0.00	0.00
CAPITAL GAINS $					0.00	1.37	0.00	0.32	0.38	0.00	0.00	0.00
EXPENSE RATIO %					0.00	0.00	0.00	2.38	2.34	2.35	2.35	2.35
INCOME RATIO %					0.00	0.00	7.88	0.00	0.00	0.00	0.00	0.00
TURNOVER RATE %					N/A	N/A	N/A	N/A	108	177	177	177
NET ASSETS $MIL					41.5	141.1	613.1	637.0	434.3	352.7	291.5	230.2

% Performance '94-'99

	Q1	Q2	Q3	Q4	Total
1994	15	60	6	-3	26
1995	-7	10	25	-18	5
1996	-8	0	11	1	3
1997	1	15	0	-34	-23
1998	9	-7	-12	52	42
1999	3	13			

Investment Style

Price / Earnings Ratio	24.9
Price / Book Ratio	4.4
%/Yr Earnings Growth	14.6%
Median Mkt Cap $M	$1,985

Composition	% of Assets
Cash	45.0
Stocks	55.0
Bonds	0.0

Portfolio Analysis

Total Stocks: 58

Top Ten Stocks

America Online	6.1%
Microsoft	5.6%
Maxim Integrated	3.5%
Keane	3.4%
Sanmina	3.2%
Texas Inst.	2.8%
Flextronics Intl.	2.8%
Compaq Computer	2.6%
Compuware	2.6%
Xilinx	2.4%

Special Securities

Private / Illiquid Securities : No

Options / Futures : No

Address : P.O. Box 9011
Princeton, NJ 08543-9011
Telephone: (800) 637-3863 or (609) 282-2800
Web: www.merrill.com
Advisor: Merrill Lynch Asset Mgmt.
Manager: Paul Meeks
States Avail: All

Minimum Purchase: $1,000
Add: $50
IRA: $100
Deferred Load: 4.00%
Management Fee: 1.00%
Expense Ratio: 2.35%
Morningstar Rating: *

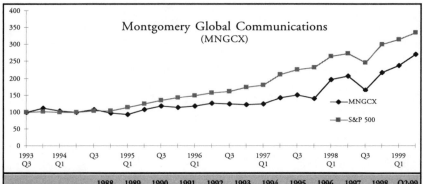

	1988	1989	1990	1991	1992	1993	1994	1995	1996	1997	1998	Q2:99
NAV						16.18	13.98	16.34	16.74	15.57	21.41	26.73
TOTAL RETURN %							-13.4	16.9	8.0	15.4	53.6	24.8
INCOME $						0.00	0.00	0.00	0.00	0.00	0.00	0.00
CAPITAL GAINS $							0.03	N/A	0.90	3.75	2.51	0.00
EXPENSE RATIO %						N/A	1.94	1.91	1.90	1.91	1.90	1.90
INCOME RATIO %							0.00	0.00	0.00	0.00	0.00	0.00
TURNOVER RATE %									104	76	80	80
NET ASSETS $MIL						220.9	216.4	220.0	165.4	138.3	282.1	311.4

% Performance '94-'99

	Q1	Q2	Q3	Q4	Total
1994	-7	-6	9	-10	-13
1995	-4	15	11	-5	17
1996	4	6	-1	-1	8
1997	1	16	6	-7	15
1998	39	6	-20	32	54
1999	9	14			

Investment Style

Price / Earnings Ratio	42.4
Price / Book Ratio	8.2
3 Yr Earnings Growth	26.0%
Median Mkt Cap $M	$13,248

Composition	% of Assets
Cash	7.9
Stocks	91.0
Bonds	1.1

Portfolio Analysis

Total Stocks: 51

Top Ten Stocks

Global Telesys	4.3%
MCI WorldCom	3%
KPN (Konin) NV	3%
Mannesmann AG	2.9%
Nokia OYG	2.8%
Swisscom AG-Reg	2.8%
Orange PLC	2.7%
Cap Gemini SA	2.6%
Network Assoc.	2.6%
Fox Entertainment	2.5%

Special Securities

Private / Illiquid Securities : No

Options / Futures : No

Address :	101 California Street	**Minimum Purchase:**	$1,000
	San Francisco, CA 94111	**Add:**	$100
Telephone:	(800) 572-3863 or (415) 268-6000	**IRA:**	$1,000
Web:	www.montgomeryfunds.com	**Front Load:**	0.00%
Advisor:	Montgomery Asset Mgmt.	**Management Fee:**	1.25%
Manager:	Oscar Castro & John Boich	**Expense Ratio:**	1.90%
States Avail:	All	**Morningstar Rating:**	* * *

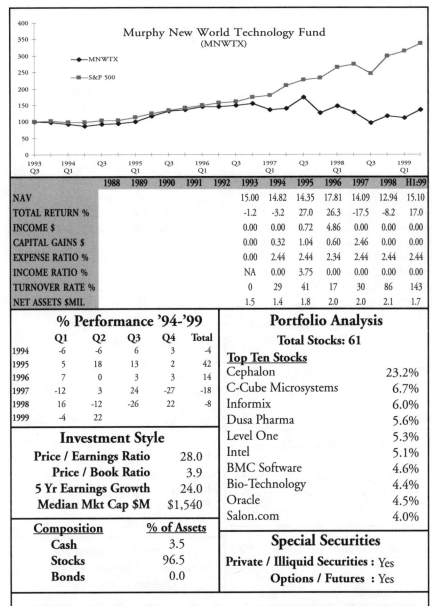

Murphy New World Technology Fund (MNWTX)

	1988	1989	1990	1991	1992	1993	1994	1995	1996	1997	1998	H1:99
NAV						15.00	14.82	14.35	17.81	14.09	12.94	15.10
TOTAL RETURN %						-1.2	-3.2	27.0	26.3	-17.5	-8.2	17.0
INCOME $						0.00	0.00	0.72	4.86	0.00	0.00	0.00
CAPITAL GAINS $						0.00	0.32	1.04	0.60	2.46	0.00	0.00
EXPENSE RATIO %						0.00	2.44	2.44	2.34	2.44	2.44	2.44
INCOME RATIO %						NA	0.00	3.75	0.00	0.00	0.00	0.00
TURNOVER RATE %						0	29	41	17	30	86	143
NET ASSETS $MIL						1.5	1.4	1.8	2.0	2.0	2.1	1.7

% Performance '94–'99

	Q1	Q2	Q3	Q4	Total
1994	-6	-6	6	3	-4
1995	5	18	13	2	42
1996	7	0	3	3	14
1997	-12	3	24	-27	-18
1998	16	-12	-26	22	-8
1999	-4	22			

Investment Style

Price / Earnings Ratio	28.0
Price / Book Ratio	3.9
5 Yr Earnings Growth	24.0
Median Mkt Cap $M	$1,540

Composition	% of Assets
Cash	3.5
Stocks	96.5
Bonds	0.0

Portfolio Analysis

Total Stocks: 61

Top Ten Stocks

Cephalon	23.2%
C-Cube Microsystems	6.7%
Informix	6.0%
Dusa Pharma	5.6%
Level One	5.3%
Intel	5.1%
BMC Software	4.6%
Bio-Technology	4.4%
Oracle	4.5%
Salon.com	4.0%

Special Securities

Private / Illiquid Securities : Yes

Options / Futures : Yes

Address : P. O. Box 308
Half Moon Bay, CA 94019
Telephone: (650) 726-8495
Web: www.ctsl.com
Advisor: Murphy Investment Mgmt.
Manager: Michael Murphy
States Avail: All

Minimum Purchase: $1,000
Add: $50
IRA: $100
Front Load: 0.00%
Management Fee: No load
Expense Ratio: 1.99%
Morningstar Rating: NR

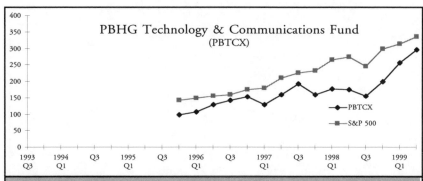

PBHG Technology & Communications Fund (PBTCX)

	1988	1989	1990	1991	1992	1993	1994	1995	1996	1997	1998	H1:99
NAV								11.60	17.56	17.28	21.45	31.84
TOTAL RETURN %								16.0	54.4	3.2	25.8	48.4
INCOME $								0.00	0.00	0.00	0.00	0.00
CAPITAL GAINS $								0.00	0.35	0.85	0.29	0.00
EXPENSE RATIO %								0.00	1.50	1.33	1.30	1.33
INCOME RATIO %								0.00	0.00	0.00	0.00	0.00
TURNOVER RATE %								0	126	289	260	276
NET ASSETS $MIL								35.9	562.6	606.1	396.3	679.7

% Performance '95-'99

	Q1	Q2	Q3	Q4	Total
1995				16	16
1996	8	20	11	8	54
1997	-17	25	20	-18	3
1998	12	-2	-11	29	26
1999	29	15			

Investment Style

Price / Earnings Ratio	53.1
Price / Book Ratio	14.3
3 Yr Earnings Growth	24.6%
Median Mkt Cap $M	$10,286

Composition	% of Assets
Cash	9.3
Stocks	90.7
Bonds	0.0

Portfolio Analysis

Total Stocks: 38

Top Ten Stocks

America Online	8.7%
Xilinx	5.9%
Microsoft	3.3%
Applied Material	3.2%
PSINet	3.1%
EMC Corp.	3%
Verio	3%
Motorola	2.8%
MCI WorldCom	2.8%
Linear Technology	2.5%

Special Securities

Private / Illiquid Securities : No
Options / Futures : No

Address : 680 E. Swedesford Rd.
Wayne, PA 19087-1658
Telephone: (800) 433-0051
Web: www.pbhgfunds.com
Advisor: Pilgrim Baxter & Assoc.
Manager: Jeffery Wrona
States Avail: All

Minimum Purchase: $2,500
Add: None
IRA: $2,000
Front Load: 0.00%
Management Fee: 0.85%
Expense Ratio: 1.34%
Morningstar Rating: ••••

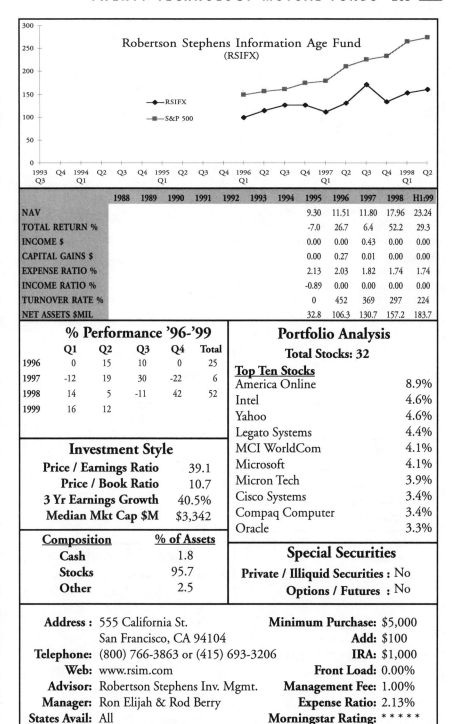

Robertson Stephens Information Age Fund (RSIFX)

	1988	1989	1990	1991	1992	1993	1994	1995	1996	1997	1998	H1:99
NAV								9.30	11.51	11.80	17.96	23.24
TOTAL RETURN %								-7.0	26.7	6.4	52.2	29.3
INCOME $								0.00	0.00	0.43	0.00	0.00
CAPITAL GAINS $								0.00	0.27	0.01	0.00	0.00
EXPENSE RATIO %								2.13	2.03	1.82	1.74	1.74
INCOME RATIO %								-0.89	0.00	0.00	0.00	0.00
TURNOVER RATE %								0	452	369	297	224
NET ASSETS $MIL								32.8	106.3	130.7	157.2	183.7

% Performance '96-'99

	Q1	Q2	Q3	Q4	Total
1996	0	15	10	0	25
1997	-12	19	30	-22	6
1998	14	5	-11	42	52
1999	16	12			

Investment Style

Price / Earnings Ratio	39.1
Price / Book Ratio	10.7
3 Yr Earnings Growth	40.5%
Median Mkt Cap $M	$3,342

Composition	% of Assets
Cash	1.8
Stocks	95.7
Other	2.5

Portfolio Analysis

Total Stocks: 32

Top Ten Stocks

America Online	8.9%
Intel	4.6%
Yahoo	4.6%
Legato Systems	4.4%
MCI WorldCom	4.1%
Microsoft	4.1%
Micron Tech	3.9%
Cisco Systems	3.4%
Compaq Computer	3.4%
Oracle	3.3%

Special Securities

Private / Illiquid Securities : No

Options / Futures : No

Address : 555 California St.
San Francisco, CA 94104
Telephone: (800) 766-3863 or (415) 693-3206
Web: www.rsim.com
Advisor: Robertson Stephens Inv. Mgmt.
Manager: Ron Elijah & Rod Berry
States Avail: All

Minimum Purchase: $5,000
Add: $100
IRA: $1,000
Front Load: 0.00%
Management Fee: 1.00%
Expense Ratio: 2.13%
Morningstar Rating: * * * * *

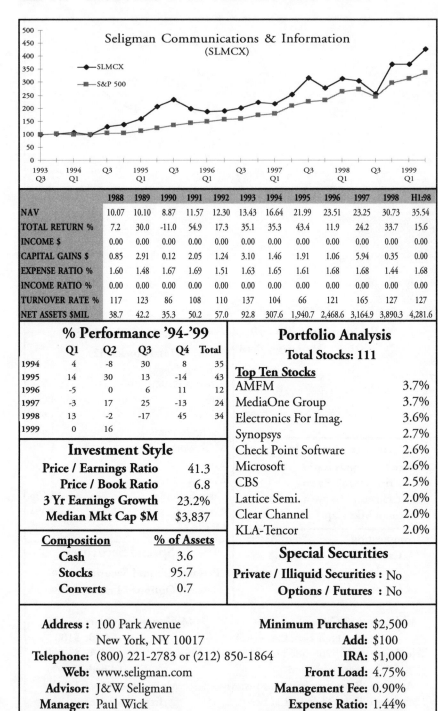

Seligman Communications & Information (SLMCX)

	1988	1989	1990	1991	1992	1993	1994	1995	1996	1997	1998	H1:98
NAV	10.07	10.10	8.87	11.57	12.30	13.43	16.64	21.99	23.51	23.25	30.73	35.54
TOTAL RETURN %	7.2	30.0	-11.0	54.9	17.3	35.1	35.3	43.4	11.9	24.2	33.7	15.6
INCOME $	0.00	0.00	0.00	0.00	0.00	0.00	0.00	0.00	0.00	0.00	0.00	0.00
CAPITAL GAINS $	0.85	2.91	0.12	2.05	1.24	3.10	1.46	1.91	1.06	5.94	0.35	0.00
EXPENSE RATIO %	1.60	1.48	1.67	1.69	1.51	1.63	1.65	1.61	1.68	1.68	1.44	1.68
INCOME RATIO %	0.00	0.00	0.00	0.00	0.00	0.00	0.00	0.00	0.00	0.00	0.00	0.00
TURNOVER RATE %	117	123	86	108	110	137	104	66	121	165	127	127
NET ASSETS $MIL	38.7	42.2	35.3	50.2	57.0	92.8	307.6	1,940.7	2,468.6	3,164.9	3,890.3	4,281.6

% Performance '94-'99

	Q1	Q2	Q3	Q4	Total
1994	4	-8	30	8	35
1995	14	30	13	-14	43
1996	-5	0	6	11	12
1997	-3	17	25	-13	24
1998	13	-2	-17	45	34
1999	0	16			

Investment Style

Price / Earnings Ratio	41.3
Price / Book Ratio	6.8
3 Yr Earnings Growth	23.2%
Median Mkt Cap $M	$3,837

Composition	% of Assets
Cash	3.6
Stocks	95.7
Converts	0.7

Portfolio Analysis

Total Stocks: 111

Top Ten Stocks

AMFM	3.7%
MediaOne Group	3.7%
Electronics For Imag.	3.6%
Synopsys	2.7%
Check Point Software	2.6%
Microsoft	2.6%
CBS	2.5%
Lattice Semi.	2.0%
Clear Channel	2.0%
KLA-Tencor	2.0%

Special Securities

Private / Illiquid Securities : No
Options / Futures : No

Address : 100 Park Avenue
New York, NY 10017
Telephone: (800) 221-2783 or (212) 850-1864
Web: www.seligman.com
Advisor: J&W Seligman
Manager: Paul Wick
States Avail: All

Minimum Purchase: $2,500
Add: $100
IRA: $1,000
Front Load: 4.75%
Management Fee: 0.90%
Expense Ratio: 1.44%
Morningstar Rating: *****

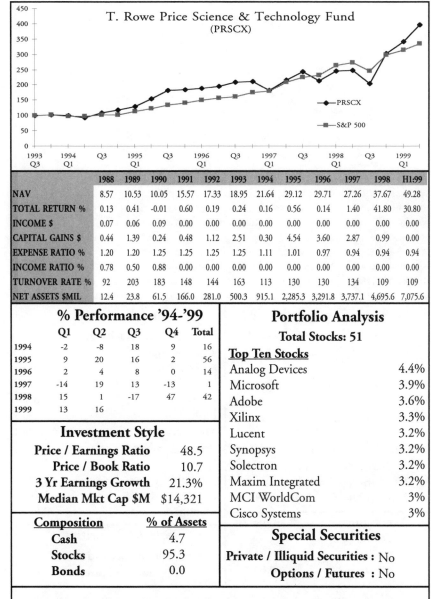

T. Rowe Price Science & Technology Fund
(PRSCX)

	1988	1989	1990	1991	1992	1993	1994	1995	1996	1997	1998	H1:99
NAV	8.57	10.53	10.05	15.57	17.33	18.95	21.64	29.12	29.71	27.26	37.67	49.28
TOTAL RETURN %	0.13	0.41	-0.01	0.60	0.19	0.24	0.16	0.56	0.14	1.40	41.80	30.80
INCOME $	0.07	0.06	0.09	0.00	0.00	0.00	0.00	0.00	0.00	0.00	0.00	0.00
CAPITAL GAINS $	0.44	1.39	0.24	0.48	1.12	2.51	0.30	4.54	3.60	2.87	0.99	0.00
EXPENSE RATIO %	1.20	1.20	1.25	1.25	1.25	1.25	1.11	1.01	0.97	0.94	0.94	0.94
INCOME RATIO %	0.78	0.50	0.88	0.00	0.00	0.00	0.00	0.00	0.00	0.00	0.00	0.00
TURNOVER RATE %	92	203	183	148	144	163	113	130	130	134	109	109
NET ASSETS $MIL	12.4	23.8	61.5	166.0	281.0	500.3	915.1	2,285.3	3,291.8	3,737.1	4,695.6	7,075.6

% Performance '94-'99

	Q1	Q2	Q3	Q4	Total
1994	-2	-8	18	9	16
1995	9	20	16	2	56
1996	2	4	8	0	14
1997	-14	19	13	-13	1
1998	15	1	-17	47	42
1999	13	16			

Investment Style

Price / Earnings Ratio	48.5
Price / Book Ratio	10.7
3 Yr Earnings Growth	21.3%
Median Mkt Cap $M	$14,321

Composition	% of Assets
Cash	4.7
Stocks	95.3
Bonds	0.0

Portfolio Analysis

Total Stocks: 51

Top Ten Stocks

Analog Devices	4.4%
Microsoft	3.9%
Adobe	3.6%
Xilinx	3.3%
Lucent	3.2%
Synopsys	3.2%
Solectron	3.2%
Maxim Integrated	3.2%
MCI WorldCom	3%
Cisco Systems	3%

Special Securities

Private / Illiquid Securities : No

Options / Futures : No

Address :	100 E. Pratt Street	**Minimum Purchase:**	$2,500
	Baltimore, MD 21202	**Add:**	$100
Telephone:	(800) 638-5660 or (410) 547-2308	**IRA:**	$1,000
Web:	www.troweprice.com	**Front Load:**	0.00%
Advisor:	T. Rowe Price Associates	**Management Fee:**	0.35%
Manager:	Chip Morris	**Expense Ratio:**	0.94%
States Avail:	All	**Morningstar Rating:**	* * * * *

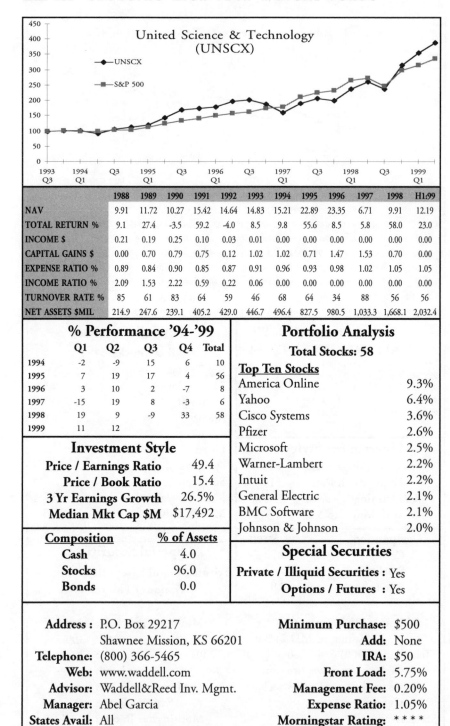

United Science & Technology (UNSCX)

◆— UNSCX
■— S&P 500

	1988	1989	1990	1991	1992	1993	1994	1995	1996	1997	1998	H1:99
NAV	9.91	11.72	10.27	15.42	14.64	14.83	15.21	22.89	23.35	6.71	9.91	12.19
TOTAL RETURN %	9.1	27.4	-3.5	59.2	-4.0	8.5	9.8	55.6	8.5	5.8	58.0	23.0
INCOME $	0.21	0.19	0.25	0.10	0.03	0.01	0.00	0.00	0.00	0.00	0.00	0.00
CAPITAL GAINS $	0.00	0.70	0.79	0.75	0.12	1.02	1.02	0.71	1.47	1.53	0.70	0.00
EXPENSE RATIO %	0.89	0.84	0.90	0.85	0.87	0.91	0.96	0.93	0.98	1.02	1.05	1.05
INCOME RATIO %	2.09	1.53	2.22	0.59	0.22	0.06	0.00	0.00	0.00	0.00	0.00	0.00
TURNOVER RATE %	85	61	83	64	59	46	68	64	34	88	56	56
NET ASSETS $MIL	214.9	247.6	239.1	405.2	429.0	446.7	496.4	827.5	980.5	1,033.3	1,668.1	2,032.4

% Performance '94-'99

	Q1	Q2	Q3	Q4	Total
1994	-2	-9	15	6	10
1995	7	19	17	4	56
1996	3	10	2	-7	8
1997	-15	19	8	-3	6
1998	19	9	-9	33	58
1999	11	12			

Investment Style

Price / Earnings Ratio	49.4
Price / Book Ratio	15.4
3 Yr Earnings Growth	26.5%
Median Mkt Cap $M	$17,492

Composition	% of Assets
Cash	4.0
Stocks	96.0
Bonds	0.0

Portfolio Analysis

Total Stocks: 58

Top Ten Stocks

America Online	9.3%
Yahoo	6.4%
Cisco Systems	3.6%
Pfizer	2.6%
Microsoft	2.5%
Warner-Lambert	2.2%
Intuit	2.2%
General Electric	2.1%
BMC Software	2.1%
Johnson & Johnson	2.0%

Special Securities

Private / Illiquid Securities : Yes
Options / Futures : Yes

Address : P.O. Box 29217		**Minimum Purchase:** $500
Shawnee Mission, KS 66201		**Add:** None
Telephone: (800) 366-5465		**IRA:** $50
Web: www.waddell.com		**Front Load:** 5.75%
Advisor: Waddell&Reed Inv. Mgmt.		**Management Fee:** 0.20%
Manager: Abel Garcia		**Expense Ratio:** 1.05%
States Avail: All		**Morningstar Rating:** ＊＊＊＊

## CHAPTER TWENTY-TWO

Seven Medical and Biotechnology Mutual Funds

There could hardly be clearer evidence that biotechnology is under-owned than the paucity of mutual funds dedicated to this sector. Wall Street's reticence to embrace the promise of biotechnology opens incredible opportunities for the individual investor in bio-tech companies and mutual funds.

As for the funds in Chapter 21, each page in this chapter shows a chart and two tables of performance data, information on investment style, the top ten holdings (pay particular attention to the percentage in biotechnology versus the percentage in traditional pharmaceuticals), and contact and fee information.

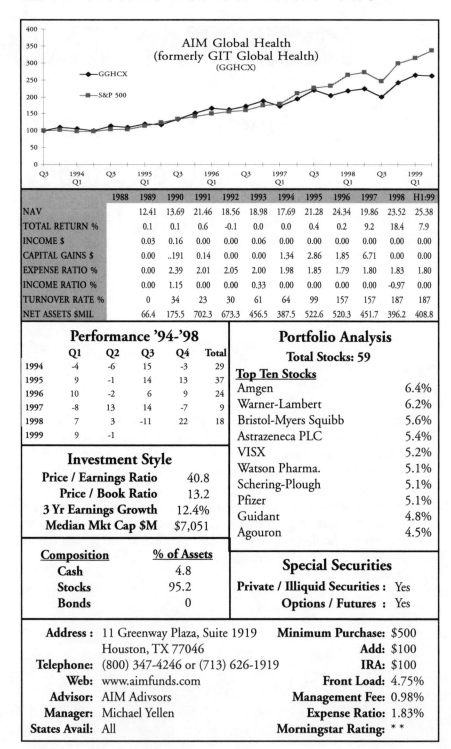

AIM Global Health
(formerly GIT Global Health)
(GGHCX)

◆ GGHCX
■ S&P 500

	1988	1989	1990	1991	1992	1993	1994	1995	1996	1997	1998	H1:99
NAV		12.41	13.69	21.46	18.56	18.98	17.69	21.28	24.34	19.86	23.52	25.38
TOTAL RETURN %		0.1	0.1	0.6	-0.1	0.0	0.0	0.4	0.2	9.2	18.4	7.9
INCOME $		0.03	0.16	0.00	0.00	0.06	0.00	0.00	0.00	0.00	0.00	0.00
CAPITAL GAINS $		0.00	..191	0.14	0.00	0.00	1.34	2.86	1.85	6.71	0.00	0.00
EXPENSE RATIO %		0.00	2.39	2.01	2.05	2.00	1.98	1.85	1.79	1.80	1.83	1.80
INCOME RATIO %		0.00	1.15	0.00	0.00	0.33	0.00	0.00	0.00	0.00	-0.97	0.00
TURNOVER RATE %		0	34	23	30	61	64	99	157	157	187	187
NET ASSETS $MIL		66.4	175.5	702.3	673.3	456.5	387.5	522.6	520.3	451.7	396.2	408.8

Performance '94-'98

	Q1	Q2	Q3	Q4	Total
1994	-4	-6	15	-3	29
1995	9	-1	14	13	37
1996	10	-2	6	9	24
1997	-8	13	14	-7	9
1998	7	3	-11	22	18
1999	9	-1			

Investment Style

Price / Earnings Ratio	40.8
Price / Book Ratio	13.2
3 Yr Earnings Growth	12.4%
Median Mkt Cap $M	$7,051

Composition	% of Assets
Cash	4.8
Stocks	95.2
Bonds	0

Portfolio Analysis

Total Stocks: 59

Top Ten Stocks

Amgen	6.4%
Warner-Lambert	6.2%
Bristol-Myers Squibb	5.6%
Astrazeneca PLC	5.4%
VISX	5.2%
Watson Pharma.	5.1%
Schering-Plough	5.1%
Pfizer	5.1%
Guidant	4.8%
Agouron	4.5%

Special Securities

Private / Illiquid Securities : Yes
Options / Futures : Yes

Address :	11 Greenway Plaza, Suite 1919	**Minimum Purchase:**	$500
	Houston, TX 77046	**Add:**	$100
Telephone:	(800) 347-4246 or (713) 626-1919	**IRA:**	$100
Web:	www.aimfunds.com	**Front Load:**	4.75%
Advisor:	AIM Adivsors	**Management Fee:**	0.98%
Manager:	Michael Yellen	**Expense Ratio:**	1.83%
States Avail:	All	**Morningstar Rating:**	* *

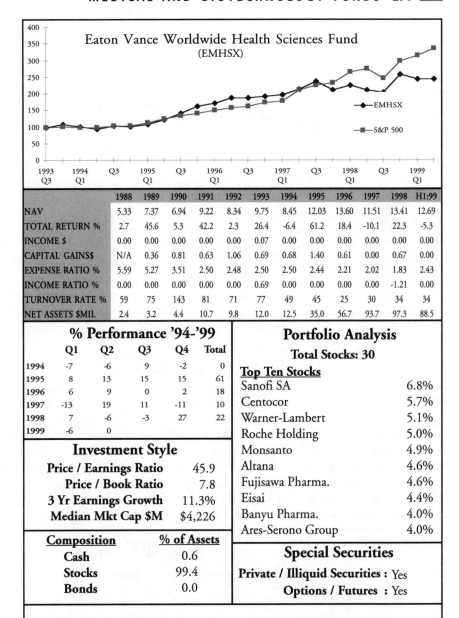

Eaton Vance Worldwide Health Sciences Fund (EMHSX)

	1988	1989	1990	1991	1992	1993	1994	1995	1996	1997	1998	H1:99
NAV	5.33	7.37	6.94	9.22	8.34	9.75	8.45	12.03	13.60	11.51	13.41	12.69
TOTAL RETURN %	2.7	45.6	5.3	42.2	2.3	26.4	-6.4	61.2	18.4	-10.1	22.3	-5.3
INCOME $	0.00	0.00	0.00	0.00	0.00	0.07	0.00	0.00	0.00	0.00	0.00	0.00
CAPITAL GAINS$	N/A	0.36	0.81	0.63	1.06	0.69	0.68	1.40	0.61	0.00	0.67	0.00
EXPENSE RATIO %	5.59	5.27	3.51	2.50	2.48	2.50	2.50	2.44	2.21	2.02	1.83	2.43
INCOME RATIO %	0.00	0.00	0.00	0.00	0.00	0.69	0.00	0.00	0.00	0.00	-1.21	0.00
TURNOVER RATE %	59	75	143	81	71	77	49	45	25	30	34	34
NET ASSETS $MIL	2.4	3.2	4.4	10.7	9.8	12.0	12.5	35.0	56.7	93.7	97.3	88.5

% Performance '94-'99

	Q1	Q2	Q3	Q4	Total
1994	-7	-6	9	-2	0
1995	8	13	15	15	61
1996	6	9	0	2	18
1997	-13	19	11	-11	10
1998	7	-6	-3	27	22
1999	-6	0			

Investment Style

Price / Earnings Ratio	45.9
Price / Book Ratio	7.8
3 Yr Earnings Growth	11.3%
Median Mkt Cap $M	$4,226

Composition	% of Assets
Cash	0.6
Stocks	99.4
Bonds	0.0

Portfolio Analysis

Total Stocks: 30

Top Ten Stocks

Sanofi SA	6.8%
Centocor	5.7%
Warner-Lambert	5.1%
Roche Holding	5.0%
Monsanto	4.9%
Altana	4.6%
Fujisawa Pharma.	4.6%
Eisai	4.4%
Banyu Pharma.	4.0%
Ares-Serono Group	4.0%

Special Securities

Private / Illiquid Securities : Yes

Options / Futures : Yes

Address : 24 Federal Street
Boston, MA 02110
Telephone: (800) 225-6265 or (617) 482-8260
Web: www.eatonvance.com
Advisor: Mehta & Isaly Asset Mgmt.
Manager: Samuel D. Isaly
States Avail: All

Minimum Purchase: $1,000
Add: $100
IRA: $50
Front Load: 5.00%
Management Fee: 1.00%
Expense Ratio: 1.83%
Morningstar Rating: * * *

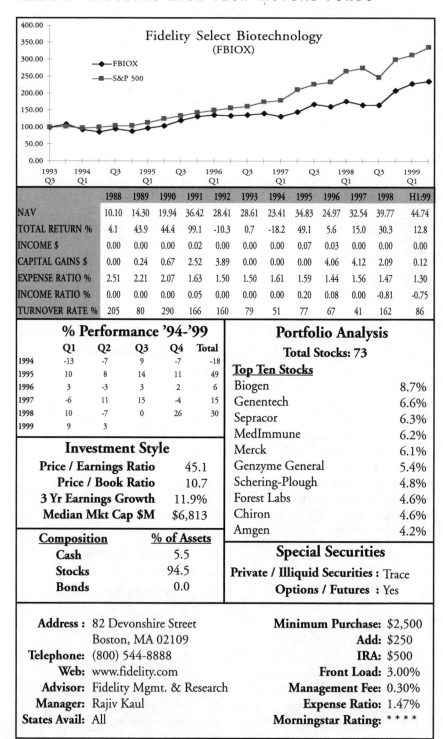

Fidelity Select Biotechnology (FBIOX)

	1988	1989	1990	1991	1992	1993	1994	1995	1996	1997	1998	H1:99
NAV	10.10	14.30	19.94	36.42	28.41	28.61	23.41	34.83	24.97	32.54	39.77	44.74
TOTAL RETURN %	4.1	43.9	44.4	99.1	-10.3	0.7	-18.2	49.1	5.6	15.0	30.3	12.8
INCOME $	0.00	0.00	0.00	0.02	0.00	0.00	0.00	0.07	0.03	0.00	0.00	0.00
CAPITAL GAINS $	0.00	0.24	0.67	2.52	3.89	0.00	0.00	0.00	4.06	4.12	2.09	0.12
EXPENSE RATIO %	2.51	2.21	2.07	1.63	1.50	1.50	1.61	1.59	1.44	1.56	1.47	1.30
INCOME RATIO %	0.00	0.00	0.00	0.05	0.00	0.00	0.00	0.20	0.08	0.00	-0.81	-0.75
TURNOVER RATE %	205	80	290	166	160	79	51	77	67	41	162	86

% Performance '94-'99

	Q1	Q2	Q3	Q4	Total
1994	-13	-7	9	-7	-18
1995	10	8	14	11	49
1996	3	-3	3	2	6
1997	-6	11	15	-4	15
1998	10	-7	0	26	30
1999	9	3			

Investment Style

Price / Earnings Ratio	45.1
Price / Book Ratio	10.7
3 Yr Earnings Growth	11.9%
Median Mkt Cap $M	$6,813

Composition	% of Assets
Cash	5.5
Stocks	94.5
Bonds	0.0

Portfolio Analysis

Total Stocks: 73

Top Ten Stocks

Biogen	8.7%
Genentech	6.6%
Sepracor	6.3%
MedImmune	6.2%
Merck	6.1%
Genzyme General	5.4%
Schering-Plough	4.8%
Forest Labs	4.6%
Chiron	4.6%
Amgen	4.2%

Special Securities

Private / Illiquid Securities : Trace

Options / Futures : Yes

Address :	82 Devonshire Street
	Boston, MA 02109
Telephone:	(800) 544-8888
Web:	www.fidelity.com
Advisor:	Fidelity Mgmt. & Research
Manager:	Rajiv Kaul
States Avail:	All

Minimum Purchase:	$2,500
Add:	$250
IRA:	$500
Front Load:	3.00%
Management Fee:	0.30%
Expense Ratio:	1.47%
Morningstar Rating:	★ ★ ★ ★

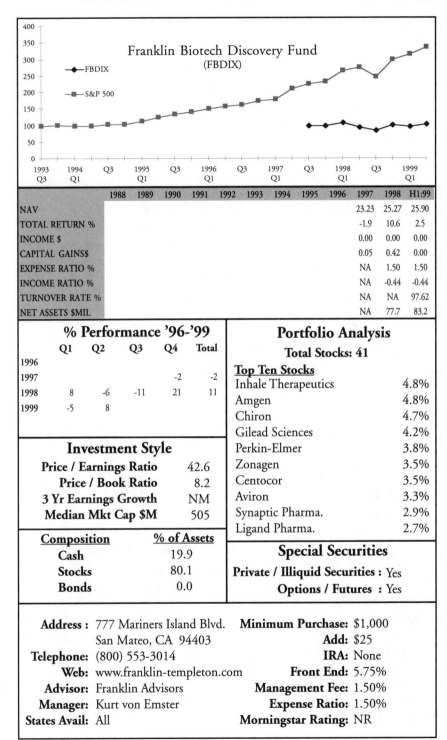

Franklin Biotech Discovery Fund (FBDIX)

◆ FBDIX
■ S&P 500

	1988	1989	1990	1991	1992	1993	1994	1995	1996	1997	1998	H1:99
NAV										23.23	25.27	25.90
TOTAL RETURN %										-1.9	10.6	2.5
INCOME $										0.00	0.00	0.00
CAPITAL GAINS$										0.05	0.42	0.00
EXPENSE RATIO %										NA	1.50	1.50
INCOME RATIO %										NA	-0.44	-0.44
TURNOVER RATE %										NA	NA	97.62
NET ASSETS $MIL										NA	77.7	83.2

% Performance '96-'99

	Q1	Q2	Q3	Q4	Total
1996					
1997				-2	-2
1998	8	-6	-11	21	11
1999	-5	8			

Investment Style

Price / Earnings Ratio	42.6
Price / Book Ratio	8.2
3 Yr Earnings Growth	NM
Median Mkt Cap $M	505

Composition	% of Assets
Cash	19.9
Stocks	80.1
Bonds	0.0

Portfolio Analysis

Total Stocks: 41

Top Ten Stocks

Inhale Therapeutics	4.8%
Amgen	4.8%
Chiron	4.7%
Gilead Sciences	4.2%
Perkin-Elmer	3.8%
Zonagen	3.5%
Centocor	3.5%
Aviron	3.3%
Synaptic Pharma.	2.9%
Ligand Pharma.	2.7%

Special Securities

Private / Illiquid Securities : Yes
Options / Futures : Yes

Address : 777 Mariners Island Blvd.
San Mateo, CA 94403
Telephone: (800) 553-3014
Web: www.franklin-templeton.com
Advisor: Franklin Advisors
Manager: Kurt von Emster
States Avail: All

Minimum Purchase: $1,000
Add: $25
IRA: None
Front End: 5.75%
Management Fee: 1.50%
Expense Ratio: 1.50%
Morningstar Rating: NR

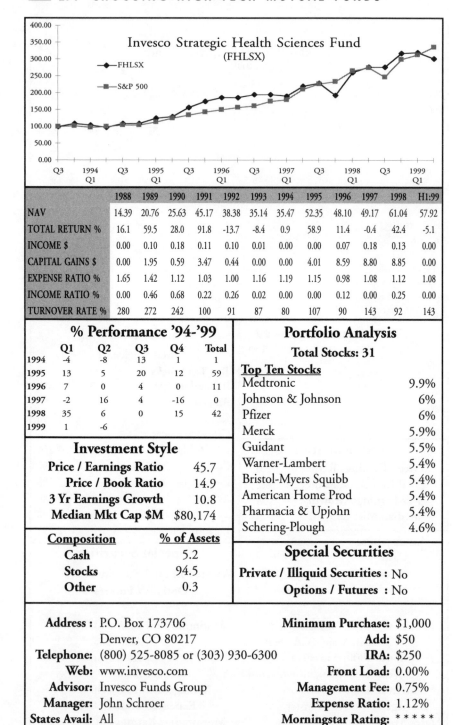

Invesco Strategic Health Sciences Fund (FHLSX)

	1988	1989	1990	1991	1992	1993	1994	1995	1996	1997	1998	H1:99
NAV	14.39	20.76	25.63	45.17	38.38	35.14	35.47	52.35	48.10	49.17	61.04	57.92
TOTAL RETURN %	16.1	59.5	28.0	91.8	-13.7	-8.4	0.9	58.9	11.4	-0.4	42.4	-5.1
INCOME $	0.00	0.10	0.18	0.11	0.10	0.01	0.00	0.00	0.07	0.18	0.13	0.00
CAPITAL GAINS $	0.00	1.95	0.59	3.47	0.44	0.00	0.00	4.01	8.59	8.80	8.85	0.00
EXPENSE RATIO %	1.65	1.42	1.12	1.03	1.00	1.16	1.19	1.15	0.98	1.08	1.12	1.08
INCOME RATIO %	0.00	0.46	0.68	0.22	0.26	0.02	0.00	0.00	0.12	0.00	0.25	0.00
TURNOVER RATE %	280	272	242	100	91	87	80	107	90	143	92	143

% Performance '94-'99

	Q1	Q2	Q3	Q4	Total
1994	-4	-8	13	1	1
1995	13	5	20	12	59
1996	7	0	4	0	11
1997	-2	16	4	-16	0
1998	35	6	0	15	42
1999	1	-6			

Investment Style

Price / Earnings Ratio	45.7
Price / Book Ratio	14.9
3 Yr Earnings Growth	10.8
Median Mkt Cap $M	$80,174

Composition	% of Assets
Cash	5.2
Stocks	94.5
Other	0.3

Portfolio Analysis

Total Stocks: 31

Top Ten Stocks

Medtronic	9.9%
Johnson & Johnson	6%
Pfizer	6%
Merck	5.9%
Guidant	5.5%
Warner-Lambert	5.4%
Bristol-Myers Squibb	5.4%
American Home Prod	5.4%
Pharmacia & Upjohn	5.4%
Schering-Plough	4.6%

Special Securities

Private / Illiquid Securities : No

Options / Futures : No

Address : P.O. Box 173706	**Minimum Purchase:** $1,000
Denver, CO 80217	**Add:** $50
Telephone: (800) 525-8085 or (303) 930-6300	**IRA:** $250
Web: www.invesco.com	**Front Load:** 0.00%
Advisor: Invesco Funds Group	**Management Fee:** 0.75%
Manager: John Schroer	**Expense Ratio:** 1.12%
States Avail: All	**Morningstar Rating:** * * * * *

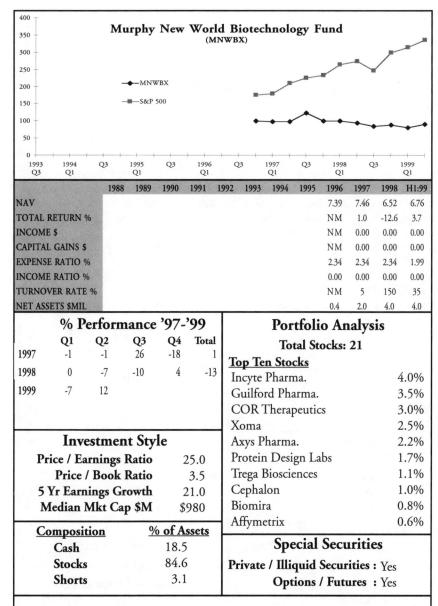

Murphy New World Biotechnology Fund
(MNWBX)

	1988	1989	1990	1991	1992	1993	1994	1995	1996	1997	1998	H1:99
NAV									7.39	7.46	6.52	6.76
TOTAL RETURN %									NM	1.0	-12.6	3.7
INCOME $									NM	0.00	0.00	0.00
CAPITAL GAINS $									NM	0.00	0.00	0.00
EXPENSE RATIO %									2.34	2.34	2.34	1.99
INCOME RATIO %									0.00	0.00	0.00	0.00
TURNOVER RATE %									NM	5	150	35
NET ASSETS $MIL									0.4	2.0	4.0	4.0

% Performance '97-'99

	Q1	Q2	Q3	Q4	Total
1997	-1	-1	26	-18	1
1998	0	-7	-10	4	-13
1999	-7	12			

Investment Style

Price / Earnings Ratio	25.0
Price / Book Ratio	3.5
5 Yr Earnings Growth	21.0
Median Mkt Cap $M	$980

Composition	% of Assets
Cash	18.5
Stocks	84.6
Shorts	3.1

Portfolio Analysis

Total Stocks: 21

Top Ten Stocks

Incyte Pharma.	4.0%
Guilford Pharma.	3.5%
COR Therapeutics	3.0%
Xoma	2.5%
Axys Pharma.	2.2%
Protein Design Labs	1.7%
Trega Biosciences	1.1%
Cephalon	1.0%
Biomira	0.8%
Affymetrix	0.6%

Special Securities

Private / Illiquid Securities : Yes
Options / Futures : Yes

Address :	P. O. Box 308	**Minimum Purchase:**	$1,000
	Half Moon Bay, CA 94019	**Add:**	$50
Telephone:	(650) 726-8495	**IRA:**	$100
Web:	www.ctsl.com	**Front Load:**	0.00%
Advisor:	Murphy Investment Mgmt.	**Management Fee:**	1.00%
Manager:	Lissa Morgenthaler	**Expense Ratio:**	1.99%
States Avail:	All	**Morningstar Rating:**	NR

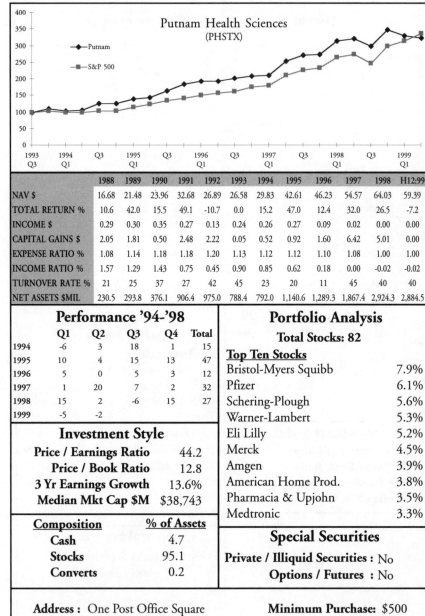

Putnam Health Sciences (PHSTX)

	1988	1989	1990	1991	1992	1993	1994	1995	1996	1997	1998	H12:99
NAV $	16.68	21.48	23.96	32.68	26.89	26.58	29.83	42.61	46.23	54.57	64.03	59.39
TOTAL RETURN %	10.6	42.0	15.5	49.1	-10.7	0.0	15.2	47.0	12.4	32.0	26.5	-7.2
INCOME $	0.29	0.30	0.35	0.27	0.13	0.24	0.26	0.27	0.09	0.02	0.00	0.00
CAPITAL GAINS $	2.05	1.81	0.50	2.48	2.22	0.05	0.52	0.92	1.60	6.42	5.01	0.00
EXPENSE RATIO %	1.08	1.14	1.18	1.18	1.20	1.13	1.12	1.12	1.10	1.08	1.00	1.00
INCOME RATIO %	1.57	1.29	1.43	0.75	0.45	0.90	0.85	0.62	0.18	0.00	-0.02	-0.02
TURNOVER RATE %	21	25	37	27	42	45	23	20	11	45	40	40
NET ASSETS $MIL	230.5	293.8	376.1	906.4	975.0	788.4	792.0	1,140.6	1,289.3	1,867.4	2,924.3	2,884.5

Performance '94-'98

	Q1	Q2	Q3	Q4	Total
1994	-6	3	18	1	15
1995	10	4	15	13	47
1996	5	0	5	3	12
1997	1	20	7	2	32
1998	15	2	-6	15	27
1999	-5	-2			

Investment Style

Price / Earnings Ratio	44.2
Price / Book Ratio	12.8
3 Yr Earnings Growth	13.6%
Median Mkt Cap $M	$38,743

Composition	% of Assets
Cash	4.7
Stocks	95.1
Converts	0.2

Portfolio Analysis

Total Stocks: 82

Top Ten Stocks

Bristol-Myers Squibb	7.9%
Pfizer	6.1%
Schering-Plough	5.6%
Warner-Lambert	5.3%
Eli Lilly	5.2%
Merck	4.5%
Amgen	3.9%
American Home Prod.	3.8%
Pharmacia & Upjohn	3.5%
Medtronic	3.3%

Special Securities

Private / Illiquid Securities : No
Options / Futures : No

Address : One Post Office Square
Boston, MA 02109
Telephone: (800) 225-1581 or (617) 292-1000
Web: www.putnaminv.com
Advisor: Putnam Investment Management
Manager: England/Parker/Carlson
States Avail: All

Minimum Purchase: $500
Add: $50
IRA: $250
Front Load: 5.75%
Management Fee: 0.70%
Expense Ratio: 1.00%
Morningstar Rating: ★ ★ ★ ★ ★

My first recommendation as a professional securities analyst at American Express Investment Management was to sell Memorex, THE hot stock of 1969 and early 1970, right at the bottom of the 1970 bear market, at $172. Yet, as the market exploded upward, Memorex dropped into the midteens, rallied to $50, and collapsed to $3. My mentor and boss, George Miller (who was the first person to say: "Don't confuse brains with a bull market"), was Director of Research and told me the key to making money on Wall Street was to be different from the consensus and to be right.

Since then I've been really, really right sometimes and really, really wrong other times. Some stocks I've recommended have returned hundreds of percent; others have gone bankrupt. The market is a very volatile place, and success requires a mind-set that can accept volatility and loss. One must be able to feel despair and not panic, but keep putting one foot in front of the other until you get through the hard times doing what you know will be best in the long run, and the cycle turns up again.

Thirty years ago I had some special training in these skills, which I would not wish on anybody; yet if I hadn't gone through it I would not have met the people who gave me a start in securities analysis and whom I thank to this day for their willingness to take a chance on me.

I may be the only Registered Investment Adviser you know who has a Presidential Pardon. As you can guess, my life before American Express had some spectacular ups and downs that made everything the stock market threw at me since seem like kid stuff.

After four years at Harvard for college and a year working in New York, I finally broke down and entered law school. It was the mid-1960s, and I read an interview with Timothy Leary about LSD. It sounded interesting to me, and at the time it was legal. In the spirit of the times, I tried it twice, but accidentally took a triple dose and had a disastrous personality breakdown. By the time I had to pull my car over to the shoulder because the whole world had suddenly turned into colored checker-boards, I should have gotten help. Instead, I dropped out of law school and tried to tough it out.

Big mistake. After my savings ran out, I borrowed money. When I couldn't pay it back I robbed a bank. I learned later this is known as white-collar bank robber syndrome—brought on when people are so confused with their lives that they commit an unthinkable crime to get caught.

When I was arrested for robbery, you might think that the nightmare was about to begin. To me, the nightmare was over. After intense psychiatric evaluations, my lawyer, the prosecutor, and the judge concluded that a bank robbery conviction was not a certainty. No one was hurt in the robbery (that would have been battery), but I was clearly guilty of putting people in fear. That's assault. I pled guilty to assault and was sentenced under the Youth Offenders Act to ten years with the possibility of parole at any time. In 1968, two years, two months, two weeks, and two days after my arrest, I was released on parole from Danbury Correctional Institution to a new life in California, a new job with American Express, and a new start thanks to a number of people who stood by me and gave me a second chance.

After eighteen months as a programmer and systems analyst, I became the computer stock analyst for American Express. I enrolled in the Chartered Financial Analyst program, receiving my CFA in 1975. In that year we sold the investment management company to The Capital Group in Los Angeles, and I worked for Capital for six years as a securities analyst and head of the statistics department. Capital is widely recognized as one of the class acts of investment management, a company in which all the securities analysts also invest real money in the stocks they follow. But in the summer of 1981, tired of commuting from San Francisco to Los Angeles every week, I left Capital to found the *California Technology Stock Letter*. We published Issue #1 in January 1982, and we are now in the 400s. I hope and expect to still be doing this when Issue 1,000 rolls off the press (or off the e-mail server, if technology keeps advancing as fast as it has).

Many people taught me the craft of financial analysis and gave me the opportunity to practice it. I thank them all, especially George Miller, Reid Dennis, and Richard H. M. Holmes at American Express, who gave me my start when I needed it most. In my six years at Capital Research, I learned much from John Lovelace, Mike Shanahan, Bob Kirby, Bill Newton, Bill Hurt, and David Fisher. The *California Technology Stock Letter* never would have succeeded without Jim McCamant during the start-up years and Lissa Morgenthaler's ongoing good sense. And thanks to Louis Rukeyser, who hosted each of them on *Wall $treet Week*.

Some people are there when you really need them. My father and mother, Jack and Jane Murphy; the late Michael Belmont and Peter Smith of Cazenove & Co.; and Dr. Bernard Berkowitz were there for me.

A number of people contributed intellectually to this book: *Upside* columnist and money manager Hal Kellman, Phil Lamoreaux of Lamoreaux Partners, Sir John Templeton, Foster Friess of Friess Associates, John Westergaard of Westergaard Research, Michael Rothschild of The Bionomics Institute, Canadian economist Nuala Beck, the editors of the *Bank Credit Analyst,* and the extended Morgenthaler family, including many hours burned by both Davids, Lindsay, Gary, and Todd.

No business succeeds without relationships that go beyond the merely commercial, so many thanks to Bill Hambrecht of W. R. Hambrecht & Co. and to Bill Timken, Diane Larson, and Chris Wagner of Hambrecht & Quist. Also to Al Krause of Access Partners, who built our circulation in the early years; Jim Grensted, our first options guru; Dick Shaffer of Technologic Partners; John Reardon at Morgan Stanley Dean Witter, and Charles and Kim Githler of InterShow.

This book benefited tremendously from Scott Weisberg's research, superb editing from Suzanne Oaks of Broadway Books (it takes one to know one), and support from her assistants, Ann Campbell and Lisa Olney. Thanks to Sandra Jordan for introducing me to Bill Shinker of Broadway, to Bill for taking on a first book on a complex subject, and to Frank Curtis of Curtis and Rembar, publishing attorney extraordinaire.

My heartfelt thanks to the *CTSL* crew, Pamela Floquet, Gia Lilly, Jennifer Phipps, Andrea De Meo, David Brown, and especially my former partner, David Jones, who shouldered an extra load while I finished the book. Finally, thanks to the *CTSL* subscribers and our money-management clients, a perceptive and demanding group who keep me on my toes trying to find that next Great Growth-Flow company just about to come public.

A Focus List of Great Growth-Flow Companies

T his was our focus list as of June 1999, with prices as of June 30. Column 1 shows the stock symbol; column 2 lists the name. Column 3 specifies the stock price in mid-1999.

Column 4, labeled "5-Year Sales Growth," is the average annual growth rate in sales for the last five fiscal years. That is the first cut on our Great Growth-Flow screen. The minimum acceptable growth rate is 15 percent per year. Some stocks that used to meet the minimum (but do not today) are still listed. We keep them in the universe if we think they can recover, but we would not buy them for a Great Growth-Flow portfolio until they produce acceptable growth again.

Column 5 shows the "Pretax Profit Margin" averaged for the last three years. It must be at least 15 percent. That's the second cut.

Column 6 lists "R&D as Percent of Sales." Our 7 percent minimum assures us the company is committed to the Virtuous Circle model. That's the third cut.

"Return on Equity" in column 7 is calculated for each year by dividing earnings for the year by the book value at the beginning of the year. That's the fourth cut, and we are willing to shade it a little for a company that has strong sales growth and high R&D spending.

Column 8 shows the "Growth Flow per Share"—the total of earnings per share plus R&D per share. Column 9 shows the "Price to Growth-Flow Ratio" as of mid-1999. As you can see, even among these great companies, there are always some bargains somewhere.

Be sure to use current prices to calculate current price/growth-flow ratios. Build your own Great Growth-Flow universe by adding new companies that meet the criteria and deleting old ones that permanently fall below the various minimums.

Symb.	Name	Price 6/30/99	5-Year Sales Growth	Pretax Profits	R&D % of Sales	Return on Equity	Growth Flow /Share	Price /GF
ACLY	Accelr8 Technology	12.25	18.65	47.0%	2.4%	12.8%	0.15	79.6
ACTL	Actel	10.75	4.76	16.6	17.0	23.5	2.05	5.2
ADPT	Adaptec	14.31	7.86	24.4	17.1	27.1	2.12	6.8
ADCT	ADC Telecomm.	36.53	40.63	14.6	10.5	22.7	1.73	21.1
ADBE	Adobe Systems	42.44	15.93	32.5	18.7	41.4	5.20	8.2
AEIS	Advanced Energy Ind.	11.63	43.57	12.0	10.4	19.5	1.12	10.4
AFCI	Adv. Fibre Comm.	40.06	105.74	21.8	9.6	26.1	0.86	46.5
ALSI	Advantage Learning	27.38	60.96	25.1	9.5	21.1	0.78	35.2
ADVS	Advent Software	42.00	32.30	21.9	19.4	22.9	2.13	19.7
ALSC	Alliance Semi.	3.53	43.39	−14.5	12.9	−8.5	−0.04	−82.9
ALTR	Altera	29.56	26.91	36.4	8.6	42.8	2.11	14.0
AZA	Alza	43.25	12.42	−45.5	33.8	−70.2	−1.22	−35.5
AMGN	Amgen	65.38	7.20	35.9	26.3	40.3	4.94	13.2
ANAD	Anadigics	13.63	48.90	20.3	16.4	14.2	2.19	6.2
ADI	Analog Devices	24.56	4.16	19.0	15.8	21.7	2.31	10.6
APM	Applied Magnetics	7.63	43.53	19.9	10.6	40.8	6.23	1.2
AMAT	Applied Materials	29.50	−1.70	19.6	13.9	27.2	2.90	10.2
AMCC	Applied Micro Circ.	25.88	33.32	20.4	17.3	17.0	1.26	20.5
AVTC	Applied Voice Tech.	23.00	31.65	2.0	11.6	2.7	0.65	35.6
ARSW	Arbor Software	31.44	73.56	15.5	12.9	22.7	1.15	27.4
ASND	Ascend Comm.	49.56	31.12	−3.9	13.4	−4.6	0.17	299.6
ASPT	Aspect Telecomm.	27.38	26.54	15.4	11.7	22.5	1.62	16.9
ATML	Atmel	13.63	−10.47	0.6	14.4	0.7	1.40	9.7
ASPX	Auspex Systems	5.44	24.50	14.4	14.5	19.0	1.51	3.6
AVNT	Avant!	24.75	38.89	6.9	20.1	6.3	1.34	18.4
BOBJY	Business Objects	16.88	40.48	10.5	12.5	17.2	0.96	17.5
CUBE	C-Cube Microsystems	18.56	5.40	19.9	19.0	38.1	2.95	6.3
CS	Cabletron Systems	13.44	−2.08	−16.0	13.2	−22.3	0.35	38.9
CDN	Cadence Design Sys.	31.25	23.53	28.3	15.3	35.7	1.49	20.9
CSCO	Cisco Systems	92.06	57.23	22.3	8.3	43.6	1.74	53.0
CTXS	Citrix Systems	68.38	178.33	52.1	5.6	32.8	1.16	58.7
CLFY	Clarify	13.50	56.63	7.1	19.0	10.9	0.97	13.9
CMOS	Credence Systems	19.00	−14.53	8.9	18.3	8.9	2.19	8.7
CYMI	Cymer	16.13	213.33	17.0	12.3	27.5	1.78	9.1
CY	Cypress Semi.	8.31	3.02	4.4	17.2	3.7	1.24	6.7
DS	Dallas Semi.	31.03	27.69	25.7	12.5	26.9	4.02	7.7
DP	Diagnostic Products	28.81	5.33	13.8	10.6	13.8	2.77	10.4
DSP	DSP Communications	13.75	−8.32	29.5	8.0	20.7	0.69	19.9
ESIO	Electro Scientific	31.56	−3.70	14.1	7.4	23.4	4.04	7.8
EGLS	Electroglas	13.06	−1.26	−8.7	14.6	−6.5	0.30	43.3
ERTS	Electronic Arts	54.00	35.04	11.9	16.1	19.2	3.16	17.1
EFII	Elec. For Imaging	21.13	21.01	28.1	11.2	29.9	2.00	10.6
ENCD	Encad	13.63	38.72	17.8	7.1	41.0	2.43	5.6
ESST	ESS Technology	4.69	10.18	1.2	11.8	1.7	0.46	10.2

Symb.	Name	Price 6/30/99	5-Year Sales Growth	Pretax Profits	R&D % of Sales	Return on Equity	Growth Flow /Share	Price /GF
ETEC	Etec Systems	35.19	65.41	22.1	14.3	27.0	3.17	11.1
XLTC	Excel Technology	8.88	14.77	19.2	7.4	24.8	1.15	7.7
FORE	Fore Systems	26.50	15.94	11.0	14.6	9.9	0.99	26.8
GSNX	Gasonics	7.00	−4.56	3.8	14.4	5.8	1.47	4.8
GMSTF	Gemstar	37.44	32.03	20.9	9.9	50.6	0.98	38.3
GEN	Genrad	19.75	28.99	15.9	8.4	32.8	2.24	8.8
GEMS	Glenayre Tech.	10.75	15.74	−11.0	8.9	−12.1	−0.62	−17.3
HBOC	HBO	35.25	26.53	19.9	7.4	26.6	0.55	64.1
IDTI	Integrated Device	7.16	9.29	2.0	20.7	2.1	1.59	4.5
ISSI	Integrated Silicon	7.00	−18.01	−8.2	24.2	−6.6	1.03	6.8
INTS	Integrated Systems	15.38	14.23	7.6	15.6	9.7	1.07	14.4
INTC	Intel	74.13	20.26	42.5	9.4	55.2	5.71	13.0
JDAS	JDA Software	29.17	91.83	22.6	12.4	30.6	1.81	16.1
KLAC	Kla-Tencor	27.69	−5.73	14.9	11.5	17.1	2.86	9.7
KLIC	Kulicke & Soffa	17.00	31.67	10.3	9.2	17.7	3.63	4.7
LRCX	Lam·Research	19.13	−21.50	−6.2	16.2	−11.1	4.43	4.3
LSCC	Lattice Semi.	28.41	20.48	34.9	13.0	19.7	3.18	8.9
LGTO	Legato Systems	39.00	50.85	30.4	17.6	26.8	0.85	46.1
LEVL	Level One Comm.	23.50	39.54	18.3	19.5	23.2	1.61	14.6
LLTC	Linear Tech.	60.31	0.39	42.2	7.3	34.7	2.23	27.0
LSI	Lsi Logic	23.06	4.16	17.4	17.5	14.3	2.75	8.4
MACR	Macromedia	18.69	5.33	−4.7	28.5	−4.2	0.64	29.3
MVSN	Macrovision	23.88	19.09	30.6	11.1	26.4	0.84	28.4
MXIM	Maxim	31.69	2.87	37.0	9.1	44.6	1.48	21.5
MCRL	Micrel	32.50	57.23	24.4	13.4	36.0	1.58	20.6
MCHP	Microchip Tech.	26.13	18.74	22.2	9.7	24.0	1.94	13.4
MSFT	Microsoft	108.38	30.99	36.7	13.3	49.3	2.23	48.5
MYLX	Mylex	6.75	−28.63	−7.6	16.1	10.2	0.66	10.2
NACT	NACT Telecomm.	19.50	70.09	22.7	8.6	19.1	0.76	25.5
NMGC	Neomagic	15.50	205.58	0.0	12.9	0.0	1.52	10.2
NETM	Netmanage	3.00	−41.18	−55.6	33.6	−35.6	−0.30	−10.0
NETA	Network Associates	47.88	45.14	5.4	13.9	9.2	0.54	88.6
NVLS	Novellus Systems	35.69	15.65	−22.7	16.8	−40.2	−0.17	−206.4
OAKT	Oak Technology	4.56	−32.50	24.4	22.1	16.0	1.42	3.2
OSII	Objective Systems	7.38	−7.52	−47.4	20.8	−33.6	−0.18	−40.9
ORCL	Oracle	24.56	25.68	18.6	10.1	44.9	1.41	17.4
OCAD	Orcad	9.75	23.79	8.8	21.8	6.3	1.06	9.2
ORTL	Ortel	15.50	−6.89	4.5	17.7	4.4	1.88	8.2
PAIR	Pairgain Tech.	17.44	37.38	27.6	11.3	33.1	1.15	15.1
PRLS	Peerless Systems	20.75	58.31	29.1	18.1	21.9	0.89	23.3
PSFT	Peoplesoft	47.00	81.23	21.6	15.9	42.2	1.06	44.2
PTEC	Phoenix Tech.	12.75	13.85	28.0	32.1	22.2	2.49	5.1
PIXR	Pixar	60.38	0.00	91.7	13.5	14.6	0.63	95.2
PLT	Plantronics	51.50	20.89	24.4	7.4	107.8	2.70	19.1
PMCS	PMC—Sierra	46.88	−32.49	39.3	18.0	55.2	1.92	24.4
PWAV	Powerwave Tech.	16.75	98.42	21.6	9.6	34.3	1.60	10.4
PRMS	Premisys Comm.	24.88	6.02	17.4	10.3	18.4	0.85	29.3
PRIA	PRI Automation	17.06	53.11	15.3	14.5	21.7	2.78	6.1
QKTN	Quickturn Design	7.31	0.75	−10.2	21.3	−12.3	1.03	7.1
RSYS	Radisys	21.50	54.78	18.9	9.3	31.3	3.48	6.2
RNBO	Rainbow Technologies	13.67	15.93	20.3	8.9	21.8	2.55	5.3
RMDY	Remedy	17.00	60.21	33.0	16.4	28.8	1.69	10.0

Symb.	Name	Price 6/30/99	5-Year Sales Growth	Pretax Profits	R&D % of Sales	Return on Equity	Growth Flow /Share	Price /GF
SIII	S3	5.06	−0.66	2.8	22.0	4.6	2.07	2.4
SNDK	Sandisk	13.81	28.33	18.6	10.8	12.2	1.29	10.7
SBSE	SBS Technologies	30.13	68.57	1.0	6.0	1.5	0.90	33.4
SMTC	Semtech	17.69	43.60	21.6	8.9	40.5	1.69	10.5
SVGI	Silicon Valley Grp.	16.06	−7.03	0.4	12.4	0.4	2.42	6.6
SIPX	Sipex	21.50	37.25	24.0	10.6	18.1	1.06	20.4
SFAM	Speedfam	18.44	44.32	15.3	10.7	18.1	3.00	6.1
SPLH	Splash Technology	17.19	74.33	−14.0	7.3	−19.8	0.81	21.2
STAA	Staar Surgical	15.56	7.84	25.7	8.7	26.1	0.86	18.2
SUPX	Supertex	12.13	7.71	25.3	10.6	23.3	1.16	10.4
SNPS	Synopsys	45.75	25.60	22.7	23.0	22.6	2.94	15.6
TKLC	Tekelec	22.38	73.50	23.8	16.8	27.6	0.96	23.4
TLAB	Tellabs	71.63	38.50	33.2	13.1	42.8	2.32	30.8
TER	Teradyne	26.75	8.08	15.3	12.8	20.6	3.48	7.7
TMBS	Timberline Software	23.56	22.96	19.8	20.6	52.5	1.69	13.9
UTEK	Ultratech Stepper	19.75	−23.85	17.0	17.9	9.5	2.12	9.3
UTR	Unitrode	11.50	33.01	26.9	9.6	30.0	1.95	5.9
VNTV	Vantive	20.50	82.57	1.2	14.9	2.4	0.42	49.1
VRTS	Veritas Software	41.38	66.50	19.6	20.8	22.8	1.04	39.8
VIAS	Viasoft	16.19	95.86	−11.0	9.2	−32.6	−0.43	−38.0
VSIO	Visio	47.75	66.69	20.5	15.6	26.6	1.08	44.0
VISX	Visx	59.50	−1.48	23.3	14.9	14.5	1.59	37.5
VTSS	Vitesse	30.88	58.75	34.8	16.0	13.8	0.69	44.6
WIND	Wind River Systems	35.88	44.38	14.6	13.0	12.0	0.66	54.7
XLNX	Xilinx	34.00	8.00	29.9	13.1	33.3	2.52	13.5

A Focus List of
Biotechnology Companies

T his was our focus list as of June 1999, with prices as of June 30. Column 1 shows the stock symbol; column 2 lists the name. Column 3 is the stock price in mid-1999.

Column 4, labeled "Mkt. Cap.," is the total market capitalization of the company—the stock price times the number of shares outstanding. This is the amount we would have to pay to buy the whole company at the listed stock price.

Column 5 shows the "Last 5 years' R&D," which is the total amount of money the company has invested in R&D for the last five years. This is the company's investment in its science.

Column 6 shows the "M Score"—column 4 divided by column 5, or the ratio of the market capitalization to the last five years' spending on R&D.

As you can see, the M Score shows a wide variation (remember that 8x to 10x is an average range) and, as with the Great-Growth Flow companies, there always are some bargains somewhere. Again, be sure to use current prices to calculate current M Scores.

Symb.	Name	Price 6/30/99	Value ($M) 6/30/98	Last 5 Yrs R&D ($M)	M Score
ATIS	Advanced Tissue	4.44	166.6	90.5	1.8
AFFX	Affymetrix	24.06	544.8	68.8	7.9
AGPH	Agouron	30.31	1006.7	299.4	3.4
ALXN	Alexion	10.00	74.5	26.9	2.8
ALKS	Alkermes	17.97	374.3	121.9	3.1
ALLP	Alliance	4.19	126.9	166.1	0.8
AMGN	Amgen	65.38	17952.0	2189.8	8.2
AMLN	Amylin	3.78	121.6	235.9	0.5
ANRG	Anergen	1.94	36.5	42.1	0.9
ARQL	ArQule	12.94	160.3	12.7	12.6
AVGN	Avigen	3.50	25.5	11.4	2.2
AVIR	Aviron	31.19	426.6	53.7	7.9
AXPH	AxyS	7.13	107.1	92.1	1.2
BTGC	Bio-Technology General	7.09	342.3	67.0	5.1
BCHE	BioChem Pharma.	26.50	2868.7	119.9	23.9
BGEN	Biogen	49.00	3748.5	535.9	7.0
KDUS	Cadus	7.75	94.7	27.5	3.4
CELG	Celgene	10.63	129.7	56.3	2.3
CEGE	Cell Genesys	8.56	198.4	125.8	1.6
CTIC	Cell Therapeutics	2.69	31.3	58.0	0.5
CLGY	Cellegy	5.56	37.1	11.0	3.4
CPRO	CellPro	3.06	44.5	73.2	0.6
CTRX	Celtrix	2.06	43.3	70.4	0.6
CWindows 2000O	Centocor	36.25	2601.7	327.8	7.9
CEPH	Cephalon	7.88	201.9	272.5	0.7
CHIR	Chiron	15.69	2793.2	1397.0	2.0
COCN	CoCensys	2.50	56.4	64.0	0.9
CCHM	CombiChem	6.94	20.5	19.1	1.1
CORR	COR Therapeutics	13.88	290.7	197.1	1.5
CORX	Cortex	1.88	15.5	15.3	1.0
CVAS	Corvas International	4.13	57.2	53.8	1.1
CLTR	Coulter	30.38	309.8	37.3	8.3
CBMI	Creative Biomolecules	4.81	159.2	83.0	1.9
CYGN	Cygnus	10.44	197.6	100.8	2.0
CYPB	Cypress Bioscience	2.97	104.6	18.1	5.8
CYP	Cypros	4.06	63.8	4.0	16.0
CYTL	Cytel	1.38	35.3	96.9	0.4
DURA	Dura	22.38	980.7	63.5	15.4
ENZN	Enzon	6.38	185.2	66.1	2.8
GELX	GelTex	18.63	253.1	55.0	4.6
GNLB	Genelabs	3.00	116.9	60.9	1.9
GNE	Genentech	67.88	8579.4	1918.8	4.5
GWindows 2000A	Genta Inc.	1.34	7.7	48.2	0.2
GENZ	Genzyme—Gen'l Div.	25.56	2017.4	266.6	7.6
GERN	Geron	9.38	98.9	48.8	2.0
GILD	Gilead Sciences	32.06	940.4	145.1	6.5
GLIA	Gliatech	16.13	118.5	54.5	2.2
HSKA	Heska	11.06	292.6	40.1	7.3
HGSI	Human Genome Sciences	35.69	768.0	163.5	4.7

Symb.	Name	Price 6/30/99	Value ($M) 6/30/98	Last 5 Yrs R&D ($M)	M Score
ICOS	Icos	19.13	757.2	136.2	5.6
IDPH	IDEC	23.56	441.6	121.6	3.6
IMCL	ImClone Systems	12.25	287.4	62.4	4.6
IMNR	Immune Response	15.00	328.2	106.2	3.1
IMNX	Immunex	66.25	2626.2	439.4	6.0
INCY	Incyte	34.13	824.5	143.5	5.7
ISV	Insite Vision	3.38	44.0	30.7	1.4
ISIP	Isis	13.69	362.2	186.8	1.9
KOSP	Kos	10.13	147.5	46.2	3.2
LJPC	La Jolla Pharma.	3.50	61.4	51.4	1.2
LGND	Ligand	12.88	426.5	225.1	1.9
LXR	LXR Biotechnology	1.94	43.0	23.9	1.8
MAGN	Magainin	5.31	104.6	81.6	1.3
MATX	Matrix	4.38	94.2	101.5	0.9
MMP	Maxim	20.50	136.7	8.0	17.2
MEDI	MedImmune	62.38	1442.7	136.2	10.6
MCDE	Microcide	6.69	72.4	40.2	1.8
MYCO	Mycogen	24.03	743.0	104.0	7.1
MYGN	Myriad Genetics	14.63	135.9	39.7	3.4
NPRO	Napro Biotherapeutics	1.25	15.1	29.2	0.5
NERX	NeoRx Corp.	4.94	89.2	43.6	2.0
Windows 2000II	Neurobiological Tech.	0.88	5.7	18.8	0.3
NBIX	Neurocrine Biosciences	7.94	144.3	46.4	3.1
NRGN	Neurogen	17.75	254.7	62.9	4.1
NXTR	Nexstar	9.97	266.1	196.6	1.4
NPSP	NPS Pharmaceuticals	7.13	85.2	48.6	1.8
ONXX	Onyx	6.13	59.5	58.9	1.0
PGNS	Pathogenesis	29.00	455.3	85.4	5.3
PCYC	Pharmacyclics	23.75	219.9	33.5	6.6
PPRT	Pharmaprint	10.25	116.4	13.2	8.8
PRCY	Procyte	0.81	10.8	41.6	0.3
PGNX	Progenics	14.88	116.0	17.8	6.5
PGEN	Progenitor	1.63	7.0	17.7	0.4
PDLI	Protein Design Labs	24.09	425.3	103.9	4.1
REGN	Regeneron	9.22	252.4	171.3	1.5
RIBI	Ribi Immunochem	5.06	101.6	28.6	3.5
RZYM	Ribozyme	4.94	36.6	50.8	0.7
SCLN	Sciclone	3.75	61.8	46.3	1.3
SCIO	Scios	8.88	320.5	179.7	1.8
SEQU	Sequus.	11.38	345.5	124.3	2.8
SERO	Serologicals	21.50	517.7	7.8	66.6
SHMN	Shaman	3.38	57.4	92.3	0.6
SIBI	Sibia Neurosciences	5.25	48.6	45.7	1.1
SUGN	Sugen	16.25	217.6	114.9	1.9
SUPG	Supergen	10.06	188.9	14.7	12.8
SNAP	Synaptic.	14.00	113.8	52.9	2.2
TGEN	Targeted Genetics	1.59	32.2	43.8	0.7
TTNP	Titan Pharma.	4.63	62.3	36.1	1.7
TRGA	Trega	3.63	49.3	40.4	1.2
VIRS	Triangle	14.88	280.7	27.2	10.3
VRTX	Vertex	22.50	545.9	186.3	2.9
VICL	Vical	16.94	262.2	46.8	5.6

Symb.	Name	Price 6/30/99	Value ($M) 6/30/98	Last 5 Yrs R&D ($M)	M Score
VPHM	Viropharma	23.25	234.6	20.6	11.4
XOMA	Xoma	4.81	191.0	132.5	1.4
ZONA	Zonagen	21.94	198.3	37.3	5.3

Selected Technology Convertible Bonds and Preferred Stocks Available to Individual Investors

Convert. Symbol (if any)	Company Name	Coupon	Year Due	Price	Yield to Maturity
	Adv. Micro Devices	6.000	2005	80.25	10.4
AGCPRC	Airtouch Pfd.	2.225	Pfd	87.00	2.4
AZA/ZR1	Alza	0.000	2014	58.50	3.1
AZA/06	Alza	5.000	2006	127.13	1.3
	Amkor Rech	5.750	2003	89.88	8.5
ADI/00	Analog Devices	3.500	2000	124.75	N/M
	Applied Magnetics	7.000	2006	44.50	23.7
ASTAL	AST Research	0.000	2013	42.00	5.8
AUD/ZR1	Automatic Data Proc.	0.000	2012	95.50	0.3
	C-Cube Microsystems	5.875	2005	89.13	8.0
CMICG	Calif. Microwave	5.250	2003	86.38	8.6
	Chiron	1.900	2000	92.00	5.7
DPT/06	Datapoint	8.875	2006	57.50	20.2
	DII Group	6.000	2002	111.75	3.0

Convert. Symbol (if any)	Company Name	Coupon	Year Due	Price	Yield to Maturity
	Dura Pharmaceuticals	3.500	2002	84.00	8.5
ESCCG	Evans & Sutherland	6.000	2012	100.00	6.1
XTONG	Executone	7.500	2011	80.00	6.1
CNVXG	Hewlett-Packard	6.000	2012	93.75	6.7
	Hewlett-Packard	0.000	2017	53.13	3.3
HXL/03	Hexcel	7.000	2003	142.38	NM
HXLDG	Hexcel	7.000	2011	103.00	6.8
	HNC Software	4.750	2003	107.75	3.0
ICN/99	ICN Pharmaceuticals	8.500	1999	115.00	6.6
	Inacom	4.500	2004	100.38	4.4
IDTIG	Integrated Device Tech.	5.500	2002	80.00	12.5
IMMCO	Interdigital Comm.	2.500	Pfd	20.88	12.5
ITXPr	International Tech.	1.750	Pfd	18.50	9.0
IOMGG	Iomega	6.750	2001	116.00	0.7
	IVAX	6.500	2001	88.25	11.1
	Learning Company	5.500	2000	96.50	7.8
GLYCG	Ligand (Glycomed)	7.500	2003	80.13	14.1
	Loral Space/Comm.	3.000	Pfd	78.75	3.8
MNS/A.A	MacNeal-Schwendler	7.875	2004	100.25	8.0
	Macronix	1.000	2007	104.50	0.5
	Metricom	8.000	2003	82.00	13.3
	Micron	7.000	2004	95.50	8.1
	MicroProse	6.500	2002	62.38	21.3
MOT/ZR0	Motorola	0.000	2009	90.00	1.0
MOT/ZR1	Motorola	0.000	2013	72.13	1.2
	National Data	5.000	2003	101.75	4.7
NERPV	NeoRx	2.440	Pfd	25.06	9.7
	Network Equipment	7.250	2014	94.25	8.0
IMGXP	Network Imaging	2.000	Pfd	10.50	19.0
	Photronics	6.000	2004	105.13	5.1
	Quantum	7.000	2004	93.88	8.4
	Richardson Electronics	7.250	2006	98.50	7.6
	Silicon Graphics	5.250	2004	86.13	8.3
	Silicon Graphics (Cray)	6.125	2011	81.25	8.7
SSAXG	System Software Asso	7.000	2002	82.00	13.0
SCTCG	Systems & Comp Tech	5.000	2004	121.75	1.4
TLXNG	Telxon	7.500	2012	117.00	5.8
	Telxon	5.750	2003	120.50	1.0
	Thermo Inst. Systems	3.750	2000	198.69	N/M
	Thermo Inst. Systems	4.000	2005	100.00	0.4
TTNP1	Titan	1.000	Pfd	14.00	7.1
	Titan	8.250	2003	184.50	NM
UIS/00	Unisys	8.250	2000	100.00	7.8
UISPrA	Unisys A	3.750	Pfd	52.19	7.2
	VLSI Technology	8.250	2005	97.38	9.0

Notes: "Yield" is yield to maturity for convertible bonds or current yield for preferred stocks.
"Pfd" indicates preferred stock, typically with no maturity date.
"N/M" means no meaningful yield to maturity, usually because the bond is well above par value based on the relatively high price of the underlying stock.

CONVERTIBLES WORKSHEET

COMPANY NAME _____ STOCK SYMBOL _____

STOCK PRICE _____ DIVIDEND, IF ANY _____

EXCHANGE _____

1. CONVERTIBLE INFORMATION

CONVERTIBLE SYMBOL, IF ANY _____

PRICE _____

COUPON _____%

YEAR DUE _____

CONVERSION RATIO _____

(How many shares per bond? Divide $1,000 by conversion price per share.)

2. VALUE CALCULATION

CONVERSION VALUE _____

(Multiply conversion ratio times price of one common share.)

PREMIUM _____

(Percentage convertible price is higher than conversion value.)

CONVERTIBLE YIELD _____

(Divide coupon by current convertible price.)

COMMON YIELD _____

(Divide dividend, if any, by current common stock price.)

YIELD ADVAWindows 2000AGE _____

(Subtract common yield from convertible yield.)

PAYBACK PERIOD _____

(Divide premium by yield advantage.)

Changing Accounting Rules to Promote R&D Investment

I t is a basic principle of accounting that in any time period, revenues should be matched to the expenses that produced them. When I became a securities analyst, companies capitalized their R&D spending, instead of charging it against current earnings, because it related to future products. When those products were shipped, the capitalized R&D was written off against revenues, as an appropriate expense.

Unfortunately, in the late 1960s, some managements were very aggressive in capitalizing anything that could remotely be called R&D in order to inflate their current earnings. Others adjusted the capitalization percentage each quarter to show smooth earnings growth. There was no consistency between companies, and analysts were reduced to comparing the "quality" of, say, IBM's earnings to those of Burroughs.

Frustrated, the Financial Accounting Standards Board (FASB) promulgated new rules that made almost all R&D related to any current product a current expense and, therefore, an immediate deduction from current earnings. Only R&D related to a project that does not yet have commercial feasibility can be capitalized. Companies now boast about not having any capitalized R&D.

But is this convenience for the accountants and analysts good for the U.S. economy? Growth-flow analysis implies that the real value of a technology company is understated because R&D of future products is treated as a current expense. That means the total reported earnings of technology companies is understated relative to old-economy companies. As a result, technology companies are systematically undervalued relative to old-economy companies.

This is important because in addition to giving you opportunities to buy into companies at depressed levels, the undervaluation means that capital flows in the economy are not properly balanced. The purpose of the capital markets is to direct capital to situations and managements that are best able to invest it. The capital markets function most efficiently when underpriced stocks are pushed up, overpriced stocks are pushed down, and companies and industries are valued fairly relative to one another.

Expensing R&D creates less-efficient capital markets. Wall Street treats a dollar of earnings from Intel the same as a dollar of earnings from Coca-Cola, even though Intel's earnings might be calculated after subtracting the investment of another dollar of R&D in future products. The higher a stock's price, the lower the cost of equity capital is to that company. If old-economy companies have, on average, higher relative valuations than technology companies, too much capital will flow into less productive areas while newer, high-growth sectors are starved. That's bad for economic growth.

If the accounting rules were changed to require the capitalization of all R&D, there would be consistency between companies. R&D would be written off only against revenues from the products it relates to, or in a one-time adjustment for failed programs and products. Technology companies would report higher earnings relative to old-economy companies than they do now, the stocks would sell for higher levels, and their cost of capital would be lower. The U.S. economy would be more efficient, more productive, and better able to compete in a rapidly changing world.

Contacts and Sources

Books

Four books I have found useful in understanding the transition to a technology economy are:

Shifting Gears: Thriving in the New Economy by Nuala Beck (Toronto: HarperCollins, 1992), for its identification of the major markers of a complete change in the economic base.

Bionomics: Economy as Ecosystem by Michael Rothschild (New York: Henry Holt, 1990), for its paradigm of the economy as a biological instead of a mechanical process ("They jump-started the economy, but now it's overheating.").

A Gale of Creative Destruction: The Coming Economic Boom 1992–2000 by Myron H. Ross (New York: Praeger, 1989) for its practical view of long-wave economics in relation to the technology revolution.

The Great Boom Ahead by Harry S. Dent, Jr. (New York: Hyperion, 1993) for its understanding of demographics as a driving force in economic cycles.

Newspapers and Magazines

BioVenture View
  Circulation: (650) 574–7128
  Web site: http://www.pjpubs.co.uk/bvv/index.html

The Economist
Circulation: (800) 456-4086; (303) 604-1464
Web site: http://www.economist.com

Forbes ASAP
Circulation: (800) 888-9896
Web site: http://www.forbes.com

Investor's Business Daily
Circulation: (800) 306-9744
Web site: http://www.investors.com

Nature Biotechnology
Circulation: (800) 524-0384
Web site: http://www.biotech.nature.com

The New York Times Tuesday and Sunday science pages
Circulation: (800) 631-2580
Web site: http://www.nytimes.com

Red Herring
Circulation: (800) 627-4931
Web site: http://www.redherring.com

San Jose Mercury News Tuesday and Sunday science pages
(sometimes picked up from The New York Times)
Circulation: (800) 870-6397
Web site: http://www.sjmercury.com

Science News
Circulation: (800) 552-4412
Web site: http://www.sciencenews.com

Scientific American
Circulation: (800) 333-1199; (515) 247-7631
Web site: http://www.sciam.com

Upside
Circulation: (888) 998-7743
Web site: http://www.upside.com

The Wall Street Journal
Circulation: (800) 369-2834 x11
Web site: http://www.wsj.com

Wall Street Transcript
Circulation: (212) 952-7400
Web site: http://www.twst.com

Wired
Circulation: (800) 769-7433
Web site: http://www.wired.com

Technology and Stock Newsletters

Michael Murphy & Lissa Morgenthaler
California Technology Stock Letter
Circulation: (800) 998-CTSL
Web site: http://www.ctsl.com

Dick Shaffer
Computer Letter
Circulation: (212) 343-1900
Web site: http://www.tpsite.com

Chris Shipley
Demo Letter
Circulation: (415) 312-0691
Web site: http://www.pcletter.com

Jim McCamant
Medical Technology Stock Letter
AgBiotech Letter
Circulation: (510) 843-1857
Web site: http://www.bioinvest.com

Harry Tracy
NeuroInvestment
Circulation: (603) 964-9640
Web site: http://www.nh.ultranet.com/~neuroinv

Steve Szirom
Semiconductor Industry & Business Survey (SIBS)
Circulation: (650) 871-4377
Web site: http://www.hte-sibs.com

Jeffrey Tartar
Softletter
Circulation: (617) 924-3944
Web site: http://www.softletter.com

Mutual Fund Rating Services

Morningstar
Circulation: (800) 735-0700
Web site: http://www.morningstar.net

Value Line Mutual Fund Survey
Circulation: (800) 634-3583
Web site: http://www.valueline.com/print3.html

Internet and Television

C/Net
TV schedule: (415) 395-7805 x 1642
Call for broadcast schedule near you, or visit the C/Net Web site
Web site: http://www.cnet.com

SEC/Edgar electronic corporate filings and reports
Web site: http://www.sec.gov

Silicon Investor
Web site: http://www.techstocks.com

Yahoo stock forums (free)
Web site: http://messages.yahoo.com/index.html

Brokerage Firms

BancBoston Robertson, Stephens & Co.
New Accounts: (415) 781-9700
Web site: http://www.rsco.com

Cowen & Co.
New Accounts: (617) 946-3700
Web site: http://www.cowen.com

DB Alex. Brown
New Accounts: (800) 638-2596
Web site: http://www.alexbrown.com

First Security Van Kasper
New Accounts: (800) 652-1747
Web site: http://www.vkco.com

Goldman Sachs
New Accounts: (212) 902-1000
Web site: http://www.gs.com

Hambrecht & Quist
New Accounts: (415) 439-3000
Web site: http: www.hamquist.com

L. H. Alton & Co.
New Accounts: (415) 391-2072

Nationsbank Montgomery Securities
New Accounts: (415) 627-2000
Web site: http://www.montgomery.com

Organizations

American Electronics Association
(800) 284-4232
Web site: http://www.aeanet.org

Semiconductor Equipment & Materials Institute
(650) 940-6902
Web site: http://www.semi.org

Accel Partners, 106
Accounting:
    for R&D by development-stage companies,
        164–65
    rule changes to promote investment in R&D,
        293–94
Adaptec, profile of, 198
Adobe Systems, 42, 98, 161, 179
    profile of, 199
Advanced Micro Devices, 63, 155
Advanced Tissue Sciences, 133–34
Advantest, 59
Advertising on the Internet, 118–19, 120
Aerospace industry, 14
AgBiotech, 44
Aging of the population, 137
Agrarian economy, 7–8, 11
AIM Global Health, 270
AIM Global Telecommunications, 249
Alliance Technology, 244, 250
Altera, 70, 174
    profile of, 200
Amazon.com, 115, 120, 123
Amdahl, Carlton, 107–108
American Academy for the Advancement of
        Science, 43
American Electronics Association (AEA), 181
America Online, 112, 119, 120, 123, 127, 128
Amgen, 138, 167
Amylin Pharmaceuticals, 130
Analog and digital chips, integration of, 75
Analog signals, 104
Analysts, 10, 15, 40, 180, 191
Andreessen, Marc, 117
Anthem Electronics, 67
Antisense, 142
Apple Computer, 9, 84, 157, 160, 178, 179
Applets, 102–103
Applied Data Research, 91
Applied Magnetics, 88
Applied Materials, 53, 55, 56, 58, 59, 189
    profile of, 201

Applied research, 37–39
Ascend Communications, 106
Asia, 13, 137
ASM International, 56
ASM Lithography, 58
Asset allocation, 4–5, 175
ATM (Asynchronous Transfer Mode), 105, 114
AT&T, 64, 77, 106, 110, 123, 196
    breakup of, 105, 108
Auditors, resignation of, 193
AutoCAD, 99, 100
Autodesk, 98, 99–100
Axys Pharmaceuticals, 140
AZT, clinical trials for, 134–35

Baan, 93
Baby Bells, 105–106, 113
BancBoston Robertson, Stephens & Co., 44,
        194
Barron's, 243
Basic research, 37–38
Bay Networks, 112
Bechtolsheim, Andy, 112
Biomet, 138
Biotechnology, 129, 130
    asset allocations, 5
    competitive strategies of, 139–40
    customers of, 138
    development-stage companies, 167, 285–88
    drug approval process, 130, 131–36
    focus list of biotech companies, 285–88
    growth cycles, impetus for, 137
    growth rate of, 13, 31, 136–37
    Internet's effect on, 141
    mutual funds, profiled, 269–76
    next big change in, 141–43
    profitability of, 137–38
    R&D spending by, 130–31, 138, 140
    seasonality rule affecting biotech stocks, 183
Bioventure View, 43
Blue Chips 2010, 196–235
Bonding step in making semiconductors, 59

Bonds, convertible technology, *see* Convertible technology bonds and stocks
Book-to-bill ratio, 51–52
Book value, Downside Risk Value and, 177
Boole & Babbage, 91
Borland, 173
Boston Scientific, 138
Brokerage firms, information from, 5, 194
Building to order, 88–89, 95
Burroughs Corporation, 76
Burroughs-Wellcome, 135
Business Week, 14, 173, 243

Cadence Design Systems, profile of, 202
California Technology Stock Letter, 5, 40, 44, 47, 162, 187
    Web site, 44
Call provision of convertible bonds, 234–35
Canon, 58
Capital spending, low-tech versus high-tech, 15–17
Cardio-Pet, 166
Carterfone vs. AT&T, 110
Cash flow, 152
CCITT, 111
C-Cube Microsystems, 73
CDNow.com, 122
Cell signaling, 142
Check Point Software, 123
Chemical-vapor-deposition (CVD) equipment, 58
Childbearing population, chart of, 17, 18
China, 137
    semiconductor-fabrication factories, building of, 50
Cirrus Logic, 69, 71, 73
Cisco Systems, 31, 107, 108, 109, 112, 123, 172, 173
    profile of, 203
Clark, Jim, 9
Client/server computing, 78, 81–82, 94, 95
CNBC, 44
C/Net, 44
CNN, "Science and Technology Week," 44
Code-division multiple-access standard, 113
Combinatorial chemistry, 142
COMDEX personal-computer trade show, 88
Commodity-product companies, stock prices of global, 17, 27–29
Communications industry:
    competitive strategies of, 110–12
    customers of, 110
    data versus telecommunications, 104–105
    growth cycles, impetus for, 109
    growth rate of, 13, 31, 108–109
    history of, 104–108
    Internet's effect on, 112–13
    next big change in, 113–14
    profitability of, 109
    R&D spending, 109
    standards in, 110–12, 113
Communism, fall of, 13

Compaq, 82, 85, 87, 172
Compaq Computer, 72
Comparative advantage, 17
Competitive strategies:
    of communications industry, 110
    of Internet companies, 127
    of mainframes and minicomputers, 81–82
    of medical technology industry, 139–40
    of personal computer industry, 88–89
    in semiconductor-equipment industry, 53–54
    in semiconductor industry, 72–73
    for software industry, 9–101
CompUSA, 40
Computer Associates, 92
Computer Letter, 44
Computers:
    large, *see* Mainframe computer industry; Minicomputer industry
    personal, *see* Personal computers
Computer Sciences, 92
Computer Television Network, 44
Conexant, 73
Congress, U.S., 63–65
Consumer-based economy, 7–8
Consumer-branded companies, stock prices of global, 17, 24–26
Control Data, 76
Convergent Technologies, 41
Convertible technology bonds and stocks, 5, 228–35
    buying new underwritings, 235
    call provision of, 234–35
    characteristics of, 229
    conversion value of, 230
    investment value of, 230
    list of, 148, 289–91
    retirement investing and, 228
    rules for picking, 232–34
CopyTele, 166
Corn prices, 31, 34
Cowen & Co., 44
Creative Technology, 73
Credence Systems, 59
Cullinet, 91
Customers:
    of communications industry, 110
    of Internet companies, 124–47
    of mainframes and minicomputers, 80
    of medical technology industry, 138
    of personal computer industry, 88
    of of semiconductor industry, 72
    of software industry, 98–99
Cygnus Therapeutics, 130
Cypress Semiconductor, 70, 174
    profile of, 204
Cyrix, 155

Database software, 92, 94–95, 96
Data communications industry, *see* Communications industry
Data General, 77, 79–80
Day-trading, 5

DB Alex. Brown, 44, 194
Defense Department, U.S., 8
Dell Computer, 85, 87, 89, 90, 95
Demo Letter, 44
Dento-Med, 166
Desktop publishing software, 103
Development-stage companies, 147, 163–70
  accounting practices of, 164–65
  biotechnology, 167, 285–88
  burn rate of, 169
  M Score, 147, 164, 167–69, 285
  overhyping of, 165, 166
  R&D spending of, 164–65, 167–69
  reasons for need of valuation method for, 165
  Statement of Changes in Financial Condition, 169
  transition to real companies, valuation methods and, 169–70
  venture capitalists and, 163, 165–66, 167
Dicing of semiconductors, 59
Diffusion furnaces, 56–58
Digital and analog chips, integration of, 75
Digital cellular telephone systems, 113–14
Digital Equipment Corporation, 8, 77, 79–80, 82, 92, 172
Digital photography, 97–98
Digital Research, 173
Digital signals, 104
Direct marketing, Internet's potential for, 119
Disco, 59
Discount brokers, 194
Diversification, 147, 190–91
Dow Jones Industry Average (DJIA), 196
  in 2010, 196–235
Downgraded stocks, 192
Downside Risk Value (DRV), 176–79
Downsizing, 82
Dragon Dictate, 103
DRAMs (dynamic random-access-memory chips), 52, 63–66, 89
  U.S. protectionist policy and, 63–65
Dresdner RCM Biotechnology, 242
Drug approval process, 130, 131–36, 167, 182

Earnings preannouncements, 191
Eaton Corp., 58
Eaton Vance Worldwide Health Sciences Fund, 245, 271
Economic indicators, technology and, 9, 14–15
Economic revolutions, 7–9
Economist, The, 43
Edgar system, 44
EDS (Electronic Data Systems), 92
Electronic data interchange (EDI), 126–27
Electro Scientific Industries, 59
EMCORE, 56
Employment, knowledge-intensive, 9
Encapsulation step in making semiconductors, 59
Epitaxial layer of a semiconductor, 56
EPROM (electronically programmable read-only memory) chips, 63

Etching of a semiconductor, 58
Etec Systems, 58
Ethernet, 105, 114
Eudora, 100
Eudora Pro, 100
Europe, 10, 13, 137, 141, 184
Excel, 97

Fairchild, 8, 63
Federal Reserve, 15, 175
FEI Corp., 59
Fiber-optic cables, 105
Fidelity Select Biotechnology, 245, 272
Fidelity Select Computer, 251
Fidelity Select Developing Communications, 245, 252
Fidelity Select Electronics, 253
Fidelity Select Software & Computer, 244, 254
Fidelity Select Technology Fund, 255
Fidelity Select Telecommunications, 256
Financial analysts, 10, 15, 40, 181, 191
Firsthand Technology Value Fund, 244, 257
First Security Van Kasper, 194
Food and Drug Administration (FDA), 13, 139
  drug approval process, 130, 131–36, 167, 182
Forbes, 243
Forbes ASAP, 43
Ford, Henry, 7–8
Ford, Mike, 99
Forrester Research, 118–19, 124
Franklin Biotech Discovery Fund, 246, 273
Franklin Dyna Tech, 258
Freeware, 77, 100–101

GaSonics International, 58, 189–90
Gates, Bill, 9
Gateway, 40, 89, 90
Genentech, 138, 165
Gene sequencing, 142
Gene therapy, 142
GenRad, 59
Genus, 58
Genzyme, 138
Gilder, George, 84
Glaxo, 135
Global economy, 13
Goldman Sachs, 44, 194
Granite Systems, 112
Great Growth-Flow companies, spotting, 147, 156–62
  Growth-Flow model, 152–55
  listing of, 281–84
  non-Great Growth-Flow stocks, investing in, 161–62
  profitability, 159
  R&D spending, 160–61
  return on equity, 159–60
  sales growth, 158–59
Greenspan, Alan, 15
Growth cycles, impetus behind:
  for communications industry, 109
  of Internet companies, 122–23

of mainframes and minicomputers, 78–79
of medical technology industry, 137
of personal computer industry, 86–87
in semiconductor-equipment industry, 50–53
in semiconductor industry, 67–69
software industry, 96–98
Growth-Flow model, 152–55
Growth rate:
  of communications industry, 13, 31, 108–109
  of Internet companies, 122
  of mainframes and minicomputers, 77–78
  of medical technology industry, 136–37
  of personal computer industry, 85–86
  of semiconductor-equipment industry, 50
  of semiconductor industry, 65–67
  of software industry, 94–96
GTE, 113

Hambrecht & Quist, 44, 184, 194
  Life Sciences Conference, 134, 183
  Technology Stock Conference, 183, 184
Hewlett-Packard, 79, 81, 82, 83, 85, 196
  profile of, 205
Hierarchical databases, 94
HMT, 88
Honeywell, 76
Hoya Glass, 58
Hyundai, 52–53

IBM, 59, 64, 71, 76, 79–80, 81, 82, 85, 172, 196
  antitrust consent decree, 91
  downsizing at, 82
  institutional versus individual shareholders of, 43
  personal computer and, 9, 47, 84
  360 series, 79
  370 series, 79
ICN Pharmaceuticals, 41–42, 134
IDEC Pharmaceuticals, 138
Illustra Information Technology, 94
Index puts, 187–88
Industrial Revolution, 8, 11
Information sources, 5, 144, 194–95, 242–43, 295–99
Information Storage Devices, 74–75
Informix, 92, 94–95, 192
  profile of, 206
Ingres, 92
Insider-trading reports, 161
Inspection of semiconductors, 59
Integrated Device Technology, 174
Intel, 8, 31, 69, 72, 73, 84, 174, 242
  Celeron processor, 87, 95
  EPROM business, 65
  IA-64 chip, 81, 97
  individual shareholders of, 43
  Merced chip, 81, 97
  Pentium chip, 81, 86–87, 97
  Pentium II chip, 81, 87, 95
  Pentium III chip, 81, 95
  profile of, 207
  R&D spending by, 155

Interactive Data Corporation, 126
International Telecommunications Union, 111
Internet:
  availability of access to, 117–18
  brownouts, 122, 123
  communications industry, effect on, 112–13
  disintermediation and, 120–21
  growth of usage of, 13, 84–85
  as information utility, 117
  investing in Internet companies, see Internet companies
  investment information on, 5, 44, 195, 196
  mainframe and minicomputer industry, effect on, 81–83
  medical technology industry, effect on, 141
  newsgroups, 90
  personal computer industry, effect on, 90
  semiconductor-equipment industry, effect on, 54
  semiconductor industry, effect on, 74–75
  software industry, effect on, 101–103
  standards, 117
Internet companies, 115–28
  advertising on the Internet and, 118–19, 120
  competitive strategies of, 127
  content companies, 116, 117, 123
  customers of, 124–27
  direct marketing opportunities and, 119
  growth cycles of, impetus for, 122–23
  growth rate of, 122
  hardware infrastructure companies, 116
  high fixed costs and low variable costs of, 118
  measuring usage, 119
  micropayments to, 127–28
  momentum investing and, 116
  next big change in, 127–28
  payment attribute of the Internet and, 118–19
  profitability of, 123–24
  R&D spending, 123
  reintermediators, 121–22
  secret of search engine companies, 127
  software infrastructure companies, 116–17, 123
  valuation of stocks of, 123–24, 125–26
  Web-portal strategy, 119–20
Internet Protocol (IP), 117
Intranets, 83, 103, 112–13
Invesco Strategic Health Sciences Fund, 274
Invesco Strategic Technology Fund, 259
Investor-relations specialists, 5, 43, 194–95, 196–97
  revenues from new products, asking about, 42
Investor's Business Daily, 195
Investo Strategic Technology, 244
Ion implementation, 58
ISDN (Integrated Services Digital Network), 106

Japan, 13, 137
  DRAM production and, 52, 63–65
  drug approval in, 136, 141

EPROM chip production and, 63
R&D spending in, 149
robotics and, 10
as technology market, 10
trade deficit, U.S./Japan, 149, 150
Java language, 103
John Hancock Global Technology, 260
Johnson & Johnson, 196
Jupiter Communications, 124
Just-in-time manufacturing, 88–89, 95

KLA Tencor, 59
Knowledge explosion, 11
Kokusai Electric, 58
Komag, 88
    profile of, 208
Korea:
    DRAM production and, 52, 65
Kulicke & Soffa Industries, 59

Lam Research, 53, 55, 58, 59, 189
    profile of, 209
LANs, see Local area networks (LANs)
Laptop computers, 73
Latin America, 13
"Learning-curve" economics, 11
Leveraged buyouts, 152
L. H. Alton & Co., 194
Licensing of software, 93, 101
Linear Technology, profile of, 210
Lipper Analytical Services, 243
Lithography step in making semiconductors, 58
Local area networks (LANs), 104, 107, 108,
        110, 114
Lotus, 173
Lotus 1-2-3, 97
LSI Logic, 70, 174
    profile of, 211
LTX, 59
Lucent Technologies, 109, 110
Lycos, 119
Lynch, Peter, 12

McAfee Associates, 100
McCamant, Jim, 44
Macromedia, profile of, 212
MacWorld, 102
Mainframe computer industry, 76–83, 92
    competitive strategies of, 81–82
    customers of, 80
    growth cycles, impetus for, 78–79
    growth rate of, 77–78, 94
    history of, 8, 76
    Internet's effect on, 83
    next big change in, 83
    profitability of, 79–80
    software developed for, 94, 96, 98–99
Managing your technology portfolio, 189–95
    buying unpopular stocks, 191–92
    diversification, 147, 190–91
    information sources, 194–95
    seasonality rules and, 191

selling, 192–94
Marcam, 92
Market risk, 175–76
Mask, 58
Mass-production economy, 8, 11, 14, 17, 19–23
Matsushita, 89
Mattson Technology, 55, 58, 59, 189–90
    profile of, 213
Maxim Integrated Products, profile of, 214
Medical-device companies, 129
    growth rate of, 137
    profitability of, 138
    R&D spending by, 138
    see also Medical technology industry
Medical technology industry, 129–43
    biotechnology, see Biotechnology
    competitive strategies of, 139–40
    customers for, 138
    growth cycles, impetus for, 137
    growth rate of, 136–37
    Internet's effect on, 141
    medical devices, see Medical-device industry
    mutual funds, profiled, 269–76
    next big change in, 141–43
    profitability of, 137–38
Medical Technology Stock Letter, 44
Megatest, 59
MEMC Electronic Materials, 56
Merck, 138, 196
Merrill Lynch Technology, 261
Metalization step in making semiconductors, 59
Microchip Technology, profile of, 215
Micro Mask, 58
Micron Electronics, 87, 108
Micron Technology, 73, 179
    profile of, 216
Microprocessors, birth of, 8–9, 77
Microsoft, 31, 84, 96, 97, 98, 123, 124, 128,
        178, 179
    DOS, 80, 87
    Excel, 97
    profile of, 217
    Windows 3.0, 87
    Windows 95, 68, 69, 87, 97
    Windows 98, 80
    Windows NT, 80
    Windows 2000, 80, 82, 83, 90, 97, 173
Miller, George, 179
Minicomputer industry, 76–83
    competitive strategies of, 81–82
    customers of, 80
    growth cycles, impetus for, 78–79, 94
    growth rate of, 78
    history of, 76–77
    Internet's effect on, 82–83
    next big change in, 83
    profitability of, 79–80
    software developed for, 92–93, 95, 99
MKE, 89
Modems, 85, 104
Molecular Applications Group, 143
Momentum investing, 116, 157, 192, 242

Monterey Mutual Fund group, 246
Montgomery Global Communications, 245, 262
Montgomery Securities, 44, 194
Moore's Law, 9, 49, 52, 62, 65
Morgan Stanley Dean Witter, 194
Morningstar service, 242, 243, 244
Motorola, profile of, 218
M score, 123, 164, 167–69, 288
Murphy New World Biotechnology Fund, 242, 246, 275
Murphy New World Technology Convertibles Fund, 246
Murphy New World Technology Fund, 246, 263
Musicboulevard.com, 122
Mutual funds, technology, 5, 239–76
    average price/earnings ratio, 243
    broad categories of, 241
    fund management, 243
    information sources on, 242–43
    medical and biotechnology funds, profiled, 269–76
    profiled, 247–76
    recommended, 243–46
    sector risk, 175
    Standard & Poors 500 versus, 242

NASDAQ 100, 188
National Institutes of Health, 135
National Semiconductor, 63, 155
National Space and Aeronautic Administration (NASA), 8
Nationsbank, 44, 194
Nature Biotechnology, 43
NCR, 76
Negreponte, Nicholas, 17
NeoMagic Corp., 73
NetFRAME Systems, 107–108
Netscape Communications, 112, 115, 117, 119, 127
    profile of, 219
Netscape/Healthion, 9
Network Associates, 100–101
Neurocrine Biosciences, 140
NeuroInvestment, 44
Newbridge Networks, 109
Newsletters, technology, 44
New York Times, The, 43
Nikon, 58
Nontechnology economy, rate of growth of, 10, 11, 12
NorTel, 112
Novell, 107, 173
Novellus Systems, 53, 58, 59, 189
    profile of, 220
Windows 2000SC standard for color television, 107
Nuance, 103

Object-relational databases, 94–95
Octel Communications, 110
Oil industry stocks, 31, 32
OPTI, 73

Oracle Corporation, 92
    profile of, 221
Organogenesis, 133–34
Orphan Drug designation, 139
Overpriced Stock Service, 166
Oxide-deposit step in making semiconductors, 59

Pacific Bell, 106
Pacific Stock Exchange High-Tech Index, 188
Packard Bell, 69, 89
PairGain Technologies, profile of, 222
Panic, Milan, 134
Paper industry stocks, 29, 31
Patented product, semiconductor companies with, 71–72
PBGH Technology & Communications Fund, 264
PCS Primeco, 113
PC World, 102
Penny-stock market, 164, 167
PeopleSoft, 92
Perot, Ross, 92
Personal computers and personal-computer industry, 84–90
    competitive strategies of, 88–89
    customers of, 88
    growth cycles, impetus for, 86–87
    growth in markets for, 13, 31, 84–85
    growth rate of, 85–86
    history of, 9, 47, 84
    Internet's effect on, 90
    next big change in, 90
    profitability of, 87–88
    software industry and, 93, 95, 96, 99
Phillips ElectronOptics, 59
Photoresist layer of a semiconductor, 58
Photoresist strip machine, 58
Photronics, 58
Picking technology stocks, 147–246
    Blue Chips 2010, 196–235
    convertible, *see* Convertible technology bonds and stocks
    development-stage companies, *see* Development-stage companies
    Growth-Flow model, 152–55
    managing your portfolio, *see* Managing your technology portfolio
    overview, 147–48
    R&D spending and, 149–52
    risk and, *see* Risk in investing in technology stocks, controlling
    spotting Great Growth-Flow companies, *see* Great Growth-flow companies, spotting
    two-step process of investing, 156, 189
Planning Research, 92
Platt, Lewis, 81
PMC Sierra, 70
Preferred stocks, convertible, 229
    see also Convertible technology bonds and stocks
Premisys, 109

Premisys Communications, profile of, 223
Preview Travel, 123
Price/earnings ratio, 154
  average mutual fund, 243
  Downside Risk Value and, 177–78
Price-revenue ratio (PRR), 124, 125–26
Productivity defined, 11
Profitability, 159
  of communications industry, 109
  gross profits versus pretax profits, 159
  of Internet companies, 123–24
  of mainframes and minicomputers, 79–80
  of medical technology industry, 137–38
  of personal computer industry, 87–88
  of semiconductor-equipment industry, 53
  of semiconductor industry, 69–72
  of software industry, 98
Protein folding, 143
Putnam Health Sciences, 276
Put options, 186–88

Qualcomm, 113
Qualcomm Corporation, 100
Quantum Corp., 88, 89

Rate of return, asset allocation and, 4
Rational-drug design, 142
R&D, see Research and development (R&D)
Read-Rite, 88
Real costs, 11
Red Herring, The, 43
Regional Bell Operating Companies (RBOCs),
  105–106, 113
Relational databases, 94, 95
Research and Development (R&D), 13, 37–42,
  157
  accounting rule changes to promote
    investment in, 293–94
  applied, 37–39
  basic, 37–38
  by biotechnology companies, 130–31, 138,
    140
  in communications industry, 109
  current reported earnings, effect on, 151
  of development-stage companies, 164–65,
    167–69
  evaluating, 41–43
  fueling growth of tech companies, 11
  by Great Growth-Flow companies, 160–61
  Growth-Flow model, 152–55
  incremental annual increases in, 161
  by Internet companies, 123
  by medical-device companies, 138
  in personal computer industry, 87, 88
  picking technology stocks and, 149–52
  quantifying, 39–41
  sheer size of spending on, 154–55
  by software industry, 98
Research and development (R&D), 11
Reticle, 58
Retirement:
  asset allocation and, 4

convertible bonds and stocks for, see
  Convertible technology bonds and stocks
Return on equity, 159–60
Ribozymes, 142
Risk in investing in technology stocks,
  controlling, 171–88
  building a ten-stock portfolio, 173–74,
    190–91
  Downside Risk Value (DRV), 176–79
  market risk, 175–76
  with put options, 186–88
  seasonality rules, 179–85
  sector risk, 175
  short-term volatility, 171
  specific-company risk, 173–74
  successful implementors of a technology,
    concentrating on, 172–73
Robertson Stephens Information Age Fund, 265
Robotics, 10, 55
Ross Systems, 93
Rules of thumb, valuation, 154–55

St. Jude Medical, 138
Sales per share, Downside Risk Value and,
  176–77
San Jose Mercury News, The, 195
SAP, 93
Schlumberger, 59, 63
Schoendorf, Joe, 106
Science, 43
Science News, 43
Scientific American, 43
Seagate Technology, 10, 40, 88, 89, 160, 161
  profile of, 224
Seasonality rules affecting tech-stock prices,
  179–85, 191
Sector risk, 175
Securities and Exchange Commission (SEC),
  134
  filings with, 44, 169
Selecting technology stocks, see Picking
  technology stocks
Seligman Communications & Information, 245,
  266
Selling, reasons for, 192–94
Semiconductor Equipment and Materials
  Institute, 51
Semiconductor-equipment industry, 49–55
  competitive strategies of, 53–54
  growth cycles, impetus for, 50–53
  growth rate of, 50
  Internet's effect on, 54
  next big change in, 54–55
  profitability of, 53
Semiconductor-fabrication factories:
  building of, 50
  cost of, 50
  semiconductor companies owning their own,
    69–70
Semiconductors and semiconductor industry,
  31, 62–75
  business models for, 69–72

companies owning their own fabrication facilities, 69–70
companies with patented product, 71–72
competitive strategies of, 72–73
constantly declining price per semiconductor function, 9, 49, 52, 62
customers of, 72
economics of making, 59–61
fabless companies, 70–71
global market, 63
growth cycles, impetus behind the, 67–69
growth rate of, 65–67
Internet's effect on, 74–75
invention of, 8
"learning-curve" economics and, 11
lowering of cost and demand for new products, 11, 62
"mixed-signal" devices, 75
Moore's Law, 9, 49, 52, 62, 65
next big change in, 75
profitability of, 69–72
steps in making, 56–61
SEMI monthly press releases, 52
Sequent Computer, 77
Sequoia Capital, 108
Shaffer, Dick, 44, 106
Shinetsu, 56
Shipley, Chris, 44
Shopping.com, 117
Short-interest data, 193–94
Short-interest ratio, 194
Short-term trading, 5
SIBS, 44
Silicon Investor, 44, 118
Silicon Valley, 9, 184
Silicon Valley Group, 58, 59
Small office/home office market, 41
SoftLetter, 44, 96
Software and software industry, 91–103
    applets, 102–103
    bugs, 68
    competitive strategies for, 99–101
    customers of, 98–99
    distribution channels, 93, 102
    growth cycles, impetus for, 96–98
    growth rate of, 94–96
    history of, 91–93
    Internet's effect on, 101–103
    minicomputers and, 92–93, 95
    next big change in, 103
    personal computers and, 93, 95, 96
    profitability of, 98
    R&D spending, 98
    see also names of specific programs
Software Publishers Association, 100
Soybean prices, 31, 35
Specialty-materials companies, 40
Specific-company risk, 173–74
SportsLine, 123
Spreadsheets, 96
Sprint PCS system, 113
Spyglass, 112

SRI (Stanford Research Institute), 37
Standard & Poor's 100 ("OEX"), 187, 188
Standard & Poor's 500, 187
Statement of Changes in Financial Condition, 169
S3, 73
Stocks, picking technology, see Picking technology stocks
Stratacom, 172, 173
Sun Microsystems, 173
    profile of, 225
Supplier investment in R&D, 40, 87, 88
Sybase, 92
Synergen, 132–33
Systems Engineering Laboratories, 77
Szirom, Steve, 44

Tartar, Jeffrey, 44, 96
Technology economy, 8–10
    economic indicators and, 9, 14–15
    information sources, 43–44
    performance of leading stocks, 31
    rate of growth of, 10, 11–12
    reasons to invest in, 7–13
    worldwide markets for, 13
Technology mutual funds, see Mutual funds, technology
Technology stocks, picking, see Picking technology stocks
Tektronix, 154
Telecommunications industry, see Communications industry
Telios Pharmaceuticals, 133
Tellabs, 109
Ten-stock tech portfolio, building a, 173–74, 190–91
Teradyne, 59
Testing of semiconductors, 59
Texas Instruments, 8, 63, 70, 73
3Com, 109, 112
Throop, Bob, 67
Time-division multiple access (TDMA) standard, 113–14
Tokyo Electron, 58
Tracy, Harry, 44
Trade deficit, U.S./Japan, 149, 150
Travel agencies, on-line, 121–22
Trends, future:
    in communications industry, 113–14
    for Internet companies, 127–28
    in mainframe and minicomputer industry, 81–82
    in medical technology industry, 141–43
    in personal computer industry, 90
    in semiconductor-equipment industry, 54–55
    in semiconductor industry, 75
    in software industry, 103
Trident Microsystems, 73
Trikon Technologies, 54–55
T. Rowe Price Science & Technology Fund, 245, 267
Trucking industry, 17, 30

Turnaround companies, 179
Two-step process of investing, 156, 189

Ultratech Stepper, 53, 58
Underwriters, 191
Unisys, 76
United Science & Technology, 268
University Computing, 92
UNIX operating system, 77, 80, 81, 82, 83
Unpopular stocks, taking advantage of, 191–92
U.S.-Japan Semiconductor Agreement, 64–65
U.S. Robotics, X2 standard, 111–12
Usenet discussion groups, 195

Valuation of stocks:
    of Internet companies, 123–24, 125–26
    rules of thumb, 154–55
Value-added resellers (VARs), software, 93
Value investors, 157
Varian Semiconductor Equipment, 58
Venture capitalists, 163, 165–66, 167
VisiCalc, 97
Vitesse Semiconductor, profile of, 226
VLSI Technology, 73
Voice-mail, 110
Voice-recognition systems, 103
Volatility, 4

Wafer stepper, 58

Walker Interactive, 93
Wall Street analysts, 10, 15, 40, 180, 191
Wall Street Journal, The, 41, 118, 157, 192
Wall Street Transcript, 44
Wal-Mart, 8
WANs, *see* Wide area networks (WANs)
Warning signs, spotting, 192–94
Watkins-Johnson, 58, 59
Westergaard, John, 115, 156
Western Digital, 88, 89
Western Electric, 105
Wheat prices, 31, 33
Wide-area networks (WANs), 104, 107, 108
Wilshire 2000 Small Cap, 187, 188
Windows operating systems, *see* Microsoft
Wire bonding, 59
Wired, 43
Word processing software, 96, 101, 103
WordStar, 93, 97
WorkSlate from Convergent Technologies, 41
World Wide Web, *see* Internet
Wozniak, Steve, 111

Xilinx, 70, 174
    profile of, 227

Yahoo, 44, 115, 118, 119, 120, 123, 128
Year 2000 problem, 94

ZDTV, 44